Generation
X

AMERICANS
BORN 1965 to 1976

Generation X

X

AMERICANS
BORN 1965 to 1976

4th EDITION

BY THE NEW STRATEGIST EDITORS

New Strategist Publications, Inc.
Ithaca, New York

New Strategist Publications, Inc.
P.O. Box 242, Ithaca, New York 14851
800/848-0842; 607/273-0913
www.newstrategist.com

ISBN 1-885070-52-7

Printed in the United States of America

Table of Contents

Chapter 4. Income

Chapter 5. Labor Force

Chapter 6. Living Arrangements

Tables

Chapter 4. Income

Chapter 5. Labor Force

Illustrations

Chapter 5. Labor Force

Chapter 6. Living Arrangements

Chapter 7. Population

Chapter 8. Spending

Chapter 9. Wealth

Introduction

Generation X gained its fame simply because it followed the Baby-Boom generation onto the stage of youth, a stage Boomers had created and made the center of the nation's attention. Generation X was everything Boomers were not—small in number, cynical rather than idealistic—and they were expected to make their way easily through life because of the swath Boomers had carved. But it didn't turn out that way. Generation Xers have struggled to compete with the masses of Boomers ahead of them. They have found jobs scarce, promotions hard to come by, and housing expensive. *Generation X: Americans Born 1965 to 1976* tells the story of the small generation that spans the ages of 27 to 39 in 2004.

Although their numbers are small, lifestage dictates that Generation X is a vital part of the nation's commerce and culture. People in their late twenties and thirties are marrying, having children, and buying houses. They are moving up in their careers, their incomes are growing, and their spending is too. *Generation X: Americans Born 1965 to 1976* shows how Gen Xers are changing and what to expect from them in the future.

Generation Xers are a diverse segment of the population, with minorities accounting for a large share of the whole. They are a generation that is moving up. Most have passed one or two of life's important milestones on the way to full adulthood, according to an AARP survey. Most have married, and most have children. But few adults under age 38 have reached other important milestones, such as divorce, the death of a parent, a midlife crisis, or a major illness.

Those milestones lie ahead for many Gen Xers. The work versus family struggle, competition in the job market, trying to get ahead economically—these are the issues that define Generation X today. While these issues seem familiar because Boomers have been there, done that, they are new to Generation X and create in them an outlook very different from that of Boomers, who are becoming empty nesters and pondering their retirement years.

It is not easy to study Generation Xers. Few government surveys focus on the generation, and the ages spanned by the members of the generation make it difficult to tease them out of the government's traditional five- or ten-year age categories. To analyze Gen X lifestyles, then, most of the tables in *Generation X: Americans Born 1965 to 1976* approximate the generation. Single-year-of-age data are shown whenever they are available, but five-year age groups are most common. When five-year age categories are shown, Gen Xers are included in three: 25-to-29, 30-to-34, and 35-to-39. In a few tables, data are available only for much broader age groups, forcing a more general analysis of trends among Gen Xers.

Critical Life Events among Young Adults, 2002

(percent of people aged 18 to 37 who have ever experienced selected life events, 2002)

	percent of people aged 37 or younger who have ever
Gotten married for the first time	57%
Become a parent for the first time	56
Gotten a divorce	27
Remarried	12
Had last child move out of the house	5
Had spouse die	2
Become a grandparent	3
Had an adult child move back home	1
Moved back into parents' home	27
Provided child care or daycare to a grandchild on a regular basis	3
Had father die	16
Had mother die	7
Experienced a midlife crisis	10
Survived a major illness	19
Made major changes in diet because of a medical condition	20
Made a major career change	41
Lost a job	29

Source: © 2002, AARP. Reprinted with permission. Boomers at Midlife: The AARP Life Stage Study, *A National Survey Conducted for AARP by Princeton Survey Research Associates, November 2002; Internet site http://www.aarp.org*

Whether Generation X age groups are exact or approximate, however, the results are clear. Generation Xers are entering the prime of life. They account for a growing share of households with incomes of $100,000 or more. Their spending is on the rise, their families are expanding, and they are moving into larger homes. One of the most distinct features of the generation is its diversity, with blacks, Hispanics, and Asians all accounting for significant proportions of the whole. Gen Xers are searching for success, and *Generation X: Americans Born 1965 to 1976* is your guide to how well they are doing.

How to use this book

Generation X: Americans Born 1965 to 1976 is designed for easy use. It is divided into nine chapters, organized alphabetically: Education, Health, Housing, Income, Labor Force, Living Arrangements, Population, Spending, and Wealth.

This edition of *Generation X* includes the latest statistics on the labor force participation, living arrangements, incomes, health, spending, and wealth of this rising generation. The socioeconomic estimates presented here reflect 2000 census results, which counted 6 million more Americans than demographers had estimated. *Generation X* presents labor force data for 2003, including the government's updated occupational classifications. It contains the Census Bureau's latest population projections—the first released by the bureau in years. New data are shown on the health of the population, including updated estimates of the overweight and the obese. *Generation X* also presents the latest data on wealth from the Survey of Consumer Finances. And because the government now breaks out the Asian population separately in its estimates, most of the all-important racial and ethnic breakdowns include Asians for the first time, along with blacks, Hispanics, and non-Hispanic whites. New to this book is a chapter on housing, revealing the surge in homeownership among Generation Xers as mortgage interest rates fell.

Most of the tables in *Generation X* are based on data collected by the federal government, in particular the Census Bureau, the Bureau of Labor Statistics, the National Center for Education Statistics, the National Center for Health Statistics, and the Federal Reserve Board. The federal government is the best source of up-to-date, reliable information on the changing characteristics of Americans.

While most of the tables in this book are based on data collected by the federal government, they are not simply reprints of government spreadsheets—as is the case in many reference books. Instead, each table is individually compiled and created by New Strategist's editors, with calculations designed to reveal the trends. Each chapter of *Generation X* includes the demographic and lifestyle data most important to researchers. Each table tells a story about Gen Xers, a story amplified by the accompanying text and chart, which analyze the data and highlight future trends. If you need more information than tables and text provide, you can plumb the original source listed at the bottom of each table.

The book contains a lengthy table list to help you locate the information you need. For a more detailed search, see the index at the back of the book. Also at the back of the book is the glossary, which defines the terms and describes the surveys commonly used in the tables and text. A list of telephone and Internet contacts also appears at the end of the book, allowing you to access government specialists and web sites.

With *Generation X: Americans Born 1965 to 1976* on your bookshelf, an in-depth understanding of this influential generation is at hand.

1

Education

■ Generation X women are better educated than their male counterparts. They are, in fact, the best-educated women in the nation. Thirty-two percent have at least a bachelor's degree, and 61 percent have at least some college experience.

■ Among Gen Xers, Asians are by far the best educated, while Hispanics have the least education. Fully 58 percent of Asian men aged 26 to 37 are college graduates. In contrast, only 58 percent of Hispanic men in the age group have even graduated from high school.

■ People aged 25 to 34 account for only 16 percent of the nation's college undergraduates. But they are fully 42 percent of graduate students.

■ Fifty-six percent of people aged 25 to 34 participated in adult education in 2001, up fully 19 percentage points from 1991.

Nearly 30 Percent of Gen X Men Are College Graduates

Many of those without a college degree will get one later in life.

The men of Generation X are well educated, although not as highly educated as Baby-Boom men. Eighty-six percent of men aged 26 to 37 are high school graduates. That leaves a substantial 14 percent who do not have a high school diploma. These men will have a difficult time making ends meet in an economy that rewards the well-educated.

Fifty-five percent of men aged 26 to 37 have attended college, but only 30 percent are college graduates, meaning that many men who start college drop out before getting their degree. Some are likely to return to school as older students to complete their education.

■ Most men are aware of the importance of education for their career. Even if they do not obtain a college degree, attending college for a year or two should boost their earnings significantly.

Most men aged 26 to 37 have at least some college experience

(percent distribution of men aged 26 to 37 by educational attainment, 2002)

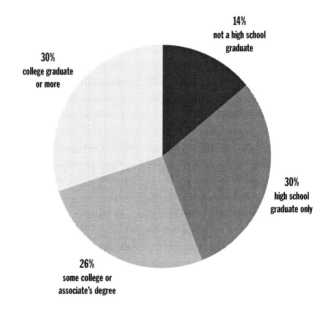

Table 1.1 Educational Attainment of Generation X Men, 2002

(number and percent distribution of men aged 25 or older, aged 26 to 37, and aged 25 to 39 in five-year age groups, by highest level of education, 2002; numbers in thousands)

	total aged 25 or older	aged 26 to 37 exactly	five-year age groups 25 to 29	30 to 34	35 to 39
Total men	**86,996**	**23,695**	**9,150**	**10,084**	**10,698**
Not a high school graduate	14,095	3,356	1,399	1,473	1,387
High school graduate only	26,947	7,197	2,767	2,984	3,466
Some college, no degree	14,661	4,255	1,843	1,747	1,843
Associate's degree	6,466	1,885	684	857	918
Bachelor's degree	15,925	5,171	2,012	2,208	2,095
Master's degree	5,595	1,268	313	570	644
Professional degree	1,795	333	93	135	208
Doctoral degree	1,514	232	39	110	138
High school graduate or more	72,903	20,341	7,751	8,611	9,312
Some college or more	45,956	13,144	4,984	5,627	5,846
Bachelor's degree or more	24,829	7,004	2,457	3,023	3,085
Total men	**100.0%**	**100.0%**	**100.0%**	**100.0%**	**100.0%**
Not a high school graduate	16.2	14.2	15.3	14.6	13.0
High school graduate only	31.0	30.4	30.2	29.6	32.4
Some college, no degree	16.9	18.0	20.1	17.3	17.2
Associate's degree	7.4	8.0	7.5	8.5	8.6
Bachelor's degree	18.3	21.8	22.0	21.9	19.6
Master's degree	6.4	5.4	3.4	5.7	6.0
Professional degree	2.1	1.4	1.0	1.3	1.9
Doctoral degree	1.7	1.0	0.4	1.1	1.3
High school graduate or more	83.8	85.8	84.7	85.4	87.0
Some college or more	52.8	55.5	54.5	55.8	54.6
Bachelor's degree or more	28.5	29.6	26.9	30.0	28.8

Source: Bureau of the Census, Educational Attainment in the United States: March 2002, *detailed tables (PPL-169); Internet site http://www.census.gov/population/www/socdemo/education/ppl-169.html; calculations by New Strategist*

Gen X Women Are Better Educated than Gen X Men

They are more likely to attend and to complete college.

As educational opportunities for women broadened over the years, increasing numbers of women took advantage of them. Women aged 26 to 37 are better educated than their male counterparts.

The women of Generation X, in fact, are the best-educated women in the nation. Thirty-two percent have at least a bachelor's degree, and 61 percent have at least some college experience. Among men aged 26 to 37, a smaller 30 percent have a bachelor's degree, while 55 percent have college experience.

The higher educational attainment of Baby-Boom and younger women is the driving factor behind the changing roles of women in society. With greater education, women expect to work and are eager to advance in their careers.

■ Among high school graduates, girls are more likely than boys to go to college. Consequently, among Generation Xers, women are more likely than men to have a college degree.

Most women aged 26 to 37 have at least some college experience

(percent distribution of women aged 26 to 37 by educational attainment, 2002)

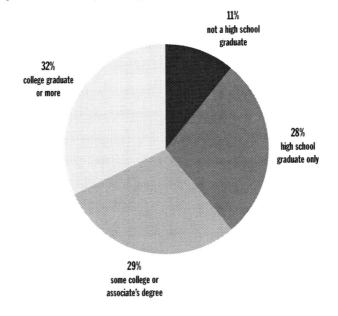

Table 1.2 Educational Attainment of Generation X Women, 2002

(number and percent distribution of women aged 25 or older, aged 26 to 37, and aged 25 to 39 in five-year age groups, by highest level of education, 2002; numbers in thousands)

	total aged 25 or older	aged 26 to 37 exactly	five-year age groups 25 to 29	30 to 34	35 to 39
Total women	**95,145**	**23,957**	**9,159**	**10,277**	**10,950**
Not a high school graduate	14,854	2,671	1,088	1,112	1,201
High school graduate only	31,509	6,681	2,433	2,805	3,388
Some college, no degree	16,330	4,600	1,903	1,905	1,997
Associate's degree	8,585	2,349	821	1,016	1,210
Bachelor's degree	16,357	5,622	2,276	2,486	2,253
Master's degree	5,893	1,524	486	725	655
Professional degree	942	339	114	139	144
Doctoral degree	676	177	39	89	102
High school graduate or more	80,292	21,292	8,072	9,165	9,749
Some college or more	48,783	14,611	5,639	6,360	6,361
Bachelor's degree or more	23,868	7,662	2,915	3,439	3,154
Total women	**100.0%**	**100.0%**	**100.0%**	**100.0%**	**100.0%**
Not a high school graduate	15.6	11.1	11.9	10.8	11.0
High school graduate only	33.1	27.9	26.6	27.3	30.9
Some college, no degree	17.2	19.2	20.8	18.5	18.2
Associate's degree	9.0	9.8	9.0	9.9	11.1
Bachelor's degree	17.2	23.5	24.8	24.2	20.6
Master's degree	6.2	6.4	5.3	7.1	6.0
Professional degree	1.0	1.4	1.2	1.4	1.3
Doctoral degree	0.7	0.7	0.4	0.9	0.9
High school graduate or more	84.4	88.9	88.1	89.2	89.0
Some college or more	51.3	61.0	61.6	61.9	58.1
Bachelor's degree or more	25.1	32.0	31.8	33.5	28.8

Source: Bureau of the Census, Educational Attainment in the United States: March 2002, *detailed tables (PPL-169); Internet site http://www.census.gov/population/www/socdemo/education/ppl-169.html; calculations by New Strategist*

Among Gen Xers, Asian Men Have the Highest Educational Attainment

Hispanics are least likely to have completed high school.

There are substantial socioeconomic differences between Americans of different racial and ethnic backgrounds. Differences in educational attainment are the primary reason for the disparity.

Among Gen X men, Asians are by far the best educated. Fully 77 percent of Asian men aged 26 to 37 have college experience and the 58 percent majority are college graduates. Among non-Hispanic white men in the age group, 62 percent have college experience and 35 percent have a college degree.

Hispanics are the least educated. Only 58 percent of Hispanic men aged 26 to 37 have even graduated from high school. Just 10 percent have a college degree. Black Gen X men are much better educated than Hispanics. The 51 percent majority has college experience, and 19 percent are college graduates.

■ The educational attainment of Hispanics is low because many are recent immigrants from countries with little educational opportunity.

Education gaps point to continued socioeconomic differences

(percent of men aged 26 to 37 with a bachelor's degree or more, by race and Hispanic origin, 2002)

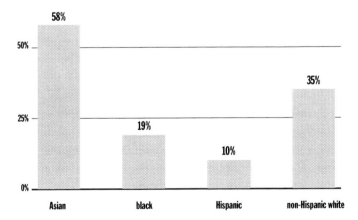

Table 1.3 Educational Attainment of Generation X Men by Race and Hispanic Origin, 2002

(number and percent distribution of men aged 26 to 37 by educational attainment, race, and Hispanic origin, 2002; numbers in thousands)

| | non-Hispanic | | | |
	Asian	black	white	Hispanic
Total men	**1,339**	**2,548**	**15,341**	**4,282**
Not a high school graduate	91	322	1,119	1,788
High school graduate only	226	933	4,698	1,255
Some college, no degree	168	628	2,832	592
Associate's degree	84	182	1,403	204
Bachelor's degree	463	407	3,945	341
Master's degree	228	48	921	67
Professional degree	47	16	250	22
Doctoral degree	40	11	171	7
High school graduate or more	1,256	2,225	14,220	2,488
Some college or more	1,030	1,292	9,522	1,233
Bachelor's degree or more	778	482	5,287	437
Total men	**100.0%**	**100.0%**	**100.0%**	**100.0%**
Not a high school graduate	6.8	12.6	7.3	41.8
High school graduate only	16.9	36.6	30.6	29.3
Some college, no degree	12.5	24.6	18.5	13.8
Associate's degree	6.3	7.1	9.1	4.8
Bachelor's degree	34.6	16.0	25.7	8.0
Master's degree	17.0	1.9	6.0	1.6
Professional degree	3.5	0.6	1.6	0.5
Doctoral degree	3.0	0.4	1.1	0.2
High school graduate or more	93.8	87.3	92.7	58.1
Some college or more	76.9	50.7	62.1	28.8
Bachelor's degree or more	58.1	18.9	34.5	10.2

Note: Numbers will not add to total because not all races are shown and Hispanics may be of any race.
Source: Bureau of the Census, Educational Attainment in the United States: March 2002, *detailed tables (PPL-169); Internet site http://www.census.gov/population/www/socdemo/education/ppl-169.html; calculations by New Strategist*

Hispanic Women Are Least Likely to Be High School Graduates

Asians are most likely to be college graduates.

Although the educational attainment of women has been rising for decades, substantial gaps persist among Gen Xers by race and Hispanic origin. From 89 to 95 percent of Asian, Black, and non-Hispanic white women aged 26 to 37 have graduated from high school versus only 64 percent of Hispanic women in the age group. The majority of Asian, black, and non-Hispanic white women have college experience compared with only 34 percent of their Hispanic counterparts.

Asians are the best-educated Gen X women. Fully 56 percent have a college degree. Among non-Hispanic white women in the age group, the proportion is 37 percent. Twenty percent of black women aged 26 to 27 have a college diploma, while the figure is just 13 percent for Hispanics.

■ The educational attainment of Hispanics will remain low as long as immigrants remain a large share of the Hispanic population.

Young Asian women have the highest educational attainment

(percent of women aged 26 to 37 with a bachelor's degree or more, by race and Hispanic origin, 2002)

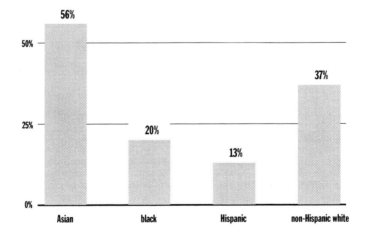

Table 1.4 Educational Attainment of Generation X Women by Race and Hispanic Origin, 2002

(number and percent distribution of women aged 26 to 37 by educational attainment, race, and Hispanic origin, 2002; numbers in thousands)

	non-Hispanic			
	Asian	black	white	Hispanic
Total women	**1,350**	**3,228**	**15,334**	**3,790**
Not a high school graduate	85	356	824	1,368
High school graduate only	246	1,119	4,106	1,117
Some college, no degree	180	783	2,983	584
Associate's degree	89	315	1,697	227
Bachelor's degree	492	496	4,208	390
Master's degree	176	120	1,154	70
Professional degree	54	26	230	28
Doctoral degree	32	9	129	4
High school graduate or more	1,269	2,868	14,507	2,420
Some college or more	1,023	1,749	10,401	1,303
Bachelor's degree or more	754	651	5,721	492
Total women	**100.0%**	**100.0%**	**100.0%**	**100.0%**
Not a high school graduate	6.3	11.0	5.4	36.1
High school graduate only	18.2	34.7	26.8	29.5
Some college, no degree	13.3	24.3	19.5	15.4
Associate's degree	6.6	9.8	11.1	6.0
Bachelor's degree	36.4	15.4	27.4	10.3
Master's degree	13.0	3.7	7.5	1.8
Professional degree	4.0	0.8	1.5	0.7
Doctoral degree	2.4	0.3	0.8	0.1
High school graduate or more	94.0	88.8	94.6	63.9
Some college or more	75.8	54.2	67.8	34.4
Bachelor's degree or more	55.9	20.2	37.3	13.0

Note: Numbers will not add to total because not all races are shown and Hispanics may be of any race.
Source: Bureau of the Census, Educational Attainment in the United States: March 2002, *detailed tables (PPL-169); Internet site http://www.census.gov/population/www/socdemo/education/ppl-169.html; calculations by New Strategist*

Many Gen Xers Are Still in School

Nearly one out of ten people aged 25 to 34 is a student.

School is a major part of life for many people in their twenties and thirties. Among 25-to-29-year-olds, 12 percent—or one in eight—are in school. The proportion drops to 7 percent among 30-to-34-year-olds. Among people aged 35 or older, only 2 percent are enrolled in school.

Women are more likely to go to college than men. This is why a larger proportion of 25-to-34-year-old women than men are enrolled in school. Ten percent of women in the age group are students versus 8 percent of men.

■ Among students in the 25-to-34 age group, women outnumber men by more than half a million.

Among Gen X students, women outnumber men

(number of people aged 25 to 34 enrolled in school, by sex, 2002)

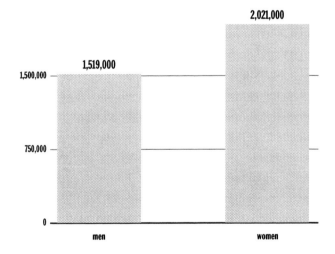

Table 1.5 School Enrollment by Sex and Age, 2002

(total number of people aged 3 or older, and number and percent enrolled in school by sex and age, 2002; numbers in thousands)

	total	enrolled	
		number	percent
Total people	**270,919**	**74,046**	**27.3%**
Under age 25	88,079	67,462	76.6
Aged 25 to 34	38,484	3,541	9.2
Aged 25 to 29	18,141	2,196	12.1
Aged 30 to 34	20,343	1,345	6.6
Aged 35 or older	144,356	3,043	2.1
Total females	**139,061**	**37,266**	**26.8**
Under age 25	43,311	33,360	77.0
Aged 25 to 34	19,450	2,021	10.4
Aged 25 to 29	9,152	1,231	13.5
Aged 30 to 34	10,298	790	7.7
Aged 35 or older	76,300	1,885	2.5
Total males	**131,858**	**36,779**	**27.9**
Under age 25	44,766	34,103	76.2
Aged 25 to 34	19,034	1,519	8.0
Aged 25 to 29	8,989	964	10.7
Aged 30 to 34	10,045	555	5.5
Aged 35 or older	68,058	1,157	1.7

Source: Bureau of the Census, School Enrollment—Social and Economic Characteristics of Students: October 2002, *detailed tables; Internet site http://www.census.gov/population/www/socdemo/school/cps2002.html; calculations by New Strategist*

Gen Xers Account for Few Undergraduates

They account for a large share of graduate students, however.

Although the college enrollment of older people has grown over the years, young adults still dominate the nation's college campuses. In 2002, fully 62 percent of college students were under age 25. People aged 25 to 34 (Gen Xers were aged 26 to 37 in that year) account for only 21 percent of college students, while people aged 35 or older accounted for 17 percent.

Students aged 25 to 34 account for only 16 percent of undergraduates, although they are a larger 28 percent share of part-time undergraduates. The 25-to-34 age group accounts for fully 42 percent of graduate students.

■ Although Generation X is small in number, they are a plurality of graduate students.

Gen Xers account for the largest share of graduate students

(percent distribution of graduate students, by age, 2002)

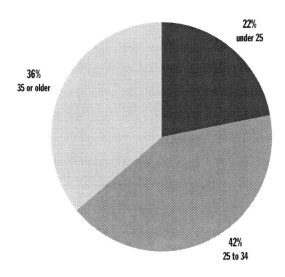

Table 1.6 College Students by Age and Attendance Status, 2002

(number and percent distribution of people aged 15 or older enrolled in institutions of higher education, by age and full- or part-time attendance status, 2002; numbers in thousands)

	total	undergraduate total	full-time	part-time	graduate total	full-time	part-time
Total enrolled	**16,497**	**13,425**	**9,735**	**3,690**	**3,072**	**1,406**	**1,666**
Under age 25	10,248	9,578	8,153	1,425	670	524	146
Aged 25 to 34	3,403	2,106	1,074	1,032	1,297	631	666
Aged 25 to 29	2,093	1,346	758	588	747	411	336
Aged 30 to 34	1,310	760	316	444	550	220	330
Aged 35 or older	2,846	1,741	508	1,233	1,105	251	854
PERCENT DISTRIBUTION BY ATTENDANCE STATUS							
Total enrolled	**100.0%**	**81.4%**	**59.0%**	**22.4%**	**18.6%**	**8.5%**	**10.1%**
Under age 25	100.0	93.5	79.6	13.9	6.5	5.1	1.4
Aged 25 to 34	100.0	61.9	31.6	30.3	38.1	18.5	19.6
Aged 25 to 29	100.0	64.3	36.2	28.1	35.7	19.6	16.1
Aged 30 to 34	100.0	58.0	24.1	33.9	42.0	16.8	25.2
Aged 35 or older	100.0	61.2	17.8	43.3	38.8	8.8	3.0
PERCENT DISTRIBUTION BY AGE							
Total enrolled	**100.0%**	**100.0%**	**100.0%**	**100.0%**	**100.0%**	**100.0%**	**100.0%**
Under age 25	62.1	71.3	83.7	38.6	21.8	37.3	8.8
Aged 25 to 34	20.6	15.7	11.0	28.0	42.2	44.9	40.0
Aged 25 to 29	12.7	10.0	7.8	15.9	24.3	29.2	20.2
Aged 30 to 34	7.9	5.7	3.2	12.0	17.9	15.6	19.8
Aged 35 or older	17.3	13.0	5.2	33.4	36.0	17.9	51.3

Source: Bureau of the Census, School Enrollment—Social and Economic Characteristics of Students: October 2002, *detailed tables; Internet site http://www.census.gov/population/www/socdemo/school/cps2002.html; calculations by New Strategist*

Generation Xers Are Most Likely to Participate in Adult Education

As Americans become increasingly educated, life-long learning is becoming more popular.

As Americans have become more educated, they have become more appreciative of education. Young adults are no exception. Fifty-six percent of people aged 25 to 34 participated in adult education in 2001, up fully 19 percentage points from 1991.

Among adults under age 55, the majority participated in adult education. Many seek training to further their careers. Older Americans are more likely to participate in adult education for personal and social reasons. As highly educated younger generations age into the 55-or-older age groups, expect to see a growing proportion of older Americans returning to the classroom to explore new interests.

■ The percentage of young adults seeking educational opportunity is likely to grow as life-long learning becomes increasingly necessary for success.

Participation in adult education is above 50 percent among Gen Xers

(percent of people aged 16 or older participating in adult education, by age, 2001)

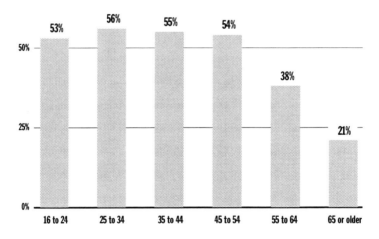

Table 1.7 Participation in Adult Education by Age, 1991 and 2001

(percent of people aged 16 or older participating in adult education activities, by age, 1991 and 2001; percentage point change, 1991–2001)

	2001	1991	percentage point change 1991–01
Total people	**47%**	**32%**	**15**
Aged 16 to 24	53	33	20
Aged 25 to 34	56	37	19
Aged 35 to 44	55	44	11
Aged 45 to 54	54	32	22
Aged 55 to 64	38	23	15
Aged 65 or older	21	10	11

Note: Adult education activities include apprenticeships, courses for basic skills, personal development, English as a second language, work-related courses, and credential programs in organizations other than postsecondary institutions. Excludes full-time participation in postsecondary institutions leading to a college degree, diploma, or certificate.
Source: National Center for Education Statistics, Adult Education and Lifelong Learning Survey of the National Household Education Surveys Program; Internet site http://nces.ed.gov/programs/coe/2003/section1/tables/t08_2.asp; calculations by New Strategist

2

Health

■ The 55 percent majority of Americans aged 18 or older say their health is excellent or very good, with the figure peaking at 64 percent in the 25-to-34 age group.

■ The majority of men and women aged 20 to 34 are overweight, and one in four is obese.

■ Most women aged 25 to 29 have had at least one child, and one in three has had two or more children. In the 30-to-34 age group, the majority has had at least two children, and one in five has had three or more.

■ Many young adults do not have health insurance, including 30 percent of those aged 18 to 24 and 25 percent of 25-to-34-year-olds.

■ Twenty-eight percent of Americans aged 18 to 44 have experienced lower back pain in the past three months, making it the most common health condition in the age group.

■ People aged 25 to 44 account for 23 percent of doctor visits. Women account for the great majority of these visits because of pregnancy and childbirth.

■ Accidents are the number-one cause of death among 25-to-34-year-olds, accounting for 28 percent of deaths in the age group. Homicide ranks second, and suicide is third.

Most Young Adults Say Their Health Is Excellent or Very Good

The proportion of people in good or excellent health declines with age.

Overall, the 55 percent majority of Americans aged 18 or older say their health is excellent or very good. The figure peaks at 64 percent in the 25-to-34 age group. Young adults are more likely than their elders to report being in tip-top shape for good reason. Although many of the conditions and diseases associated with aging have diminished in severity thanks to healthier lifestyles and better medical care, health deteriorates with age as chronic conditions become common.

Older Americans are less likely than younger adults to report excellent or very good health. Nevertheless, the proportion of Americans who say they are in poor health remains below 10 percent, regardless of age.

■ Basic biology dictates that young adults will always feel more fit than their elders.

People aged 25 to 34 are most likely to report excellent or very good health

(percent of people aged 18 or older who say their health is excellent or very good, by age, 2002)

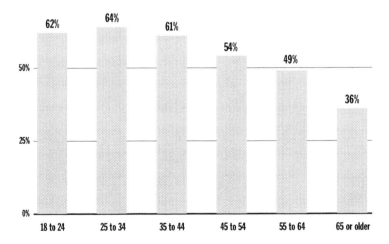

Table 2.1 Health Status by Age, 2002

(percent distribution of people aged 18 or older by self-reported health status, by age, 2002)

	excellent	very good	good	fair	poor
Total people	**21.4%**	**33.8%**	**29.8%**	**10.4%**	**3.9%**
Aged 18 to 24	25.4	37.0	29.5	6.0	0.8
Aged 25 to 34	26.6	37.5	27.4	5.8	1.2
Aged 35 to 44	24.8	35.8	27.6	8.1	2.4
Aged 45 to 54	21.1	32.6	29.6	10.7	4.1
Aged 55 to 64	18.8	30.0	30.2	13.5	6.5
Aged 65 or older	11.4	25.0	33.6	19.7	8.7

Source: Centers for Disease Control and Prevention, Behavioral Risk Factor Surveillance System Prevalence Data, 2002; Internet site http://apps.nccd.cdc.gov/brfss/index.asp

Weight Problems Are the Norm, Even for Young Adults

The majority of young adults are overweight and many are trying to shed pounds.

Americans have a weight problem. The 64 percent majority of people aged 20 or older are overweight, and 30 percent are obese, according to the latest data from the National Center for Health Statistics. Within the 20-to-34 age group, the shares of the overweight and the obese are below the national averages—but still alarmingly high. Fifty-eight percent of men in the age group are overweight, including 24 percent who are obese. Among women, 52 percent are overweight, including 26 percent who are obese.

Not surprisingly, many Americans are trying to lose weight. Among 25-to-34-year-olds, 38 percent are trying to shed pounds. Only 12 percent say they are eating fewer calories to lose or maintain their weight. More than two out of three say they are exercising to lose or maintain their weight. Although most people in the age group are overweight, only 8 percent have been advised by a health professional to lose weight.

Many people claim to exercise, but only 34 percent of adults aged 25 to 44 participate regularly in leisure-time physical activity, according to government data. The proportion of those who engage in regular physical activity falls with age.

■ Many young adults lack the willpower to eat less or exercise more, and their weight problems are likely to increase as they get older.

More than half of 20-to-34-year-olds are overweight

(percent of people aged 20 to 34 who are overweight, by sex, 1999–2000)

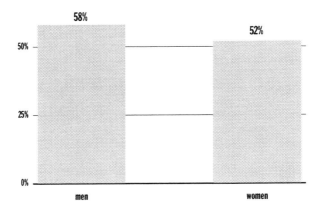

Table 2.2 Overweight and Obese by Sex and Age, 1999–2000

(percent of people aged 20 or older who are overweight or obese, by sex and age, 1999–2000)

	overweight	obese
TOTAL PEOPLE*	**64.3%**	**30.3%**
Total men*	**66.5**	**27.5**
Aged 20 to 34	58.0	24.1
Aged 35 to 44	67.6	25.2
Aged 45 to 54	71.3	30.1
Aged 55 to 64	72.5	32.9
Aged 65 to 74	77.2	33.4
Aged 75 or older	66.4	20.4
Total women*	**62.0**	**34.0**
Aged 20 to 34	51.5	25.8
Aged 35 to 44	63.6	33.9
Aged 45 to 54	64.7	38.1
Aged 55 to 64	73.1	43.1
Aged 65 to 74	70.1	38.8
Aged 75 or older	59.6	25.1

* Aged 20 to 74.
Note: Being overweight is defined as having a body mass index of 25 or higher. Obesity is defined as having a body mass index of 30 or higher. Body mass index is calculated by dividing weight in kilograms by height in meters squared.
Source: National Center for Health Statistics, Health, United States, 2003, *Internet site http://www.cdc.gov/nchs/hus.htm*

Table 2.3 Weight Loss Behavior by Age, 2000

(percent of people aged 18 or older engaging in selected weight loss behaviors, by age, 2000)

	total	18 to 24	25 to 34	35 to 44	45 to 54	55 to 64	65 or older
Trying to lose weight	38.0%	30.2%	38.0%	40.4%	44.7%	42.6%	30.6%
Trying to maintain weight	58.9	51.9	56.9	59.8	63.1	60.8	58.4
Eating fewer calories to lose/maintain weight*	13.5	11.4	12.1	13.9	15.2	13.2	12.0
Eating less fat to lose/maintain weight*	27.4	25.3	25.8	27.7	28.3	29.1	29.4
Eating fewer calories and less fat to lose/maintain weight*	29.6	25.5	27.0	30.1	32.6	33.0	29.0
Using physical activity or exercise to lose/maintain weight*	60.7	74.7	67.7	64.0	60.5	55.4	43.3
Advised by health professional to lose weight	11.7	4.0	8.4	11.3	16.0	17.7	11.2

* Among those trying to lose or maintain weight.
Source: Centers for Disease Control and Prevention, Behavioral Risk Factor Surveillance System Prevalence Data, 2000; Internet site http://apps.nccd.cdc.gov/brfss/index.asp

Table 2.4 Leisure-Time Physical Activity Level by Sex and Age, 1999–2001

(percent distribution of people aged 18 or older by leisure-time physical activity level, percent participating in regular leisure-time physical activity by level, and percent participating in strengthening activities, by sex and age, 1999–2001)

| | total | physically inactive | at least some physical activity | regular physical activity | | | strengthening activities |
				any	light–moderate	vigorous	
Total people	**100.0%**	**38.4%**	**61.6%**	**31.4%**	**15.5%**	**22.6%**	**23.2%**
Aged 18 to 24	100.0	29.9	70.1	39.7	17.8	31.7	36.5
Aged 25 to 44	100.0	33.7	66.3	34.3	15.4	26.6	27.2
Aged 45 to 64	100.0	40.5	59.5	29.3	15.1	19.9	18.6
Aged 65 to 74	100.0	46.6	53.4	26.3	17.0	13.4	12.4
Aged 75 or older	100.0	60.8	39.2	15.6	11.2	6.2	9.2
Total men	**100.0**	**35.4**	**64.6**	**35.1**	**16.8**	**26.6**	**27.5**
Aged 18 to 24	100.0	25.3	74.7	46.6	20.6	39.1	45.3
Aged 25 to 44	100.0	31.4	68.6	37.0	16.3	29.9	31.6
Aged 45 to 64	100.0	39.8	60.2	31.5	15.7	22.5	20.5
Aged 65 to 74	100.0	42.1	57.9	30.4	18.7	16.9	14.3
Aged 75 or older	100.0	54.4	45.6	20.7	14.5	9.4	11.9
Total women	**100.0**	**41.2**	**58.8**	**28.0**	**14.3**	**18.9**	**19.3**
Aged 18 to 24	100.0	34.4	65.6	32.8	15.1	24.5	27.8
Aged 25 to 44	100.0	36.0	64.0	31.7	14.6	23.3	23.0
Aged 45 to 64	100.0	41.3	58.7	27.3	14.5	17.4	16.9
Aged 65 to 74	100.0	50.3	49.7	22.9	15.6	10.6	10.9
Aged 75 or older	100.0	65.0	35.0	12.3	9.1	4.2	7.4

Note: "Physically inactive" means no light to moderate or vigorous leisure-time physical activity. "At least some" includes light to moderate or vigorous leisure-time physical activities. "Regular physical activity" includes activities done at least three to five times per week. Regular "light to moderate" activity is defined as engaging in light to moderate activity at least five times per week for at least thirty minutes each time. Regular "vigorous" activity is defined as engaging in vigorous activity at least three times per week for at least twenty minutes each time. "Any" regular activity is defined as meeting either criterion or both critera. Light to moderate activity is leisure-time physical activity that causes only light sweating or a light to moderate increase in breathing or heart rate and is done for at least ten minutes per episode. Vigorous activity is leisure-time physical activity that causes heavy sweating or large increases in breathing or heart rate and is done for at least ten minutes per episode. "Strengthening" activities are those designed to strengthen muscles such as weight lifting or calisthenics. Minimum duration and frequency were not asked. Those engaging in strengthening activities may be included in the physically inactive if they did not engage in any other type of physical activity. Numbers will not add to 100 because people may be in more than one category.
Source: National Center for Health Statistics, Health Behaviors of Adults: United States, 1999–2001, Vital and Health Statistics, Series 10, No. 219, 2004

Birth Rate Is Rising among Women Aged 30 or Older

Rate is falling among women under age 30.

The nation's birth rate has been falling for decades, but since 1990 the trend has reversed itself among older women. Between 1960 and 2002, the birth rate among women aged 25 to 29 fell from 197 to 114 births per 1,000 women. During those same years, the birth rate among women aged 30 to 34 fell from 113 to 92. But the 2002 birth rate among 30-to-34-year-olds was 11 percent higher in 2002 than in 1990. In each successively older age group, the birth rate has increased by an ever-larger amount since 1990. In contrast, birth rates continued to fall among women under age 30 between 1990 and 2002.

In 1960, women aged 20 to 24 had the highest birth rate. In 2002, the highest birth rate was found in the 25-to-29 age group.

■ Because the majority of today's young women go to college and then enter the work force, they are delaying childbearing until their later twenties and catching up in their thirties.

Birth rates are unlikely to return to 1960 levels

(births per 1,000 women in age group, 1960 and 2002)

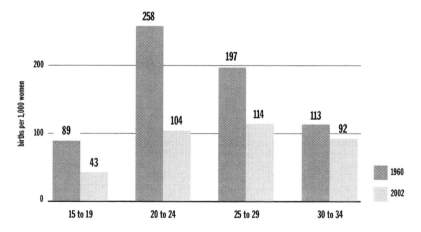

Table 2.5 Birth Rates by Age of Mother, 1990 to 2002

(number of live births per 1,000 women in age group and percent change in rate, 1990–2002)

	15 to 19	20 to 24	25 to 29	30 to 34	35 to 39	40 to 44	45 to 49
2002	43.0	103.6	113.6	91.5	41.4	8.3	0.5
2001	45.3	106.2	113.4	91.9	40.6	8.1	0.5
2000	47.7	109.7	113.5	91.2	39.7	8.0	0.5
1999	48.8	107.9	111.2	87.1	37.8	7.4	0.4
1998	50.3	108.4	110.2	85.2	36.9	7.4	0.4
1997	51.3	107.3	108.3	83.0	35.7	7.1	0.4
1996	53.5	107.8	108.6	82.1	34.9	6.8	0.3
1995	56.0	107.5	108.8	81.1	34.0	6.6	0.3
1994	58.2	109.2	111.0	80.4	33.4	6.4	0.3
1993	59.0	111.3	113.2	79.9	32.7	6.1	0.3
1992	60.3	113.7	115.7	79.6	32.3	5.9	0.3
1991	61.8	115.3	117.2	79.2	31.9	5.5	0.2
1990	59.9	116.5	120.2	80.8	31.7	5.5	0.2
Percent change							
1990 to 2002	−28.2%	−11.1%	−5.5%	13.2%	30.6%	50.9%	150.0%

Source: National Center for Health Statistics, Revised Birth and Fertility Rates for the 1990s and New Rates for the Hispanic Populations 2000 and 2001: United States, *National Vital Statistics Report, Vol. 51, No. 12, 2003; calculations by New Strategist*

Most Women Aged 25 to 29 Have Borne Children

One in three has had two or more children.

The proportion of women who have not given birth falls from 91 percent among 15-to-19-year-olds to a much smaller (but still substantial) 18 percent among women aged 40 to 44. Most women become mothers during their twenties. By their early thirties, the majority (51 percent) has had at least two children, and one in five has had three or more.

Among women who gave birth in the past year, 70 percent were between the ages of 20 and 34. Fully 30 percent were not married, including 36 percent of those having their first child. More than half of those having borne a child in the past year were in the labor force, including 60 percent of those having borne their first child.

■ Childbearing has changed greatly over the past few decades. Today, single mothers are far more common and working mothers are the norm.

Most new mothers are in the labor force

(percent distribution of women who gave birth to their first child in the past year by labor force status, 2002)

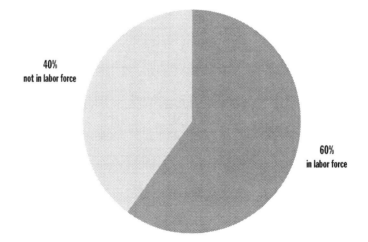

40%
not in labor force

60%
in labor force

Table 2.6 Number of Children Born to Women Aged 15 to 44, 2002

(total number of women aged 15 to 44, and percent distribution of women by number of children ever borne, by age, 2002; numbers in thousands)

	total		number of children						
	number	percent	none	one	two	three	four	five	six or more
Aged 15 to 44	**61,361**	**100.0%**	**43.5%**	**17.5%**	**22.2%**	**11.2%**	**3.8%**	**1.5%**	**0.3%**
Aged 15 to 19	9,809	100.0	91.2	5.2	2.4	0.8	0.2	0.1	0.0
Aged 20 to 24	9,683	100.0	67.0	19.6	9.3	3.2	0.6	0.3	0.1
Aged 25 to 29	9,221	100.0	45.2	22.2	19.8	9.1	2.7	0.9	0.1
Aged 30 to 34	10,284	100.0	27.6	21.8	29.6	14.1	4.7	1.9	0.2
Aged 35 to 39	10,803	100.0	20.2	18.6	32.4	18.8	6.9	2.6	0.5
Aged 40 to 44	11,561	100.0	17.9	17.4	35.4	18.9	6.8	2.8	0.8

Source: Bureau of the Census, Fertility of American Women: June 2002, *detailed tables, Internet site http://www.census.gov/population/www/socdemo/fertility/cps2002.html*

Table 2.7 Characteristics of Women Aged 15 to 44 Who Gave Birth in the Past Year, 2002

(total number of women aged 15 to 44, percent childless, number and percent distribution of those who gave birth in the past year and had a first birth in past year, by selected characteristics, 2002; numbers in thousands)

	total	percent childless	gave birth in past year number	gave birth in past year percent distribution	first birth in past year number	first birth in past year percent distribution
Total aged 15 to 44	**61,361**	**43.5%**	**3,766**	**100.0%**	**1,415**	**100.0%**
Aged 15 to 19	9,809	91.2	549	14.6	272	19.2
Aged 20 to 24	9,683	67.0	872	23.2	438	31.0
Aged 25 to 29	9,221	45.2	897	23.8	306	21.6
Aged 30 to 34	10,284	27.6	859	22.8	272	19.2
Aged 35 to 39	10,803	20.2	452	12.0	85	6.0
Aged 40 to 44	11,561	17.9	137	3.6	42	3.0
Marital Status						
Married, husband present	27,828	18.5	2,382	63.3	825	58.3
Married, husband absent/separated	2,446	21.1	124	3.3	42	3.0
Widowed or divorced	5,303	21.1	143	3.8	35	2.5
Never married	25,782	77.2	1,118	29.7	513	36.3
Race and Hispanic origin						
Asian	3,267	50.8	181	4.8	89	6.3
Black	8,846	39.0	571	15.2	197	13.9
Hispanic	9,141	35.8	750	19.9	278	19.6
Non-Hispanic white	40,017	45.6	2,262	60.1	854	60.4
Educational attainment						
Not a high school graduate	13,096	58.8	812	21.6	264	18.7
High school, four years	16,644	30.7	1,005	26.7	380	26.9
Some college, no degree	12,451	45.9	750	19.9	298	21.1
Associate's degree	5,113	33.0	221	5.9	79	5.6
Bachelor's degree	10,592	46.6	683	18.1	266	18.8
Graduate or professional degree	3,465	44.6	294	7.8	128	9.0
Labor force status						
In labor force	43,360	44.0	2,056	54.6	846	59.8
Not in labor force	18,001	42.4	1,710	45.4	568	40.1
Employment status						
Employed	40,150	43.2	1,867	49.6	741	52.4
Unemployed	3,210	52.8	189	5.0	106	7.5
Not in labor force	18,001	42.4	1,710	45.4	568	40.1

	total	percent childless	gave birth in past year		first birth in past year	
			number	percent distribution	number	percent distribution
Occupation						
Managerial and professional	13,021	43.8%	717	19.0%	309	21.8%
Technical, sales, admin. support	17,163	44.0	770	20.4	326	23.0
Service occupations	9,102	46.6	436	11.6	165	11.7
Farming, forestry, and fishing	493	47.8	16	0.4	2	0.1
Precision prod., craft and repair	819	33.9	37	1.0	13	0.9
Operators, fabricators, and laborers	2,884	32.9	118	3.1	38	2.7
Unemployed	452	83.7	25	0.7	25	1.8
Not in labor force	17,421	42.2	1,646	43.7	535	37.8
Household income						
Under $10,000	4,203	40.0	355	9.4	128	9.0
$10,000 to $19,999	5,760	39.9	472	12.5	200	14.1
$20,000 to $24,999	3,348	38.2	215	5.7	73	5.2
$25,000 to $29,999	3,464	41.9	194	5.2	55	3.9
$30,000 to $34,999	3,612	43.7	264	7.0	84	5.9
$35,000 to $49,999	8,477	43.0	457	12.1	161	11.4
$50,000 to $74,999	10,613	43.6	554	14.7	247	17.5
$75,000 and over	13,771	47.2	826	21.9	294	20.8
Region						
Northeast	11,616	46.1	694	18.4	247	17.5
Midwest	14,041	43.8	780	20.7	303	21.4
South	21,680	40.9	1,453	38.6	561	39.6
West	14,024	45.1	838	22.3	305	21.6
Metropolitan status						
In central cities	18,804	46.4	1,163	30.9	430	30.4
Outside central cities	31,950	43.8	1,869	49.6	719	50.8
Nonmetropolitan	10,606	37.3	734	19.5	266	18.8
Nativity						
Native born	52,428	44.8	3,129	83.1	1,153	81.5
Foreign born	8,933	35.6	637	16.9	262	18.5

Source: Bureau of the Census, Fertility of American Women: June 2002, *detailed tables, Internet site http://www.census.gov/population/www/socdemo/fertility/cps2002.html*

Half of Babies Are Born to Women Aged 25 to 34

More than one-third are born to women under age 25.

Despite an increase in the number of older mothers during the past few decades, the great majority of new mothers continue to be in their twenties and thirties. The women of Generation X, now aging out of the 25-to-34 age group, account for half of the nation's births. Only 14 percent of newborns in 2002 had a mother aged 35 or older, while a substantial 36 percent had a mother under age 25.

Among women aged 25 to 34 who gave birth in 2002, 33 percent were having their first child and a slightly larger 35 percent were having their second child. A substantial 27 percent were having their third or subsequent child.

Sixty-one percent of babies born to women aged 25 to 34 had a non-Hispanic white mother. The non-Hispanic white share is slightly larger among older women, and much lower among younger women. Only 48 percent of babies born to women under age 25 had a non-Hispanic white mother.

■ Generation Xers account for half of births today, but the share will shrink rapidly as they age into their late thirties.

The women of Generation X account for half of births

(percent distribution of births by age of mother, 2002)

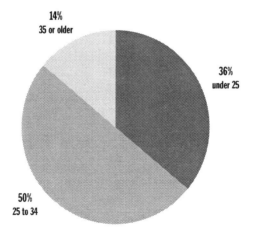

14%
35 or older

36%
under 25

50%
25 to 34

Table 2.8 Births to Women by Age and Birth Order, 2002

(number and percent distribution of births by mother's age and birth order, 2002)

	total births	first child	second child	third child	fourth or later child
Total births	**4,021,726**	**1,594,921**	**1,306,786**	**675,270**	**434,527**
Under age 25	1,454,914	816,186	424,389	154,360	56,357
Aged 25 to 34	2,011,610	654,757	705,222	394,522	252,227
Aged 25 to 29	1,060,391	378,647	362,440	199,106	117,622
Aged 30 to 34	951,219	276,110	342,782	195,416	134,605
Aged 35 to 39	453,927	102,180	148,922	105,468	96,042
Aged 40 or older	101,275	21,798	28,253	20,920	29,901
PERCENT DISTRIBUTION BY AGE					
Total births	**100.0%**	**100.0%**	**100.0%**	**100.0%**	**100.0%**
Under age 25	36.2	51.2	32.5	22.9	13.0
Aged 25 to 34	50.0	41.1	54.0	58.4	58.1
Aged 25 to 29	26.4	23.7	27.7	29.5	27.1
Aged 30 to 34	23.7	17.3	26.2	28.9	31.0
Aged 35 to 39	11.3	6.4	11.4	15.6	22.1
Aged 40 or older	2.5	1.4	2.2	3.1	6.9
PERCENT DISTRIBUTION BY BIRTH ORDER					
Total births	**100.0%**	**39.7%**	**32.5%**	**16.8%**	**10.8%**
Under age 25	100.0	56.1	29.2	10.6	3.9
Aged 25 to 34	100.0	32.5	35.1	19.6	12.5
Aged 25 to 29	100.0	35.7	34.2	18.8	11.1
Aged 30 to 34	100.0	29.0	36.0	20.5	14.2
Aged 35 to 39	100.0	22.5	32.8	23.2	21.2
Aged 40 or older	100.0	21.5	27.9	20.7	29.5

Note: Numbers will not add to total because not stated is not included.
Source: National Center for Health Statistics, Births: Final Data for 2002, *National Vital Statistics Report, Vol. 52, No. 10, 2002, calculations by New Strategist*

Table 2.9 Births by Age, Race, and Hispanic Origin of Mother, 2002

(number and percent distribution of births by age, race, and Hispanic origin of mother, 2002)

	total	American Indian	Asian	black	white	Hispanic	non-Hispanic white
			race			Hispanic origin	
Total births	**4,021,726**	**42,368**	**210,907**	**593,691**	**3,174,760**	**876,642**	**2,298,156**
Under age 25	1,454,914	22,183	38,172	301,687	1,092,872	395,556	700,157
Aged 25 to 34	2,011,610	16,477	132,859	231,597	1,630,677	394,030	1,235,082
Aged 25 to 29	1,060,391	10,139	62,519	136,591	851,142	236,143	614,909
Aged 30 to 34	951,219	6,338	70,340	95,006	779,535	157,887	620,173
Aged 35 to 39	453,927	2,976	32,730	48,388	369,833	71,480	297,436
Aged 40 or older	101,275	732	7,146	12,019	81,378	15,576	65,481
PERCENT DISTRIBUTION BY AGE							
Total births	**100.0%**	**100.0%**	**100.0%**	**100.0%**	**100.0%**	**100.0%**	**100.0%**
Under age 25	36.2	52.4	18.1	50.8	34.4	45.1	30.5
Aged 25 to 34	50.0	38.9	63.0	39.0	51.4	44.9	53.7
Aged 25 to 29	26.4	23.9	29.6	2.3	26.8	26.9	26.8
Aged 30 to 34	23.7	15.0	33.4	1.6	24.6	18.0	27.0
Aged 35 to 39	11.3	7.0	15.5	8.2	11.6	8.2	12.9
Aged 40 or older	2.5	1.7	3.4	2.0	2.6	1.8	2.8
PERCENT DISTRIBUTION BY RACE AND HISPANIC ORIGIN							
Total births	**100.0%**	**1.1%**	**5.2%**	**14.8%**	**78.9%**	**21.8%**	**57.1%**
Under age 25	100.0	1.5	2.6	20.7	75.1	27.2	48.1
Aged 25 to 34	100.0	0.8	6.6	11.5	81.1	19.6	61.4
Aged 25 to 29	100.0	1.0	5.9	12.9	80.3	22.3	58.0
Aged 30 to 34	100.0	0.7	7.4	10.0	82.0	16.6	65.2
Aged 35 to 39	100.0	0.7	7.2	10.7	81.5	15.7	65.5
Aged 40 or older	100.0	0.7	7.1	11.9	80.4	15.4	64.7

Note: Numbers will not add to total because Hispanics may be of any race and not stated is not included.
Source: National Center for Health Statistics, Births: Final Data for 2002, National Vital Statistics Report, Vol. 52, No. 10, 2002, calculations by New Strategist

Many Generation X Mothers Are Not Married

The percentage of babies born to unmarried women falls with age.

Slightly more than one-third of babies born in 2002 had a mother who was not married. There are sharp differences by age in the percentage of new mothers who are not married, however. The younger the woman, the more likely she is to give birth out of wedlock.

The 60 percent majority of babies born to women under age 25 in 2002 were born to single mothers. The figure stood at a much smaller 20 percent among babies born to women aged 25 to 34. Among those born to women aged 40 or older, only 17 percent had an unmarried mother.

Black women are most likely to be single mothers. Fully 52 percent of babies born in 2002 to black women aged 25 to 34 were out-of-wedlock. Among Hispanics, the share was 32 percent. Among non-Hispanic whites, it was a much smaller 12 percent.

■ The differences in out-of-wedlock childbearing by race and Hispanic origin result in different lifestyles among adults in their twenties and thirties.

The percentage of babies born to single mothers varies by race and Hispanic origin

(percent of babies born to unmarried women aged 25 to 34, by race and Hispanic origin, 2002)

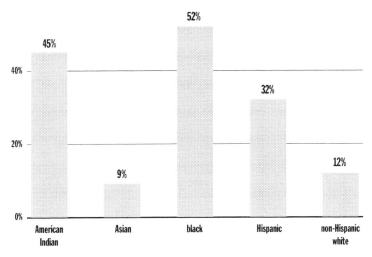

Table 2.10 Births by Age, Marital Status, Race, and Hispanic Origin of Mother, 2002

(total number of births and number and percent to unmarried women by age, race, and Hispanic origin of mother, 2002)

		race				Hispanic origin	
	total	American Indian	Asian	black	white	Hispanic	non-Hispanic white
Total births	**4,021,726**	**42,368**	**210,907**	**593,691**	**3,174,760**	**876,642**	**2,298,156**
Under age 25	1,454,914	22,183	38,172	301,687	1,092,872	395,556	700,157
Aged 25 to 34	2,011,610	16,477	132,859	231,597	1,630,677	394,030	1,235,082
Aged 25 to 29	1,060,391	10,139	62,519	136,591	851,142	236,143	614,909
Aged 30 to 34	951,219	6,338	70,340	95,006	779,535	157,887	620,173
Aged 35 to 39	453,927	2,976	32,730	48,388	369,833	71,480	297,436
Aged 40 or older	101,275	732	7,146	12,019	81,378	15,576	65,481
BIRTHS TO UNMARRIED WOMEN							
Total births	**1,365,966**	**25,297**	**31,344**	**404,864**	**904,461**	**381,466**	**528,535**
Under age 25	874,936	16,355	16,505	260,825	581,251	233,118	351,288
Aged 25 to 34	407,520	7,468	11,988	120,321	267,743	125,289	144,454
Aged 25 to 29	268,312	4,993	7,318	79,946	176,055	83,035	94,304
Aged 30 to 34	139,208	2,475	4,670	40,375	91,688	42,254	50,150
Aged 35 to 39	66,036	1,176	2,218	18,958	43,684	18,566	25,472
Aged 40 or older	17,474	298	633	4,760	11,783	4,493	7,321
PERCENT OF BIRTHS TO UNMARRIED WOMEN							
Total births	**34.0%**	**59.7%**	**14.9%**	**68.2%**	**28.5%**	**43.5%**	**23.0%**
Under age 25	60.1	73.7	43.2	86.5	53.2	58.9	50.2
Aged 25 to 34	20.3	45.3	9.0	52.0	16.4	31.8	11.7
Aged 25 to 29	25.3	49.2	11.7	58.5	20.7	35.2	15.3
Aged 30 to 34	14.6	39.1	6.6	42.5	11.8	26.8	8.1
Aged 35 to 39	14.5	39.5	6.8	39.2	11.8	26.0	8.6
Aged 40 or older	17.3	40.7	8.9	39.6	14.5	28.8	11.2

Note: Births by race and Hispanic origin will not add to total because Hispanics may be of any race, not all races are shown, and not stated is not included.
Source: National Center for Health Statistics, Births: Final Data for 2002, National Vital Statistics Report, Vol. 52, No. 10, 2002, calculations by New Strategist

Caesarean Deliveries Are Common among Women of All Ages

The rate is highest among older women, however.

Delayed childbearing can have an unanticipated cost. The older a woman is when she has a child, the greater the likelihood of complications that necessitate Caesarean delivery.

Among babies born in 2002, more than one in four (26 percent) were Caesarean deliveries. Only 20 percent of babies born to women under age 25 were delivered by Caesarean section, but the share stood at 27 percent among women aged 25 to 34, and topped 40 percent among women aged 40 or older.

Many women whose first child is delivered by Caesarean hope that subsequent children can be delivered vaginally. Age influences the likelihood of a subsequent Caesarean delivery, however. Repeat Caesareans are more common among older women.

■ As women delay childbearing, the rate of Caesarean delivery increases. With new fertility technologies enabling more women to have children later in life, the rate is likely to rise further.

Young women are least likely to require Caesarean deliveries

(percent of births delivered by Caesarean section, by age of mother, 2002)

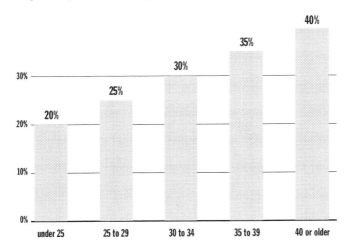

Table 2.11 Birth Delivery Method by Age, 2002

(number and percent distribution of births by age and method of delivery, 2002)

		vaginal		Caesarean		
	total	total	after previous Caesarean	total	first	repeat
Total births	**4,021,726**	**2,958,423**	**59,248**	**1,043,846**	**634,426**	**409,420**
Under age 25	1,454,914	1,153,190	12,416	295,802	212,688	83,114
Aged 25 to 34	2,011,610	1,452,342	34,270	549,028	316,028	233,000
Aged 25 to 29	1,060,391	788,776	16,294	266,452	159,869	106,583
Aged 30 to 34	951,219	663,566	17,976	282,576	156,159	126,417
Aged 35 to 39	453,927	293,251	10,278	158,005	82,497	75,508
Aged 40 or older	101,275	59,640	2,284	41,011	23,213	17,798
PERCENT DISTRIBUTION BY AGE						
Total births	**100.0%**	**100.0%**	**100.0%**	**100.0%**	**100.0%**	**100.0%**
Under age 25	36.2	39.0	21.0	28.3	33.5	20.3
Aged 25 to 34	50.0	49.1	57.8	52.6	49.8	56.9
Aged 25 to 29	26.4	26.7	27.5	25.5	25.2	26.0
Aged 30 to 34	23.7	22.4	30.3	27.1	24.6	30.9
Aged 35 to 39	11.3	9.9	17.3	15.1	1.3	18.4
Aged 40 or older	2.5	2.0	3.9	3.9	3.7	4.3
PERCENT DISTRIBUTION BY DELIVERY METHOD						
Total births	**100.0%**	**73.6%**	**1.5%**	**26.0%**	**15.8%**	**10.2%**
Under age 25	100.0	79.3	0.9	20.3	14.6	5.7
Aged 25 to 34	100.0	72.2	1.7	27.3	15.7	11.6
Aged 25 to 29	100.0	74.4	1.5	25.1	15.1	10.1
Aged 30 to 34	100.0	69.8	1.9	29.7	16.4	13.3
Aged 35 to 39	100.0	64.6	2.3	34.8	18.2	16.6
Aged 40 or older	100.0	58.9	2.3	40.5	22.9	17.6

Note: Numbers will not add to total because not stated is not included.
Source: National Center for Health Statistics, Births: Final Data for 2002, *National Vital Statistics Report, Vol. 52, No. 10, 2002, calculations by New Strategist*

One-Quarter of Gen Xers Smoke, Two-Thirds Drink

Most have tried to quit.

The percentage of Americans who smoke cigarettes is down sharply from what it was a few decades ago. Nevertheless, in 2002, a substantial 23 percent of people aged 18 or older were current smokers. The figure peaks among 18-to-24-year-olds at 31 percent. In the 25-to-34 age group, a smaller 26 percent smoke. Among those who do, more than half (57 percent) have tried to quit smoking in the past twelve months.

Drinking alcohol is much more popular than smoking. Overall, 63 percent of people aged 18 or older are current drinkers, with men much more likely than women to drink (69 versus 57 percent). The proportion of people who drink alcohol peaks in the 25-to-44 age group, then declines with age. A minority of people aged 65 or older are drinkers.

■ Generation X is aging out of the risk-taking age groups. The percentage of Gen Xers who smoke and drink will decline as they get older.

Many Generation Xers have tried to quit smoking

(percent of people aged 25 to 34 who smoke cigarettes and share of smokers who have tried to quit in the past twelve months, 2002)

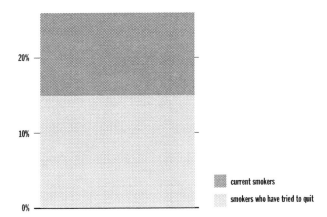

current smokers

smokers who have tried to quit

Table 2.12 Cigarette Smoking and Attempts to Quit by Age, 2002

(percent of people aged 18 or older who currently smoke cigarettes and percent of smokers who quit smoking for at least one day in the past twelve months, by age, 2002)

	current smokers	smokers who quit on one or more days
Total people	**23.0%**	**51.8%**
Aged 18 to 24	31.2	65.4
Aged 25 to 34	25.9	56.9
Aged 35 to 44	27.2	49.3
Aged 45 to 54	24.8	47.9
Aged 55 to 64	20.8	44.2
Aged 65 or older	10.0	42.0

Source: Centers for Disease Control and Prevention, Behavioral Risk Factor Surveillance System Prevalence Data, 2002; Internet site http://apps.nccd.cdc.gov/brfss/index.asp

Table 2.13 Alcohol Use by Age, 2001

(percent of people aged 18 or older who are current drinkers, by age and sex, 2001)

	total	men	women
Total people	**62.5%**	**68.8%**	**56.8%**
Aged 18 to 24	63.6	69.6	57.7
Aged 25 to 44	70.8	76.8	65.0
Aged 45 to 54	65.6	70.1	61.2
Aged 55 to 64	57.6	64.2	51.6
Aged 65 or older	42.0	50.9	35.5

Source: National Center for Health Statistics, Health, United States, 2003, Internet site http://www.cdc.gov/nchs/hus.htm

Most Generation Xers Have Used Illicit Drugs

Generation X is much less likely to have used illicit drugs in the past month than 18-to-25-year-olds, however.

People aged 18 to 25 are most likely to be current drug users. Twenty percent of them have used illicit drugs in the past month. The percentage of current users falls to 13 percent among 26-to-29-year-olds and to just 9 percent among 30-to-34-year-olds.

More than half of Generation Xers have used illicit drugs at some time during their life, with the percentage standing at 57 to 59 percent in the 26-to-34 age group. The figure rises to 61 percent in the 35-to-39 age group and peaks at 66 percent among the youngest Baby Boomers, aged 40 to 44.

■ Although drug use among young adults is a serious concern, chronic use drops sharply as people age into their late twenties, establish careers, and start families.

Generation Xers are less likely than Boomers to have ever used illicit drugs

(percent of people aged 12 or older who have ever used any illicit drug, by age, 2002)

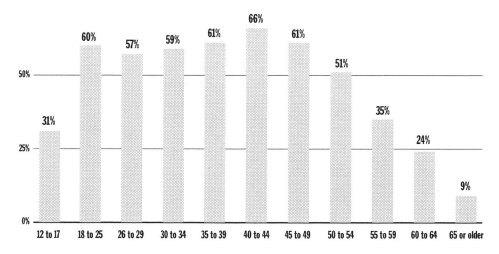

Table 2.14 Drug Use by Age, 2002

(percent of people aged 12 or older who ever used any illicit drug, who used an illicit drug in the past year, and who used an illicit drug in the past month, by age, 2002)

	ever used	used in past year	used in past month
Total people	**46.0%**	**14.9%**	**8.3%**
Aged 12 to 17	30.9	22.2	11.6
Aged 18 to 25	59.8	35.5	20.2
Aged 26 to 29	57.4	22.4	12.8
Aged 30 to 34	59.0	17.2	8.8
Aged 35 to 39	61.0	15.5	8.6
Aged 40 to 44	66.4	14.4	7.8
Aged 45 to 49	60.9	12.3	7.5
Aged 50 to 54	51.1	6.5	3.4
Aged 55 to 59	35.0	3.3	1.9
Aged 60 to 64	23.7	4.1	2.5
Aged 65 or older	9.2	1.3	0.8

Note: Illicit drugs include marijuana/hashish, cocaine (including crack), heroin, hallucinogens, inhalants, or any prescription-type psychotherapeutic used nonmedically.
Source: SAMHSA, Office of Applied Studies, National Survey on Drug Use and Health, 2002; Internet site http://www.samhsa.gov/

One in Four Generation Xers Has No Health Insurance

The figure is even higher among 18-to-24-year-olds.

People aged 18 to 34 are more likely than middle-aged or older adults to be without health insurance. Entering the workforce at the age of 18, or graduating from college at the age of 21, usually means health insurance coverage is no longer available through a parent's plan. This reality partly explains why a substantial 30 percent of the nation's 18-to-24-year-olds and 25 percent of 25-to-34-year-olds have no health insurance.

Most Americans obtain health insurance coverage through their employer, but ever fewer employers offer health insurance coverage. Among 25-to-34-year-olds, only 63 percent had employment-based coverage in 2002. Among 18-to-44-year-olds without health insurance in 2000, the single biggest reason for not having coverage was the high cost (cited by 44 percent), followed by losing employment (22 percent). In third place, 16 percent said their employer did not offer health insurance.

■ The health insurance needs of young adults are a problem without an easy solution since few can afford to buy private insurance.

More than one in four people under age 35 lack health insurance

(percent of people aged 18 to 34 who do not have health insurance, 2002)

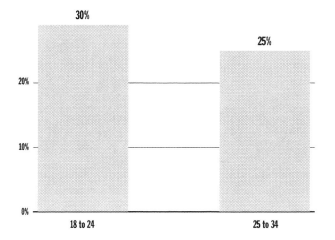

Table 2.15 Health Insurance Coverage by Age, 2002

(number and percent distribution of people by age and health insurance coverage status, 2002; numbers in thousands)

| | | covered by private or government health insurance | | | | | | | not |
| | | private health insurance | | | government health insurance | | | | covered |
	total	total	total	employment based	total	Medicaid	Medicare	military	
Total people	285,933	242,360	198,973	175,296	73,624	33,246	38,448	10,063	43,574
Under age 18	73,312	64,781	49,473	46,182	19,662	17,526	524	2,148	8,531
Aged 18 to 24	27,438	19,310	16,562	13,429	3,738	2,909	183	779	8,128
Aged 25 to 34	39,243	29,474	26,492	24,800	3,944	2,801	455	922	9,769
Aged 35 to 44	44,074	36,292	33,240	31,180	4,240	2,728	881	1,121	7,781
Aged 45 to 54	40,234	34,648	31,724	29,617	4,345	2,227	1,382	1,351	5,586
Aged 55 to 64	27,399	23,879	20,797	18,505	4,882	1,773	2,392	1,482	3,521
Aged 65 or older	34,234	33,976	20,685	11,583	32,813	3,283	32,631	2,259	258
PERCENT DISTRIBUTION BY AGE									
Total people	100.0%	100.0%	100.0%	100.0%	100.0%	100.0%	100.0%	100.0%	100.0%
Under age 18	25.6	26.7	24.9	26.3	26.7	52.7	1.4	21.3	19.6
Aged 18 to 24	9.6	8.0	8.3	7.7	5.1	8.7	0.5	7.7	18.7
Aged 25 to 34	13.7	12.2	13.3	14.1	5.4	8.4	1.2	9.2	22.4
Aged 35 to 44	15.4	15.0	16.7	17.8	5.8	8.2	2.3	11.1	17.9
Aged 45 to 54	14.1	14.3	15.9	16.9	5.9	6.7	3.6	13.4	12.8
Aged 55 to 64	9.6	9.9	10.5	10.6	6.6	5.3	6.2	14.7	8.1
Aged 65 or older	12.0	14.0	10.4	6.6	44.6	9.9	84.9	22.4	0.6
PERCENT DISTRIBUTION BY TYPE OF COVERAGE									
Total people	100.0%	84.8%	69.6%	61.3%	25.7%	11.6%	13.4%	3.5%	15.2%
Under age 18	100.0	88.4	67.5	63.0	26.8	23.9	0.7	2.9	11.6
Aged 18 to 24	100.0	70.4	60.4	48.9	13.6	10.6	0.7	2.8	29.6
Aged 25 to 34	100.0	75.1	67.5	63.2	10.1	7.1	1.2	2.3	24.9
Aged 35 to 44	100.0	82.3	75.4	70.7	9.6	6.2	2.0	2.5	17.7
Aged 45 to 54	100.0	86.1	78.8	73.6	10.8	5.5	3.4	3.4	13.9
Aged 55 to 64	100.0	87.2	75.9	67.5	17.8	6.5	8.7	5.4	12.9
Aged 65 or older	100.0	99.2	60.4	33.8	95.8	9.6	95.3	6.6	0.8

Note: Numbers may not add to total because some people have more than one type of health insurance coverage.
Source: Bureau of the Census, 2003 Current Population Survey, Internet site http://www.census.gov/hhes/hlthins/historic/hihistt2.html; calculations by New Strategist

Table 2.16 People Aged 18 to 44 by Health Insurance Coverage Status and Reason for No Coverage, 2000

(number and percent distribution of people aged 18 to 44 by health insurance coverage status and reasons for no coverage, by sex, 2000; numbers in thousands)

	total		men		women	
	number	percent	number	percent	number	percent
Total people aged 18 to 44	**108,472**	**100.0%**	**53,442**	**100.0%**	**55,030**	**100.0%**
With health insurance	84,925	78.3	40,641	76.1	44,284	80.5
Without health insurance	23,547	21.7	12,801	24.0	10,746	19.5
Without health insurance	**23,547**	**100.0**	**12,801**	**100.0**	**10,746**	**100.0**
Lost job or change in employment	5,201	22.1	2,871	22.4	2,330	21.7
Change in marital status or death of parent	551	2.3	141	1.1	410	3.8
Ineligible due to age/left school	2,580	11.0	1,630	12.7	950	8.8
Employer didn't offer insurance/ company refused	3,676	15.6	2,233	17.4	1,443	13.4
Cost	10,334	43.9	5,727	44.7	4,606	42.9
Medicaid stopped	1,782	7.6	428	3.3	1,353	12.6
Other	1,201	5.1	701	5.5	499	4.6

Note: Numbers may not sum to total because people can report more than one reason.
Source: National Center for Health Statistics, Summary Health Statistics for the U.S. Population: National Health Interview Survey, 2000, Vital and Health Statistics, Series 10, No. 214, 2003

Health Problems Are Few in the 18-to-44 Age Group

Lower back pain is by far the most common health condition in the age group.

Twenty-eight percent of Americans aged 18 to 44 have experienced lower back pain for at least one full day in the past three months, making it the most common health condition in the age group. Migraines or severe headaches are second, with 20 percent having the problem. Sinusitis is third, mentioned by 16 percent. The 18-to-44 age group accounts for more than half of those suffering from hay fever and asthma.

Few adults aged 18 to 44 have hearing or vision problems. But they are just as likely as older adults to have emotional problems. The proportion of people saying they feel sad, hopeless, or worthless at least some of the time does not vary much by age. Young and middle-aged adults are more likely to be nervous and restless at least some of the time than Americans aged 65 or older.

While 10 percent of people aged 16 to 64 have a health problem that prevents them from working or limits the kind of work they can do, the proportion is a smaller 6 percent among 25-to-34-year-olds and rises to 9 percent in the 35-to-44 age group. But the less educated the young adult is, the more likely he or she is to have a work disability.

People with AIDS are often counted among the nation's disabled. As of mid-2002, more than 800,000 people had been diagnosed with AIDS, most of them Baby-Boom men. People aged 20 to 29 account for only 16 percent of those diagnosed with AIDS. Those aged 30 to 39 account for a much larger 44 percent.

■ As Generation Xers age into their forties, the number with chronic conditions such as heart disease, arthritis, and hearing problems will rise.

The top five health conditions among people aged 18 to 44

(percent of people aged 18 to 44 with selected health conditions, 2001)

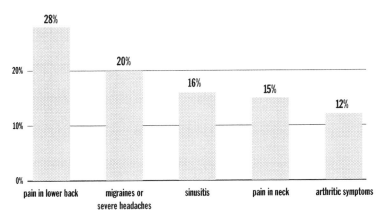

Table 2.17 Number of People Aged 18 or Older with Selected Health Conditions, 2001

(number of people aged 18 or older with selected health conditions, by type of condition and age, 2001; numbers in thousands)

	total	18 to 44	45 to 64	65 or older
Total people	**203,832**	**108,436**	**62,531**	**32,864**
Heart disease	23,482	4,996	8,173	10,313
Coronary	12,719	1,057	4,748	6,914
Hypertension	41,764	7,604	17,900	16,260
Stroke	4,836	478	1,416	2,942
Emphysema	2,984	200	1,100	1,684
Asthma	22,169	12,795	6,508	2,866
Hay fever	20,405	10,834	7,218	2,353
Sinusitis	35,462	17,203	13,281	4,979
Chronic bronchitis	11,199	4,913	4,074	2,211
Cancer	14,003	2,379	5,151	6,473
Breast cancer	2,256	176	987	1,092
Cervical cancer	1,172	597	423	151
Prostate cancer	1,499	3	225	1,274
Diabetes	13,006	2,167	5,834	5,005
Ulcers	18,901	7,025	7,211	4,665
Kidney disease	3,301	1,019	1,124	1,158
Liver disease	2,697	927	1,337	432
Arthritic symptoms	41,185	12,987	16,850	11,348
Migraines, severe headaches	33,899	21,616	10,027	2,255
Pain in neck	34,084	15,801	13,117	5,167
Pain in lower back	63,253	30,783	22,010	10,460
Pain in face or jaw	10,789	5,991	3,657	1,141
Hearing				
Good	168,207	99,096	49,678	19,433
A little trouble	28,411	8,199	10,822	9,389
A lot of trouble or deaf	6,996	1,116	1,988	3,893
Vision				
No trouble	183,272	101,587	54,778	26,907
Trouble	20,378	6,786	7,675	5,917
Absence of teeth	17,211	2,370	5,793	9,047
Sadness				
All or most of the time	6,862	3,455	2,337	1,070
Some of the time	19,529	9,692	6,319	3,519
Hopelessness				
All or most of the time	4,377	2,275	1,491	611
Some of the time	9,038	4,937	2,900	1,202
Worthlessness				
All or most of the time	3,850	1,824	1,432	594
Some of the time	7,031	3,516	2,442	1,073

	total	18 to 44	45 to 64	65 or older
Everything is an effort				
All or most of the time	11,464	6,319	3,596	1,549
Some of the time	18,362	10,285	5,455	2,622
Nervousness				
All or most of the time	9,147	4,540	3,177	1,431
Some of the time	28,279	15,921	8,671	3,687
Restlessness				
All or most of the time	11,171	6,187	3,563	1,421
Some of the time	26,962	15,001	8,387	3,573

Note: From heart disease through arthritic symptoms, respondents were asked whether they had been told by a doctor or other health professional in the past twelve months whether they had the condition; from migraines through pain in face or jaw, respondents were asked whether they had experienced pain for one full day or more during the past three months; from sadness through restlessness, respondents were asked how often they had the feeling in the past thirty days; numbers will not add to total because people may have more than one condition.
Source: National Center for Health Statistics, Summary Health Statistics for U.S. Adults: National Health Interview Survey, 2001, Series 10, No. 218, 2004; calculations by New Strategist

Table 2.18 Percent of People Aged 18 or Older with Selected Health Conditions, 2001

(percent of people aged 18 or older with selected health conditions, by type of condition and age, 2001)

	total	18 to 44	45 to 64	65 or older
Total people	100.0%	100.0%	100.0%	100.0%
Heart disease	11.5	4.6	13.1	31.4
Coronary	6.2	1.0	7.6	21.0
Hypertension	20.5	7.0	28.6	49.5
Stroke	2.4	0.4	2.3	9.0
Emphysema	1.5	0.2	1.8	5.1
Asthma	10.9	11.8	10.4	8.7
Hay fever	10.0	10.0	11.5	7.2
Sinusitis	17.4	15.9	21.2	15.2
Chronic bronchitis	5.5	4.5	6.5	6.7
Cancer	6.9	2.2	8.2	19.7
Breast cancer	1.1	0.2	1.6	3.3
Cervical cancer	0.6	0.6	0.7	0.5
Prostate cancer	0.7	0.0	0.4	3.9
Diabetes	6.4	2.0	9.3	15.2
Ulcers	9.3	6.5	11.5	14.2
Kidney disease	1.6	0.9	1.8	3.5
Liver disease	1.3	0.9	2.1	1.3
Arthritic symptoms	20.2	12.0	26.9	34.5
Migraines, severe headaches	16.6	19.9	16.0	6.9
Pain in neck	16.7	14.6	21.0	15.7
Pain in lower back	31.0	28.4	35.2	31.8
Pain in face or jaw	5.3	5.5	5.8	3.5
Hearing				
Good	82.5	91.4	79.4	59.1
A little trouble	13.9	7.6	17.3	28.6
A lot of trouble or deaf	3.4	1.0	3.2	11.8
Vision				
No trouble	89.9	93.7	87.6	81.9
Trouble	10.0	6.3	12.3	18.0
Absence of teeth	8.4	2.2	9.3	27.5
Sadness				
All or most of the time	3.4	3.2	3.7	3.3
Some of the time	9.6	8.9	10.1	10.7
Hopelessness				
All or most of the time	2.1	2.1	2.4	1.9
Some of the time	4.4	4.6	4.6	3.7
Worthlessness				
All or most of the time	1.9	1.7	2.3	1.8
Some of the time	3.4	3.2	3.9	3.3

	total	18 to 44	45 to 64	65 or older
Everything is an effort				
All or most of the time	5.6%	5.8%	5.8%	4.7%
Some of the time	9.0	9.5	8.7	8.0
Nervousness				
All or most of the time	4.5	4.2	5.1	4.4
Some of the time	13.9	14.7	13.9	11.2
Restlessness				
All or most of the time	5.5	5.7	5.7	4.3
Some of the time	13.2	13.8	13.4	10.9

Note: From heart disease through arthritic symptoms, respondents were asked whether they had been told by a doctor or other health professional in the past twelve months whether they had the condition; from migraines through pain in face or jaw, respondents were asked whether they had experienced pain for one full day or more during the past three months; from sadness through restlessness, respondents were asked how often they had the feeling in the past thirty days; numbers will not add to total because people may have more than one condition.
Source: National Center for Health Statistics, Summary Health Statistics for U.S. Adults: National Health Interview Survey, 2001, *Series 10, No. 218, 2004; calculations by New Strategist*

Table 2.19 Percent Distribution of People Aged 18 or Older with Selected Health Conditions, 2001

(percent distribution of people aged 18 or older with selected health conditions, by type of condition and age, 2001)

	total	18 to 44	45 to 64	65 or older
Total people	**100.0%**	**53.2%**	**30.7%**	**16.1%**
Heart disease	100.0	21.3	34.8	43.9
Coronary	100.0	8.3	37.3	54.4
Hypertension	100.0	18.2	42.9	38.9
Stroke	100.0	9.9	29.3	60.8
Emphysema	100.0	6.7	36.9	56.4
Asthma	100.0	57.7	29.4	12.9
Hay fever	100.0	53.1	35.4	11.5
Sinusitis	100.0	48.5	37.5	14.0
Chronic bronchitis	100.0	43.9	36.4	19.7
Cancer	100.0	17.0	36.8	46.2
Breast cancer	100.0	7.8	43.8	48.4
Cervical cancer	100.0	50.9	36.1	12.9
Prostate cancer	100.0	0.2	15.0	85.0
Diabetes	100.0	16.7	44.9	38.5
Ulcers	100.0	37.2	38.2	24.7
Kidney disease	100.0	30.9	34.1	35.1
Liver disease	100.0	34.4	49.6	16.0
Arthritic symptoms	100.0	31.5	40.9	27.6
Migraines, severe headaches	100.0	63.8	29.6	6.7
Pain in neck	100.0	46.4	38.5	15.2
Pain in lower back	100.0	48.7	34.8	16.5
Pain in face or jaw	100.0	55.5	33.9	10.6
Hearing				
Good	100.0	58.9	29.5	11.6
A little trouble	100.0	28.9	38.1	33.0
A lot of trouble or deaf	100.0	16.0	28.4	55.6
Vision				
No trouble	100.0	55.4	29.9	14.7
Trouble	100.0	33.3	37.7	29.0
Absence of teeth	100.0	13.8	33.7	52.6
Sadness				
All or most of the time	100.0	50.3	34.1	15.6
Some of the time	100.0	49.6	32.4	18.0
Hopelessness				
All or most of the time	100.0	52.0	34.1	14.0
Some of the time	100.0	54.6	32.1	13.3

	total	18 to 44	45 to 64	65 or older
Worthlessness				
All or most of the time	100.0%	47.4%	37.2%	15.4%
Some of the time	100.0	50.0	34.7	15.3
Everything is an effort				
All or most of the time	100.0	55.1	31.4	13.5
Some of the time	100.0	56.0	29.7	14.3
Nervousness				
All or most of the time	100.0	49.6	34.7	15.6
Some of the time	100.0	56.3	30.7	13.0
Restlessness				
All or most of the time	100.0	55.4	31.9	12.7
Some of the time	100.0	55.6	31.1	13.3

Note: From heart disease through arthritic symptoms, respondents were asked whether they had been told by a doctor or other health professional in the past twelve months whether they had the condition; from migraines through pain in face or jaw, respondents were asked whether they had experienced pain for one full day or more during the past three months; from sadness through restlessness, respondents were asked how often they had the feeling in the past thirty days; numbers will not add to total because people may have more than one condition.
Source: National Center for Health Statistics, Summary Health Statistics for U.S. Adults: National Health Interview Survey, 2001, *Series 10, No. 218, 2004; calculations by New Strategist*

Table 2.20 People Aged 25 to 44 with a Work Disability, 2002

(number and percent of people aged 16 to 64 and 25 to 44 with a work disability, by education and severity of disability, 2002; numbers in thousands)

| | | with a work disability | | | | | |
| | | total | | not severe | | severe | |
	total	number	percent	number	percent	number	percent
Total aged 16 to 64	**183,018**	**18,120**	**9.9%**	**5,487**	**3.0%**	**12,632**	**6.9%**
Not a high school graduate	33,185	5,041	15.2	801	2.4	4,240	12.8
High school graduate	54,676	6,579	12.0	1,878	3.4	4,701	8.6
Associate's degree or some college	50,118	4,442	8.9	1,776	3.5	2,666	5.3
Bachelor's degree or more	45,038	2,058	4.6	1,032	2.3	1,026	2.3
Total aged 25 to 34	**38,402**	**2,284**	**5.9**	**783**	**2.0**	**1,501**	**3.9**
Not a high school graduate	5,070	510	10.1	90	1.8	419	8.3
High school graduate	10,924	952	8.7	287	2.6	666	6.1
Associate's degree or some college	10,646	548	5.1	263	2.5	285	2.7
Bachelor's degree or more	11,762	274	2.3	143	1.2	131	1.1
Total aged 35 to 44	**44,003**	**3,839**	**8.7**	**1,174**	**2.7**	**2,665**	**6.1**
Not a high school graduate	5,138	946	18.4	131	2.5	817	15.9
High school graduate	14,258	1,495	10.5	448	3.1	1,047	7.3
Associate's degree or some college	12,077	1,004	8.3	398	3.3	606	5.0
Bachelor's degree or more	12,529	393	3.1	198	1.6	195	1.6

Note: A person is considered to have a work disability if one or more of the following conditions are met: 1) identified by the March supplement question "Does anyone in this household have a health problem or disability which prevents them from working or which limits the kind or amount of work they can do?"; 2) identified by the March supplement question "Is there anyone in this household who ever retired or left a job for health reasons?"; 3) identified by the core questionnaire as currently not in the labor force because of a disability; 4) identified by the March supplement as a person who did not work at all in the previous year because of illness or disability; 5) under 65 years old and covered by Medicare in previous year; 6) under 65 years old and received Supplemental Security Income in previous year; 7) received Veterans Administration disability income in previous year. If one or more of conditions 3, 4, 5, and 6 are met, the person is considered to have a severe work disability.
Source: Bureau of the Census, 2002 Current Population Survey Annual Demographic Supplement, Internet site http://www .census.gov/hhes/www/disable/cps/cps102.html

Table 2.21 AIDS Cases by Sex and Age, through June 2002

(cumulative number and percent distribution of AIDS cases by age at diagnosis and sex for those aged 13 or older, through June 2002)

	number	percent of total cases
Total cases	**831,112**	**100.0%**
Under age 1	3,249	0.4
Aged 1 to 12	5,558	0.7
Aged 13 to 19	4,627	0.6
Aged 20 to 29	134,170	16.1
Aged 30 to 39	365,924	44.0
Aged 40 to 49	223,467	26.9
Aged 50 to 59	68,988	8.3
Aged 60 or older	25,129	3.0
Females		
Aged 13 or older	145,696	17.5
Aged 13 to 19	1,995	0.2
Aged 20 to 29	29,996	3.6
Aged 30 to 39	63,504	7.6
Aged 40 to 49	35,168	4.2
Aged 50 to 59	10,243	1.2
Aged 60 or older	4,790	0.6
Males		
Aged 13 or older	676,609	81.4
Aged 13 to 19	2,632	0.3
Aged 20 to 29	104,174	12.5
Aged 30 to 39	302,420	36.4
Aged 40 to 49	188,299	22.7
Aged 50 to 59	58,745	7.1
Aged 60 or older	20,339	2.4

Source: National Center for Health Statistics, Health, United States, *2003; calculations by New Strategist*

Adults Aged 25 to 44 Account for Nearly One in Four Physician Visits

Among 25-to-44-year-olds, women make 66 percent of physician visits.

In 2001, Americans visited physicians a total of 880 million times. People aged 25 to 44 made 23 percent of visits. Women account for the great majority of physician visits by those in the age group because of pregnancy and childbirth.

People aged 25 to 44 account for 25 percent of visits to hospital outpatient departments. Among outpatient visitors in the 25-to-44 age group, 43 percent have an acute problem. A smaller one-third visit the outpatient department because of a chronic problem.

People aged 25 to 44 account for the largest share of visits to hospital emergency departments (30 percent) among age groups. This makes sense since so many people in the age group lack health insurance, and many people without health insurance end up in emergency rooms. Among emergency room visits by people aged 25 to 44, only 18 percent are classified as having "emergent" problems, or conditions that need to be addressed within 15 minutes.

■ Without better health insurance coverage, more patients will be seen in emergency rooms rather than doctor's office or health clinics.

People aged 25 to 44 see a doctor about twice a year

(average number of physician visits per person per year, by age, 2001)

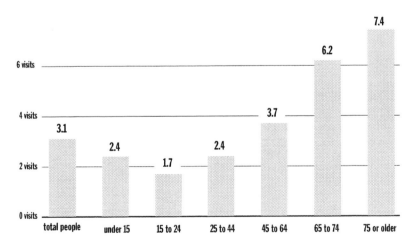

Table 2.22   Physician Office Visits by Sex and Age, 2001

(total number, percent distribution, and number of physician office visits per person per year, by sex and age, 2001; numbers in thousands)

	total	percent distribution	average visits per year
Total visits	**880,487**	**100.0%**	**3.1**
Under age 15	146,683	16.7	2.4
Aged 15 to 24	65,632	7.5	1.7
Aged 25 to 44	200,636	22.8	2.4
Aged 45 to 64	239,106	27.2	3.7
Aged 65 to 74	112,978	12.8	6.2
Aged 75 or older	115,452	13.1	7.4
Visits by females	**520,110**	**59.1**	**3.6**
Under age 15	69,614	7.9	2.4
Aged 15 to 24	42,071	4.8	2.2
Aged 25 to 44	131,664	15.0	3.1
Aged 45 to 64	142,657	16.2	4.3
Aged 65 to 74	64,029	7.3	6.5
Aged 75 or older	70,075	8.0	7.3
Visits by males	**360,377**	**40.9**	**2.6**
Under age 15	77,069	8.8	2.5
Aged 15 to 24	23,562	2.7	1.2
Aged 25 to 44	68,971	7.8	1.7
Aged 45 to 64	96,449	11.0	3.1
Aged 65 to 74	48,950	5.6	6.0
Aged 75 or older	45,376	5.2	7.6

Source: National Center for Health Statistics, National Ambulatory Medical Care Survey: 2001 Summary, *Advance Data No. 337, 2003*

Table 2.23 Hospital Outpatient Department Visits by Age and Reason, 2001

(number and percent distribution of visits to hospital outpatient departments by age and major reason for visit, 2001; numbers in thousands)

		major reason for visit					
	total	acute problem	chronic problem, routine	chronic problem, flare-up	pre- or post- surgery	preventive care	unknown
Total visits	**83,715**	**31,738**	**26,017**	**6,619**	**3,230**	**12,969**	**3,142**
Under age 15	18,319	7,970	4,258	1,106	588	3,936	460
Aged 15 to 24	9,834	3,881	1,977	663	272	2,737	304
Aged 25 to 44	20,576	8,790	5,243	1,643	795	3,267	838
Aged 45 to 64	21,590	7,128	8,750	2,033	911	1,831	938
Aged 65 to 74	7,299	2,190	3,044	665	376	661	363
Aged 75 or older	6,097	1,779	2,745	510	288	536	238
PERCENT DISTRIBUTION BY AGE							
Total visits	**100.0%**	**100.0%**	**100.0%**	**100.0%**	**100.0%**	**100.0%**	**100.0%**
Under age 15	21.9	25.1	16.4	16.7	18.2	30.3	14.6
Aged 15 to 24	11.7	12.2	7.6	10.0	8.4	21.1	9.7
Aged 25 to 44	24.6	27.7	20.2	24.8	24.6	25.2	26.7
Aged 45 to 64	25.8	22.5	33.6	30.7	28.2	14.1	29.9
Aged 65 to 74	8.7	6.9	11.7	10.1	11.6	5.1	11.6
Aged 75 or older	7.3	5.6	10.6	7.7	8.9	4.1	7.6
PERCENT DISTRIBUTION BY MAJOR REASON							
Total visits	**100.0%**	**37.9%**	**31.1%**	**7.9%**	**3.9%**	**15.5%**	**3.8%**
Under age 15	100.0	43.5	23.2	6.0	3.2	21.5	2.5
Aged 15 to 24	100.0	39.5	20.1	6.7	2.8	27.8	3.1
Aged 25 to 44	100.0	42.7	25.5	8.0	3.9	15.9	4.1
Aged 45 to 64	100.0	33.0	40.5	9.4	4.2	8.5	4.3
Aged 65 to 74	100.0	30.0	41.7	9.1	5.2	9.1	5.0
Aged 75 or older	100.0	29.2	45.0	8.4	4.7	8.8	3.9

Source: National Center for Health Statistics, National Hospital Ambulatory Medical Care Survey: 2001 Outpatient Department Summary, *Advance Data No. 338, 2003*

Table 2.24 Emergency Department Visits by Age and Urgency of Problem, 2001

(number of visits to emergency rooms and percent distribution by age and urgency of problem, 2001; numbers in thousands)

| | number | percent distribution | percent distribution by urgency of problem | | | | | |
			total	emergent	urgent	semiurgent	nonurgent	unknown
Total visits	**107,490**	**100.0%**	**100.0%**	**19.2%**	**31.7%**	**16.3%**	**9.1%**	**23.6%**
Under age 15	22,245	20.7	100.0	14.9	31.2	17.6	8.7	27.6
Aged 15 to 24	17,371	16.2	100.0	15.7	31.4	18.5	11.4	22.9
Aged 25 to 44	32,732	30.5	100.0	17.9	32.2	17.1	10.2	22.6
Aged 45 to 64	19,260	17.9	100.0	22.6	31.5	14.8	8.6	22.5
Aged 65 to 74	6,551	6.1	100.0	26.7	31.3	13.4	6.4	22.1
Aged 75 or older	9,332	8.7	100.0	29.0	32.0	11.4	5.0	22.6

Note: Emergent is a visit in which the patient should be seen in less than 15 minutes; urgent is a visit in which the patient should be seen within 15 to 60 minutes; semiurgent is a visit in which the patient should be seen within 61 to 120 minutes; nonurgent is a visit in which the patient should be seen within 121 minutes to 24 hours; unknown is a visit with no mention of immediacy or triage, or the patient was dead on arrival.
Source: National Center for Health Statistics, National Hospital Ambulatory Medical Care Survey: 2001 Emergency Department Summary, *Advance Data No. 335, 2003*

Most Deaths of Young Adults Are Preventable

Accidents are the leading killers of 25-to-34-year-olds.

When adults under age 35 die, it is often preventable. Accidents are the most important cause of death among 25-to-34-year-olds, accounting for 28 percent of the total. Homicide ranks second, and suicide is third. Among 35-to-44-year-olds, cancer is the leading cause of death followed by accidents. HIV infection ranks sixth as a cause of death among 25-to-34-year-olds and a higher fifth among 35-to-44-year-olds.

Although more could be done to reduce deaths among young adults, some progress has been made. The life expectancy of Americans continues to rise. At age 25, life expectancy is another 54 years. At age 35, another 44 years of life remain. If middle age is defined as the point at which people have lived half their lives, then 35-year-olds are not there yet since they have, on average, more than 40 years left to live.

■ Young adults are not as safety-conscious as middle-aged and older adults. Accidents and homicide will always rank as more important causes of death among young adults than among older Americans.

More than half of deaths among 25-to-34-year-olds are preventable

(percent of deaths among 25-to-34-year-olds caused by top three causes of death, 2001)

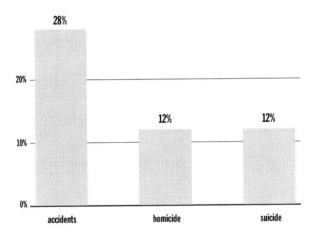

Table 2.25 Leading Causes of Death for People Aged 25 to 34, 2001

(number and percent distribution of deaths for the ten leading causes of death for people aged 25 to 34, 2001)

		number	percent
All causes		**41,683**	**100.0%**
1.	Accidents (5)	11,839	28.4
2.	Homicide (13)	5,204	12.5
3.	Suicide (11)	5,070	12.2
4.	Malignant neoplasms (2)	3,994	9.6
5.	Diseases of heart (1)	3,160	7.6
6.	Human immunodeficiency virus infection	2,101	5.0
7.	Cerebrovascular diseases (3)	601	1.4
8.	Diabetes mellitus (6)	595	1.4
9.	Congenital malformations, deformations	458	1.1
10.	Chronic liver disease and cirrhosis (12)	387	0.9
	All other causes	8,274	19.8

Note: Number in parentheses shows rank for all age groups if the cause of death is among top fifteen.
Source: National Center for Health Statistics, Deaths: Leading Causes for 2001. *National Vital Statistics Report, Vol. 52, No. 9, 2003; calculations by New Strategist*

Table 2.26 Leading Causes of Death for People Aged 35 to 44, 2001

(number and percent distribution of deaths for the ten leading causes of death for people aged 35 to 44, 2001)

		number	percent
All causes		**91,674**	**100.0%**
1.	Malignant neoplasms (2)	16,569	18.1
2.	Accidents (5)	15,945	17.4
3.	Diseases of heart (1)	13,326	14.5
4.	Suicide (11)	6,635	7.2
5.	Human immunodeficiency virus infection	5,867	6.4
6.	Homicide (13)	4,268	4.7
7.	Chronic liver disease and cirrhosis (12)	3,336	3.6
8.	Cerebrovascular diseases (3)	2,491	2.7
9.	Diabetes mellitus (6)	1,958	2.1
10.	Influenza and pneumonia (7)	983	1.1
	All other causes	20,296	22.1

Note: Number in parentheses shows rank for all age groups if the cause of death is among top fifteen.
Source: National Center for Health Statistics, Deaths: Leading Causes for 2001. *National Vital Statistics Report, Vol. 52, No. 9, 2003; calculations by New Strategist*

Table 2.27 Life Expectancy by Age and Sex, 2002

(years of life remaining at selected ages, by sex, 2002)

	total	females	males
At birth	77.4	79.9	74.7
Aged 1	76.9	79.4	74.3
Aged 5	73.0	75.5	70.4
Aged 10	68.1	70.6	65.4
Aged 15	63.1	65.6	60.5
Aged 20	58.3	60.7	55.8
Aged 25	53.6	55.9	51.1
Aged 30	48.8	51.0	46.5
Aged 35	44.1	46.2	41.8
Aged 40	39.4	41.5	37.2
Aged 45	34.9	36.8	32.7
Aged 50	30.4	32.2	28.4
Aged 55	26.2	27.8	24.2
Aged 60	22.0	23.5	20.3
Aged 65	18.2	19.5	16.6
Aged 70	14.7	15.8	13.3
Aged 75	11.6	12.5	10.4
Aged 80	8.9	9.5	8.0
Aged 85	6.7	7.0	5.9
Aged 90	4.9	5.1	4.4
Aged 95	3.7	3.8	3.3
Aged 100	2.8	2.8	2.6

Source: National Center for Health Statistics, Deaths: Preliminary Data for 2002, *National Vital Statistics Report, Vol. 52, No. 13, 2004*

3

Housing

■ The nation's homeownership rate has climbed by more than 4 percentage points since 1990 to a record high of 68.3 percent in 2003. The homeownership rate of Gen Xers rose slightly faster than average during those years.

■ Generation X is in transition from renting to homeowning. The 60 percent majority of householders aged 25 to 29 are renters. Among householders aged 30 to 34, only 43 percent are renters.

■ The 53 percent majority of non-Hispanic white householders aged 25 to 34 owned a home, according to the 2000 census. Blacks in the age group were only about half as likely to own a home, with a homeownership rate of 27 percent.

■ Forty-two percent of people aged 25 to 29 live in apartment buildings, but the figure falls to just 28 percent among 30-to-34-year-olds as people buy detached single-family homes.

■ Median monthly housing costs for married-couple homeowners aged 25 to 29 stood at $914 in 2001, and costs exceeded $1,000 a month for couples aged 30 to 44.

■ Between March 2002 and March 2003, a substantial 28 percent of people aged 25 to 29 moved to a different home. Among those aged 30 to 34, one in five moved during the year.

Homeownership Is Up among Gen Xers

Homeownership has been rising among Gen Xers because of low interest rates.

The nation's homeownership rate has climbed considerably since 1990, up by more than 4 percentage points to a record high of 68.3 percent in 2003. The homeownership rate of Gen Xers (Gen Xers were aged 27 to 38 in 2003) rose slightly faster than average. In 2003, 40 percent of householders aged 25 to 29 and 57 percent of those aged 30 to 34 were homeowners.

It's no coincidence that the majority of householders aged 30 to 34 are homeowners. This is the age group in which marriage becomes the norm for men (most women are married in their late twenties), and making the mortgage payment usually requires two incomes. As Gen Xers have married, they have taken advantage of low interest rates and gone shopping for a home of their own.

■ The homeownership rate of the youngest adults—under age 25—has increased the most since 1990. Their Boomer parents may be behind the rise, helping their children buy homes while interest rates are low.

Homeownership is higher for young adults today

(percentage point change in homeownership rate, by age of householder, 1990 to 2003)

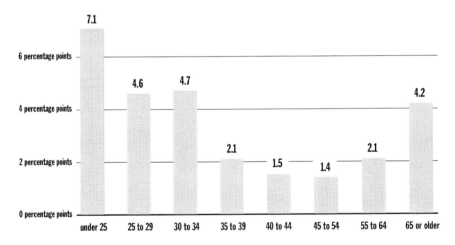

Table 3.1 Homeownership by Age of Householder, 1990 to 2003

(percentage of householders who own their home by age of householder, 1990 to 2003; percentage point change for selected years)

| | 2003 | 2000 | 1990 | percentage point change | |
				2000–03	1990–03
Total households	**68.3%**	**67.4%**	**63.9%**	**0.9**	**4.4**
Under age 25	22.8	21.7	15.7	1.1	7.1
Aged 25 to 29	39.8	38.1	35.2	1.7	4.6
Aged 30 to 34	56.5	54.6	51.8	1.9	4.7
Aged 35 to 39	65.1	65.0	63.0	0.1	2.1
Aged 40 to 44	71.3	70.6	69.8	0.7	1.5
Aged 45 to 54	76.6	76.5	75.2	0.1	1.4
Aged 55 to 64	81.4	80.3	79.3	1.1	2.1
Aged 65 or older	80.5	80.4	76.3	0.1	4.2

Source: Bureau of the Census, Housing Vacancy Surveys, Internet site http://www.census.gov/hhes/www/housing/hvs/annual03/ann03ind.html; calculations by New Strategist

Homeownership Rises with Age

Most of the nation's renters are under age 40.

Generation X is in transition from renting to homeowning. The 60 percent majority of house-holders aged 25 to 29 were renters in 2003 (Gen Xers were aged 27 to 38 in that year). Among householders aged 30 to 34, the proportion who rent their home drops to the 43 percent minority. Only slightly more than one-third of householders aged 35 to 39 rent their home.

The homeownership rate climbs steeply as people enter their thirties and forties. During the past two decades, Boomers have filled those age groups, fueling the real estate, construction, and home improvement industries. Now it's the turn of Generation X to shop for a home. Because Gen X is small, it won't have the same impact that Boomers have had on the housing market. But Gen X will add more fuel to the fire and help keep the housing industry vibrant in an otherwise lackluster economy.

■ As the large Millennial generation replaces Generation X in the young-adult age group, the rental market should get a boost.

Homeownership becomes the norm in the 30-to-34 age group

(percent distribution of householders aged 25 to 34 by homeownership status, 2003)

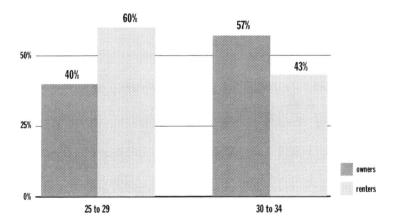

Table 3.2 Owners and Renters by Age of Householder, 2003

(number and percent distribution of householders by age and homeownership status, 2003; numbers in thousands)

	total	owners			renters		
		number	percent distribution	share of total	number	percent distribution	share of total
Total households	**105,560**	**72,054**	**100.0%**	**68.3%**	**33,506**	**100.0%**	**31.7%**
Under age 25	6,441	1,469	2.0	22.8	4,972	14.8	77.2
Aged 25 to 29	8,213	3,272	4.5	39.8	4,941	14.7	60.2
Aged 30 to 34	10,084	5,698	7.9	56.5	4,386	13.1	43.5
Aged 35 to 39	10,777	7,018	9.7	65.1	3,759	11.2	34.9
Aged 40 to 44	11,748	8,376	11.6	71.3	3,372	10.1	28.7
Aged 45 to 54	21,535	16,499	22.9	76.6	5,036	15.0	23.4
Aged 55 to 64	15,326	12,468	17.3	81.4	2,858	8.5	18.6
Aged 65 or older	21,436	17,253	23.9	80.5	4,183	12.5	19.5

Source: Bureau of the Census, Housing Vacancy Survey, Internet site http://www.census.gov/hhes/www/housing/hvs/historic/histt12.html; calculations by New Strategist

Married Couples Are Likely to Be Homeowners

Two incomes make homes more affordable.

The homeownership rate among all married couples was a lofty 83 percent in 2003, much higher than the 68 percent rate for all households. Couples in their twenties and thirties are less likely than average to own a home. Among couples aged 25 to 29, 58 percent were homeowners. The figure is a much higher 72 percent among couples aged 30 to 34, and rises to 79 percent in the 35-to-39 age group.

Homeownership is much lower for other types of households in the 25-to-39 age group. Among female-headed family householders in the age group, the homeownership rate ranges from 23 to 43 percent. The figures are similar for men and women who live alone. Homeownership rates are higher for male-headed family householders, ranging from 39 percent among those aged 25 to 29 to the 54 percent majority of those aged 35 to 39.

■ The majority of householders aged 45 or older own a home, regardless of household type.

Most married couples in their late twenties and thirties own a home

(percent of married-couple householders aged 25 to 39 who own their home. 2003)

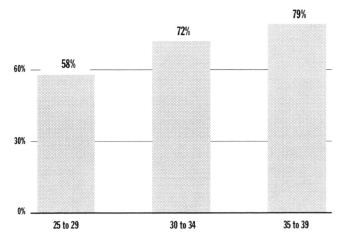

Table 3.3   Homeownership Rate by Age of Householder and Type of Household, 2003

(percent of households owning their home, by age of householder and type of household, 2003)

		family households			people living alone	
	total	married couples	female householder, no spouse present	male householder, no spouse present	females	males
Total households	**68.3%**	**83.3%**	**49.6%**	**57.9%**	**59.1%**	**50.0%**
Under age 25	22.8	32.8	23.1	40.4	12.7	16.0
Aged 25 to 29	39.8	57.9	23.0	39.0	23.8	28.2
Aged 30 to 34	56.5	71.6	33.3	49.2	37.3	38.1
Aged 35 to 39	65.1	78.9	43.2	53.5	45.2	44.6
Aged 40 to 44	71.3	84.9	51.6	63.7	49.8	49.6
Aged 45 to 49	75.4	88.3	60.0	69.6	54.2	50.4
Aged 50 to 54	77.9	90.2	61.1	71.5	60.9	55.4
Aged 55 to 59	80.9	91.6	65.8	75.2	65.4	58.7
Aged 60 to 64	81.9	92.2	71.3	75.0	68.6	61.4
Aged 65 or older	80.5	92.1	81.6	81.9	70.0	67.8

Source: Bureau of the Census, Housing Vacancy Survey, Internet site http://www.census.gov/hhes/www/housing/hvs/annual03/ann03t15.html

Non-Hispanic Whites Have the Highest Homeownership Rate

Among Gen Xers, only non-Hispanic whites are likely to be homeowners.

Nationally, the homeownership rate of non-Hispanic whites stood at 72 percent, according to the 2000 census. The rate was a much lower 53 percent among Asians, and below the 50 percent majority among blacks and Hispanics. Regardless of race and Hispanic origin, however, homeownership rises with age as people acquire the savings and income needed to become homeowners.

Among 25-to-34-year-old householders in 2000 (Gen Xers were aged 24 to 35 in that year), the 53 percent majority of non-Hispanic whites owned a home. But blacks in the age group were only about half as likely to own a home, with a homeownership rate of just 27 percent. Thirty-two percent of Asian and 33 percent of Hispanic householders aged 25 to 34 owned a home.

■ Blacks are less likely to be homeowners because a smaller share of their households are headed by married couples.

Among 25-to-34-year-olds, most non-Hispanic whites are homeowners

(homeownership rate of householders aged 25 to 34 by race and Hispanic origin, 2000)

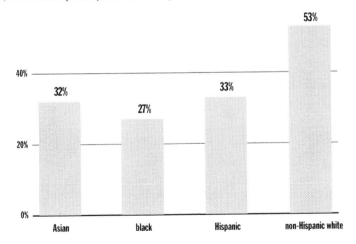

Table 3.4 Homeowners by Age, Race, and Hispanic Origin of Householder, 2000 Census

(percent of households owning their home by age, race, and Hispanic origin of householder, 2000)

	total	Asian	black	Hispanic	non-Hispanic white
Total households	**66.2%**	**52.8%**	**46.0%**	**45.7%**	**72.4%**
Under age 25	17.9	11.3	10.4	15.3	20.5
Aged 25 to 34	45.6	32.1	27.2	32.9	53.0
Aged 35 to 44	66.2	57.8	44.4	48.8	73.2
Aged 45 to 54	74.9	67.9	55.2	56.8	80.3
Aged 55 to 64	79.8	71.2	61.6	61.9	84.1
Aged 65 or older	78.1	62.0	64.3	62.8	80.6

Note: Each racial category includes those who identified themselves as being of the race alone and those who identified themselves as being of the race in combination with one or more other races. Hispanics may be of any race. Non-Hispanic whites include only those who identified themselves as white alone and non-Hispanic.
Source: Bureau of the Census, Census 2000, American Factfinder, Internet site http://factfinder.census.gov/home/saff/main.html?_lang=en

Most Americans Live in Single-Family Homes

Many Gen Xers live in apartment buildings or mobile homes, however.

The 63 percent majority of American households live in detached single-family homes. Older householders are most likely to live in this type of home, where the median age of householders is 49.

Fifty-seven percent of householders under age 25 live in multi-unit buildings, as do 34 percent of those aged 25 to 34. The share drops sharply within the 25-to-34 age group because many people buy homes as they enter their thirties. While 42 percent of people aged 25 to 29 live in apartment buildings, the figure falls to just 28 percent among those aged 30 to 34. The median age of householders living in apartment buildings is just 39.

Seven percent of people aged 25 to 34 live in mobile homes, a figure that does not vary much by age. Generation Xers account for 19 percent of mobile home householders. The 45-or-older age group accounts for more than half of householders living in mobile homes.

■ The demand for apartments is likely to rise as the large Millennial generation replaces small Generation X in the age group where apartment living is most popular.

Young adults are most likely to live in multi-unit buildings

(percent of households living in multi-unit buildings, by age of householder, 2001)

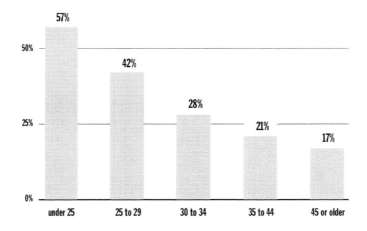

Table 3.5 Number of Units in Structure by Age of Householder, 2001

(number and percent distribution of households by age of householder and number of units in structure of home, 2001; numbers in thousands)

	total	one, detached	one, attached	multi-unit dwellings						mobile homes
				total	2 to 4	5 to 9	10 to 19	20 to 49	50 or more	
Total households	**106,261**	**67,129**	**7,305**	**24,609**	**8,200**	**4,994**	**4,620**	**3,253**	**3,543**	**7,219**
Under age 25	6,206	1,613	632	3,545	1,022	887	838	468	330	416
Aged 25 to 34	18,597	9,111	1,750	6,392	2,275	1,386	1,333	788	612	1,345
Aged 25 to 29	8,143	3,260	803	3,435	1,188	760	739	428	321	646
Aged 30 to 34	10,454	5,851	947	2,957	1,087	626	594	360	291	699
Aged 35 to 44	23,882	15,803	1,541	4,900	1,789	975	1,034	607	496	1,638
Aged 45 or older	57,575	40,601	3,383	9,771	3,114	1,746	1,415	1,391	2,105	3,819
Median age	47	49	43	39	39	37	36	41	52	46

PERCENT DISTRIBUTION BY AGE OF HOUSEHOLDER

	total	one, detached	one, attached	multi-unit dwellings						mobile homes
				total	2 to 4	5 to 9	10 to 19	20 to 49	50 or more	
Total households	**100.0%**	**100.0%**	**100.0%**	**100.0%**	**100.0%**	**100.0%**	**100.0%**	**100.0%**	**100.0%**	**100.0%**
Under age 25	5.8	2.4	8.7	14.4	12.5	17.8	18.1	14.4	9.3	5.8
Aged 25 to 34	17.5	13.6	24.0	26.0	27.7	27.8	28.9	24.2	17.3	18.6
Aged 25 to 29	7.7	4.9	11.0	14.0	14.5	15.2	16.0	13.2	9.1	8.9
Aged 30 to 34	9.8	8.7	13.0	12.0	13.3	12.5	12.9	11.1	8.2	9.7
Aged 35 to 44	22.5	23.5	21.1	19.9	21.8	19.5	22.4	18.7	14.0	22.7
Aged 45 or older	54.2	60.5	46.3	39.7	38.0	35.0	30.6	42.8	59.4	52.9

PERCENT DISTRIBUTION BY UNITS IN STRUCTURE

	total	one, detached	one, attached	multi-unit dwellings						mobile homes
				total	2 to 4	5 to 9	10 to 19	20 to 49	50 or more	
Total households	**100.0%**	**63.2%**	**6.9%**	**23.2%**	**7.7%**	**4.7%**	**4.3%**	**3.1%**	**3.3%**	**6.8%**
Under age 25	100.0	26.0	10.2	57.1	16.5	14.3	13.5	7.5	5.3	6.7
Aged 25 to 34	100.0	49.0	9.4	34.4	12.2	7.5	7.2	4.2	3.3	7.2
Aged 25 to 29	100.0	40.0	9.9	42.2	14.6	9.3	9.1	5.3	3.9	7.9
Aged 30 to 34	100.0	56.0	9.1	28.3	10.4	6.0	5.7	3.4	2.8	6.7
Aged 35 to 44	100.0	66.2	6.5	20.5	7.5	4.1	4.3	2.5	2.1	6.9
Aged 45 or older	100.0	70.5	5.9	17.0	5.4	3.0	2.5	2.4	3.7	6.6

Source: Bureau of the Census, American Housing Survey for the United States in 2001. *Internet site http://www.census.gov/hhes/www/housing/ahs/ahs01/ahs01.html*

Generation Xers Are Most Likely to Live in New Homes

Older homeowners are least likely to live in recently built homes.

New homes are the province of the young. Overall, only 6 percent of homeowners live in a new home—meaning one built in the past four years. The share is much greater among younger homeowners, however. Among 25-to-34-year-olds, 14 percent live in a new home. The figure is a slightly higher 15 percent among those aged 25 to 29. Among homeowners aged 45 or older, only 4 percent live in new homes. Generation Xers account for a substantial 27 percent of homeowners living in newly built homes.

Overall, 3 percent of the nation's renters live in newly built housing units. The figure is a higher 7 percent among householders under age 25, then varies little by age.

■ The large Millennial generation is likely to boost sales of new homes as they replace Generation X in the ages of first-home buying.

Many young homeowners live in new homes

(percent of homeowners living in homes built in the past four years, by age of householder, 2001)

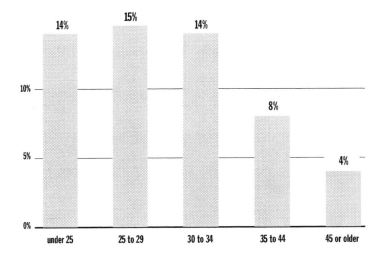

Table 3.6 Owners and Renters of New Homes by Age of Householder, 2001

(number of total occupied housing units, number and percent built in the past four years, and percent distribution of new units by housing tenure and age of householder, 2001; numbers in thousands)

		in new homes		
	total	number	percent of total	percent distribution
Total households	**106,261**	**5,853**	**5.5%**	**100.0%**
Under age 25	6,206	502	8.1	8.6
Aged 25 to 34	18,597	1,616	8.7	27.6
Aged 25 to 29	8,143	683	8.4	11.7
Aged 30 to 34	10,454	933	8.9	15.9
Aged 35 to 44	23,882	1,502	6.3	25.7
Aged 45 or older	57,575	2,232	3.9	38.1
Owners	**72,265**	**4,690**	**6.5**	**100.0**
Under age 25	1,320	182	13.8	3.9
Aged 25 to 34	8,967	1,274	14.2	27.2
Aged 25 to 29	3,256	494	15.2	10.5
Aged 30 to 34	5,711	780	13.7	16.6
Aged 35 to 44	16,359	1,310	8.0	27.9
Aged 45 or older	45,619	1,924	4.2	41.0
Renters	**33,996**	**1,163**	**3.4**	**100.0**
Under age 25	4,886	321	6.6	27.6
Aged 25 to 34	9,630	342	3.6	29.4
Aged 25 to 29	4,887	189	3.9	16.3
Aged 30 to 34	4,743	153	3.2	13.2
Aged 35 to 44	7,524	191	2.5	16.4
Aged 45 or older	11,956	308	2.6	26.5

Source: Bureau of the Census, American Housing Survey for the United States in 2001. Internet site http://www.census.gov/hhes/www/housing/ahs/ahs01/ahs01.html

Housing Costs Are High for Generation Xers

Costs are lowest for homeowners aged 65 or older.

Monthly housing costs for the average household in 2001 stood at a median of $658, including mortgage interest and utilities. For homeowners, the median monthly housing cost was $685, and for renters the figure was a slightly smaller $632.

Among married-couple homeowners, housing costs are highest for those aged 25 to 44, not only because their homes are larger than average to make room for children but also because many are recent homeowners with hefty mortgage interest charges. The median monthly housing cost for married-couple homeowners aged 25 to 29 stood at $914 in 2001 and exceeded $1,000 for those aged 30 to 44.

Housing costs are lowest for homeowning married couples aged 65 or older. For older renters, however, housing costs do not decline with age. Among married householders aged 65 or older, homeowners paid a median of $383 for housing while renters paid a median of $651.

■ The financial advantages of homeownership grow as householders age and pay off their mortgages.

Housing costs are highest for 25-to-44-year-old married couples

(median monthly housing costs for married couples, by age of householder, 2001)

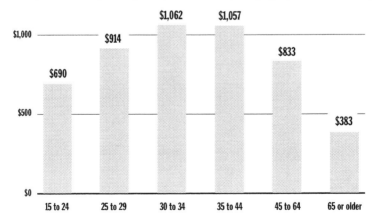

Table 3.7 Median Monthly Housing Costs of Married Couples by Age of Householder, 2001

(median monthly housing costs and indexed costs of married-couple households by age of householder and housing tenure, 2001)

	median monthly cost			indexed cost		
	total	owners	renters	total	owners	renters
TOTAL HOUSEHOLDS	**$658**	**$685**	**$632**	**100**	**104**	**96**
Married couples	**783**	**811**	**721**	**119**	**123**	**110**
Aged 15 to 24	638	690	622	97	105	95
Aged 25 to 29	796	914	691	121	139	105
Aged 30 to 34	928	1,062	737	141	161	112
Aged 35 to 44	979	1,057	775	149	161	118
Aged 45 to 64	815	833	740	124	127	113
Aged 65 or older	395	383	651	60	58	99

Source: Bureau of the Census, American Housing Survey for the United States in 2001, Internet site http://www.census.gov/hhes/ www/housing/ahs/ahs01/ahs01.html; calculations by New Strategist

Many Young Adults Own Highly Valued Homes

Home values rise as young couples trade in their starter homes for more expensive models.

The median value of America's owned homes stood at $124,624 in 2001. Median home value is an even higher $139,364 among the nation's married couples. Home values peak among couples aged 35 to 44, with a median value of $147,327.

The value of the homes owned by married couples under age 30 is below average because many have small starter homes. Among couples aged 30 to 34, however, home values are higher as they trade in their starter homes for bigger models with more room for children. The median value of the homes owned by couples aged 30 to 34 is close to the married-couple average, at $135,904 in 2001. More than one in four own a home worth at least $200,000.

■ Home values have been rising steadily and are now significantly higher than the 2001 figures shown in this table.

Home values peak in the 35-to-44 age group

(median value of homes owned by married couples, by age of householder, 2001)

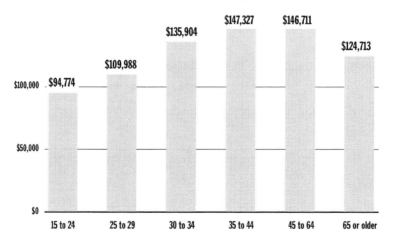

Table 3.8 Value of Homes Owned by Married Couples by Age of Householder, 2001

(total number of married-couple homeowners and percent distribution by value of home, median value of housing unit, and indexed median value, by age of householder, 2001)

	total number (in 000s)	total percent	under $100,000	$100,000 to $149,999	$150,000 to $199,999	$200,000 to $249,999	$250,000 to $299,999	$300,000 or more	median value of home	indexed median value
TOTAL HOMEOWNERS	**72,265**	**100.0%**	**39.3%**	**21.6%**	**14.1%**	**7.9%**	**5.2%**	**11.8%**	**$124,624**	**100**
Married couples	**44,618**	**100.0**	**32.8**	**21.9**	**15.5**	**9.4**	**6.3**	**14.1**	**139,364**	**112**
Under age 25	490	100.0	53.7	19.2	11.2	6.5	3.1	5.9	94,774	76
Aged 25 to 29	2,039	100.0	44.9	25.7	14.4	6.0	3.4	5.6	109,988	88
Aged 30 to 34	3,744	100.0	31.8	25.3	15.7	9.6	7.0	10.6	135,904	109
Aged 35 to 44	11,182	100.0	29.1	22.0	16.5	10.2	7.1	15.1	147,327	118
Aged 45 to 64	18,681	100.0	30.0	21.4	15.8	10.0	6.4	16.5	146,711	118
Aged 65 or older	8,482	100.0	39.8	20.6	14.1	8.3	5.4	11.8	124,713	100

Source: Bureau of the Census, American Housing Survey for the United States in 2001. Internet site http://www.census.gov/hhes/www/housing/ahs/ahs01/ahs01.html

Generation Xers Are on the Move

Young adults are more likely than older Americans to change houses.

Young adults are far more likely than their elders to move from one home to another. Only 7 percent of people aged 40 or older move in a typical year, but the proportion of adults in their twenties and thirties who change homes is substantially higher. Between March 2002 and March 2003, a substantial 28 percent of people aged 25 to 29 moved to a different home. One in five people aged 30 to 34 moved during the year.

Most movers—even among Generation Xers— stay within the same county. Fifty-eight percent of movers aged 25 to 39 moved within the same county. Only 19 percent moved to a different state.

Among 25-to-29-year-old movers, the largest share (48 percent) moved for housing-related reasons. Twelve percent were renters who bought a home, and 17 percent moved because they wanted a better home or apartment. Twenty-seven percent of 25-to-29-year-olds said they moved for family-related reasons, and 19 percent moved for job-related reasons.

■ Americans are moving less than they once did. Several factors are behind the lower mobility rate, including the aging of the population, the rise in homeownership, and the proliferation of dual-income couples.

Mobility rate falls sharply with age

(percent of people who moved between March 2002 and March 2003, by age)

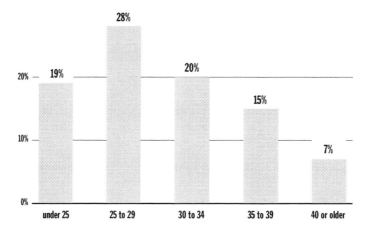

Table 3.9 Geographical Mobility by Age, 2002 to 2003

(total number and percent distribution of people aged 1 or older by mobility status between March 2002 and March 2003, by selected age groups; numbers in thousands)

	total	nonmovers	total movers	same county	different county, same state	different state, same division	different division, same region	different region	abroad
Total, aged 1 or older	**282,556**	**242,463**	**40,093**	**23,468**	**7,728**	**3,752**	**1,181**	**2,695**	**1,269**
Under age 25	97,372	79,100	18,268	11,143	3,455	1,504	517	1,142	507
Total aged 25 to 39	60,526	47,962	12,565	7,311	2,397	1,134	368	842	513
Aged 25 to 29	18,721	13,470	5,252	3,010	1,020	483	155	339	245
Aged 30 to 34	20,521	16,460	4,061	2,391	742	378	108	294	148
Aged 35 to 39	21,284	18,032	3,252	1,910	635	273	105	209	120
Aged 40 or older	124,657	115,401	9,255	5,013	1,875	1,114	294	711	248

PERCENT DISTRIBUTION BY AGE

	total	nonmovers	total movers	same county	different county, same state	different state, same division	different division, same region	different region	abroad
Total, aged 1 or older	**100.0%**	**100.0%**	**100.0%**	**100.0%**	**100.0%**	**100.0%**	**100.0%**	**100.0%**	**100.0%**
Under age 25	34.5	32.6	45.6	47.5	44.7	40.1	43.8	42.4	40.0
Total aged 25 to 39	21.4	19.8	31.3	31.2	31.0	30.2	31.2	31.2	40.4
Aged 25 to 29	6.6	5.6	13.1	12.8	13.2	12.9	13.1	12.6	19.3
Aged 30 to 34	7.3	6.8	10.1	10.2	9.6	10.1	9.1	10.9	11.7
Aged 35 to 39	7.5	7.4	8.1	8.1	8.2	7.3	8.9	7.8	9.5
Aged 40 or older	44.1	47.6	23.1	21.4	24.3	29.7	24.9	26.4	19.5

PERCENT DISTRIBUTION BY MOBILITY STATUS

	total	nonmovers	total movers	same county	different county, same state	different state, same division	different division, same region	different region	abroad
Total, aged 1 or older	**100.0%**	**85.8%**	**14.2%**	**8.3%**	**2.7%**	**1.3%**	**0.4%**	**1.0%**	**0.4%**
Under age 25	100.0	81.2	18.8	11.4	3.5	1.5	0.5	1.2	0.5
Total aged 25 to 39	100.0	79.2	20.8	12.1	4.0	1.9	0.6	1.4	0.8
Aged 25 to 29	100.0	72.0	28.1	16.1	5.4	2.6	0.8	1.8	1.3
Aged 30 to 34	100.0	80.2	19.8	11.7	3.6	1.8	0.5	1.4	0.7
Aged 35 to 39	100.0	84.7	15.3	9.0	3.0	1.3	0.5	1.0	0.6
Aged 40 or older	100.0	92.6	7.4	4.0	1.5	0.9	0.2	0.6	0.2

PERCENT DISTRIBUTION OF MOVERS BY TYPE OF MOVE

	total	nonmovers	total movers	same county	different county, same state	different state, same division	different division, same region	different region	abroad
Total, aged 1 or older	–	–	**100.0%**	**58.5%**	**19.3%**	**9.4%**	**2.9%**	**6.7%**	**3.2%**
Under age 25	–	–	100.0	61.0	18.9	8.2	2.8	6.3	2.8
Total aged 25 to 39	–	–	100.0	58.2	19.1	9.0	2.9	6.7	4.1
Aged 25 to 29	–	–	100.0	57.3	19.4	9.2	3.0	6.5	4.7
Aged 30 to 34	–	–	100.0	58.9	18.3	9.3	2.7	7.2	3.6
Aged 35 to 39	–	–	100.0	58.7	19.5	8.4	3.2	6.4	3.7
Aged 40 or older	–	–	100.0	54.2	20.3	12.0	3.2	7.7	2.7

Note: (–) means not applicable.
Source: Bureau of the Census, Geographical Mobility: March 2002 to March 2003, Detailed Tables for P20-549, 2003 Current Population Survey, Internet site http://www.census.gov/population/www/socdemo/migrate/p20-549.html; calculations by New Strategist

Table 3.10 Reason for Moving by Age, 2002 to 2003

(number and percent distribution of movers between March 2002 and March 2003 by primary reason for move and age; numbers in thousands)

	total	under 25	25 to 29	30 to 44	45 to 64	65 or older
TOTAL MOVERS	**40,093**	**18,272**	**5,252**	**9,996**	**5,203**	**1,371**
Family reasons	**10,548**	**5,274**	**1,401**	**2,322**	**1,151**	**401**
Change in marital status	2,679	1,108	396	752	358	65
To establish own household	2,814	1,558	460	540	224	33
Other family reason	5,055	2,608	545	1,030	569	303
Job reasons	**6,247**	**2,558**	**992**	**1,769**	**859**	**69**
New job or job transfer	3,546	1,449	566	1,048	460	23
To look for work or lost job	749	326	126	196	102	–
To be closer to work/easier commute	1,275	563	213	334	158	5
Retired	101	5	1	19	45	32
Other job-related reason	576	215	86	172	94	9
Housing reasons	**20,578**	**9,195**	**2,518**	**5,394**	**2,830**	**636**
Wanted own home, not rent	4,078	1,687	636	1,172	532	50
Wanted new or better home/apartment	7,942	3,737	916	2,074	1,034	181
Wanted better neighborhood/ less crime	1,530	702	179	410	199	39
Wanted cheaper housing	2,622	1,177	286	684	358	116
Other housing reason	4,406	1,892	501	1,054	707	250
Other reasons	**2,722**	**1,246**	**341**	**509**	**364**	**261**
To attend or leave college	1,010	688	176	121	21	3
Change of climate	160	26	15	46	46	26
Health reasons	565	113	35	96	124	197
Other reasons	987	419	115	246	173	35

PERCENT DISTRIBUTION BY REASON	total	under 25	25 to 29	30 to 44	45 to 64	65 or older
TOTAL MOVERS	100.0%	100.0%	100.0%	100.0%	100.0%	100.0%
Family reasons	**26.3**	**28.9**	**26.7**	**23.2**	**22.1**	**29.2**
Change in marital status	6.7	6.1	7.5	7.5	6.9	4.7
To establish own household	7.0	8.5	8.8	5.4	4.3	2.4
Other family reason	12.6	14.3	10.4	10.3	10.9	22.1
Job reasons	**15.6**	**14.0**	**18.9**	**17.7**	**16.5**	**5.0**
New job or job transfer	8.8	7.9	10.8	10.5	8.8	1.7
To look for work or lost job	1.9	1.8	2.4	2.0	2.0	–
To be closer to work/easier commute	3.2	3.1	4.1	3.3	3.0	0.4
Retired	0.3	0.0	0.0	0.2	0.9	2.3
Other job-related reason	1.4	1.2	1.6	1.7	1.8	0.7
Housing reasons	**51.3**	**50.3**	**47.9**	**54.0**	**54.4**	**46.4**
Wanted own home, not rent	10.2	9.2	12.1	11.7	10.2	3.6
Wanted new or better home/apartment	19.8	20.5	17.4	20.7	19.9	13.2
Wanted better neighborhood/less crime	3.8	3.8	3.4	4.1	3.8	2.8
Wanted cheaper housing	6.5	6.4	5.4	6.8	6.9	8.5
Other housing reason	11.0	10.4	9.5	10.5	13.6	18.2
Other reasons	**6.8**	**6.8**	**6.5**	**5.1**	**7.0**	**19.0**
To attend or leave college	2.5	3.8	3.4	1.2	0.4	0.2
Change of climate	0.4	0.1	0.3	0.5	0.9	1.9
Health reasons	1.4	0.6	0.7	1.0	2.4	14.4
Other reasons	2.5	2.3	2.2	2.5	3.3	2.6

PERCENT DISTRIBUTION BY AGE	total	under 25	25 to 29	30 to 44	45 to 64	65 or older
TOTAL MOVERS	100.0%	45.6%	13.1%	24.9%	13.0%	3.4%
Family reasons	**100.0**	**50.0**	**13.3**	**22.0**	**10.9**	**3.8**
Change in marital status	100.0	41.4	14.8	28.1	13.4	2.4
To establish own household	100.0	55.4	16.3	19.2	8.0	1.2
Other family reason	100.0	51.6	10.8	20.4	11.3	6.0
Job reasons	**100.0**	**40.9**	**15.9**	**28.3**	**13.8**	**1.1**
New job or job transfer	100.0	40.9	16.0	29.6	13.0	0.6
To look for work or lost job	100.0	43.5	16.8	26.2	13.6	–
To be closer to work/easier commute	100.0	44.2	16.7	26.2	12.4	0.4
Retired	100.0	5.0	1.0	18.8	44.6	31.7
Other job-related reason	100.0	37.3	14.9	29.9	16.3	1.6
Housing reasons	**100.0**	**44.7**	**12.2**	**26.2**	**13.8**	**3.1**
Wanted own home, not rent	100.0	41.4	15.6	28.7	13.1	1.2
Wanted new or better home/apartment	100.0	47.1	11.5	26.1	13.0	2.3
Wanted better neighborhood/						
less crime	100.0	45.9	11.7	26.8	13.0	2.5
Wanted cheaper housing	100.0	44.9	10.9	26.1	13.7	4.4
Other housing reason	100.0	42.9	11.4	23.9	16.1	5.7
Other reasons	**100.0**	**45.8**	**12.5**	**18.7**	**13.4**	**9.6**
To attend or leave college	100.0	68.1	17.4	12.0	2.1	0.3
Change of climate	100.0	16.2	9.4	28.7	28.7	16.2
Health reasons	100.0	20.0	6.2	17.0	21.9	34.9
Other reasons	100.0	42.5	11.7	24.9	17.5	3.5

Note: (–) means number is less than 500 or sample is too small to make a reliable estimate.
Source: Bureau of the Census, Geographical Mobility: March 2002 to March 2003, Detailed Tables for P20-549, *2003 Current Population Survey, Internet site http://www.census.gov/population/www/socdemo/migrate/p20-549.html; calculations by New Strategist*

4

Income

■ Between 2000 and 2002, the median income of households headed by people aged 25 to 34 fell 2 percent, after adjusting for inflation. Despite the decline, their median income was higher in 2002 than in 1990 or 1980.

■ The median income of householders aged 25 to 29, at $41,338 in 2002, was below the national median of $42,409. But householders aged 30 to 34 had a median income well above the national average, at $48,698.

■ Among households headed by people aged 25 to 34, married couples have the highest incomes (a median of $57,454 in 2002), and female-headed families have the lowest (a median of $23,162).

■ Between 1980 and 2002, the median income of men aged 25 to 34 fell 5 percent. The decline was an even larger 9 percent for those aged 35 to 44. In contrast, women's incomes have soared over the past two decades.

■ Generation Xers are slightly less likely to be poor than is the average American. Overall, 12 percent of Americans lived in poverty in 2002. Among people aged 26 to 37, however, a smaller 11 percent are poor.

Household Incomes of Gen Xers Are Down

But incomes are higher than they were ten or twenty years ago.

Between 2000 and 2002, the median income of households headed by people aged 25 to 34 fell 2 percent, after adjusting for inflation (Generation Xers were aged 26 to 37 in 2002). The median income of householders aged 35 to 44 fell 4.7 percent during those years. Behind the decline was the recession of 2001 and the loss of millions of jobs. Despite the decline since 2000, the median incomes of householders aged 25 to 44 were higher in 2002 than they were in 1990 or 1980.

The $45,330 median income of householders aged 25 to 34 was just slightly higher than the national median of $42,409. The median income of householders aged 35 to 44, at $53,521, was well above the national median.

■ Householders in almost every age group have lost ground since 2000, the biggest decline in median income occurring for those aged 35 to 44.

Household incomes of 25-to-44-year-olds have fallen since 2000

(median income of households headed by people aged 25 to 44, 2000–02; in 2002 dollars)

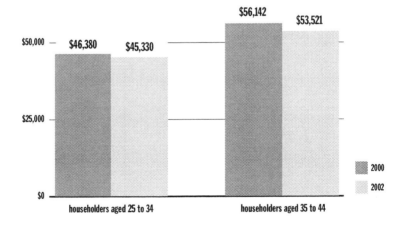

Table 4.1 Median Income of Households Headed by People Aged 25 to 44, 1980 to 2002

(median income of total households and households headed by people aged 25 to 44, 1980 to 2002; percent change for selected years; in 2002 dollars)

	total households	25 to 34	35 to 44
2002	$42,409	$45,330	$53,521
2001	42,899	45,797	54,168
2000	43,848	46,380	56,142
1999	44,044	45,510	54,897
1998	42,844	44,148	53,384
1997	41,346	42,653	51,798
1996	40,503	40,954	50,690
1995	39,931	40,662	50,932
1994	38,725	39,790	50,012
1993	38,287	38,336	50,078
1992	38,482	39,239	50,060
1991	38,790	39,713	50,666
1990	39,949	40,504	51,447
1989	40,484	41,768	52,709
1988	39,766	41,494	53,394
1987	39,453	40,823	53,266
1986	38,975	40,542	51,326
1985	37,648	39,986	49,520
1984	36,921	39,096	49,059
1983	35,774	37,248	47,411
1982	35,986	37,966	47,045
1981	36,042	38,762	47,966
1980	36,608	39,972	48,839
Percent change			
2000–2002	–3.3%	–2.3%	–4.7%
1990–2002	6.2	11.9	4.0
1980–2002	15.8	13.4	9.6

Source: Bureau of the Census, data from the Current Population Survey Annual Demographic Supplements, Internet site http:// www.census.gov/hhes/income/histinc/h10.html; calculations by New Strategist

Household Income Rises with Age

Household income exceeds the average in the 30-to-34 age group.

The median income of householders aged 25 to 29, at $41,338 in 2002, was below the national median of $42,409. But householders aged 30 to 34 had a median income well above the national average, at $48,698. Behind the substantially higher incomes of the 30-to-34 age group is their lifestyle. At this age, most men and women are married and most couples have two incomes.

In the nation as a whole, more than 15 million households have incomes of $100,000 or more. Just over 2 million of those householders are aged 25 to 39. Among all households, 14 percent have incomes of $100,000 or more. For householders aged 25 to 29, the figure is just 8 percent. It rises to 13 percent among 30-to-34-year-olds and surpasses the national figure among 35-to-39-year-olds, at 17 percent.

■ The household incomes of Gen Xers are kept in check partly because they are competing for jobs with two much larger generations—the older Boomers and the younger Millennials.

Householders aged 25 to 29 have below-average incomes

(median income of total households and households headed by people aged 25 to 39, 2002)

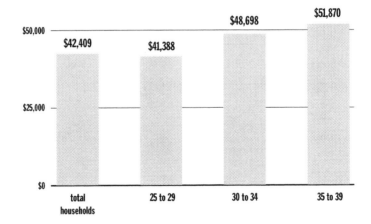

Table 4.2 Income of Households Headed by People Aged 25 to 39, 2002: Total Households

(number and percent distribution of total households and households headed by people aged 25 to 39 by income, 2002; households in thousands as of 2003)

	total	aged 25 to 34 total	25 to 29	30 to 34	aged 35 to 39
Total households	**111,278**	**19,055**	**8,535**	**10,521**	**11,486**
Under $10,000	10,090	1,347	673	675	674
$10,000 to $19,999	15,063	1,912	968	944	982
$20,000 to $29,999	14,362	2,515	1,213	1,302	1,296
$30,000 to $39,999	12,795	2,546	1,223	1,325	1,250
$40,000 to $49,999	10,743	2,160	1,029	1,131	1,271
$50,000 to $59,999	9,226	1,929	857	1,073	1,146
$60,000 to $69,999	7,633	1,685	716	969	905
$70,000 to $79,999	6,695	1,340	549	791	893
$80,000 to $89,999	5,039	966	369	598	641
$90,000 to $99,999	3,952	599	226	373	504
$100,000 or more	15,676	2,057	713	1,344	1,921
Median income	$42,409	$45,330	$41,388	$48,698	$51,870
Total households	**100.0%**	**100.0%**	**100.0%**	**100.0%**	**100.0%**
Under $10,000	9.1	7.1	7.9	6.4	5.9
$10,000 to $19,999	13.5	10.0	11.3	9.0	8.5
$20,000 to $29,999	12.9	13.2	14.2	12.4	11.3
$30,000 to $39,999	11.5	13.4	14.3	12.6	10.9
$40,000 to $49,999	9.7	11.3	12.1	10.7	11.1
$50,000 to $59,999	8.3	10.1	10.0	10.2	10.0
$60,000 to $69,999	6.9	8.8	8.4	9.2	7.9
$70,000 to $79,999	6.0	7.0	6.4	7.5	7.8
$80,000 to $89,999	4.5	5.1	4.3	5.7	5.6
$90,000 to $99,999	3.6	3.1	2.6	3.5	4.4
$100,000 or more	14.1	10.8	8.4	12.8	16.7

Source: Bureau of the Census, data from the 2003 Current Population Survey Annual Social and Economic Supplement, Internet site http://ferret.bls.census.gov/macro/032003/hhinc/new02_000.htm; calculations by New Strategist

Incomes Are Highest for Asian Households

The incomes of 25-to-39-year-old Asian householders are far higher than those of other racial or ethnic groups.

The median income of households headed by Asians aged 25 to 34 stood at $52,224 in 2002 (Gen Xers were aged 26 to 37 in that year). Among Asian householders aged 35 to 39, median income was an even higher $66,174. The income of non-Hispanic whites aged 25 to 34 was slightly lower than that of Asians, at $51,324. The incomes of black and Hispanic householders in the age group was much lower, $34,129 for Hispanics and $30,385 for blacks.

Behind the income differences by race and Hispanic origin is the number of earners per household. Because Asian and non-Hispanic white households are more likely than black or Hispanic households to be two-earner married couples, their incomes are considerably higher. Education also accounts for some of the gap. Asians are the best educated Americans, followed by non-Hispanic whites. Hispanics are the least educated.

■ Black and Hispanic householders will not close the income gap until dual-earner couples make up a larger share of their households and college graduation rates approach those of Asians and non-Hispanic whites.

Incomes of young householders vary by race and Hispanic origin

(median income of households headed by people aged 25 to 34, by race and Hispanic origin, 2002)

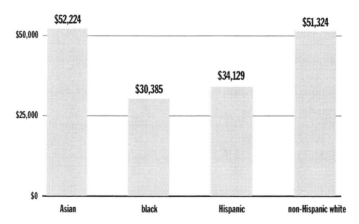

Table 4.3 Income of Households Headed by People Aged 25 to 39, 2002: Asian Households

(number and percent distribution of total Asian households and households headed by Asians aged 25 to 39 by income, 2002; households in thousands as of 2003)

| | total | aged 25 to 34 | | | aged 35 to 39 |
		total	25 to 29	30 to 34	
Total Asian households	**4,079**	**998**	**420**	**578**	**546**
Under $10,000	329	62	40	21	31
$10,000 to $19,999	379	72	34	38	50
$20,000 to $29,999	407	106	44	61	43
$30,000 to $39,999	436	118	50	66	55
$40,000 to $49,999	359	107	45	62	30
$50,000 to $59,999	355	101	48	54	39
$60,000 to $69,999	270	75	31	43	41
$70,000 to $79,999	261	58	19	39	46
$80,000 to $89,999	228	58	16	43	45
$90,000 to $99,999	166	37	15	21	20
$100,000 or more	889	204	77	128	145
Median income	$52,285	$52,224	$49,304	$56,720	$66,174
Total Asian households	**100.0%**	**100.0%**	**100.0%**	**100.0%**	**100.0%**
Under $10,000	8.1	6.2	9.5	3.6	5.7
$10,000 to $19,999	9.3	7.2	8.1	6.6	9.2
$20,000 to $29,999	10.0	10.6	10.5	10.6	7.9
$30,000 to $39,999	10.7	11.8	11.9	11.4	10.1
$40,000 to $49,999	8.8	10.7	10.7	10.7	5.5
$50,000 to $59,999	8.7	10.1	11.4	9.3	7.1
$60,000 to $69,999	6.6	7.5	7.4	7.4	7.5
$70,000 to $79,999	6.4	5.8	4.5	6.7	8.4
$80,000 to $89,999	5.6	5.8	3.8	7.4	8.2
$90,000 to $99,999	4.1	3.7	3.6	3.6	3.7
$100,000 or more	21.8	20.4	18.3	22.1	26.6

Note: Asian householders include those who identified themselves as Asian alone and those who identified themselves as Asian in combination with one or more other races.
Source: Bureau of the Census, data from the 2003 Current Population Survey Annual Social and Economic Supplement. Internet site http://ferret.bls.census.gov/macro/032003/hhinc/new02_000.htm; calculations by New Strategist

Table 4.4 Income of Households Headed by People Aged 25 to 39, 2002: Black Households

(number and percent distribution of total black households and households headed by blacks aged 25 to 39 by income, 2002; households in thousands as of 2003)

	total	aged 25 to 34 total	aged 25 to 34 25 to 29	aged 25 to 34 30 to 34	aged 35 to 39
Total black households	**13,778**	**2,695**	**1,214**	**1,481**	**1,524**
Under $10,000	2,432	384	201	183	176
$10,000 to $19,999	2,486	467	246	221	225
$20,000 to $29,999	2,111	477	215	259	245
$30,000 to $39,999	1,809	432	194	237	189
$40,000 to $49,999	1,190	220	95	125	174
$50,000 to $59,999	918	177	67	110	141
$60,000 to $69,999	698	163	67	96	96
$70,000 to $79,999	566	122	52	71	85
$80,000 to $89,999	384	84	22	61	37
$90,000 to $99,999	280	32	13	19	37
$100,000 or more	904	140	44	95	118
Median income	$29,177	$30,385	$27,658	$32,797	$35,811
Total black households	**100.0%**	**100.0%**	**100.0%**	**100.0%**	**100.0%**
Under $10,000	17.7	14.2	16.6	12.4	11.5
$10,000 to $19,999	18.0	17.3	20.3	14.9	14.8
$20,000 to $29,999	15.3	17.7	17.7	17.5	16.1
$30,000 to $39,999	13.1	16.0	16.0	1.6	12.4
$40,000 to $49,999	8.6	8.2	7.8	8.4	11.4
$50,000 to $59,999	6.7	6.6	5.5	7.4	9.3
$60,000 to $69,999	5.1	6.1	5.5	6.5	6.3
$70,000 to $79,999	4.1	4.5	4.3	4.8	5.6
$80,000 to $89,999	2.8	3.1	1.8	4.1	2.4
$90,000 to $99,999	2.0	1.2	1.1	1.3	2.4
$100,000 or more	6.6	5.2	3.6	6.4	7.7

Note: Black householders include those who identified themselves as black alone and those who identified themselves as black in combination with one or more other races.
Source: Bureau of the Census, data from the 2003 Current Population Survey Annual Social and Economic Supplement, Internet site http://ferret.bls.census.gov/macro/032003/hhinc/new02_000.htm; calculations by New Strategist

Table 4.5 Income of Households Headed by People Aged 25 to 39, 2002: Hispanic Households

(number and percent distribution of total Hispanic households and households headed by Hispanics aged 25 to 39 by income, 2002; households in thousands as of 2003)

		aged 25 to 34			
	total	total	25 to 29	30 to 34	aged 35 to 39
Total Hispanic households	**11,339**	**2,980**	**1,368**	**1,612**	**1,625**
Under $10,000	1,247	257	125	132	112
$10,000 to $19,999	1,879	472	215	257	237
$20,000 to $29,999	1,949	577	265	312	292
$30,000 to $39,999	1,574	417	202	215	245
$40,000 to $49,999	1,109	331	163	168	168
$50,000 to $59,999	945	276	115	161	165
$60,000 to $69,999	693	201	90	111	106
$70,000 to $79,999	505	138	55	83	84
$80,000 to $89,999	372	103	41	64	62
$90,000 to $99,999	249	62	29	35	42
$100,000 or more	815	144	69	75	113
Median income	$33,103	$34,129	$33,485	$34,650	$36,870
Total Hispanic households	**100.0%**	**100.0%**	**100.0%**	**100.0%**	**100.0%**
Under $10,000	11.0	8.6	9.1	8.2	6.9
$10,000 to $19,999	16.6	15.8	15.7	15.9	14.6
$20,000 to $29,999	17.2	19.4	19.4	19.4	18.0
$30,000 to $39,999	13.9	14.0	14.8	13.3	15.1
$40,000 to $49,999	9.8	11.1	11.9	10.4	10.3
$50,000 to $59,999	8.3	9.3	8.4	10.0	10.2
$60,000 to $69,999	6.1	6.7	6.6	6.9	6.5
$70,000 to $79,999	4.5	4.6	4.0	5.1	5.2
$80,000 to $89,999	3.3	3.5	3.0	4.0	3.8
$90,000 to $99,999	2.2	2.1	2.1	2.2	2.6
$100,000 or more	7.2	4.8	5.0	4.7	7.0

Note: Hispanics may be of any race.
Source: Bureau of the Census, data from the 2003 Current Population Survey Annual Social and Economic Supplement. Internet site http://ferret.bls.census.gov/macro/032003/hhinc/new02_000.htm; calculations by New Strategist

Table 4.6　Income of Households Headed by People Aged 25 to 39, 2002:
Non-Hispanic White Households

(number and percent distribution of total non-Hispanic white households and households headed by non-Hispanic whites aged 25 to 39 by income, 2002; households in thousands as of 2003)

		aged 25 to 34			
	total	total	25 to 29	30 to 34	aged 35 to 39
Total non-Hispanic					
white households	**81,166**	**12,247**	**5,465**	**6,782**	**7,702**
Under $10,000	5,977	625	297	328	342
$10,000 to $19,999	10,170	882	466	417	466
$20,000 to $29,999	9,797	1,339	674	664	715
$30,000 to $39,999	8,829	1,537	755	782	749
$40,000 to $49,999	7,982	1,489	722	769	883
$50,000 to $59,999	6,958	1,371	625	747	791
$60,000 to $69,999	5,926	1,249	529	721	658
$70,000 to $79,999	5,301	1,007	415	591	672
$80,000 to $89,999	4,034	722	290	434	492
$90,000 to $99,999	3,235	466	170	296	401
$100,000 and over	12,958	1,558	523	1,035	1,533
Median income	$46,900	$51,324	$46,816	$55,426	$58,424
Total non-Hispanic					
white households	**100.0%**	**100.0%**	**100.0%**	**100.0%**	**100.0%**
Under $10,000	7.4	5.1	5.4	4.8	4.4
$10,000 to $19,999	12.5	7.2	8.5	6.1	6.1
$20,000 to $29,999	12.1	10.9	12.3	9.8	9.3
$30,000 to $39,999	10.9	12.6	13.8	11.5	9.7
$40,000 to $49,999	9.8	12.2	13.2	11.3	11.5
$50,000 to $59,999	8.6	11.2	11.4	11.0	10.3
$60,000 to $69,999	7.3	10.2	9.7	10.6	8.5
$70,000 to $79,999	6.5	8.2	7.6	8.7	8.7
$80,000 to $89,999	5.0	5.9	5.3	6.4	6.4
$90,000 to $99,999	4.0	3.8	3.1	4.4	5.2
$100,000 and over	16.0	12.7	9.6	15.3	19.9

Note: Non-Hispanic white householders include only those who identified themselves as white alone and non-Hispanic.
Source: Bureau of the Census, data from the 2003 Current Population Survey Annual Social and Economic Supplement, Internet site http://ferret.bls.census.gov/macro/032003/hhinc/new02_000.htm; calculations by New Strategist

Dual Earners Give Gen Xers Higher Incomes

Single mothers have the lowest incomes.

The incomes of households headed by people aged 25 to 34 vary sharply by household type. Married couples have the highest incomes by far. Among households headed by people aged 25 to 34 (Gen Xers were aged 26 to 37 in 2002), married couples had a median income of $57,454 in 2002. In the 35-to-39 age group, the median income of married couples was a lofty $67,395. Behind their higher incomes is the fact that most are dual-earner couples.

Female-headed families in the 25-to-34 age group had a median income of only $23,162 in 2002. Most are single parents. The median income of male-headed families was nearly twice that of female-headed families ($42,411). The median income of women aged 25 to 34 who live alone was almost as high as that of their male counterparts, $32,301 versus $32,595.

■ Female-headed families have the lowest incomes because their households usually include only one earner and the presence of children makes them less flexible in their job choices.

The incomes of Gen X couples are above average

(median income of householders aged 25 to 34, by household type, 2002)

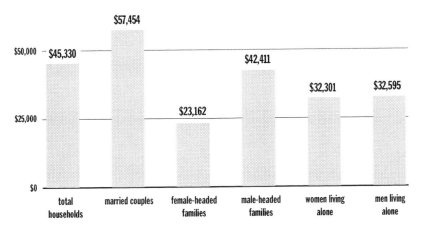

Table 4.7 Income of Households by Household Type, 2002: Aged 25 to 34

(number and percent distribution of households headed by people aged 25 to 34 by income and household type,
2002; households in thousands as of 2003)

| | | family households | | | nonfamily households | | | |
| | | | | | female householder | | male householder | |
	total	married couples	female hh, no spouse present	male hh, no spouse present	total	living alone	total	living alone
Total householders								
aged 25 to 34	**19,055**	**9,536**	**2,892**	**1,010**	**2,274**	**1,596**	**3,343**	**2,212**
Under $10,000	1,347	218	568	43	233	206	286	260
$10,000 to $19,999	1,912	552	681	94	226	193	358	316
$20,000 to $29,999	2,515	927	556	166	349	286	519	398
$30,000 to $39,999	2,546	1,029	443	154	418	352	502	388
$40,000 to $49,999	2,160	1,094	214	128	288	206	433	296
$50,000 to $59,999	1,929	1,168	118	118	208	127	316	167
$60,000 to $69,999	1,685	1,063	98	105	162	82	254	123
$70,000 to $79,999	1,340	916	65	74	109	43	175	88
$80,000 to $89,999	966	660	54	34	85	20	134	55
$90,000 to $99,999	599	422	17	22	51	33	86	17
$100,000 or more	2,057	1,485	79	70	144	48	279	106
Median income	$45,330	$57,454	$23,162	$42,411	$37,691	$32,301	$40,093	$32,595
Total householders								
aged 25 to 34	**100.0%**	**100.0%**	**100.0%**	**100.0%**	**100.0%**	**100.0%**	**100.0%**	**100.0%**
Under $10,000	7.1	2.3	19.6	4.3	10.2	12.9	8.6	11.8
$10,000 to $19,999	10.0	5.8	23.5	9.3	9.9	12.1	10.7	14.3
$20,000 to $29,999	13.2	9.7	19.2	16.4	15.3	17.9	15.5	18.0
$30,000 to $39,999	13.4	10.8	15.3	15.2	18.4	22.1	15.0	17.5
$40,000 to $49,999	11.3	11.5	7.4	12.7	12.7	12.9	13.0	13.4
$50,000 to $59,999	10.1	12.2	4.1	11.7	9.1	8.0	9.5	7.5
$60,000 to $69,999	8.8	11.1	3.4	10.4	7.1	5.1	7.6	5.6
$70,000 to $79,999	7.0	9.6	2.2	7.3	4.8	2.7	5.2	4.0
$80,000 to $89,999	5.1	6.9	1.9	3.4	3.7	1.3	4.0	2.5
$90,000 to $99,999	3.1	4.4	0.6	2.2	2.2	2.1	2.6	0.8
$100,000 or more	10.8	15.6	2.7	6.9	6.3	3.0	8.3	4.8

Source: Bureau of the Census, data from the 2003 Current Population Survey Annual Social and Economic Supplement, Internet
site http://ferret.bls.census.gov/macro/032003/hhinc/new02_000.htm; calculations by New Strategist

Table 4.8 Income of Households by Household Type, 2002: Aged 25 to 29

(number and percent distribution of households headed by people aged 25 to 29, by income and household type, 2002; households in thousands as of 2003)

| | | family households | | | nonfamily households | | | |
| | | | | | female householder | | male householder | |
	total	married couples	female hh, no spouse present	male hh, no spouse present	total	living alone	total	living alone
Total householders aged 25 to 29	**8,535**	**3,760**	**1,391**	**508**	**1,223**	**783**	**1,653**	**1,021**
Under $10,000	673	99	303	26	103	86	141	120
$10,000 to $19,999	968	250	356	54	121	101	188	163
$20,000 to $29,999	1,213	429	245	80	195	154	265	201
$30,000 to $39,999	1,223	459	192	90	235	191	246	182
$40,000 to $49,999	1,029	489	100	55	171	117	214	131
$50,000 to $59,999	857	485	53	57	106	45	158	65
$60,000 to $69,999	716	409	46	49	85	40	124	61
$70,000 to $79,999	549	358	35	24	59	20	73	25
$80,000 to $89,999	369	212	18	19	52	3	66	27
$90,000 to $99,999	226	141	6	16	22	8	42	6
$100,000 or more	713	428	36	38	76	16	134	39
Median income	$41,388	$52,728	$21,270	$40,408	$37,815	$31,833	$39,082	$31,016
Total householders aged 25 to 29	**100.0%**	**100.0%**	**100.0%**	**100.0%**	**100.0%**	**100.0%**	**100.0%**	**100.0%**
Under $10,000	7.9	2.6	21.8	5.1	8.4	11.0	8.5	11.8
$10,000 to $19,999	11.3	6.6	25.6	10.6	9.9	12.9	11.4	16.0
$20,000 to $29,999	14.2	11.4	17.6	15.7	15.9	19.7	16.0	19.7
$30,000 to $39,999	14.3	12.2	13.8	17.7	19.2	24.4	14.9	17.8
$40,000 to $49,999	12.1	1.3	7.2	10.8	14.0	14.9	12.9	12.8
$50,000 to $59,999	10.0	12.9	3.8	11.2	8.7	5.7	9.6	6.4
$60,000 to $69,999	8.4	10.9	3.3	9.6	7.0	5.1	7.5	6.0
$70,000 to $79,999	6.4	9.5	2.5	4.7	4.8	2.6	4.4	2.4
$80,000 to $89,999	4.3	5.6	1.3	3.7	4.3	0.4	4.0	2.6
$90,000 to $99,999	2.6	3.8	0.4	3.1	1.8	1.0	2.5	0.6
$100,000 or more	8.4	11.4	2.6	7.5	6.2	2.0	8.1	3.8

Source: Bureau of the Census, data from the 2003 Current Population Survey Annual Social and Economic Supplement, Internet site http://ferret.bls.census.gov/macro/032003/hhinc/new02_000.htm; calculations by New Strategist

Table 4.9 Income of Households by Household Type, 2002: Aged 30 to 34

(number and percent distribution of households headed by people aged 30 to 34, by income and household type, 2002; households in thousands as of 2003)

| | | family households | | | nonfamily households | | | |
| | | | | | female householder | | male householder | |
	total	married couples	female hh, no spouse present	male hh, no spouse present	total	living alone	total	living alone
Total householders aged 30 to 34	**10,521**	**5,776**	**1,501**	**503**	**1,051**	**814**	**1,690**	**1,191**
Under $10,000	675	118	265	17	129	119	144	139
$10,000 to $19,999	944	301	326	41	105	92	171	153
$20,000 to $29,999	1,302	498	309	87	155	131	252	196
$30,000 to $39,999	1,325	569	251	64	184	161	258	206
$40,000 to $49,999	1,131	605	114	73	118	88	220	167
$50,000 to $59,999	1,073	684	66	62	101	81	157	103
$60,000 to $69,999	969	655	51	55	78	42	130	61
$70,000 to $79,999	791	559	29	51	49	23	103	60
$80,000 to $89,999	598	446	36	14	32	15	68	29
$90,000 to $99,999	373	281	11	7	29	26	43	11
$100,000 or more	1,344	1,057	43	32	67	32	145	66
Median income	$48,698	$61,242	$24,817	$45,608	$37,579	$33,293	$40,538	$34,936
Total householders aged 30 to 34	**100.0%**	**100.0%**	**100.0%**	**100.0%**	**100.0%**	**100.0%**	**100.0%**	**100.0%**
Under $10,000	6.4	2.0	17.7	3.4	12.3	14.6	8.5	11.7
$10,000 to $19,999	9.0	5.2	21.7	8.2	10.0	11.3	10.1	12.8
$20,000 to $29,999	12.4	8.6	20.6	17.3	14.7	16.1	14.9	16.5
$30,000 to $39,999	12.6	9.9	16.7	12.7	17.5	19.8	15.3	17.3
$40,000 to $49,999	10.7	10.5	7.6	14.5	11.2	10.8	13.0	14.0
$50,000 to $59,999	10.2	11.8	4.4	12.3	9.6	10.0	9.3	8.6
$60,000 to $69,999	9.2	11.3	3.4	10.9	7.4	5.2	7.7	5.1
$70,000 to $79,999	7.5	9.7	1.9	10.1	4.7	2.8	6.1	5.0
$80,000 to $89,999	5.7	7.7	2.4	2.8	3.0	1.8	4.0	2.4
$90,000 to $99,999	3.5	4.9	0.7	1.4	2.8	3.2	2.5	0.9
$100,000 or more	12.8	18.3	2.9	6.4	6.4	3.9	8.6	5.5

Source: Bureau of the Census, data from the 2003 Current Population Survey Annual Social and Economic Supplement, Internet site http://ferret.bls.census.gov/macro/032003/hhinc/new02_000.htm; calculations by New Strategist

Table 4.10 Income of Households by Household Type, 2002: Aged 35 to 39

(number and percent distribution of households headed by people aged 35 to 39, by income and household type, 2002; households in thousands as of 2003)

| | | family households | | | nonfamily households | | | |
| | | | | | female householder | | male householder | |
	total	married couples	female hh, no spouse present	male hh, no spouse present	total	living alone	total	living alone
Total householders aged 35 to 39	**11,486**	**6,640**	**1,826**	**498**	**943**	**771**	**1,578**	**1,178**
Under $10,000	674	119	256	23	127	123	148	132
$10,000 to $19,999	982	283	392	45	95	90	168	145
$20,000 to $29,999	1,296	480	358	83	120	109	257	225
$30,000 to $39,999	1,250	551	244	81	172	152	204	163
$40,000 to $49,999	1,271	658	222	76	112	91	203	145
$50,000 to $59,999	1,146	679	152	63	85	62	167	111
$60,000 to $69,999	905	679	56	36	36	28	98	67
$70,000 to $79,999	893	696	41	27	53	37	78	50
$80,000 to $89,999	641	517	24	15	30	23	57	37
$90,000 to $99,999	504	429	18	8	23	3	26	11
$100,000 or more	1,921	1,552	65	42	89	53	173	90
Median income	$51,870	$67,395	$26,853	$41,725	$36,638	$33,393	$40,504	$35,771
Total householders aged 35 to 39	**100.0%**	**100.0%**	**100.0%**	**100.0%**	**100.0%**	**100.0%**	**100.0%**	**100.0%**
Under $10,000	5.9	1.8	14.0	4.6	13.5	16.0	9.4	11.2
$10,000 to $19,999	8.5	4.3	21.5	9.0	10.1	11.7	10.6	12.3
$20,000 to $29,999	11.3	7.2	19.6	16.7	12.7	14.1	16.3	19.1
$30,000 to $39,999	10.9	8.3	13.4	16.3	18.2	19.7	12.9	13.8
$40,000 to $49,999	11.1	9.9	12.2	15.3	11.9	11.8	12.9	12.3
$50,000 to $59,999	10.0	10.2	8.3	12.7	9.0	8.0	10.6	9.4
$60,000 to $69,999	7.9	10.2	3.1	7.2	3.8	3.6	6.2	5.7
$70,000 to $79,999	7.8	10.5	2.2	5.4	5.6	4.8	4.9	4.2
$80,000 to $89,999	5.6	7.8	1.3	3.0	3.2	3.0	3.6	3.1
$90,000 to $99,999	4.4	6.5	1.0	1.6	2.4	0.4	1.6	0.9
$100,000 or more	16.7	23.4	3.6	8.4	9.4	6.9	11.0	7.6

Source: Bureau of the Census, data from the 2003 Current Population Survey Annual Social and Economic Supplement, Internet site http://ferret.bls.census.gov/macro/032003/hhinc/new02_000.htm; calculations by New Strategist

Incomes of Men Aged 25 to 44 Are below 1980 Levels

Both men and women have lost ground since 2000.

The incomes of men aged 25 to 44 fell between 2000 and 2002, after adjusting for inflation, by 3 percent for men aged 25 to 34 and by 4 percent for those aged 35 to 44 (Gen Xers were aged 26 to 37 in 2002). Women also experienced a decline, the median income of those aged 25 to 34 falling 2 percent and that of women aged 35 to 44 down 3 percent.

Behind the recent income decline is recession and the loss of millions of jobs. But for men, the income decline began long before the recession of 2001. Between 1980 and 2002, the median income of men aged 25 to 34 fell 5 percent, and the decline was an even larger 9 percent for those aged 35 to 44. In contrast, women's incomes have soared over the past two decades. Women aged 25 to 34 saw their median income rise 50 percent between 1980 and 2002, while those aged 35 to 44 experienced an even larger 67 percent gain, after adjusting for inflation.

■ Women's incomes have grown over the past two decades because a growing proportion have joined the workforce.

Incomes of women have soared since 1980

(median income of people aged 25 to 44, by sex, 1980 and 2002; in 2002 dollars)

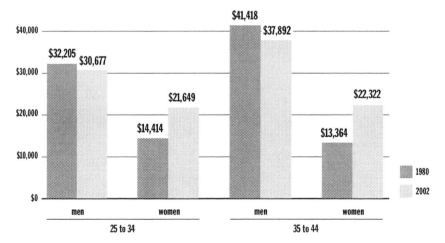

Table 4.11 **Median Income of Men Aged 25 to 44, 1980 to 2002**

(median income of men aged 15 or older and aged 25 to 44, 1980 to 2002; percent change for selected years; in 2002 dollars)

	total men	25 to 34	35 to 44
2002	$29,238	$30,677	$37,892
2001	29,564	30,995	38,950
2000	29,597	31,593	39,600
1999	29,433	32,226	39,082
1998	29,189	30,980	38,759
1997	28,170	29,046	36,705
1996	27,199	28,734	36,709
1995	26,439	27,665	36,818
1994	26,070	27,134	36,857
1993	25,862	26,873	37,185
1992	25,694	27,003	37,044
1991	26,357	27,806	37,729
1990	27,075	28,542	39,723
1989	27,861	29,925	41,227
1988	27,618	30,356	41,695
1987	26,925	30,167	40,938
1986	26,791	29,998	40,971
1985	26,000	29,748	40,422
1984	25,696	29,802	40,464
1983	25,061	28,785	38,437
1982	24,888	29,287	38,623
1981	25,459	30,408	39,903
1980	25,900	32,205	41,418
Percent change			
2000–2002	–1.2%	–2.9%	–4.3%
1990–2002	8.0	7.5	–4.6
1980–2002	12.9	–4.7	–8.5

Source: Bureau of the Census, data from the Current Population Survey Annual Demographic Supplements, Internet site http:// www.census.gov/hhes/income/histinc/p08.html; calculations by New Strategist

Table 4.12 Median Income of Women Aged 25 to 44, 1980 to 2002

(median income of women aged 15 or older and aged 25 to 44, 1980 to 2002; percent change for selected years; in 2002 dollars)

	total women	25 to 34	35 to 44
2002	$16,812	$21,649	$22,322
2001	16,878	21,814	22,828
2000	16,774	21,980	23,054
1999	16,523	20,931	22,319
1998	15,899	20,116	22,350
1997	15,311	19,718	20,900
1996	14,624	18,697	21,052
1995	14,215	18,229	20,386
1994	13,762	17,865	19,431
1993	13,537	17,143	19,418
1992	13,458	17,122	19,365
1991	13,489	16,692	19,475
1990	13,435	16,796	19,351
1989	13,479	17,130	19,335
1988	12,977	16,892	18,326
1987	12,558	16,621	18,159
1986	11,914	16,140	17,320
1985	11,504	15,748	16,378
1984	11,313	15,470	15,749
1983	10,823	14,565	15,177
1982	10,502	14,223	14,006
1981	10,313	14,357	13,919
1980	10,170	14,414	13,364
Percent change			
2000–2002	0.2%	–1.5%	–3.2%
1990–2002	25.1	28.9	15.4
1980–2002	65.3	50.2	67.0

Source: Bureau of the Census, data from the Current Population Survey Annual Demographic Supplements, Internet site http:// www.census.gov/hhes/income/histinc/p08.html; calculations by New Strategist

Men's Income Rises above Average in the 30-to-34 Age Group

Asian and non-Hispanic white men have the highest incomes.

The incomes of men rise sharply during their twenties and thirties as they advance in their career. Median income grows from a below-average $27,256 in the 25-to-29 age group to an above-average $36,942 among those aged 35 to 39 (Gen Xers were aged 26 to 37 in 2002). Income rises in part because a growing proportion of men work full-time. The figure rises from 69 percent in the 25-to-29 age group to 76 percent for men aged 35 to 39.

Among men aged 25 to 34 working full-time, Asians have the highest median income, $43,711 in 2002. Non-Hispanic white men follow, with a median income of $38,272. In the 35-to-39 age group, however, non-Hispanic white men who work full-time have a higher median income than their Asian counterparts.

Black and Hispanic men have the lowest incomes. Among black men aged 25 to 34 who work full-time, median income was $30,620 in 2002. Hispanic men who work full-time had an even lower income of $25,688. Hispanic men also have the lowest incomes among full-time workers aged 35 to 39—just $27,189 versus the high of $47,176 for non-Hispanic white men in the age group.

■ Black and Hispanic men have lower incomes than Asian or non-Hispanic white men because they are much less educated.

Among men aged 25 to 34, Hispanics have the lowest incomes

(median income of men aged 25 to 34 who work full-time, by race and Hispanic origin, 2002)

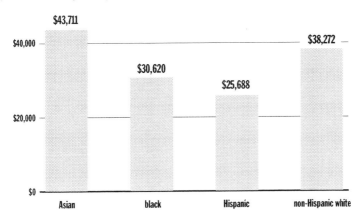

Table 4.13 Income of Men Aged 25 to 39, 2002: Total Men

(number and percent distribution of men aged 16 or older and aged 25 to 39 by income, 2002; median income by work status, and percent working year-round, full-time; men in thousands as of 2003)

	total	aged 25 to 34 total	aged 25 to 34 25 to 29	aged 25 to 34 30 to 34	aged 35 to 39
TOTAL MEN	**108,814**	**19,564**	**9,382**	**10,182**	**10,510**
Without income	**9,026**	**869**	**527**	**342**	**381**
With income	**99,788**	**18,695**	**8,855**	**9,840**	**10,129**
Under $10,000	16,061	1,845	1,013	833	802
$10,000 to $19,999	18,536	3,305	1,828	1,477	1,317
$20,000 to $29,999	16,206	3,818	1,991	1,827	1,693
$30,000 to $39,999	13,528	3,381	1,657	1,723	1,640
$40,000 to $49,999	9,485	2,256	989	1,265	1,220
$50,000 to $59,999	7,048	1,396	527	869	945
$60,000 to $69,999	4,735	937	330	606	617
$70,000 to $79,999	3,769	575	194	381	508
$80,000 to $89,999	2,355	305	104	201	310
$90,000 to $99,999	1,512	197	57	139	208
$100,000 or more	6,556	682	164	518	867
Median income of men with income	$29,238	$30,677	$27,256	$33,426	$36,942
Median income of full-time workers	40,507	35,147	31,356	37,744	41,956
Percent working full-time	54.0%	71.9%	68.6%	75.0%	75.9%
TOTAL MEN	**100.0%**	**100.0%**	**100.0%**	**100.0%**	**100.0%**
Without income	**8.3**	**4.4**	**5.6**	**3.4**	**3.6**
With income	**91.7**	**95.6**	**94.4**	**96.6**	**96.4**
Under $10,000	14.8	9.4	10.8	8.2	7.6
$10,000 to $19,999	17.0	16.9	19.5	14.5	12.5
$20,000 to $29,999	14.9	19.5	21.2	17.9	16.1
$30,000 to $39,999	12.4	17.3	17.7	16.9	15.6
$40,000 to $49,999	8.7	11.5	10.5	12.4	11.6
$50,000 to $59,999	6.5	7.1	5.6	8.5	9.0
$60,000 to $69,999	4.4	4.8	3.5	6.0	5.9
$70,000 to $79,999	3.5	2.9	2.1	3.7	4.8
$80,000 to $89,999	2.2	1.6	1.1	2.0	2.9
$90,000 to $99,999	1.4	1.0	0.6	1.4	2.0
$100,000 or more	6.0	3.5	1.7	5.1	8.2

Source: Bureau of the Census, data from the 2003 Current Population Survey Annual Social and Economic Supplement, Internet site http://ferret.bls.census.gov/macro/032003/perinc/toc.htm; calculations by New Strategist

Table 4.14 Income of Men Aged 25 to 39, 2002: Asian Men

(number and percent distribution of Asian men aged 16 or older and aged 25 to 39 by income, 2002; median income by work status, and percent working year-round, full-time; men in thousands as of 2003)

	total	aged 25 to 34 total	25 to 29	30 to 34	aged 35 to 39
TOTAL ASIAN MEN	4,688	1,116	543	572	534
Without income	549	68	56	11	23
With income	4,139	1,048	487	561	511
Under $10,000	708	115	69	45	35
$10,000 to $19,999	701	153	67	87	75
$20,000 to $29,999	589	157	76	81	78
$30,000 to $39,999	536	170	90	80	62
$40,000 to $49,999	371	103	50	52	62
$50,000 to $59,999	235	80	41	39	39
$60,000 to $69,999	206	79	35	43	38
$70,000 to $79,999	199	55	16	41	28
$80,000 to $89,999	141	35	8	27	27
$90,000 to $99,999	95	20	9	11	15
$100,000 or more	360	82	25	57	53
Median income of men with income	$30,839	$35,145	$31,665	$37,133	$40,746
Median income of full-time workers	42,448	43,711	40,250	47,675	45,843
Percent working full-time	56.2%	66.2%	61.0%	71.2%	78.1%
TOTAL ASIAN MEN	100.0%	100.0%	100.0%	100.0%	100.0%
Without income	11.7	6.1	10.3	1.9	4.3
With income	88.3	93.9	89.7	98.1	95.7
Under $10,000	15.1	10.3	12.7	7.9	6.6
$10,000 to $19,999	15.0	13.7	12.3	15.2	14.0
$20,000 to $29,999	12.6	14.1	14.0	14.2	14.6
$30,000 to $39,999	11.4	15.2	16.6	14.0	11.6
$40,000 to $49,999	7.9	9.2	9.2	9.1	11.6
$50,000 to $59,999	5.0	7.2	7.6	6.8	7.3
$60,000 to $69,999	4.4	7.1	6.4	7.5	7.1
$70,000 to $79,999	4.2	4.9	2.9	7.2	5.2
$80,000 to $89,999	3.0	3.1	1.5	4.7	5.1
$90,000 to $99,999	2.0	1.8	1.7	1.9	2.8
$100,000 or more	7.7	7.3	4.6	10.0	9.9

Note: Asians include those who identified themselves as Asian alone and those who identified themselves as Asian in combination with one or more other races.
Source: Bureau of the Census, data from the 2003 Current Population Survey Annual Social and Economic Supplement. Internet site http://ferret.bls.census.gov/macro/032003/perinc/toc.htm: calculations by New Strategist

Table 4.15 Income of Men Aged 25 to 39, 2002: Black Men

(number and percent distribution of black men aged 16 or older and aged 25 to 39 by income, 2002; median income by work status, and percent working year-round, full-time; men in thousands as of 2003)

	total	aged 25 to 34 total	25 to 29	30 to 34	aged 35 to 39
TOTAL BLACK MEN	**12,188**	**2,328**	**1,111**	**1,217**	**1,211**
Without income	**2,092**	**244**	**138**	**106**	**116**
With income	**10,096**	**2,084**	**973**	**1,111**	**1,095**
Under $10,000	2,416	354	214	141	121
$10,000 to $19,999	2,254	430	233	198	203
$20,000 to $29,999	1,813	471	199	273	236
$30,000 to $39,999	1,373	365	164	200	207
$40,000 to $49,999	829	202	75	126	96
$50,000 to $59,999	527	104	36	68	85
$60,000 to $69,999	264	65	20	46	43
$70,000 to $79,999	214	29	13	16	46
$80,000 to $89,999	115	24	7	16	20
$90,000 to $99,999	70	11	4	7	11
$100,000 or more	221	31	10	21	28
Median income of men with income	$21,509	$24,752	$21,738	$26,913	$29,280
Median income of full-time workers	31,966	30,620	27,560	31,590	33,886
Percent working full-time	45.2%	60.4%	55.4%	64.8%	67.5%
TOTAL BLACK MEN	**100.0%**	**100.0%**	**100.0%**	**100.0%**	**100.0%**
Without income	**17.2**	**10.5**	**12.4**	**8.7**	**9.6**
With income	**82.8**	**89.5**	**87.6**	**91.3**	**90.4**
Under $10,000	19.8	15.2	19.3	11.6	10.0
$10,000 to $19,999	18.5	18.5	21.0	16.3	16.8
$20,000 to $29,999	14.9	20.2	17.9	22.4	19.5
$30,000 to $39,999	11.3	15.7	14.8	16.4	17.1
$40,000 to $49,999	6.8	8.7	6.8	10.4	7.9
$50,000 to $59,999	4.3	4.5	3.2	5.6	7.0
$60,000 to $69,999	2.2	2.8	1.8	3.8	3.6
$70,000 to $79,999	1.8	1.2	1.2	1.3	3.8
$80,000 to $89,999	0.9	1.0	0.6	1.3	1.7
$90,000 to $99,999	0.6	0.5	0.4	0.6	0.9
$100,000 or more	1.8	1.3	0.9	1.7	2.3

Note: Blacks include those who identified themselves as black alone and those who identified themselves as black in combination with one or more other races.
Source: Bureau of the Census, data from the 2003 Current Population Survey Annual Social and Economic Supplement. Internet site http://ferret.bls.census.gov/macro/032003/perinc/toc.htm; calculations by New Strategist

Table 4.16 Income of Men Aged 25 to 39, 2002: Hispanic Men

(number and percent distribution of Hispanic men aged 16 or older and aged 25 to 39 by income, 2002; median income by work status, and percent working year-round, full-time; men in thousands as of 2003)

	total	total	25 to 29	30 to 34	aged 35 to 39
			aged 25 to 34		
TOTAL HISPANIC MEN	**14,353**	**3,998**	**2,114**	**1,884**	**1,653**
Without income	**1,729**	**187**	**117**	**70**	**76**
With income	**12,624**	**3,811**	**1,997**	**1,814**	**1,577**
Under $10,000	2,395	456	265	191	152
$10,000 to $19,999	3,629	1,147	640	506	405
$20,000 to $29,999	2,715	960	512	447	414
$30,000 to $39,999	1,526	577	295	283	220
$40,000 to $49,999	869	275	129	146	151
$50,000 to $59,999	566	178	63	116	88
$60,000 to $69,999	304	95	42	54	55
$70,000 to $79,999	201	43	18	24	34
$80,000 to $89,999	104	25	14	11	18
$90,000 to $99,999	63	13	2	11	5
$100,000 or more	251	38	14	24	37
Median income of men with income	$20,702	$22,017	$21,179	$23,502	$24,867
Median income of full-time workers	26,137	25,688	24,591	26,708	27,189
Percent working full-time	57.0%	72.7%	70.8%	74.8%	73.3%
TOTAL HISPANIC MEN	**100.0%**	**100.0%**	**100.0%**	**100.0%**	**100.0%**
Without income	**12.1**	**4.7**	**5.5**	**3.7**	**4.6**
With income	**88.0**	**95.3**	**94.5**	**96.3**	**95.4**
Under $10,000	16.7	11.4	12.5	10.1	9.2
$10,000 to $19,999	25.3	28.7	30.3	26.9	24.5
$20,000 to $29,999	18.9	24.0	24.2	23.7	25.1
$30,000 to $39,999	10.6	14.4	14.0	15.0	13.3
$40,000 to $49,999	6.1	6.9	6.1	7.7	9.1
$50,000 to $59,999	3.9	4.5	3.0	6.2	5.3
$60,000 to $69,999	2.1	2.4	2.0	2.9	3.3
$70,000 to $79,999	1.4	1.1	0.9	1.3	2.1
$80,000 to $89,999	0.7	0.6	0.7	0.6	1.1
$90,000 to $99,999	0.4	0.3	0.1	0.6	0.3
$100,000 or more	1.7	1.0	0.7	1.3	2.2

Note: Hispanics may be of any race.
Source: Bureau of the Census, data from the 2003 Current Population Survey Annual Social and Economic Supplement. Internet site http://ferret.bls.census.gov/macro/032003/perinc/toc.htm; calculations by New Strategist

Table 4.17 Income of Men Aged 25 to 39, 2002: Non-Hispanic White Men

(number and percent distribution of non-Hispanic white men aged 16 or older and aged 25 to 39 by income, 2002; median income by work status, and percent working year-round, full-time; men in thousands as of 2003)

	total	aged 25 to 34 total	25 to 29	30 to 34	aged 35 to 39
TOTAL NON-HISPANIC					
WHITE MEN	**76,722**	**11,989**	**5,565**	**6,425**	**7,021**
Without income	**4,576**	**352**	205	147	160
With income	**72,146**	**11,637**	**5,360**	**6,278**	**6,861**
Under $10,000	10,338	888	451	437	480
$10,000 to $19,999	11,849	1,558	881	676	628
$20,000 to $29,999	10,984	2,220	1,198	1,021	957
$30,000 to $39,999	8,664	1,110	1,139	2,323	1,206
$40,000 to $49,999	6,633	728	936	1,844	942
$50,000 to $59,999	5,164	381	643	1,556	825
$60,000 to $69,999	3,841	496	311	740	558
$70,000 to $79,999	3,139	448	149	300	403
$80,000 to $89,999	1,973	218	75	144	243
$90,000 to $99,999	1,270	152	39	112	176
$100,000 or more	5,703	526	112	414	749
Median income of men with income	$32,034	$34,254	$30,797	$38,113	$41,809
Median income of full-time workers	45,153	38,272	34,447	41,809	47,176
Percent working full-time	54.8%	74.8%	71.3%	77.7%	78.0%
TOTAL NON-HISPANIC					
WHITE MEN	**100.0%**	**100.0%**	**100.0%**	**100.0%**	**100.0%**
Without income	**6.0**	**2.9**	**3.7**	**2.3**	**2.3**
With income	**94.0**	**97.1**	**96.3**	**97.7**	**97.7**
Under $10,000	13.5	7.4	8.1	6.8	6.8
$10,000 to $19,999	15.4	13.0	15.8	10.5	8.9
$20,000 to $29,999	14.3	18.5	21.5	15.9	13.6
$30,000 to $39,999	11.3	9.3	20.5	36.2	17.2
$40,000 to $49,999	8.6	6.1	16.8	28.7	13.4
$50,000 to $59,999	6.7	3.2	11.6	24.2	11.8
$60,000 to $69,999	5.0	4.1	5.6	11.5	7.9
$70,000 to $79,999	4.1	3.7	2.7	4.7	5.7
$80,000 to $89,999	2.6	1.8	1.3	2.2	3.5
$90,000 to $99,999	1.7	1.3	0.7	1.7	2.5
$100,000 or more	7.4	4.4	2.0	6.4	10.7

Note: Non-Hispanic whites include only those who identified themselves as white alone and non-Hispanic.
Source: Bureau of the Census, data from the 2003 Current Population Survey Annual Social and Economic Supplement, Internet site http://ferret.bls.census.gov/macro/032003/perinc/toc.htm; calculations by New Strategist

Women's Incomes Do Not Rise Much with Age

Asian and non-Hispanic white women have the highest incomes.

The median income of women does not change much as they age through their twenties and thirties. Among women aged 25 to 39, median income was $21,376 in 2002 for 25-to-29-year-olds and an almost identical $21,726 for 35-to-39-year-olds (Gen Xers were aged 26 to 37 in 2002). One reason women's incomes are relatively flat is that only 48 to 50 percent work full-time. Another reason is that many women choose lower-paying careers that allow them to spend more time with their children.

Among women aged 25 to 34 working full-time, Asians have the highest median income, $32,259 in 2002. Non-Hispanic white women follow, with a median income of $31,725. In the 35-to-39 age group, the median income of Asian women who work full-time continues to surpass that of non-Hispanic whites, although not by much.

Black and Hispanic women have the lowest incomes. Among black women aged 25 to 34 who work full-time, median income was $27,471 in 2002. Hispanic women who work full-time had an even lower income of $24,082. Hispanic women also have the lowest incomes among full-time workers aged 35 to 39—just $23,530 versus the high of $35,065 for their Asian counterparts.

■ Black and Hispanic women have lower incomes than Asian or non-Hispanic white women because they are much less educated.

Among women aged 25 to 34, Hispanics have the lowest incomes

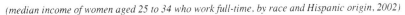

(median income of women aged 25 to 34 who work full-time, by race and Hispanic origin, 2002)

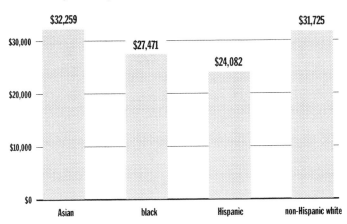

Table 4.18 Income of Women Aged 25 to 39, 2002: Total Women

(number and percent distribution of women aged 16 or older and aged 25 to 39 by income, 2002; median income by work status, and percent working year-round, full-time; women in thousands as of 2003)

		aged 25 to 34			
	total	total	25 to 29	30 to 34	aged 35 to 39
TOTAL WOMEN	116,436	19,679	9,339	10,340	10,774
Without income	13,949	2,343	1,168	1,175	974
With income	102,487	17,336	8,171	9,165	9,800
Under $10,000	33,026	4,289	1,996	2,292	2,489
$10,000 to $19,999	24,289	3,615	1,772	1,844	1,994
$20,000 to $29,999	16,626	3,550	1,824	1,725	1,781
$30,000 to $39,999	11,180	2,727	1,287	1,440	1,363
$40,000 to $49,999	6,784	1,391	621	769	858
$50,000 to $59,999	3,886	740	291	449	464
$60,000 to $69,999	2,264	383	157	226	232
$70,000 to $79,999	1,428	243	92	151	190
$80,000 to $89,999	787	104	41	63	119
$90,000 to $99,999	558	89	32	57	77
$100,000 or more	1,658	208	58	150	233
Median income of women with income	$16,812	$21,649	$21,376	$21,918	$21,726
Median income of full-time workers	30,970	30,370	29,051	31,246	31,692
Percent working full-time	36.0%	48.4%	48.2%	48.5%	49.5%
TOTAL WOMEN	**100.0%**	**100.0%**	**100.0%**	**100.0%**	**100.0%**
Without income	**12.0**	**11.9**	**12.5**	**11.4**	**9.0**
With income	**88.0**	**88.1**	**87.5**	**88.6**	**91.0**
Under $10,000	28.4	21.8	21.4	22.2	23.1
$10,000 to $19,999	20.9	18.4	19.0	17.8	18.5
$20,000 to $29,999	14.3	18.0	19.5	16.7	16.5
$30,000 to $39,999	9.6	13.9	13.8	13.9	12.7
$40,000 to $49,999	5.8	7.1	6.6	7.4	8.0
$50,000 to $59,999	3.3	3.8	3.1	4.3	4.3
$60,000 to $69,999	1.9	1.9	1.7	2.2	2.2
$70,000 to $79,999	1.2	1.2	1.0	1.5	1.8
$80,000 to $89,999	0.7	0.5	0.4	0.6	1.1
$90,000 to $99,999	0.5	0.5	0.3	0.6	0.7
$100,000 or more	1.4	1.1	0.6	1.5	2.2

Source: Bureau of the Census, data from the 2003 Current Population Survey Annual Social and Economic Supplement, Internet site http://ferret.bls.census.gov/macro/032003/perinc/toc.htm; calculations by New Strategist

Table 4.19 Income of Women Aged 25 to 39, 2002: Asian Women

(number and percent distribution of Asian women aged 16 or older and aged 25 to 39 by income, 2002; median income by work status, and percent working year-round, full-time; women in thousands as of 2003)

	total	aged 25 to 34 total	25 to 29	30 to 34	aged 35 to 39
TOTAL ASIAN WOMEN	5,131	1,192	563	629	565
Without income	994	219	105	114	68
With income	4,137	973	458	515	497
Under $10,000	1,373	266	134	132	127
$10,000 to $19,999	804	155	75	79	97
$20,000 to $29,999	642	175	98	75	72
$30,000 to $39,999	396	119	49	71	58
$40,000 to $49,999	291	81	27	53	39
$50,000 to $59,999	214	77	40	37	21
$60,000 to $69,999	118	23	9	15	20
$70,000 to $79,999	92	33	7	26	11
$80,000 to $89,999	45	5	4	1	16
$90,000 to $99,999	40	13	8	5	8
$100,000 or more	125	25	6	19	28
Median income of women with income	$17,898	$22,337	$21,211	$26,177	$23,510
Median income of full-time workers	32,031	32,259	31,223	33,935	35,065
Percent working full-time	37.0%	43.3%	40.5%	45.8%	47.8%
TOTAL ASIAN WOMEN	100.0%	100.0%	100.0%	100.0%	100.0%
Without income	19.4	18.4	18.7	18.1	12.0
With income	80.6	81.6	81.3	81.9	88.0
Under $10,000	26.8	22.3	23.8	21.0	22.5
$10,000 to $19,999	15.7	1.3	13.3	12.6	17.2
$20,000 to $29,999	12.5	14.7	17.4	11.9	12.7
$30,000 to $39,999	7.7	10.0	8.7	11.3	10.3
$40,000 to $49,999	5.7	6.8	4.8	8.4	6.9
$50,000 to $59,999	4.2	6.5	7.1	5.9	3.7
$60,000 to $69,999	2.3	1.9	1.6	2.4	3.5
$70,000 to $79,999	1.8	2.8	1.2	4.1	1.9
$80,000 to $89,999	0.9	0.4	0.7	0.2	2.8
$90,000 to $99,999	0.8	1.1	1.4	0.8	1.4
$100,000 or more	2.4	2.1	1.1	3.0	5.0

Note: Asians include those who identified themselves as Asian alone and those who identified themselves as Asian in combination with one or more other races.
Source: Bureau of the Census, data from the 2003 Current Population Survey Annual Social and Economic Supplement. Internet site http://ferret.bls.census.gov/macro/032003/perinc/toc.htm; calculations by New Strategist

Table 4.20 Income of Women Aged 25 to 39, 2002: Black Women

(number and percent distribution of black women aged 16 or older and aged 25 to 39 by income, 2002; median income by work status, and percent working year-round, full-time; women in thousands as of 2003)

	total	aged 25 to 34 total	25 to 29	30 to 34	aged 35 to 39
TOTAL BLACK WOMEN	14,887	2,848	1,372	1,476	1,510
Without income	2,222	285	138	147	96
With income	12,665	2,563	1,234	1,329	1,414
Under $10,000	4,069	564	296	268	264
$10,000 to $19,999	3,156	680	356	325	355
$20,000 to $29,999	2,196	539	253	284	310
$30,000 to $39,999	1,434	415	201	215	206
$40,000 to $49,999	774	176	71	105	117
$50,000 to $59,999	411	81	22	58	58
$60,000 to $69,999	260	48	18	32	36
$70,000 to $79,999	143	25	7	18	25
$80,000 to $89,999	71	14	7	7	12
$90,000 to $99,999	50	1	–	1	17
$100,000 or more	100	18	2	16	14
Median income of women with income	$16,671	$20,539	$18,893	$21,833	$22,607
Median income of full-time workers	27,703	27,471	26,554	28,748	28,734
Percent working full-time	40.7%	53.5%	50.7%	56.2%	62.1%
TOTAL BLACK WOMEN	100.0%	100.0%	100.0%	100.0%	100.0%
Without income	14.9	1.0	10.1	10.0	6.4
With income	85.1	90.0	89.9	90.0	93.6
Under $10,000	27.3	19.8	21.6	18.2	17.5
$10,000 to $19,999	21.2	23.9	25.9	22.0	23.5
$20,000 to $29,999	14.8	18.9	18.4	19.2	20.5
$30,000 to $39,999	9.6	14.6	14.7	14.6	13.6
$40,000 to $49,999	5.2	6.2	5.2	7.1	7.7
$50,000 to $59,999	2.8	2.8	1.6	3.9	3.8
$60,000 to $69,999	1.7	1.7	1.3	2.2	2.4
$70,000 to $79,999	1.0	0.9	0.5	1.2	1.7
$80,000 to $89,999	0.5	0.5	0.5	0.5	0.8
$90,000 to $99,999	0.3	0.0	–	0.1	1.1
$100,000 or more	0.7	0.6	0.1	1.1	0.9

Note: Blacks include those who identified themselves as black alone and those who identified themselves as black in combination with one or more other races. (–) means number is less than 500 or sample is too small to make a reliable estimate.
Source: Bureau of the Census, data from the 2003 Current Population Survey Annual Social and Economic Supplement, Internet site http://ferret.bls.census.gov/macro/032003/perinc/toc.htm; calculations by New Strategist

Table 4.21 Income of Women Aged 25 to 39, 2002: Hispanic Women

(number and percent distribution of Hispanic women aged 16 or older and aged 25 to 39 by income, 2002; median income by work status, and percent working year-round, full-time; women in thousands as of 2003)

		aged 25 to 34			
	total	total	25 to 29	30 to 34	aged 35 to 39
TOTAL HISPANIC WOMEN	13,607	3,439	1,724	1,715	1,535
Without income	3,589	864	454	410	313
With income	10,018	2,575	1,270	1,305	1,222
Under $10,000	3,822	799	404	396	344
$10,000 to $19,999	2,821	701	349	353	367
$20,000 to $29,999	1,602	534	280	252	232
$30,000 to $39,999	839	283	130	155	138
$40,000 to $49,999	444	130	61	69	70
$50,000 to $59,999	215	68	27	40	32
$60,000 to $69,999	110	24	7	17	10
$70,000 to $79,999	64	15	5	9	13
$80,000 to $89,999	30	3	–	3	8
$90,000 to $99,999	10	5	1	4	2
$100,000 or more	63	12	6	6	7
Median income of women with income	$13,364	$16,443	$15,983	$16,960	$16,633
Median income of full-time workers	22,355	24,082	23,565	25,008	23,530
Percent working full-time	33.7%	40.7%	39.1%	42.4%	44.2%
TOTAL HISPANIC WOMEN	100.0%	100.0%	100.0%	100.0%	100.0%
Without income	26.4	25.1	26.3	23.9	20.4
With income	73.6	74.9	73.7	76.1	79.6
Under $10,000	28.1	23.2	23.4	23.1	22.4
$10,000 to $19,999	20.7	20.4	20.2	20.6	23.9
$20,000 to $29,999	11.8	15.5	16.2	14.7	15.1
$30,000 to $39,999	6.2	8.2	7.5	9.0	9.0
$40,000 to $49,999	3.3	3.8	3.5	4.0	4.6
$50,000 to $59,999	1.6	2.0	1.6	2.3	2.1
$60,000 to $69,999	0.8	0.7	0.4	1.0	0.7
$70,000 to $79,999	0.5	0.4	0.3	0.5	0.8
$80,000 to $89,999	0.2	0.1	–	0.2	0.5
$90,000 to $99,999	0.1	0.1	0.1	0.2	0.1
$100,000 or more	0.5	0.3	0.3	0.3	0.5

Note: Hispanics may be of any race. (–) means number is less than 500 or sample is too small to make a reliable estimate.
Source: Bureau of the Census, data from the 2003 Current Population Survey Annual Social and Economic Supplement, Internet site http://ferret.bls.census.gov/macro/032003/perinc/toc.htm; calculations by New Strategist

Table 4.22   Income of Women Aged 25 to 39, 2002: Non-Hispanic White Women

(number and percent distribution of non-Hispanic white women aged 16 or older and aged 25 to 39 by income, 2002; median income by work status, and percent working year-round, full-time; women in thousands as of 2003)

	total	aged 25 to 34 total	aged 25 to 34 25 to 29	aged 25 to 34 30 to 34	aged 35 to 39
TOTAL NON-HISPANIC WHITE WOMEN	**81,851**	**12,075**	**5,606**	**6,469**	**7,104**
Without income	**7,037**	**960**	**470**	**490**	**491**
With income	**74,814**	**11,115**	**5,136**	**5,979**	**6,613**
Under $10,000	23,423	2,589	1,114	1,475	1,741
$10,000 to $19,999	17,326	2,066	988	1,077	1,175
$20,000 to $29,999	12,052	2,296	1,190	1,107	1,143
$30,000 to $39,999	8,440	1,894	899	995	957
$40,000 to $49,999	5,230	998	455	543	625
$50,000 to $59,999	3,018	516	199	316	347
$60,000 to $69,999	1,760	289	124	165	164
$70,000 to $79,999	1,120	169	71	97	140
$80,000 to $89,999	631	81	29	51	84
$90,000 to $99,999	452	68	24	47	49
$100,000 or more	1,360	149	45	104	184
Median income of women with income	$17,389	$23,396	$23,445	$23,341	$22,454
Median income of full-time workers	32,347	31,725	30,701	32,833	34,222
Percent working full-time	35.6%	50.3%	51.6%	49.1%	48.3%
TOTAL NON-HISPANIC WHITE WOMEN	**100.0%**	**100.0%**	**100.0%**	**100.0%**	**100.0%**
Without income	**8.6**	**8.0**	**8.4**	**7.6**	**6.9**
With income	**91.4**	**92.1**	**91.6**	**92.4**	**93.1**
Under $10,000	28.6	21.4	19.9	22.8	24.5
$10,000 to $19,999	21.2	17.1	17.6	16.6	16.5
$20,000 to $29,999	14.7	19.0	21.2	17.1	16.1
$30,000 to $39,999	10.3	15.7	16.0	15.4	13.5
$40,000 to $49,999	6.4	8.3	8.1	8.4	8.8
$50,000 to $59,999	3.7	4.3	3.5	4.9	4.9
$60,000 to $69,999	2.2	2.4	2.2	2.6	2.3
$70,000 to $79,999	1.4	1.4	1.3	1.5	2.0
$80,000 to $89,999	0.8	0.7	0.5	0.8	1.2
$90,000 to $99,999	0.6	0.6	0.4	0.7	0.7
$100,000 or more	1.7	1.2	0.8	1.6	2.6

Note: Non-Hispanic whites include only those who identified themselves as white alone and non-Hispanic.
Source: Bureau of the Census, data from the 2003 Current Population Survey Annual Social and Economic Supplement, Internet site http://ferret.bls.census.gov/macro/032003/perinc/toc.htm; calculations by New Strategist

Earnings Rise with Education

The highest earners are men with professional degrees.

For many years, a college degree has been well worth its cost. The higher the educational level, the greater the earnings. Among men aged 25 to 34 in 2002 (Gen Xers were aged 26 to 37 in that year), those with professional degrees (such as physicians and lawyers) who worked full-time had median earnings of $72,370. Their counterparts in the 35-to-44 age group had median earnings of $100,000 or more. Among women aged 25 to 34 who work full-time, median earnings were also highest for those with professional degrees, at $56,243 in 2002. Among women in the 35-to-44 age group who work full-time, those with doctorates come out on top with median earnings of $65,528.

Among men aged 25 to 44 who dropped out of high school, the earnings of those who work full-time ranged from $22,744 to $26,451 in 2002. For their counterparts with at least a college degree, earnings ranged from $49,390 to $66,836. The pattern is the same for women. Among women aged 25 to 44 working full-time who dropped out of high school, earnings ranged from $17,085 to $18,483. Among college graduates, earnings were a higher $40,069 to $45,312.

■ The steeply rising cost of a college degree combined with competition from well-educated but lower-paid workers in other countries may reduce the financial return of a college education in the years ahead.

The college bonus is still big

(median earnings of men aged 25 to 34 who work full-time, by education, 2002)

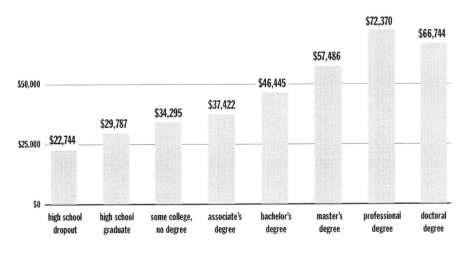

Table 4.23 Earnings of Men by Education, 2002: Aged 25 to 34

(number and percent distribution of men aged 25 to 34 by earnings and education, 2002; men in thousands as of 2003)

	total	less than 9th grade	9th to 12th grade, no degree	high school graduate, including GED	some college, no degree	associate's degree	bachelor's degree or more				
							total	bachelor's degree	master's degree	professional degree	doctoral degree
TOTAL MEN AGED 25 TO 34	**19,564**	**1,651**	**1,831**	**6,028**	**3,745**	**1,507**	**5,466**	**4,136**	**946**	**252**	**131**
Without earnings	**987**	**122**	**274**	**569**	**334**	**64**	**288**	**201**	**64**	**15**	**7**
With earnings	**17,913**	**865**	**1,557**	**5,459**	**3,411**	**1,443**	**5,178**	**3,935**	**882**	**237**	**124**
Under $10,000	1,547	139	236	511	334	84	244	216	17	9	2
$10,000 to $19,999	3,180	387	502	1,193	525	172	402	308	71	17	5
$20,000 to $29,999	3,731	209	436	1,446	757	297	586	489	81	11	5
$30,000 to $39,999	3,289	79	203	1,059	736	299	912	756	103	26	26
$40,000 to $49,999	2,189	30	101	553	486	243	778	611	130	29	8
$50,000 to $59,999	1,363	6	35	315	259	146	601	481	96	11	12
$60,000 to $69,999	896	8	13	140	124	103	509	356	116	27	11
$70,000 to $79,999	567	3	19	69	81	47	349	253	75	8	12
$80,000 to $89,999	314	2	6	48	36	27	195	121	55	11	9
$90,000 to $99,999	186	–	1	24	17	12	132	88	30	9	5
$100,000 or more	651	2	9	101	56	13	470	255	108	78	28
Median earnings of men with earnings	$30,883	$17,323	$20,614	$26,546	$30,681	$35,298	$44,885	$41,772	$51,966	$62,728	$64,232
Median earnings of full-time workers	34,665	19,042	22,744	29,787	34,295	37,422	49,390	46,445	57,486	72,370	66,744
Percent working full-time	71.9%	64.6%	63.1%	70.7%	70.0%	77.0%	77.5%	77.7%	75.8%	79.0%	80.2%

	total	less than 9th grade	9th to 12th grade, no degree	high school graduate, including GED	some college, no degree	associate's degree	bachelor's degree or more				
							total	bachelor's degree	master's degree	professional degree	doctoral degree
TOTAL MEN AGED 25 TO 34	100.0%	100.0%	100.0%	100.0%	100.0%	100.0%	100.0%	100.0%	100.0%	100.0%	100.0%
Without earnings	8.4	12.4	15.0	9.4	8.9	4.2	5.3	4.9	6.8	6.0	5.3
With earnings	91.6	87.6	85.0	90.6	91.1	95.8	94.7	95.1	93.2	94.1	94.7
Under $10,000	7.9	14.1	12.9	8.5	8.9	5.6	4.5	5.2	1.8	3.6	1.5
$10,000 to $19,999	16.3	39.2	27.4	19.8	14.0	11.4	7.4	7.4	7.5	6.7	3.8
$20,000 to $29,999	19.1	21.2	23.8	24.0	20.2	19.7	10.7	11.8	8.6	4.4	3.8
$30,000 to $39,999	16.8	8.0	11.1	17.6	19.7	19.8	16.7	18.3	10.9	10.3	19.8
$40,000 to $49,999	11.2	3.0	5.5	9.2	13.0	16.1	14.2	14.8	13.7	11.5	6.1
$50,000 to $59,999	7.0	0.6	1.9	5.2	6.9	9.7	11.0	11.6	10.1	4.4	9.2
$60,000 to $69,999	4.6	0.8	0.7	2.3	3.3	6.8	9.3	8.6	12.3	10.7	8.4
$70,000 to $79,999	2.9	0.3	1.0	1.1	2.2	3.1	6.4	6.1	7.9	3.2	9.2
$80,000 to $89,999	1.6	0.2	0.3	0.8	1.0	1.8	3.6	2.9	5.8	4.4	6.9
$90,000 to $99,999	1.0	–	0.1	0.4	0.5	0.8	2.4	2.1	3.2	3.6	3.8
$100,000 or more	3.3	0.2	0.5	1.7	1.5	0.9	8.6	6.2	11.4	31.0	21.4

Note: (–) means number is less than 500 or sample is too small to make a reliable estimate.
Source: Bureau of the Census, data from the 2003 Current Population Survey Annual Social and Economic Supplement, Internet site http://ferret.bls.census.gov/macro/032003/perinc/new03_000.htm; calculations by New Strategist

Table 4.24 Earnings of Men by Education, 2002: Aged 35 to 44

(number and percent distribution of men aged 35 to 44 by earnings and education, 2002; men in thousands as of 2003)

	total	less than 9th grade	9th to 12th grade, no degree	high school graduate, including GED	some college, no degree	associate's degree	bachelor's degree or more				
							total	bachelor's degree	master's degree	professional degree	doctoral degree
TOTAL MEN AGED 35 TO 44	21,733	1,013	1,906	7,066	3,665	1,768	6,314	4,228	1,385	402	299
Without earnings	1,795	163	333	710	270	78	240	167	60	9	4
With earnings	19,938	850	1,573	6,356	3,395	1,690	6,074	4,061	1,325	393	295
Under $10,000	1,268	117	216	504	199	89	142	105	27	6	5
$10,000 to $19,999	2,329	325	387	919	282	123	292	220	62	2	9
$20,000 to $29,999	3,235	232	428	1,421	524	248	380	300	64	9	7
$30,000 to $39,999	3,340	100	282	1,351	647	320	640	488	113	20	20
$40,000 to $49,999	2,436	31	121	808	563	306	607	433	123	22	30
$50,000 to $59,999	1,984	21	69	575	399	215	707	514	148	20	26
$60,000 to $69,999	1,314	12	34	318	260	137	553	378	142	18	16
$70,000 to $79,999	1,145	2	17	193	167	86	678	432	174	31	39
$80,000 to $89,999	612	–	4	86	109	50	363	245	78	14	25
$90,000 to $99,999	442	2	–	48	59	34	299	181	82	19	18
$100,000 or more	1,833	8	17	130	185	83	1,410	767	311	229	103
Median earnings of men with earnings	$38,947	$19,568	$23,025	$31,477	$40,477	$41,296	$62,353	$58,764	$67,443	$100,000	$77,364
Median earnings of full-time workers	42,211	21,335	26,451	34,204	42,401	44,277	66,836	61,324	70,809	100,000	79,280
Percent working full-time	76.6%	62.8%	60.5%	73.5%	76.2%	82.5%	85.7%	85.6%	83.8%	92.0%	86.6%

	total	less than 9th grade	9th to 12th grade, no degree	high school graduate, including GED	some college, no degree	associate's degree	bachelor's degree or more				
							total	bachelor's degree	master's degree	professional degree	doctoral degree
TOTAL MEN AGED 35 TO 44	**100.0%**	**100.0%**	**100.0%**	**100.0%**	**100.0%**	**100.0%**	**100.0%**	**100.0%**	**100.0%**	**100.0%**	**100.0%**
Without earnings	**8.3**	**16.1**	**17.5**	**10.1**	**7.4**	**4.4**	**3.8**	**3.9**	**4.3**	**2.2**	**1.3**
With earnings	**91.7**	**83.9**	**82.5**	**90.0**	**92.6**	**95.6**	**96.2**	**96.1**	**95.7**	**97.8**	**98.7**
Under $10,000	5.8	11.5	11.3	7.1	5.4	5.0	2.2	2.5	1.9	1.5	1.7
$10,000 to $19,999	10.7	32.1	20.3	13.3	7.7	7.0	4.6	5.2	4.5	0.5	3.0
$20,000 to $29,999	14.9	22.9	22.5	20.1	14.3	14.0	6.0	7.1	4.6	2.2	2.3
$30,000 to $39,999	15.4	9.9	14.8	19.1	17.7	18.1	10.1	11.5	8.2	5.0	6.7
$40,000 to $49,999	11.2	3.1	6.3	11.4	15.4	17.3	9.6	10.2	8.9	5.5	10.0
$50,000 to $59,999	9.1	2.1	3.6	8.1	10.9	12.2	11.2	12.2	10.7	5.0	8.7
$60,000 to $69,999	6.1	1.2	1.8	4.5	7.1	7.7	8.8	8.9	10.3	4.5	5.4
$70,000 to $79,999	5.3	0.2	0.9	2.7	4.6	4.9	10.7	10.2	12.6	7.7	13.0
$80,000 to $89,999	2.8	–	0.2	1.2	3.0	2.8	5.7	5.8	5.6	3.5	8.4
$90,000 to $99,999	2.0	0.2	–	0.7	1.6	1.9	4.7	4.3	5.9	4.7	6.0
$100,000 or more	8.4	0.8	0.9	1.8	5.1	4.7	22.3	18.1	22.5	57.0	34.4

Note: (–) means number is less than 500 or sample is too small to make a reliable estimate.
Source: Bureau of the Census, data from the 2003 Current Population Survey Annual Social and Economic Supplement, Internet site http://ferret.bls.census.gov/macro/ 032003/perinc/new03_000.htm; calculations by New Strategist

Table 4.25 Earnings of Women by Education, 2002: Aged 25 to 34

(number and percent distribution of women aged 25 to 34 by earnings and education, 2002; women in thousands as of 2003)

	total	less than 9th grade	9th to 12th grade, no degree	high school graduate, including GED	some college, no degree	associate's degree	bachelor's degree or more				
							total	bachelor's degree	master's degree	professional degree	doctoral degree
TOTAL WOMEN AGED 25 TO 34	19,679	751	1,503	5,364	3,864	1,870	6,325	4,713	1,270	238	105
Without earnings	4,496	409	640	1,409	747	287	1,001	763	198	28	12
With earnings	15,183	342	863	3,955	3,117	1,583	5,324	3,950	1,072	210	93
Under $10,000	2,871	166	333	944	660	252	516	445	60	6	5
$10,000 to $19,999	3,415	121	326	1,224	755	369	618	449	144	16	9
$20,000 to $29,999	3,398	42	142	1,046	906	434	828	691	117	17	2
$30,000 to $39,999	2,567	10	40	485	495	277	1,261	946	268	23	24
$40,000 to $49,999	1,282	4	14	160	163	129	811	576	183	35	18
$50,000 to $59,999	707	–	1	41	83	60	524	366	118	32	7
$60,000 to $69,999	369	–	1	13	31	31	291	191	86	11	5
$70,000 to $79,999	227	–	2	18	10	21	176	119	32	21	5
$80,000 to $89,999	83	–	–	4	3	1	76	54	11	9	–
$90,000 to $99,999	82	–	–	5	1	5	72	33	16	18	5
$100,000 or more	177	–	2	14	9	3	149	81	37	19	11
Median earnings of women with earnings	$23,299	$10,286	$12,090	$18,243	$21,224	$23,442	$35,350	$32,793	$38,102	$51,099	$42,269
Median earnings of full-time workers	29,655	15,250	17,085	23,399	26,097	28,155	40,069	38,224	41,344	56,243	–
Percent working full-time	48.4%	20.2%	30.1%	43.8%	49.5%	54.2%	57.5%	57.4%	55.9%	66.8%	64.8%

TOTAL WOMEN AGED 25 TO 34	total	less than 9th grade	9th to 12th grade, no degree	high school graduate, including GED	some college, no degree	associate's degree	bachelor's degree or more				
							total	bachelor's degree	master's degree	professional degree	doctoral degree
	100.0%	100.0%	100.0%	100.0%	100.0%	100.0%	100.0%	100.0%	100.0%	100.0%	100.0%
Without earnings	**22.8**	**54.5**	**42.6**	**26.3**	**19.3**	**15.3**	**15.8**	**16.2**	**15.6**	**11.8**	**11.4**
With earnings	**77.2**	**45.5**	**57.4**	**73.7**	**80.7**	**84.7**	**84.2**	**83.8**	**84.4**	**88.2**	**88.6**
Under $10,000	14.6	22.1	22.2	17.6	17.1	13.5	8.2	9.4	4.7	2.5	4.8
$10,000 to $19,999	17.4	16.1	21.7	22.8	19.5	19.7	9.8	9.5	11.3	6.7	8.6
$20,000 to $29,999	17.3	5.6	9.4	19.5	23.4	23.2	13.1	14.7	9.2	7.1	1.9
$30,000 to $39,999	13.0	1.3	2.7	9.0	12.8	14.8	19.9	20.1	21.1	9.7	22.9
$40,000 to $49,999	6.5	0.5	0.9	3.0	4.2	6.9	12.8	12.2	14.4	14.7	17.1
$50,000 to $59,999	3.6	–	0.1	0.8	2.1	3.2	8.3	7.8	9.3	13.4	6.7
$60,000 to $69,999	1.9	–	0.1	0.2	0.8	1.7	4.6	4.1	6.8	4.6	4.8
$70,000 to $79,999	1.2	–	0.1	0.3	0.3	1.1	2.8	2.5	2.5	8.8	4.8
$80,000 to $89,999	0.4	–	–	0.1	0.1	0.1	1.2	1.1	0.9	3.8	–
$90,000 to $99,999	0.4	–	–	0.1	0.0	0.3	1.1	0.7	1.3	7.6	4.8
$100,000 or more	0.9	–	0.1	0.3	0.2	0.2	2.4	1.7	2.9	8.0	10.5

Note: (–) means number is less than 500 or sample is too small to make a reliable estimate.
Source: Bureau of the Census, data from the 2003 Current Population Survey Annual Social and Economic Supplement, Internet site http://ferret.bls.census.gov/macro/032003/perinc/new03_000.htm; calculations by New Strategist

Table 4.26 Earnings of Women by Education, 2002: Aged 35 to 44

(number and percent distribution of women aged 35 to 44 by earnings and education, 2002; women in thousands as of 2003)

	total	less than 9th grade	9th to 12th grade, no degree	high school graduate, including GED	some college, no degree	associate's degree	bachelor's degree or more				
							total	bachelor's degree	master's degree	professional degree	doctoral degree
TOTAL WOMEN AGED 35 TO 44	22,341	814	1,548	6,828	3,996	2,496	6,658	4,687	1,498	284	189
Without earnings	4,838	387	547	1,531	793	375	1,204	934	213	34	23
With earnings	17,502	427	1,001	5,297	3,203	2,121	5,454	3,753	1,285	250	166
Under $10,000	2,863	132	292	1,015	527	289	609	484	108	8	8
$10,000 to $19,999	3,773	213	406	1,492	701	382	579	451	103	14	12
$20,000 to $29,999	3,766	70	218	1,456	834	498	691	581	86	13	11
$30,000 to $39,999	2,726	11	56	713	549	439	957	666	239	37	14
$40,000 to $49,999	1,705	1	15	332	275	264	817	514	253	36	12
$50,000 to $59,999	969	1	5	137	147	135	544	325	169	24	26
$60,000 to $69,999	533	–	3	64	62	52	351	231	93	11	17
$70,000 to $79,999	396	–	–	48	49	34	264	164	75	10	17
$80,000 to $89,999	241	–	4	10	27	12	187	110	46	20	10
$90,000 to $99,999	142	–	–	8	3	4	127	72	36	11	9
$100,000 or more	389	–	–	22	28	12	327	155	77	64	32
Median earnings of women with earnings	$25,110	$13,663	$14,733	$20,642	$23,942	$27,022	$38,401	$35,368	$42,109	$55,599	$60,041
Median earnings of full-time workers	31,039	16,403	18,483	24,568	29,418	32,223	45,312	41,737	50,125	61,296	65,528
Percent working full-time	51.6%	30.7%	37.5%	52.2%	53.2%	56.4%	53.9%	52.6%	54.5%	65.5%	64.6%

	total	less than 9th grade	9th to 12th grade, no degree	high school graduate, including GED	some college, no degree	associate's degree	bachelor's degree or more				
							total	bachelor's degree	master's degree	professional degree	doctoral degree
TOTAL WOMEN AGED 35 TO 44	100.0%	100.0%	100.0%	100.0%	100.0%	100.0%	100.0%	100.0%	100.0%	100.0%	100.0%
Without earnings	21.7	47.5	35.3	22.4	19.8	15.0	18.1	19.9	14.2	12.0	12.2
With earnings	78.3	52.5	64.7	77.6	80.2	85.0	81.9	80.1	85.8	88.0	87.8
Under $10,000	12.8	16.2	18.9	14.9	13.2	11.6	9.1	10.3	7.2	2.8	4.2
$10,000 to $19,999	16.9	26.2	26.2	21.9	17.5	15.3	8.7	9.6	6.9	4.9	6.3
$20,000 to $29,999	16.9	8.6	14.1	21.3	20.9	20.0	10.4	12.4	5.7	4.6	5.8
$30,000 to $39,999	12.2	1.4	3.6	10.4	13.7	17.6	14.4	14.2	16.0	13.0	7.4
$40,000 to $49,999	7.6	0.1	1.0	4.9	6.9	10.6	12.3	11.0	16.9	12.7	6.3
$50,000 to $59,999	4.3	0.1	0.3	2.0	3.7	5.4	8.2	6.9	11.3	8.5	13.8
$60,000 to $69,999	2.4	–	0.2	0.9	1.6	2.1	5.3	4.9	6.2	3.9	9.0
$70,000 to $79,999	1.8	–	–	0.7	1.2	1.4	4.0	3.5	5.0	3.5	9.0
$80,000 to $89,999	1.1	–	0.3	0.1	0.7	0.5	2.8	2.3	3.1	7.0	5.3
$90,000 to $99,999	0.6	–	–	0.1	0.1	0.2	1.9	1.5	2.4	3.9	4.8
$100,000 or more	1.7	–	–	0.3	0.7	0.5	4.9	3.3	5.1	22.5	16.9

Note: (–) means number is less than 500 or sample is too small to make a reliable estimate.
Source: Bureau of the Census, data from the 2003 Current Population Survey Annual Social and Economic Supplement, Internet site http://ferret.bls.census.gov/macro/032003/perinc/new03_000.htm; calculations by New Strategist

Wage and Salary Income Is Most Important for Gen Xers

Interest income is the second most common type of income.

Earnings from wages and salaries are the most common source of income for adults aged 25 to 44. The percentage of those who received wage or salary income in 2002 ranged from 88 to 92 percent among men and from 81 to 85 percent among women in the age group.

Interest is the second most common source of income for adults aged 25 to 44. About half of men and women in the age group receive interest income, but the amount is not enough to boost their lifestyle by much. The median amount of interest income received by 25-to-44-year-olds stood at about $1,300 in 2002.

Nearly one in ten women aged 25 to 44 receives child support income, the median amount ranging from $3,200 to $3,900 in 2002. Nine percent of men aged 35 to 44 receive income from self-employment. Those with self-employment income made a median of $21,468 from it in 2002.

■ The percentage of people receiving wage or salary income falls slightly with age as self-employment becomes a more important source of income.

Most men and women aged 25 to 44 have wage or salary income

(percent of people aged 25 to 44 with wage or salary income, by sex, 2002)

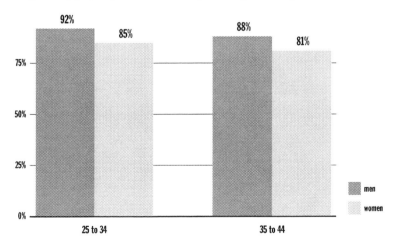

Table 4.27 Sources of Income for Men Aged 25 to 34, 2002

(number and percent distribution of men aged 25 to 34 with income and median income for those with income, by selected sources of income, 2002; men in thousands as of 2003)

	number	percent with income	median income
Total men aged 25 to 34 with income	**18,695**	**100.0%**	**$30,677**
Earnings	17,913	95.8	30,883
Wages and salary	17,143	91.7	30,879
Nonfarm self-employment	1,171	6.3	15,927
Farm self-employment	225	1.2	2,397
Social Security	228	1.2	7,354
SSI (Supplemental Security Income)	245	1.3	6,019
Public assistance	80	0.4	1,926
Veterans' benefits	100	0.5	3,464
Survivor benefits	20	0.1	–
Disability benefits	63	0.3	–
Unemployment compensation	1,247	6.7	3,081
Workers' compensation	226	1.2	2,256
Property income	7,626	40.8	1,338
Interest	7,243	38.7	1,292
Dividends	1,961	10.5	1,354
Rents, royalties, estates or trusts	439	2.3	1,974
Retirement income	120	0.6	5,614
Pension income	58	0.3	–
Alimony	0	0.0	–
Child support	52	0.3	–
Educational assistance	891	4.8	3,130
Financial assistance from other household	215	1.2	3,999
Other income	42	0.2	–

Note: (–) means sample is too small to make a reliable estimate.
Source: Bureau of the Census, data from the 2003 Current Population Survey Annual Social and Economic Supplement, Internet site http://ferret.bls.census.gov/macro/032003/perinc/new08_000.htm; calculations by New Strategist

Table 4.28 Sources of Income for Men Aged 35 to 44, 2002

(number and percent distribution of men aged 35 to 44 with income and median income for those with income, by selected sources of income, 2002; men in thousands as of 2003)

	number	percent with income	median income
Total men aged 35 to 44 with income	**20,979**	**100.0%**	**$37,892**
Earnings	19,938	95.0	38,947
Wages and salary	18,511	88.2	39,649
Nonfarm self-employment	1,976	9.4	21,468
Farm self-employment	306	1.5	2,268
Social Security	568	2.7	7,989
SSI (Supplemental Security Income)	388	1.8	5,611
Public assistance	90	0.4	1,983
Veterans' benefits	202	1.0	5,461
Survivor benefits	53	0.3	–
Disability benefits	114	0.5	8,148
Unemployment compensation	1,423	6.8	3,732
Workers' compensation	295	1.4	4,128
Property income	10,909	52.0	1,421
Interest	10,336	49.3	1,331
Dividends	3,579	17.1	1,385
Rents, royalties, estates or trusts	1,127	5.4	1,950
Retirement income	320	1.5	10,478
Pension income	206	1.0	12,190
Alimony	5	0.0	–
Child support	134	0.6	2,354
Educational assistance	349	1.7	2,415
Financial assistance from other household	111	0.5	3,629
Other income	92	0.4	1,931

Note: (–) means sample is too small to make a reliable estimate.
Source: Bureau of the Census, data from the 2003 Current Population Survey Annual Social and Economic Supplement, Internet site http://ferret.bls.census.gov/macro/032003/perinc/new08_000.htm; calculations by New Strategist

Table 4.29 Sources of Income for Women Aged 25 to 34, 2002

(number and percent distribution of women aged 25 to 34 with income and median income for those with income, by selected sources of income, 2002; women in thousands as of 2003)

	number	percent with income	median income
Total women aged 25 to 34 with income	**17,336**	**100.0%**	**$21,649**
Earnings	15,183	87.6	23,299
Wages and salary	14,698	84.8	23,510
Nonfarm self-employment	799	4.6	5,438
Farm self-employment	140	0.8	1,782
Social Security	391	2.3	6,310
SSI (Supplemental Security Income)	366	2.1	5,534
Public assistance	527	3.0	2,293
Veterans' benefits	25	0.1	–
Survivor benefits	39	0.2	–
Disability benefits	87	0.5	3,755
Unemployment compensation	761	4.4	2,990
Workers' compensation	117	0.7	2,229
Property income	8,257	47.6	1,322
Interest	7,927	45.7	1,285
Dividends	1,876	10.8	1,339
Rents, royalties, estates or trusts	379	2.2	1,857
Retirement income	151	0.9	3,336
Pension income	42	0.2	–
Alimony	35	0.2	–
Child support	1,712	9.9	3,232
Educational assistance	1,105	6.4	3,001
Financial assistance from other household	332	1.9	2,176
Other income	90	0.5	1,668

Note: (–) means sample is too small to make a reliable estimate.
Source: Bureau of the Census, data from the 2003 Current Population Survey Annual Social and Economic Supplement, Internet site http://ferret.bls.census.gov/macro/032003/perinc/new08_000.htm; calculations by New Strategist

Table 4.30 Sources of Income for Women Aged 35 to 44, 2002

(number and percent distribution of women aged 35 to 44 with income and median income for those with income, by selected sources of income, 2002; women in thousands as of 2003)

	number	percent with income	median income
Total women aged 35 to 44 with income	**20,487**	**100.0%**	**$22,322**
Earnings	17,502	85.4	25,110
Wages and salary	16,587	81.0	25,484
Nonfarm self-employment	1,311	6.4	9,963
Farm self-employment	172	0.8	1,561
Social Security	681	3.3	7,052
SSI (Supplemental Security Income)	515	2.5	5,837
Public assistance	399	1.9	2,950
Veterans' benefits	63	0.3	–
Survivor benefits	98	0.5	10,276
Disability benefits	156	0.8	5,983
Unemployment compensation	953	4.7	3,095
Workers' compensation	245	1.2	2,861
Property income	11,363	55.5	1,396
Interest	10,849	53.0	1,323
Dividends	3,270	16.0	1,375
Rents, royalties, estates or trusts	1,021	5.0	1,764
Retirement income	307	1.5	5,647
Pension income	112	0.5	6,146
Alimony	108	0.5	4,839
Child support	2,007	9.8	3,936
Educational assistance	509	2.5	2,142
Financial assistance from other household	182	0.9	3,770
Other income	152	0.7	1,950

Note: (–) means sample is too small to make a reliable estimate.
Source: Bureau of the Census, data from the 2003 Current Population Survey Annual Social and Economic Supplement, Internet site http://ferret.bls.census.gov/macro/032003/perinc/new08_000.htm; calculations by New Strategist

Poverty Rate Is below Average for Gen Xers

Poverty falls below average in the 25-to-34 age group.

Generation Xers (aged 26 to 37 in 2002) are slightly less likely to be poor than is the average American. Overall, 12 percent of Americans lived in poverty in 2002. Among people aged 26 to 37, however, a smaller 11 percent are poor. People under age 25 are more likely than average to be poor, with a poverty rate of 17 percent. But in the 25-to-34 age group, the poverty rate falls to 11.9 percent. Only 9 percent of people aged 35 to 44 are poor.

Black and Hispanic Gen Xers are about twice as likely as Asian and non-Hispanic white Gen Xers to be poor. Nineteen percent of blacks and Hispanics aged 26 to 37 live below the poverty level versus 8 to 9 percent of Asians and non-Hispanic whites. Blacks and Hispanics, together, account for the majority of poor Gen Xers, while non-Hispanic whites account for the 43 percent minority.

■ Blacks are more likely to be poor than Asians and non-Hispanic whites because they are less likely to live in married-couple families, the most affluent household type.

The young are most likely to be poor

(percent of people with incomes below poverty level, by age, 2002)

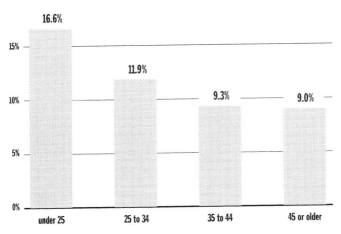

Table 4.31 People below Poverty Level by Age, Race and Hispanic Origin, 2002

(number, percent, and percent distribution of people below poverty level, by age, race and Hispanic origin, 2002; people in thousands as of 2003)

	total	Asian	black	Hispanic	non-Hispanic white
NUMBER IN POVERTY					
TOTAL PEOPLE	34,570	1,243	8,884	8,555	15,567
Generation X					
(aged 26 to 37)	5,447	234	1,162	1,637	2,357
Under age 25	16,669	564	4,936	4,796	6,255
Aged 25 to 34	4,674	207	1,018	1,410	1,980
Aged 35 to 44	4,087	212	968	1,016	1,854
Aged 45 or older	9,140	259	1,963	1,332	5,479
PERCENT IN POVERTY					
TOTAL PEOPLE	12.1%	10.0%	23.9%	21.8%	8.0%
Generation X					
(aged 26 to 37)	11.4	8.5	18.6	18.9	7.9
Under age 25	16.6	12.6	30.5	26.6	10.3
Aged 25 to 34	11.9	9.0	19.7	19.0	8.2
Aged 35 to 44	9.3	10.2	17.4	17.2	6.1
Aged 45 or older	9.0	7.2	19.1	17.0	6.9
PERCENT DISTRIBUTION OF POOR BY AGE					
TOTAL PEOPLE	100.0%	100.0%	100.0%	100.0%	100.0%
Generation X					
(aged 26 to 37)	15.8	18.8	13.1	19.1	15.1
Under age 25	48.2	45.4	55.6	56.1	40.2
Aged 25 to 34	13.5	16.7	11.5	16.5	12.7
Aged 35 to 44	11.8	17.1	10.9	11.9	11.9
Aged 45 or older	26.4	20.8	22.1	15.6	35.2
PERCENT DISTRIBUTION OF POOR BY RACE AND HISPANIC ORIGIN					
TOTAL PEOPLE	100.0%	3.6%	25.7%	24.7%	45.0%
Generation X					
(aged 26 to 37)	100.0	4.3	21.3	30.1	43.3
Under age 25	100.0	3.4	29.6	28.8	37.5
Aged 25 to 34	100.0	4.4	21.8	30.2	42.4
Aged 35 to 44	100.0	5.2	23.7	24.9	45.4
Aged 45 or older	100.0	2.8	21.5	14.6	59.9

Note: Numbers will not add to total because each racial category includes those who identified themselves as being of the race alone and those who identified themselves as being of the race in combination with one or more other races, because Hispanics may be of any race, and because not all races are shown. Non-Hispanic whites include only those who identified themselves as white alone and non-Hispanic.
Source: Bureau of the Census, data from the 2003 Current Population Survey Annual Social and Economic Supplement, Internet sites http://ferret.bls.census.gov/macro/032003/pov/new34_100.htm and http://ferret.bls.census.gov/macro/032003/pov/new01_000.htm; calculations by New Strategist

Labor Force

■ Generation Xers are at the age when men and women embark on a career. But their labor force participation rates are down because of the loss of millions of jobs over the past few years.

■ Among men aged 25 to 39, from 91 to 93 percent are in the labor force. Among women, the figure stands at 74 percent throughout the age group.

■ Only 4.7 percent of Asian men aged 25 to 39 were unemployed in 2003. For their black counterparts, unemployment stood at more than 10 percent.

■ The 68 percent majority of couples aged 25 to 39 are dual earners, while the husband is the only one in the labor force in another 28 percent.

■ Only 7 percent of all workers are self-employed. The figure is an even smaller 5 percent among those aged 25 to 34. In contrast, fully 19 percent of workers aged 65 or older are self-employed.

■ Between 2003 and 2012, Generation X will fill the 35-to-44 age group (Gen Xers will be aged 36 to 47 in 2012). Consequently, the number of workers in the age group will decline by 6 percent.

Fewer Young Adults Are at Work

Labor force participation rates are down for men and women.

Generation Xers are at the age when men and women embark on their career. But their labor force participation rates are down, thanks to the loss of millions of jobs over the past few years.

Among men aged 25 to 39, the labor force participation rate has fallen by 2 to 3 percentage points since 1990. Among women in the age group, the labor force participation rate was higher in 2003 than in 1990 for most, but it fell sharply between 2000 and 2003. The labor force participation rate of women aged 25 to 34 fell from 76 percent in 2000 to 74 percent in 2003.

While some women (and men) may be opting to stay home with young children for a few years, it's more likely that the decline in labor force participation is a consequence of job losses. If jobs become plentiful again, the labor force participation rate in the age group will rise.

■ Although labor force participation rates are down for Generation Xers, the great majority of both men and women are still in the labor force.

A shrinking share of 25-to-34-year-olds are in the labor force

(percent of people aged 25 to 34 in the labor force, by sex, 2000 and 2003)

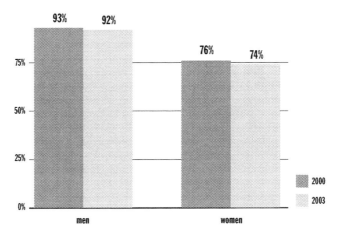

Table 5.1 Labor Force Participation of People Aged 25 to 39 by Sex, 1990 to 2003

(civilian labor force participation rate of people aged 16 or older and aged 25 to 39, by sex, 1990 to 2003; percentage point change, 2000–2003 and 1990–2003)

				percentage point change	
	2003	2000	1990	2000–03	1990–03
Men aged 16 or older	**73.5%**	**74.8%**	**76.4%**	**–1.3**	**–2.9**
Aged 25 to 34	91.8	93.4	94.1	–1.6	–2.3
Aged 25 to 29	90.6	92.5	93.7	–1.9	–3.1
Aged 30 to 34	92.9	94.2	94.5	–1.3	–1.6
Aged 35 to 39	92.8	93.2	94.8	–0.4	–2.0
Women aged 16 or older	**59.5**	**59.9**	**57.5**	**–0.4**	**2.0**
Aged 25 to 34	74.1	76.1	73.5	–2.0	0.6
Aged 25 to 29	74.4	76.7	73.6	–2.3	0.8
Aged 30 to 34	73.8	75.5	73.3	–1.7	0.5
Aged 35 to 39	74.5	75.7	75.5	–1.2	–1.0

Source: Bureau of Labor Statistics, Public Query Data Tool, Internet site http://www.bls.gov/data; calculations by New Strategist

More than 80 Percent of Generation Xers Are in the Labor Force

Among men, labor force participation is over 90 percent.

Eighty-three percent of people aged 25 to 39 were in the labor force in 2003 (Generation Xers were aged 27 to 38 in that year). The labor force participation rate varies little within the age group. Among men aged 25 to 39, from 91 to 93 percent are in the labor force. Among women, the figure stands at 74 percent throughout the age group.

Generation Xers are slightly less likely to be unemployed than the average worker. While 6.0 percent of all workers were unemployed in 2003, among those aged 25 to 39 the figure was a slightly smaller 5.7 percent. The 25-to-39 age group is far less likely to be unemployed than those under age 25, who had an unemployment rate of 12.4 percent in 2003. Generation Xers are more likely to be hunting for a job than older workers, however. Among workers aged 40 to 64, a smaller 4.3 percent were unemployed in 2003.

■ The labor force participation rates of men and women in their twenties and thirties is likely to rise when jobs become more plentiful.

Most men and women of Generation X are in the labor force

(percent of people aged 25 to 39 in the labor force, by sex, 2003)

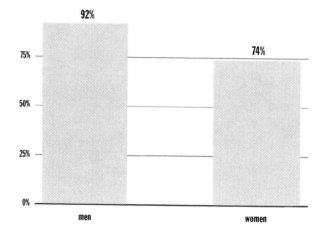

Table 5.2 Employment Status by Sex and Age, 2003

(number and percent of people aged 16 or older in the civilian labor force by sex, age, and employment status, 2003; numbers in thousands)

	civilian noninstitutional population	civilian labor force total	percent of population	employed	unemployed number	percent of labor force
Total aged 16 or older	**221,168**	**146,510**	**66.2%**	**137,736**	**8,774**	**6.0%**
Under age 25	35,897	22,098	61.6	19,352	2,746	12.4
Aged 25 to 39	60,071	49,914	83.1	47,046	2,867	5.7
Aged 25 to 29	18,625	15,357	82.5	14,339	1,018	6.6
Aged 30 to 34	20,396	16,986	83.3	16,044	941	5.5
Aged 35 to 39	21,050	17,571	83.5	16,663	908	5.2
Aged 40 to 64	90,946	69,707	76.6	66,730	2,978	4.3
Aged 65 or older	34,253	4,792	14.0	4,608	183	3.8
Men aged 16 or older	**106,435**	**78,238**	**73.5**	**73,332**	**4,906**	**6.3**
Under age 25	18,041	11,520	63.9	9,982	1,538	13.4
Aged 25 to 39	29,687	27,361	92.2	25,785	1,577	5.8
Aged 25 to 29	9,262	8,395	90.6	7,817	578	6.9
Aged 30 to 34	10,085	9,371	92.9	8,853	519	5.5
Aged 35 to 39	10,340	9,595	92.8	9,115	480	5.0
Aged 40 to 64	44,212	36,662	82.9	34,980	1,684	4.6
Aged 65 or older	14,496	2,692	18.6	2,585	107	4.0
Women aged 16 or older	**114,733**	**68,272**	**59.5**	**64,404**	**3,868**	**5.7**
Under age 25	17,858	10,577	59.2	9,369	1,208	11.4
Aged 25 to 39	30,385	22,552	74.2	21,260	1,291	5.7
Aged 25 to 29	9,363	6,962	74.4	6,522	440	6.3
Aged 30 to 34	10,312	7,614	73.8	7,191	423	5.6
Aged 35 to 39	10,710	7,976	74.5	7,547	428	5.4
Aged 40 to 64	46,734	33,045	70.7	31,751	1,293	3.9
Aged 65 or older	19,758	2,099	10.6	2,023	76	3.6

Source: Bureau of Labor Statistics, 2003 Current Population Survey, Internet site http://www.bls.gov/cps/home.htm; calculations by New Strategist

Generation X Asian Men Are Least Likely to Be Unemployed

One in ten black men aged 25 to 39 is unemployed.

Most men of Generation X are in the labor force, but there are differences in labor force participation and unemployment by race and Hispanic origin. Among Hispanic and white men aged 25 to 39, fully 93 to 94 percent are in the labor force. Among Asian men in the age group, 88 percent are in the labor force, and among black men the figure is 86 percent.

Asian men aged 25 to 39 are less likely to be unemployed than others. In 2003, only 4.7 percent were unemployed, lower than the 6.2 percent average for all Asian men and less than the 5.1 percent rate among white men in the age group. A larger 7.3 percent of Hispanic men aged 25 to 39 were unemployed. Among blacks in the age group, more than 10 percent were unemployed in 2003.

■ High unemployment among black men contributes to their lower labor force participation rate. Discouraged by the lack of prospects for work in their communities, some black men have given up looking for jobs.

Unemployment rates differ by race and Hispanic origin

(percent of men aged 25 to 39 who are unemployed, by race and Hispanic origin, 2003)

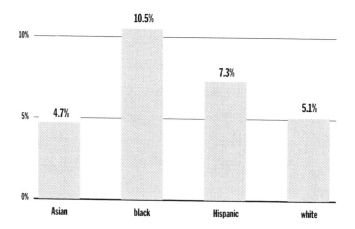

Table 5.3 Employment Status of Men by Race, Hispanic Origin, and Age, 2003

(number and percent of men aged 16 or older in the civilian labor force by race, Hispanic origin, age, and employment status, 2003; numbers in thousands)

	civilian noninstitutional population	civilian labor force total	percent of population	employed	unemployed number	percent of labor force
ASIAN MEN						
Total aged 16 or older	**4,338**	**3,277**	**75.5%**	**3,073**	**204**	**6.2%**
Under age 25	723	373	51.6	325	48	12.9
Aged 25 to 39	1,531	1,344	87.8	1,281	63	4.7
Aged 25 to 29	491	409	83.3	386	23	5.6
Aged 30 to 34	548	484	88.3	463	21	4.4
Aged 35 to 39	492	451	91.7	432	19	4.2
Aged 40 to 64	1,676	1,478	88.2	1,387	90	6.1
Aged 65 or older	409	83	20.3	79	4	4.5
BLACK MEN						
Total aged 16 or older	**11,454**	**7,711**	**67.3**	**6,820**	**891**	**11.6**
Under age 25	2,467	1,283	52.0	960	324	25.3
Aged 25 to 39	3,375	2,899	85.9	2,596	303	10.5
Aged 25 to 29	1,075	878	81.7	755	123	14.0
Aged 30 to 34	1,135	994	87.6	905	89	9.0
Aged 35 to 39	1,165	1,027	88.2	936	91	8.8
Aged 40 to 64	4,519	3,343	74.0	3,089	255	7.6
Aged 65 or older	1,093	186	17.0	176	10	5.6
HISPANIC MEN						
Total aged 16 or older	**14,098**	**11,288**	**80.1**	**10,479**	**809**	**7.2**
Under age 25	3,206	2,174	67.8	1,900	273	14.4
Aged 25 to 39	5,721	5,351	93.5	5,029	392	7.3
Aged 25 to 29	2,073	1,927	93.0	1,807	120	6.2
Aged 30 to 34	1,961	1,849	94.3	1,730	119	6.4
Aged 35 to 39	1,687	1,575	93.4	1,492	153	5.3
Aged 40 to 64	4,310	3,612	83.8	3,405	208	6.1
Aged 65 or older	862	150	17.4	144	5	3.6
WHITE MEN						
Total aged 16 or older	**88,249**	**65,509**	**74.2**	**61,866**	**3,643**	**5.6**
Under age 25	14,246	9,515	66.8	8,408	1,107	13.2
Aged 25 to 39	24,001	22,422	93.4	21,270	1,153	5.1
Aged 25 to 29	7,442	6,883	92.5	6,470	413	6.0
Aged 30 to 34	8,127	7,646	94.1	7,261	385	5.0
Aged 35 to 39	8,432	7,893	93.6	7,539	355	4.5
Aged 40 to 64	37,185	31,186	83.9	29,894	1,292	4.3
Aged 65 or older	12,818	2,386	18.6	2,295	91	3.8

Note: Race is shown only for those selecting that race group only. People who selected more than one race are not included. Hispanics may be of any race.
Source: Bureau of Labor Statistics, 2003 Current Population Survey, Internet site http://www.bls.gov/cps/home.htm; calculations by New Strategist

Labor Force Participation of Gen X Women Varies by Race and Ethnicity

Asian and Hispanic women are least likely to be in the labor force.

Black women aged 25 to 39 are more likely than Asian, Hispanic, or white women to be in the labor force. Eighty percent of black women in the age group were working or looking for work in 2003 compared with 74 percent of white, 68 percent of Asian, and just 64 percent of Hispanic women in the age group.

Unemployment is greater among black and Hispanic women than among Asian or white women. Nearly 10 percent of black women aged 25 to 39 were unemployed in 2003. Among their Hispanic counterparts, the figure was a slightly smaller 8.2 percent. For Asian women aged 25 to 39, unemployment stood at 5.7 percent, while for white women it was 4.8 percent.

■ Among young adults, Hispanic women are less likely to work than black or white women because a larger proportion of them are married and caring for young children.

Labor force participation rate is highest for black women

(labor force participation rate of women aged 25 to 39, by race and Hispanic origin, 2003)

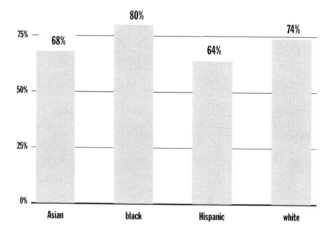

Table 5.4 Employment Status of Women by Race, Hispanic Origin, and Age, 2003

(number and percent of women aged 16 or older in the civilian labor force by race, Hispanic origin, age, and employment status, 2003; numbers in thousands)

	civilian noninstitutional population	total	percent of population	employed	unemployed number	percent of labor force
ASIAN WOMEN						
Total aged 16 or older	**4,882**	**2,845**	**58.3%**	**2,683**	**162**	**5.7%**
Under age 25	732	329	44.9	298	31	9.4
Aged 25 to 39	1,701	1,159	68.1	1,092	66	5.7
Aged 25 to 29	531	347	65.3	330	17	4.8
Aged 30 to 34	614	414	67.4	385	29	6.9
Aged 35 to 39	556	398	71.6	377	20	5.1
Aged 40 to 64	1,895	1,309	69.1	1,245	64	4.9
Aged 65 or older	555	48	8.7	47	1	3.1
BLACK WOMEN						
Total aged 16 or older	**14,232**	**8,815**	**61.9**	**7,919**	**895**	**10.2**
Under age 25	2,688	1,379	51.3	1,073	306	22.2
Aged 25 to 39	4,234	3,368	79.5	3,036	333	9.9
Aged 25 to 29	1,342	1,045	77.9	919	126	12.1
Aged 30 to 34	1,426	1,143	80.2	1,039	104	9.1
Aged 35 to 39	1,466	1,180	80.5	1,078	103	8.7
Aged 40 to 64	5,556	3,886	69.9	3,639	248	6.4
Aged 65 or older	1,753	180	10.3	171	10	5.3
HISPANIC WOMEN						
Total aged 16 or older	**13,452**	**7,525**	**55.9**	**6,894**	**631**	**8.4**
Under age 25	2,870	1,458	50.8	1,267	192	13.2
Aged 25 to 39	5,023	3,225	64.2	2,962	264	8.2
Aged 25 to 29	1,736	1,071	61.7	970	102	9.5
Aged 30 to 34	1,737	1,112	64.0	1,034	78	7.0
Aged 35 to 39	1,550	1,042	67.2	958	84	8.0
Aged 40 to 64	4,396	2,732	62.1	2,560	172	6.3
Aged 65 or older	1,166	109	9.4	105	4	4.4
WHITE WOMEN						
Total aged 16 or older	**93,043**	**55,037**	**59.2**	**52,369**	**2,668**	**4.8**
Under age 25	13,817	8,521	61.7	7,707	814	9.6
Aged 25 to 39	23,664	17,445	73.7	16,600	845	4.8
Aged 25 to 29	7,214	5,358	74.3	5,080	278	5.2
Aged 30 to 34	8,005	5,865	73.3	5,588	277	4.7
Aged 35 to 39	8,445	6,222	73.7	5,932	290	4.7
Aged 40 to 64	38,346	27,216	71.0	26,273	943	3.5
Aged 65 or older	17,216	1,852	10.8	1,788	64	3.5

Note: Race is shown only for those selecting that race group only. People who selected more than one race are not included. Hispanics may be of any race.
Source: Bureau of Labor Statistics, 2003 Current Population Survey, Internet site http://www.bls.gov/cps/home.htm; calculations by New Strategist

Most Generation X Couples Are Dual Earners

The husband is the sole support of only 28 percent of couples.

Dual incomes are by far the norm among married couples. Both husband and wife are in the labor force in 56 percent of the nation's couples. In another 22 percent, the husband is the only worker. Not far behind are the 17 percent of couples in which neither spouse is in the labor force. The wife is the sole worker among 6 percent of couples.

Sixty-eight percent of couples aged 25 to 39 are dual earners, while the husband is the only one in the labor force in another 28 percent. The dual-earner lifestyle accounts for an even larger share of couples aged 40 to 54 because their children are grown and wives are more likely to work. The dual-earner share falls to just 46 percent among couples aged 55 to 64, in part because of early retirement.

■ The dual-earner share of couples will rise in the older age groups as early retirement becomes less common.

Few Generation X couples are supported solely by the husband

(percent distribution of married couples aged 25 to 39 by labor force status of husband and wife, 2002)

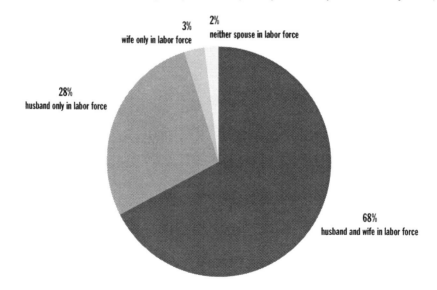

3%
wife only in labor force

2%
neither spouse in labor force

28%
husband only in labor force

68%
husband and wife in labor force

Table 5.5 Labor Force Status of Married-Couple Family Groups by Age of Reference Person, 2002

(number and percent distribution of married-couple family groups by age of reference person and labor force status of husband and wife, 2002; numbers in thousands)

		husband and/or wife in labor force			neither husband nor wife
	total	husband and wife	husband only	wife only	in labor force
Total married-couple family groups	**57,919**	**32,194**	**12,672**	**3,470**	**9,583**
Under age 25	1,711	1,018	582	69	41
Aged 25 to 39	16,571	11,289	4,583	425	274
Aged 25 to 29	3,763	2,586	1,033	87	57
Aged 30 to 34	5,889	3,964	1,693	131	102
Aged 35 to 39	6,919	4,739	1,857	207	115
Aged 40 to 44	7,499	5,424	1,686	261	128
Aged 45 to 54	13,375	9,457	2,774	683	460
Aged 55 to 64	9,062	4,206	2,003	1,127	1,726
Aged 65 or older	9,702	797	1,045	905	6,953
PERCENT DISTRIBUTION					
Total married-couple family groups	**100.0%**	**55.6%**	**21.9%**	**6.0%**	**16.5%**
Under age 25	100.0	59.5	34.0	4.0	2.4
Aged 25 to 39	100.0	68.1	27.7	2.6	1.7
Aged 25 to 29	100.0	68.7	27.5	2.3	1.5
Aged 30 to 34	100.0	67.3	28.7	2.2	1.7
Aged 35 to 39	100.0	68.5	26.8	3.0	1.7
Aged 40 to 44	100.0	72.3	22.5	3.5	1.7
Aged 45 to 54	100.0	70.7	20.7	5.1	3.4
Aged 55 to 64	100.0	46.4	22.1	12.4	19.1
Aged 65 or older	100.0	8.2	10.8	9.3	71.7

Note: Number of married-couple family groups exceeds number of married-couple householders because some households contain more than one married couple.
Source: Bureau of the Census, 2002 Current Population Survey Annual Demographic Supplement, Internet site http:// www.census.gov/population/www/socdemo/hh-fam/cps2002.html; calculations by New Strategist

Generation Xers Are Overrepresented in Technical Jobs

They are also overrepresented in jobs requiring physical stamina.

Only 22 percent of the nation's 138 million employed workers are aged 25 to 34—roughly the age of Generation X (aged 28 to 37 in 2003), but the share varies widely by occupation. Not surprisingly, Gen Xers account for just 17 percent of managers. But they are overrepresented in technical occupations. They account for fully 32 percent of computer programmers and 38 percent of computer software engineers.

Generation Xers make up a large share of employees in jobs requiring physical stamina. Thirty percent of actors are aged 25 to 34, for example. Thirty-six percent of firefighters and 35 percent of police patrol officers are in the age group as well. So are 42 percent of physical therapists.

■ Generation X was raised on computers, which is why they are disproportionately well represented in high-tech jobs.

Many computer workers are aged 25 to 34

(percent of workers aged 25 to 34. by occupation. 2003)

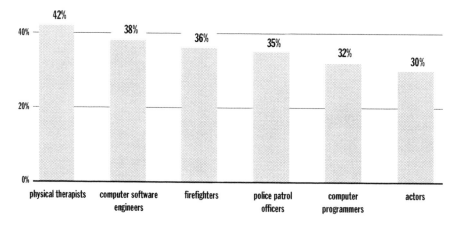

Table 5.6 Occupations of Workers Aged 25 to 44, 2003

(number of employed workers aged 16 or older, median age of workers, and number of workers aged 25 to 44, by occupation, 2003; numbers in thousands)

	total	median age	aged 25 to 44 total	25 to 34	35 to 44
TOTAL WORKERS	**137,736**	**40.4**	**65,264**	**30,383**	**34,881**
Management and professional occupations	**47,929**	**42.6**	**23,828**	**10,822**	**13,006**
Management, business and financial operations	19,934	44.0	9,512	3,839	5,673
Management	14,468	44.7	6,697	2,526	4,171
Business and financial operations	5,465	42.1	2,815	1,313	1,502
Professional and related occupations	27,995	41.5	14,317	6,984	7,333
Computer and mathematical	3,122	38.6	1,982	1,050	932
Architecture and engineering	2,727	41.5	1,462	650	812
Life, physical, and social sciences	1,375	41.2	718	383	335
Community and social services	2,184	43.1	989	497	492
Legal	1,508	43.1	755	360	395
Education, training, and library	7,768	42.6	3,573	1,782	1,791
Arts, design, entertainment, sports, and media	2,663	40.0	1,366	677	689
Health care practitioner and technician	6,648	41.9	3,470	1,584	1,886
Service occupations	**22,086**	**36.3**	**9,712**	**4,847**	**4,865**
Health care support	2,926	38.1	1,449	720	729
Protective service	2,727	39.9	1,413	663	750
Food preparation and serving	7,254	28.6	2,725	1,533	1,192
Building and grounds cleaning and maintenance	4,947	40.8	2,237	993	1,244
Personal care and service	4,232	37.9	1,889	938	951
Sales and office occupations	**35,496**	**39.7**	**15,582**	**7,293**	**8,289**
Sales and related occupations	15,960	38.8	6,887	3,258	3,629
Office and administrative support	19,536	40.5	8,695	4,035	4,660
Natural resources, construction, and maintenance occupations	**14,205**	**38.9**	**7,457**	**3,562**	**3,895**
Farming, fishing, and forestry	1,050	36.7	502	260	242
Construction and extraction	8,114	38.2	4,391	2,151	2,240
Installation, maintenance, and repair	5,041	40.4	2,565	1,152	1,413
Production, transportation, and material moving occupations	**18,020**	**40.7**	**8,683**	**3,858**	**4,825**
Production	9,700	41.1	4,800	2,088	2,712
Transportation and material moving	8,320	40.1	3,884	1,770	2,114

Source: Bureau of Labor Statistics, unpublished data from the 2003 Current Population Survey; calculations by New Strategist

Table 5.7 Distribution of Workers Aged 25 to 44 by Occupation, 2003

(percent distribution of employed people aged 16 or older and aged 25 to 44 by occupation, 2003)

	total	aged 25 to 44 total	aged 25 to 44 25 to 34	aged 25 to 44 35 to 44
TOTAL WORKERS	100.0%	100.0%	100.0%	100.0%
Management and professional occupations	**34.8**	**36.5**	**35.6**	**37.3**
Management, business and financial operations	14.5	14.6	12.6	16.3
Management	10.5	10.3	8.3	12.0
Business and financial operations	4.0	4.3	4.3	4.3
Professional and related occupations	20.3	21.9	23.0	21.0
Computer and mathematical	2.3	3.0	3.5	2.7
Architecture and engineering	2.0	2.2	2.1	2.3
Life, physical, and social sciences	1.0	1.1	1.3	1.0
Community and social services	1.6	1.5	1.6	1.4
Legal	1.1	1.2	1.2	1.1
Education, training, and library	5.6	5.5	5.9	5.1
Arts, design, entertainment, sports, and media	1.9	2.1	2.2	2.0
Health care practitioner and technician	4.8	5.3	5.2	5.4
Service occupations	**16.0**	**14.9**	**16.0**	**13.9**
Health care support	2.1	2.2	2.4	2.1
Protective service	2.0	2.2	2.2	2.2
Food preparation and serving	5.3	4.2	5.1	3.4
Building and grounds cleaning and maintenance	3.6	3.4	3.3	3.6
Personal care and service	3.1	2.9	3.1	2.7
Sales and office occupations	**25.8**	**23.9**	**2.4**	**23.8**
Sales and related occupations	11.6	10.6	10.7	10.4
Office and administrative support	14.2	13.3	13.3	13.4
Natural resources, construction, and maintenance occupation	**10.3**	**11.4**	**11.7**	**11.2**
Farming, fishing, and forestry	0.8	0.8	0.9	0.7
Construction and extraction	5.9	6.7	7.1	6.4
Installation, maintenance, and repair	3.7	3.9	3.8	4.1
Production, transportation, and material moving occupations	**13.1**	**13.3**	**12.7**	**13.8**
Production	7.0	7.4	6.9	7.8
Transportation and material moving	6.0	6.0	5.8	6.1

Source: Calculations by New Strategist based on Bureau of Labor Statistics' unpublished 2003 Current Population Survey data

Table 5.8 Share of Workers Aged 25 to 44 by Occupation, 2003

(employed persons aged 25 to 44 as a percent of total employed people aged 16 or older by occupation, 2003)

	total	aged 25 to 44		
		total	25 to 34	35 to 44
TOTAL WORKERS	**100.0%**	**47.4%**	**22.1%**	**25.3%**
Management and professional occupations	**100.0**	**49.7**	**22.6**	**27.1**
Management, business and financial operations	100.0	47.7	19.3	28.5
Management	100.0	46.3	17.5	28.8
Business and financial operations	100.0	51.5	24.0	27.5
Professional and related occupations	100.0	51.1	24.9	26.2
Computer and mathematical	100.0	63.5	33.6	29.9
Architecture and engineering	100.0	53.6	23.8	29.8
Life, physical, and social sciences	100.0	52.2	27.9	24.4
Community and social services	100.0	45.3	22.8	22.5
Legal	100.0	50.1	23.9	26.2
Education, training, and library	100.0	46.0	22.9	23.1
Arts, design, entertainment, sports, and media	100.0	51.3	25.4	25.9
Health care practitioner and technician	100.0	52.2	23.8	28.4
Service occupations	**100.0**	**44.0**	**21.9**	**22.0**
Health care support	100.0	49.5	24.6	24.9
Protective service	100.0	51.8	24.3	27.5
Food preparation and serving	100.0	37.6	21.1	16.4
Building and grounds cleaning and maintenance	100.0	45.2	20.1	25.1
Personal care and service	100.0	44.6	22.2	22.5
Sales and office occupations	**100.0**	**43.9**	**20.5**	**23.4**
Sales and related occupations	100.0	43.2	20.4	22.7
Office and administrative support	100.0	44.5	20.7	23.9
Natural resources, construction, and maintenance occupations	**100.0**	**52.5**	**25.1**	**27.4**
Farming, fishing, and forestry	100.0	47.8	24.8	23.1
Construction and extraction	100.0	54.1	26.5	27.6
Installation, maintenance, and repair	100.0	50.9	22.9	28.0
Production, transportation, and material moving occupations	**100.0**	**48.2**	**21.4**	**26.8**
Production	100.0	49.5	21.5	28.0
Transportation and material moving	100.0	46.7	21.3	25.4

Source: Calculations by New Strategist based on Bureau of Labor Statistics' unpublished 2003 Current Population Survey data

Table 5.9 Workers Aged 25 to 44 by Detailed Occupation, 2003

(number of employed workers aged 16 or older, median age, and number and percent aged 25 to 44, by selected detailed occupation, 2003; numbers in thousands)

	total workers	median age	total aged 25 to 44		aged 25 to 34		aged 35 to 44	
			number	percent of total	number	percent of total	number	percent of total
Total workers	**137,736**	**40.4**	**65,264**	**47.4%**	**30,383**	**22.1%**	**34,881**	**25.3%**
Chief executives	1,617	48.2	614	38.0	153	9.5	461	28.5
Legislators	14	53.2	4	28.6	–	–	4	28.6
Marketing and sales managers	888	41.6	515	58.0	227	25.6	288	32.4
Computer and information systems managers	347	41.7	202	58.2	83	23.9	119	34.3
Financial managers	1,041	42.1	567	54.5	233	22.4	334	32.1
Human resources managers	263	45.1	125	47.5	45	17.1	80	30.4
Farmers and ranchers	825	54.0	226	27.4	82	9.9	144	17.5
Education administrators	748	48.9	262	35.0	94	12.6	168	22.5
Food service managers	875	39.5	452	51.7	220	25.1	232	26.5
Medical, health services managers	480	46.1	202	42.1	76	15.8	126	26.2
Accountants and auditors	1,639	41.1	903	55.1	436	26.6	467	28.5
Computer scientists and systems analysts	722	40.4	407	56.4	194	26.9	213	29.5
Computer programmers	563	38.7	365	64.8	182	32.3	183	32.5
Computer software engineers	758	38.3	524	69.1	287	37.9	237	31.3
Architects	180	42.0	101	56.1	51	28.3	50	27.8
Civil engineers	278	42.9	142	51.1	67	24.1	75	27.0
Electrical engineers	363	42.7	194	53.4	72	19.8	122	33.6
Mechanical engineers	285	41.0	164	57.5	77	27.0	87	30.5
Medical scientists	101	39.9	62	61.4	32	31.7	30	29.7
Psychologists	185	50.2	64	34.6	31	16.8	33	17.8
Social workers	673	41.4	349	51.9	182	27.0	167	24.8
Clergy	410	49.9	135	32.9	52	12.7	83	20.2
Lawyers	952	44.4	475	49.9	224	23.5	251	26.4
Postsecondary teachers	1,121	43.8	497	44.3	252	22.5	245	21.9
Preschool, kindergarten teachers	665	38.9	341	51.3	192	28.9	149	22.4
Elementary and middle school teachers	2,557	42.7	1,267	49.6	651	25.5	616	24.1
Secondary school teachers	1,124	43.7	530	47.2	280	24.9	250	22.2
Librarians	194	49.6	52	26.8	25	12.9	27	13.9
Teacher assistants	932	41.8	400	42.9	153	16.4	247	26.5
Artists	212	43.8	96	45.3	42	19.8	54	25.5
Actors	30	36.6	15	50.0	9	30.0	6	20.0
Athletes	215	30.1	97	45.1	57	26.5	40	18.6
Editors	163	40.8	82	50.3	47	28.8	35	21.5
Writers and authors	190	44.8	88	46.3	38	20.0	50	26.3
Dentists	188	46.0	84	44.7	29	15.4	55	29.3
Pharmacists	232	42.1	125	53.9	66	28.4	59	25.4
Physicians and surgeons	819	44.2	419	51.2	171	20.9	248	30.3
Registered nurses	2,449	43.1	1,249	51.0	533	21.8	716	29.2

	total workers	median age	total aged 25 to 44		aged 25 to 34		aged 35 to 44	
			number	percent of total	number	percent of total	number	percent of total
Physical therapists	182	37.6	120	65.9%	77	42.3%	43	23.6%
Licensed practical nurses	531	43.3	252	47.5	98	18.5	154	29.0
Nursing, psychiatric, and home health aides	1,811	39.2	863	47.7	415	22.9	448	24.7
Firefighters	258	38.3	182	70.5	93	36.1	89	34.5
Police and sheriff's patrol officers	612	38.7	432	70.6	216	35.3	216	35.3
Security guards and gaming surveillance officers	781	40.7	288	36.9	153	19.6	135	17.3
Chefs and head cooks	281	37.8	152	54.1	79	28.1	73	26.0
Cooks	1,814	32.1	793	43.7	423	23.3	370	20.4
Food preparation workers	612	29.4	216	35.3	118	19.3	98	16.0
Waiters and waitresses	1,842	24.6	624	33.9	390	21.2	234	12.7
Janitors and building cleaners	1,973	43.2	790	40.0	310	15.7	480	24.3
Maids, housekeeping cleaners	1,370	42.2	651	47.5	274	20.0	377	27.5
Grounds maintenance workers	1,135	34.1	542	47.8	285	25.1	257	22.6
Hairdressers, hair stylists, and cosmetologists	718	39.0	390	54.3	192	26.7	198	27.6
Child care workers	1,284	35.4	533	41.5	289	22.5	244	19.0
Cashiers	2,903	26.1	874	30.1	490	16.9	384	13.2
Retail salespersons	3,113	35.9	1,136	36.5	560	18.0	576	18.5
Insurance sales agents	552	44.1	260	47.1	113	20.5	147	26.6
Securities, commodities, and financial services sales agents	389	39.8	236	60.7	126	32.4	110	28.3
Sales representatives, wholesale and manufacturing	1,399	41.7	743	53.1	317	22.7	426	30.5
Real estate brokers, sales agents	850	48.6	325	38.2	144	16.9	181	21.3
Bookkeeping, accounting, and auditing clerks	1,545	44.5	659	42.7	263	17.0	396	25.6
Customer service representatives	1,747	36.0	879	50.3	486	27.8	393	22.5
Receptionists, information clerks	1,376	36.9	495	36.0	266	19.3	229	16.6
Stock clerks and order fillers	1,360	33.6	526	38.7	271	19.9	255	18.8
Secretaries and admin. assistants	3,632	43.7	1,567	43.1	626	17.2	941	25.9
Misc. agricultural workers	741	33.8	362	48.9	201	27.1	161	21.7
Carpenters	1,595	37.4	888	55.7	448	28.1	440	27.6
Construction laborers	1,151	34.8	599	52.0	315	27.4	284	24.7
Automotive service technicians and mechanics	884	37.6	450	50.9	220	24.9	230	26.0
Misc. assemblers, fabricators	1,080	39.9	556	51.5	266	24.6	290	26.9
Machinists	454	42.3	212	46.7	86	18.9	126	27.8
Aircraft pilots, flight engineers	116	44.2	55	47.4	19	16.4	36	31.0
Driver/sales workers and truck drivers	3,214	42.1	1,602	49.8	713	22.2	889	27.7
Freight, stock and material movers, hand laborers	1,748	33.4	763	43.6	386	22.1	377	21.6

Note: (–) means number is less than 500 or sample is too small to make a reliable estimate.
Source: Bureau of Labor Statistics, unpublished tables from the 2003 Current Population Survey; calculations by New Strategist

Few Generation Xers Work Part-time

Among workers aged 25 to 34, full-time work is the norm.

The majority of workers aged 25 to 34 had full-time jobs in 2003 (Generation X was aged 27 to 38 in that year). Among employed men in the age group, 94 percent work full-time. Among women, the figure is 80 percent. With both men and women embarking on a career at this age, full-time work is usually a necessity. Only 6 percent of men and 20 percent of women in the age group have part-time jobs.

Men and women aged 25 to 34 account for about one in four full-time workers—about the same as their share of the total labor force. They account for a much smaller share of part-time workers. Men aged 25 to 34 who work part-time account for only 13 percent of all men who work part-time. Among women, the figure is 16 percent. Young adults under age 25, many of them high school or college students, account for a much larger share of part-time workers.

■ Although part-time work might appeal to many Gen Xers with young children at home, most cannot afford to live on a part-time income.

Most Generation Xers work full-time

(percent of workers aged 25 to 34 who work full-time, by sex, 2003)

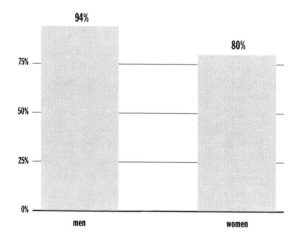

Table 5.10 Full- and Part-time Workers by Age and Sex, 2003

(number and percent distribution of employed people aged 16 or older in the civilian labor force by full- and part-time employment status. by age and sex, 2003; numbers in thousands)

	men			women		
	total	full-time	part-time	total	full-time	part-time
Total employed	**73,332**	**65,379**	**7,953**	**64,405**	**47,946**	**16,459**
Under age 25	9,983	6,477	3,506	9,369	4,882	4,487
Aged 25 to 34	16,670	15,666	1,004	13,713	11,034	2,679
Aged 35 to 44	18,774	18,039	735	16,106	12,667	3,439
Aged 45 to 64	25,321	23,653	1,668	23,192	18,441	4,751
Aged 65 or older	2,585	1,544	1,041	2,023	920	1,103
PERCENT DISTRIBUTION BY AGE						
Total employed	**100.0%**	**100.0%**	**100.0%**	**100.0%**	**100.0%**	**100.0%**
Under age 25	13.6	9.9	44.1	14.5	10.2	27.3
Aged 25 to 34	22.7	24.0	12.6	21.3	23.0	16.3
Aged 35 to 44	25.6	27.6	9.2	25.0	26.4	20.9
Aged 45 to 64	34.5	36.2	21.0	36.0	38.5	28.9
Aged 65 or older	3.5	2.4	13.1	3.1	1.9	6.7
PERCENT DISTRIBUTION BY EMPLOYMENT STATUS						
Total employed	**100.0%**	**89.2%**	**10.8%**	**100.0%**	**74.4%**	**25.6%**
Under age 25	100.0	64.9	35.1	100.0	52.1	47.9
Aged 25 to 34	100.0	94.0	6.0	100.0	80.5	19.5
Aged 35 to 44	100.0	96.1	3.9	100.0	78.6	21.4
Aged 45 to 64	100.0	93.4	6.6	100.0	79.5	20.5
Aged 65 or older	100.0	59.7	40.3	100.0	45.5	54.5

Source: Unpublished data from the Bureau of Labor Statistics; calculations by New Strategist

Few Gen Xers Work for Themselves

Self-employment requires experience, which is why self-employment rises with age.

Although many people may prefer self-employment, few have the skills until they are older to strike out on their own. Only 7 percent of all workers are self-employed. The figure is an even smaller 5 percent among those aged 25 to 34. In contrast, fully 19 percent of workers aged 65 or older are self-employed.

At every age, men are more likely than women to be self-employed. Among 25-to-34-year-olds, 5.9 percent of men and a smaller 4.6 percent of women are self-employed. The 25-to-34 age group accounts for only 16 percent of the nation's 10 million self-employed.

■ Self-employment is becoming a more difficult proposition for Americans because the cost of buying private health insurance can be prohibitive, especially for those starting businesses.

Few Gen Xers are self-employed

(percent of workers who are self-employed, by age, 2003)

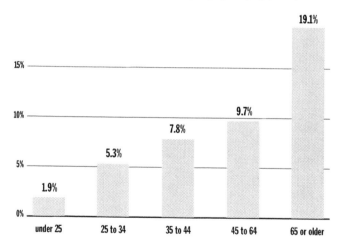

Table 5.11 Self-Employed Workers by Sex and Age, 2003

(number of employed workers aged 16 or older, number and percent who are self-employed, and percent distribution of self-employed, by sex and age, 2003; numbers in thousands)

	total	self-employed number	self-employed percent	percent distribution of self-employed by age
Total workers	**137,736**	**10,295**	**7.5%**	**100.0%**
Under age 25	19,351	359	1.9	3.5
Aged 25 to 34	30,383	1,609	5.3	15.6
Aged 35 to 44	34,881	2,717	7.8	26.4
Aged 45 to 64	48,512	4,729	9.7	45.9
Aged 65 or older	4,608	880	19.1	8.5
Total men	**73,331**	**6,430**	**8.8**	**100.0**
Under age 25	9,982	244	2.4	3.8
Aged 25 to 34	16,670	982	5.9	15.3
Aged 35 to 44	18,775	1,635	8.7	25.4
Aged 45 to 64	25,320	2,978	11.8	46.3
Aged 65 or older	2,585	590	22.8	9.2
Total women	**64,404**	**3,866**	**6.0**	**100.0**
Under age 25	9,368	117	1.2	3.0
Aged 25 to 34	13,714	628	4.6	16.2
Aged 35 to 44	16,106	1,082	6.7	28.0
Aged 45 to 64	23,191	1,750	7.5	45.3
Aged 65 or older	2,023	291	14.4	7.5

Source: Bureau of Labor Statistics, 2003 Current Population Survey, Internet site http://www.bls.gov/cps/home.htm; calculations by New Strategist

Job Tenure Has Changed Little for Men Aged 25 to 34

Long-term employment is much less common, however.

Job tenure (the number of years a worker has been with his current employer) has been declining among men for many years. Among men aged 25 to 34, however, job tenure has changed little—down only 0.2 years between 1991 and 2002 and up slightly since 2000. The numbers are similar for women in the age group.

Long-term employment has fallen among young and middle-aged workers, however. The percentage of 25-to-44-year-olds who have been with their current employer for ten or more years fell steeply between 1991 and 2002, especially among men aged 30 to 44.

■ The decline in long-term employment is a result of changes in the economy, the recession of 2001, and massive job cuts in many industrial sectors.

Fewer men aged 25 to 44 have long-term jobs

(percent of men aged 25 to 44 who have worked for their current employer for ten or more years, 1991 and 2002)

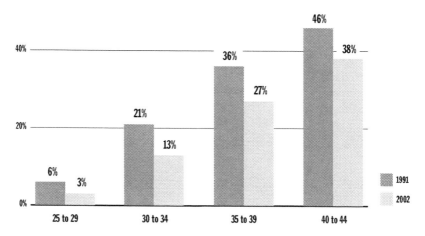

Table 5.12 Job Tenure by Sex and Age, 1991 to 2002

(median number of years that employed wage and salary workers aged 25 or older have been with their current employer, by sex and age, 1991 to 2002; change in years, 2000–2002 and 1991–2002)

	2002	2000	1991	change in years	
				2000–02	1991–02
Total workers aged 25 or older	**4.7**	**4.7**	**4.8**	**0.0**	**–0.1**
Aged 25 to 34	2.7	2.6	2.9	0.1	–0.2
Aged 35 to 44	4.6	4.8	5.4	–0.2	–0.8
Aged 45 to 54	7.6	8.2	8.9	–0.6	–1.3
Aged 55 to 64	9.9	10.0	11.1	–0.1	–1.2
Aged 65 or older	8.7	9.5	8.1	–0.8	0.6
Total men aged 25 or older	**4.9**	**5.0**	**5.4**	**–0.1**	**–0.5**
Aged 25 to 34	2.9	2.7	3.1	0.2	–0.2
Aged 35 to 44	5.1	5.4	6.5	–0.3	–1.4
Aged 45 to 54	9.1	9.5	11.2	–0.4	–2.1
Aged 55 to 64	10.2	10.2	13.4	0.0	–3.2
Aged 65 or older	8.1	9.1	7.0	–1.0	1.1
Total women aged 25 or older	**4.4**	**4.4**	**4.3**	**0.0**	**0.1**
Aged 25 to 34	2.5	2.5	2.7	0.0	–0.2
Aged 35 to 44	4.3	4.3	4.5	0.0	–0.2
Aged 45 to 54	6.5	7.3	6.7	–0.8	–0.2
Aged 55 to 64	9.6	9.9	9.9	–0.3	–0.3
Aged 65 or older	9.5	9.7	9.5	–0.2	0.0

Source: Bureau of Labor Statistics, Internet site http://www.bls.gov/news.release/tenure.t01.htm; calculations by New Strategist

Table 5.13 Long-Term Employment of People Aged 25 to 44 by Sex, 1991 to 2002

(percent of employed wage and salary workers aged 25 or older and aged 25 to 44 who have been with their current employer for ten or more years, by sex and age, 1991 to 2002; percentage point change in share, 2000–2002 and 1991–2002)

	2002	2000	1991	percentage point change 2000–02	1991–02
Total workers aged 25 or older	**31.0%**	**31.7%**	**32.2%**	**–0.7**	**–1.2**
Aged 25 to 29	2.2	2.5	5.1	–0.3	–2.9
Aged 30 to 34	11.8	14.0	19.3	–2.2	–7.5
Aged 35 to 39	25.3	26.2	31.1	–0.9	–5.8
Aged 40 to 44	34.1	35.9	39.3	–1.8	–5.2
Men aged 25 or older	**33.0**	**33.6**	**35.9**	**–0.6**	**–2.9**
Aged 25 to 29	2.6	3.0	5.7	–0.4	–3.1
Aged 30 to 34	13.1	15.3	21.1	–2.2	–8.0
Aged 35 to 39	27.3	29.5	35.6	–2.2	–8.3
Aged 40 to 44	37.7	40.4	46.3	–2.7	–8.6
Women aged 25 or older	**28.8**	**29.5**	**28.2**	**–0.7**	**0.6**
Aged 25 to 29	1.8	1.9	4.4	–0.1	–2.6
Aged 30 to 34	10.2	12.6	17.3	–2.4	–7.1
Aged 35 to 39	23.0	22.4	26.1	0.6	–3.1
Aged 40 to 44	30.2	31.4	32.0	–1.2	–1.8

Source: Bureau of Labor Statistics, Internet site http://www.bls.gov/news.release/tenure.t02.htm; calculations by New Strategist

Few Generation Xers Have Alternative Work Arrangements

Only 4 percent are independent contractors.

Among the nation's 12 million alternative workers, only 2 million (17 percent) are aged 25 to 34. The Bureau of Labor Statistics defines alternative workers as independent contractors, on-call workers (such as substitute teachers), temporary-help agency workers, and people who work for contract firms (such as lawn or janitorial service companies).

The most popular alternative work arrangement is independent contracting—which includes most of the self-employed. Among the 12.5 million alternative workers, 8.6 million are independent contractors—or 69 percent. Among alternative workers aged 25 to 34, slightly more than 1 million (62 percent) are independent contractors. About 300,000 are temp workers and another 355,000 are on-call workers.

The percentage of workers with alternative work arrangements rises with age as independent contracting becomes more popular. Nearly one in eight workers aged 45 or older has an alternative work arrangement, with nearly one in ten being an independent contractor.

■ Older workers have more skills and experience, making it easier for them to earn a living by self-employment.

Few young workers are independent contractors

(percent of employed workers who are independent contractors, by age, 2001)

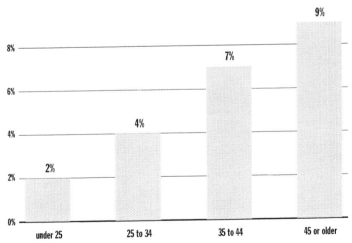

Table 5.14 Alternative Work Arrangements by Age, 2001

(number and percent distribution of employed people aged 16 or older with alternative work arrangements by age and type of alternative work, 2001; numbers in thousands)

	employed	with traditional work arrangements	with alternative work arrangements total	independent contractors	on-call workers	temporary help agency workers	workers provided by contract firms
Total people	134,605	121,917	12,476	8,585	2,089	1,169	633
Under age 25	19,856	18,573	1,187	339	511	261	76
Aged 25 to 34	30,079	27,905	2,127	1,314	355	310	148
Aged 35 to 44	36,740	33,194	3,498	2,486	538	291	183
Aged 45 or older	47,930	42,244	5,664	4,446	684	307	227
PERCENT DISTRIBUTION BY ALTERNATIVE WORK STATUS							
Total people	100.0%	90.6%	9.3%	6.4%	1.6%	0.9%	0.5%
Under age 25	100.0	93.5	6.0	1.7	2.6	1.3	0.4
Aged 25 to 34	100.0	92.8	7.1	4.4	1.2	1.0	0.5
Aged 35 to 44	100.0	90.3	9.5	6.8	1.5	0.8	0.5
Aged 45 or older	100.0	88.1	11.8	9.3	1.4	0.6	0.5
PERCENT DISTRIBUTION BY AGE							
Total people	100.0%	100.0%	100.0%	100.0%	100.0%	100.0%	100.0%
Under age 25	14.8	15.2	9.5	3.9	24.5	22.3	12.0
Aged 25 to 34	22.3	22.9	17.1	15.3	17.0	26.5	23.4
Aged 35 to 44	27.3	27.2	28.0	29.0	25.8	24.9	28.9
Aged 45 or older	35.6	34.6	45.4	51.8	32.7	26.3	35.9

Note: Numbers may not add to total because the total employed includes day laborers, an alternative arrangement not shown separately, and a small number of workers who were both on call and provided by contract firms. Independent contractors are self-employed (except incorporated) or wage and salary workers who obtain customers on their own to provide a product or service. On-call workers are in a pool of workers who are called to work only as needed, such as substitute teachers and construction workers supplied by a union hiring hall. Temporary help agency workers are those who said they are paid by a temporary help agency. Workers provided by contract firms are those employed by a company that provides employees or their services to others under contract, such as security, landscaping, and computer programming.
Source: Bureau of Labor Statistics, Contingent and Alternative Employment Arrangements, February 2001, *USDL 01-153, Internet site http://www.bls.gov/news.release/conemp.toc.htm; calculations by New Strategist*

Many Workers Have Flexible Schedules

Men are more likely than women to have flexible schedules.

Twenty-nine percent of the nation's wage and salary workers have flexible schedules—meaning they may vary the time they begin or end work, according to the Bureau of Labor Statistics. Men are more likely than women to have flexible schedules—30 versus 27 percent in 2001.

The percentage of full-time wage and salary workers with flexible schedules varies little by age. But men and women aged 25 to 34 are slightly more likely than the average worker to have flexible schedules. Many seek out jobs that allow them this flexibility because they have young children at home.

Fifteen percent of wage and salary workers do not work a regular daytime schedule. The youngest workers are most likely to work shifts—23 percent of those aged 16 to 24 work the evening, night, or other shifts. The figure falls to 14 percent among those aged 25 to 34.

■ Younger workers are less likely to work a regular daytime shift because many are in school during the day.

Generation Xers are slightly more likely than average to have flexible schedules

(percent of full-time wage and salary workers who have flexible work schedules, by sex and age, 2001)

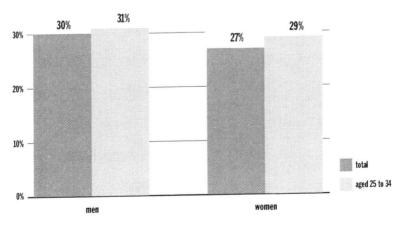

Table 5.15 Workers with Flexible Work Schedules by Age, 2001

(number and percent distribution of full-time wage and salary workers aged 16 or older with flexible work schedules, by sex and age, 2001; numbers in thousands)

	total	with flexible schedules	
		number	percent
Full-time wage and salary workers	**99,631**	**28,724**	**28.8%**
Under age 25	11,104	2,666	24.0
Aged 25 to 34	24,552	7,434	30.3
Aged 35 to 44	28,702	8,578	29.9
Aged 45 or older	35,274	10,046	28.5
Men	**56,066**	**16,792**	**30.0**
Under age 25	6,207	1,370	22.1
Aged 25 to 34	14,058	4,370	31.1
Aged 35 to 44	16,522	5,120	31.0
Aged 45 or older	19,280	5,933	30.8
Women	**43,566**	**11,931**	**27.4**
Under age 25	4,897	1,295	26.4
Aged 25 to 34	10,494	3,064	29.2
Aged 35 to 44	12,180	3,458	28.4
Aged 45 or older	15,994	4,113	25.7

Note: Flexible schedules are those that allow workers to vary the time they begin or end work.
Source: Bureau of Labor Statistics, Workers on Flexible and Shift Schedules in 2001, USDL 02-225, 2002, Internet site http://www.bls.gov/news.release/flex.toc.htm; calculations by New Strategist

Table 5.16 Workers by Shift Usually Worked and Age, 2001

(number of full-time wage and salary workers aged 16 or older and percent distribution by age and shift usually worked, 2001; numbers in thousands)

	total	16 to 24	25 to 34	35 to 44	45 to 54	55 to 64	65 or older
Total full-time wage and salary workers, number	**99,631**	**11,104**	**24,552**	**28,702**	**23,946**	**9,971**	**1,357**
Total full-time wage and salary workers, percent	**100.0%**	**100.0%**	**100.0%**	**100.0%**	**100.0%**	**100.0%**	**100.0%**
Regular daytime schedule	84.8	76.6	84.9	86.2	86.3	86.3	84.9
Shift workers	14.5	22.5	14.4	13.2	13.1	13.2	15.0
Evening shift	4.8	9.4	4.9	3.7	4.1	4.5	3.9
Night shift	3.3	4.8	3.3	3.3	2.9	3.1	2.1
Rotating shift	2.3	3.3	2.3	2.3	2.3	1.7	1.7
Split shift	0.4	0.3	0.6	0.4	0.3	0.4	1.3
Employer-arranged irregular schedule	2.8	3.8	2.4	2.8	2.6	2.8	5.5
Other	0.7	0.8	0.8	0.6	0.8	0.6	0.5

Source: Bureau of Labor Statistics, Workers on Flexible and Shift Schedules in 2001, *USDL 02-225, 2002, Internet site http://www.bls.gov/news.release/flex.toc.htm*

Few Gen Xers Work for Minimum Wage

Only 2 percent of workers aged 25 to 44 make minimum wage or less.

Among the nation's 73 million workers who are paid hourly rates, only 2 million (3 percent) make minimum wage or less, according to the Bureau of Labor Statistics. Among those making minimum wage or less, the 74 percent majority make even less than minimum wage, which stood at $5.15 per hour in 2002.

Fully 53 percent of minimum-wage workers are under age 25. Only 29 percent are between the ages of 25 and 44. Among hourly workers in the 25-to-44 age group, only 2 percent make minimum wage or less.

■ Younger workers are most likely to earn minimum wage or less because many are entry-level and/or part-time workers.

Most minimum wage workers are under age 25

(percent distribution of workers making minimum wage or less, by age, 2002)

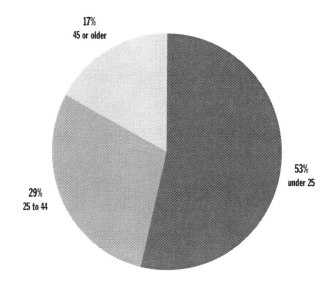

17%
45 or older

53%
under 25

29%
25 to 44

Table 5.17 Workers Earning Minimum Wage by Age, 2002

(number and percent distribution of workers paid hourly rates and workers paid at or below minimum wage, by age, 2002; numbers in thousands)

	total paid hourly rates	at or below minimum wage		
		total	at $5.15/hour	below $5.15/hour
Total aged 16 or older	**72,720**	**2,168**	**570**	**1,598**
Under age 25	16,191	1,158	340	818
Aged 25 to 44	40,174	639	140	499
Aged 25 to 29	8,120	208	48	160
Aged 30 to 34	8,237	167	33	134
Aged 35 to 39	8,408	139	33	106
Aged 40 to 44	8,744	125	26	99
Aged 45 or older	23,022	371	90	281
PERCENT DISTRIBUTION BY AGE				
Total aged 16 or older	**100.0%**	**100.0%**	**100.0%**	**100.0%**
Under age 25	22.3	53.4	59.6	51.2
Aged 25 to 44	55.2	29.3	26.1	30.4
Aged 25 to 29	11.2	9.6	8.4	10.0
Aged 30 to 34	11.3	7.7	5.8	8.4
Aged 35 to 39	11.6	6.4	5.8	6.6
Aged 40 to 44	12.0	5.8	4.6	6.2
Aged 45 or older	31.7	17.1	15.8	17.6
PERCENT DISTRIBUTION BY WAGE STATUS				
Total aged 16 or older	**100.0%**	**3.0%**	**0.8%**	**2.2%**
Under age 25	100.0	7.2	2.1	5.1
Aged 25 to 44	100.0	1.6	0.4	1.2
Aged 25 to 29	100.0	2.6	0.6	2.0
Aged 30 to 34	100.0	2.0	0.4	1.6
Aged 35 to 39	100.0	1.7	0.4	1.3
Aged 40 to 44	100.0	1.4	0.3	1.1
Aged 45 or older	100.0	1.6	0.4	1.2

Source: Bureau of Labor Statistics, Characteristics of Minimum Wage Workers, *2002, Internet site http://www.bls.gov/cps/minwage2002.htm; calculations by New Strategist*

Few 25-to-34-Year-Olds Belong to Unions

Men are more likely than women to be union members.

Union membership has fallen sharply over the past few decades. In 1970, 30 percent of nonagricultural workers were members of labor unions. In 2003, only 13 percent were union members. A slightly larger 14 percent of workers are represented by unions.

The percentage of workers who belong to a union peaks in the 45-to-54 age group at 20 percent of men and 16 percent of women. A larger percentage of men are union members because they are more likely to work in jobs that are traditional strongholds of labor unions. In fact, the decline of labor unions is partly the result of the shift in jobs from manufacturing to services. Among 25-to-34-year-olds, only 12 percent of men and 10 percent of women are union members.

■ Union membership will continue to decline because the increasingly cut-throat economy rewards companies with more flexible workforces.

Few workers belong to unions

(percent of employed wage and salary workers who are members of unions, by age, 2003)

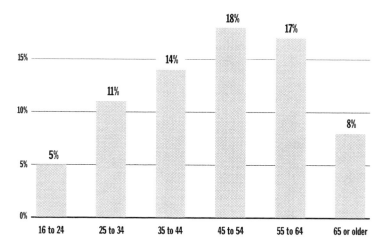

Table 5.18 Union Membership by Sex and Age, 2003

(number and percent of employed wage and salary workers aged 16 or older by union affiliation, sex, and age, 2003; numbers in thousands)

	total employed	represented by unions		members of unions	
		number	percent	number	percent
Total aged 16+	**122,358**	**17,448**	**14.3%**	**15,776**	**12.9%**
Aged 16 to 24	18,904	1,124	5.9	966	5.1
Aged 25 to 34	28,179	3,455	12.3	3,097	11.0
Aged 35 to 44	30,714	4,717	15.4	4,308	14.0
Aged 45 to 54	27,567	5,307	19.3	4,848	17.6
Aged 55 to 64	13,633	2,547	18.7	2,300	16.9
Aged 65 or older	3,361	297	8.8	258	7.7
Men aged 16+	**63,236**	**9,848**	**15.6**	**9,044**	**14.3**
Aged 16 to 24	9,683	685	7.1	595	6.1
Aged 25 to 34	15,263	2,005	13.1	1,826	12.0
Aged 35 to 44	16,080	2,735	17.0	2,535	15.8
Aged 45 to 54	13,723	2,891	21.1	2,684	19.6
Aged 55 to 64	6,776	1,377	20.3	1,271	18.8
Aged 65 or older	1,710	155	9.0	133	7.8
Women aged 16+	**59,122**	**7,601**	**12.9**	**6,732**	**11.4**
Aged 16 to 24	9,221	439	4.8	371	4.0
Aged 25 to 34	12,916	1,451	11.2	1,270	9.8
Aged 35 to 44	14,634	1,982	13.5	1,773	12.1
Aged 45 to 54	13,844	2,416	17.5	2,163	15.6
Aged 55 to 64	6,857	1,170	17.1	1,029	15.0
Aged 65 or older	1,651	142	8.6	125	7.6

Source: Bureau of Labor Statistics, 2003 Current Population Survey, Internet site http://www.bls.gov/cps/home.htm

Little Change Seen in Generation X Labor Force Participation

The number of workers aged 35 to 44 will decline as Generation X fills the age group.

Between 2003 and 2012, the small Generation X will fill the 35-to-44 age group (Gen Xers will be aged 36 to 47 in 2012). The number of workers in the age group will decline by 6 percent. The 25-to-34 age group, in contrast, will be filling with the larger Millennial generation. Consequently the number of workers aged 25 to 34 will expand by 10 percent. The labor force participation rate of Gen X men is projected to remain stable through the decade, while that of Gen X women should rise by 3 percentage points, to nearly 80 percent.

The number of older workers is projected to soar during the coming decade. The Bureau of Labor Statistics projects a 42 percent increase in the number of workers aged 55 or older between 2003 and 2012. In contrast, the number of workers under age 55 should grow by just 5 percent during those years.

■ Generation Xers may find it difficult to advance in their career as Boomers, working well into their sixties, clog the ranks of upper management.

The number of workers aged 35 to 44 will decline

(percent change in number of workers by sex and selected age, 2003–12)

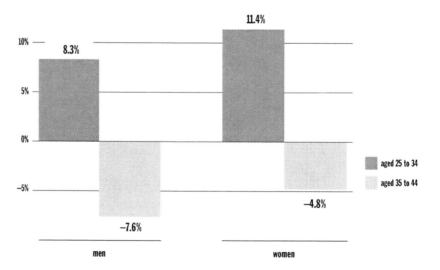

Table 5.19 Projections of the Labor Force by Sex and Age, 2003 to 2012

(number and percent of people aged 16 or older in the civilian labor force by sex and age, 2003 and 2012; percent change in number and percentage point change in participation rate, 2003–12; numbers in thousands)

	number			participation rate		
	2003	2012	percent change 2003–12	2003	2012	percentage point change 2003–12
Total labor force	**147,003**	**162,269**	**10.4%**	**67.1%**	**67.2%**	**0.1**
Total men in labor force	**78,560**	**85,252**	**8.5**	**74.4**	**73.1**	**–1.3**
Under age 25	11,884	12,461	4.9	66.6	65.7	–0.9
Aged 25 to 34	17,602	19,069	8.3	93.2	92.5	–0.7
Aged 25 to 29	8,326	9,436	13.3	92.2	91.1	–1.1
Aged 30 to 34	9,276	9,633	3.8	94.0	93.9	–0.1
Aged 35 to 44	19,734	18,244	–7.6	92.3	92.3	0.0
Aged 35 to 39	9,529	8,817	–7.5	93.1	93.0	–0.1
Aged 40 to 44	10,205	9,428	–7.6	91.6	91.6	0.0
Aged 45 to 54	17,511	19,122	9.2	88.3	88.6	0.3
Aged 55 to 64	9,232	12,714	37.7	69.3	69.9	0.6
Aged 65 or older	2,598	3,641	40.1	18.3	20.8	2.5
Total women in labor force	**68,443**	**77,017**	**12.5**	**60.4**	**61.6**	**1.2**
Under age 25	10,980	11,916	8.5	61.3	63.2	1.9
Aged 25 to 34	14,660	16,337	11.4	75.5	78.2	2.7
Aged 25 to 29	7,038	8,164	16.0	75.9	78.0	2.1
Aged 30 to 34	7,623	8,174	7.2	75.2	78.4	3.2
Aged 35 to 44	17,002	16,189	–4.8	76.8	79.9	3.1
Aged 35 to 39	8,029	7,674	–4.4	75.8	79.1	3.3
Aged 40 to 44	8,973	8,515	–5.1	77.7	80.6	2.9
Aged 45 to 54	15,824	17,905	13.2	76.3	79.8	3.5
Aged 55 to 64	8,043	11,902	48.0	55.8	60.6	4.8
Aged 65 or older	1,934	2,769	43.2	10.3	12.1	1.8

Source: Bureau of Labor Statistics, Internet site http://www.bls.gov/emp/emplab1.htm; calculations by New Strategist

6

Living Arrangements

■ Among householders aged 25 to 29, the 44 percent minority are married couples. The figure rises to the 55 percent majority in the 30-to-34 age group and climbs to 58 percent among householders aged 35 to 39.

■ Married couples account for fully 57 percent of Hispanic householders aged 25 to 39. Among Asians, the figure is 36 percent, and among blacks it's an even smaller 30 percent.

■ More than half the households headed by people aged 25 to 34 include children under age 18. The proportion rises from the 45 percent minority of those aged 25 to 29 to the 59 percent majority of those aged 30 to 34.

■ More than two-thirds of Hispanic households headed by 25-to-34-year-olds include children under age 18. Among Asian householders in the age group, just 37 percent have children in their home.

■ Among 25–to-29-year-olds, only 37 percent of men and 47 percent of women live with a spouse. In the 30-to-34 age group, the proportions rise to the 54 and 61 percent majorities, respectively.

Married Couples Become the Norm in the 30-to-34 Age Group

Female-headed families account for a large share of households in the 25-to-39 age group.

As people age from their mid-twenties through their thirties, life gets serious. Most embark on a career, marry for the first time, have children, and buy a home.

Among householders aged 25 to 29, the 44 percent minority are married couples. The figure rises to the 55 percent majority in the 30-to-34 age group and climbs to 58 percent among householders aged 35 to 39. Nonfamilies (people living alone or with nonrelatives) account for fully 34 percent of households headed by 25-to-29-year-olds. More than one in five householders in their late twenties live alone. As more people marry, the proportion living in nonfamily households falls to 22 percent by the 35-to-39 age group.

Fifteen percent of householders in the 25-to-39 age group are women heading families without a spouse, making it the second-most common household type. Men who live alone rank third, accounting for 10 to 12 percent of householders aged 25 to 39. Women who live alone account for only 7 to 9 percent of householders in the age group, and men heading families without a spouse are just 4 to 6 percent.

■ People in their twenties and thirties are undergoing many changes, making these years not only exciting, but also stressful.

Most householders in their thirties are married

(married couples as a percent of householders aged 25 to 39, by age, 2003)

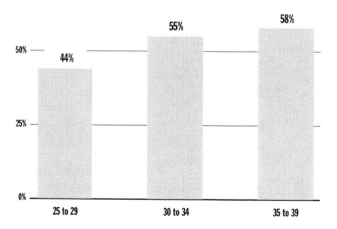

Table 6.1 **Households Headed by People Aged 25 to 39 by Household Type, 2003: Total Households**

(number and percent distribution of total households and households headed by people aged 25 to 39, by household type, 2003; numbers in thousands)

	total	aged 25 to 39			
		total	25 to 29	30 to 34	35 to 39
Total households	**111,278**	**30,542**	**8,535**	**10,521**	**11,486**
Family households	75,596	22,403	5,659	7,779	8,965
Married couples	57,320	16,176	3,760	5,776	6,640
Female householder, no spouse present	13,620	4,718	1,391	1,501	1,826
Male householder, no spouse present	4,656	1,509	508	503	498
Nonfamily households	35,682	8,138	2,876	2,741	2,521
Female householder	19,662	3,217	1,223	1,051	943
Living alone	16,919	2,368	783	814	771
Male householder	16,020	4,921	1,653	1,690	1,578
Living alone	12,511	3,390	1,021	1,191	1,178
PERCENT DISTRIBUTION BY TYPE					
Total households	**100.0%**	**100.0%**	**100.0%**	**100.0%**	**100.0%**
Family households	67.9	73.4	66.3	73.9	78.1
Married couples	51.5	53.0	44.1	54.9	57.8
Female householder, no spouse present	12.2	15.4	16.3	14.3	15.9
Male householder, no spouse present	4.2	4.9	6.0	4.8	4.3
Nonfamily households	32.1	26.6	33.7	26.1	21.9
Female householder	17.7	10.5	14.3	10.0	8.2
Living alone	15.2	7.8	9.2	7.7	6.7
Male householder	14.4	16.1	19.4	16.1	13.7
Living alone	11.2	11.1	12.0	11.3	10.3
PERCENT DISTRIBUTION BY AGE					
Total households	**100.0%**	**27.4%**	**7.7%**	**9.5%**	**10.3%**
Family households	100.0	29.6	7.5	10.3	11.9
Married couples	100.0	28.2	6.6	10.1	11.6
Female householder, no spouse present	100.0	34.6	10.2	11.0	13.4
Male householder, no spouse present	100.0	32.4	10.9	10.8	10.7
Nonfamily households	100.0	22.8	8.1	7.7	7.1
Female householder	100.0	16.4	6.2	5.3	4.8
Living alone	100.0	14.0	4.6	4.8	4.6
Male householder	100.0	30.7	10.3	10.5	9.9
Living alone	100.0	27.1	8.2	9.5	9.4

Source: Bureau of the Census, 2003 Current Population Survey, Annual Social and Economic Supplement, Internet site http:// ferret.bls.census.gov/macro/032003/hhinc/new02_000.htm; calculations by New Strategist

Hispanics and Blacks Head Many Gen X Households

Non-Hispanic whites head fewer than half of female-headed families.

Among all households headed by people aged 25 to 39, non-Hispanic whites head the 65 percent majority. But the figure varies greatly by type of household. Non-Hispanic whites head only 46 percent of female-headed families in the 25-to-39 age group, for example, but they head fully 70 percent of nonfamily households. Blacks account for 34 percent of female family householders aged 25 to 39.

Although blacks and Hispanics are nearly equal in number in the U.S. population, Hispanic married couples greatly outnumber black couples. Among couples aged 25 to 39, 16 percent are Hispanic, 8 percent are black, and 5 percent are Asian.

■ As the Millennial generation enters its late twenties and thirties, the non-Hispanic white share of households will shrink, regardless of household type.

Hispanics account for a large share of Gen X couples

(percent distribution of married couples aged 25 to 39, by race and Hispanic origin, 2003)

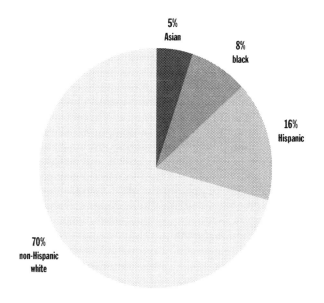

5%
Asian

8%
black

16%
Hispanic

70%
non-Hispanic
white

Table 6.2 Households Headed by People Aged 25 to 39 by Household Type, Race, and Hispanic Origin, 2003

(number and percent distribution of households headed by people aged 25 to 39, by household type, race, and Hispanic origin, 2003; numbers in thousands)

	total	Asian	black	Hispanic	non-Hispanic white
Total householders aged 25 to 39	**30,542**	**1,544**	**4,219**	**4,605**	**19,949**
Family households	22,403	1,042	3,125	3,841	14,232
Married couples	16,176	841	1,285	2,639	11,305
Female householder, no spouse present	4,718	108	1,604	822	2,155
Male householder, no spouse present	1,509	93	236	381	771
Nonfamily households	8,138	502	1,094	765	5,717
Female householder	3,217	218	479	231	2,265
Living alone	2,368	156	413	162	1,622
Male householder	4,921	284	615	533	3,452
Living alone	3,390	196	481	318	2,370

PERCENT DISTRIBUTION BY RACE AND HISPANIC ORIGIN

Total householders aged 25 to 39	**100.0%**	**5.1%**	**13.8%**	**15.1%**	**65.3%**
Family households	100.0	4.7	13.9	17.1	63.5
Married couples	100.0	5.2	7.9	16.3	69.9
Female householder, no spouse present	100.0	2.3	34.0	17.4	45.7
Male householder, no spouse present	100.0	6.2	15.6	25.2	51.1
Nonfamily households	100.0	6.2	13.4	9.4	70.3
Female householder	100.0	6.8	14.9	7.2	70.4
Living alone	100.0	6.6	17.4	6.8	68.5
Male householder	100.0	5.8	12.5	10.8	70.1
Living alone	100.0	5.8	14.2	9.4	69.9

Note: Numbers will not add to total because each racial group includes householders identifying themselves as the race alone and householders identifying themselves as the race in combination with other races. Hispanics may be of any race. Non-Hispanic white households include only householders identifying themselves as white alone and non-Hispanic.
Source: Bureau of the Census, 2003 Current Population Survey, Annual Social and Economic Supplement, Internet site http:// ferret.bls.census.gov/macro/032003/hhinc/new02_000.htm; calculations by New Strategist

Asian Gen Xers Are in Transition

Single in their twenties, they are married by their thirties.

Although married couples accounted for the majority of Asian households headed by 25-to-39-year-olds in 2003 (Generation Xers were aged 27 to 38 in that year), there are stark differences in living arrangements within the age group. Among Asian householders aged 25 to 29, only 35 percent are married couples. A much larger 50 percent head nonfamily households—meaning they live alone (30 percent) or with nonrelatives (20 percent). The figures change dramatically among 30-to-34-year olds. Married couples head the 58 percent majority of households in the age group, and the nonfamily share drops to 31 percent. The trend continues in the 35-to-39 age group, with couples heading 66 percent of households and nonfamilies only 21 percent.

Single-parent families account for few Asian households. Women head only 7 percent of families among Asian householders aged 25 to 39. Men head an even smaller 6 percent.

■ Asians are by far the best-educated segment of the American population. Many live alone or with nonrelatives during their twenties because they are attending school.

Many Asian Gen Xers live alone

(percent distribution of households headed by Asians aged 25 to 39, by household type, 2003)

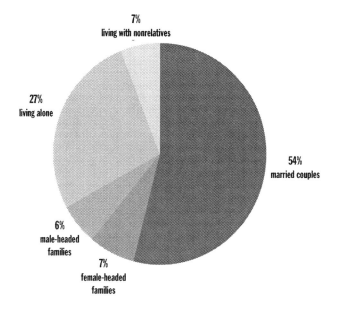

7%
living with nonrelatives

27%
living alone

54%
married couples

6%
male-headed
families

7%
female-headed
families

Table 6.3 Households Headed by People Aged 25 to 39 by Household Type, 2003: Asian Households

(number and percent distribution of total households headed by Asians and households headed by Asians aged 25 to 39, by household type, 2003; numbers in thousands)

	total	aged 25 to 39			
		total	25 to 29	30 to 34	35 to 39
Total Asian households	**4,079**	**1,544**	**420**	**578**	**546**
Family households	2,939	1,042	211	397	434
Married couples	2,344	841	147	335	359
Female householder, no spouse present	354	108	29	34	45
Male householder, no spouse present	241	93	35	28	30
Nonfamily households	1,140	502	209	181	112
Female householder	567	218	92	78	48
Living alone	435	156	54	58	44
Male householder	573	284	117	103	64
Living alone	411	196	72	79	45
PERCENT DISTRIBUTION BY TYPE					
Total Asian households	**100.0%**	**100.0%**	**100.0%**	**100.0%**	**100.0%**
Family households	72.1	67.5	50.2	68.7	79.5
Married couples	57.5	54.5	35.0	58.0	65.8
Female householder, no spouse present	8.7	7.0	6.9	5.9	8.2
Male householder, no spouse present	5.9	6.0	8.3	4.8	5.5
Nonfamily households	27.9	32.5	49.8	31.3	20.5
Female householder	13.9	14.1	21.9	13.5	8.8
Living alone	10.7	10.1	12.9	10.0	8.1
Male householder	14.1	18.4	27.9	17.8	11.7
Living alone	10.1	12.7	17.1	13.7	8.2
PERCENT DISTRIBUTION BY AGE					
Total Asian households	**100.0%**	**37.9%**	**10.3%**	**14.2%**	**13.4%**
Family households	100.0	35.5	7.2	13.5	14.8
Married couples	100.0	35.9	6.3	14.3	15.3
Female householder, no spouse present	100.0	30.5	8.2	9.6	12.7
Male householder, no spouse present	100.0	38.6	14.5	11.6	12.4
Nonfamily households	100.0	44.0	18.3	15.9	9.8
Female householder	100.0	38.4	16.2	13.8	8.5
Living alone	100.0	35.9	12.4	13.3	10.1
Male householder	100.0	49.6	20.4	18.0	11.2
Living alone	100.0	47.7	17.5	19.2	10.9

Note: Number of Asian households includes both those identifying themselves as Asian alone and those identifying themselves as Asian in combination with other races.
Source: Bureau of the Census, 2003 Current Population Survey, Annual Social and Economic Supplement, Internet site http://ferret.bls.census.gov/macro/032003/hhinc/new02_000.htm; calculations by New Strategist

Female-Headed Families Are Common among Gen X Blacks

Married couples head a minority of black households.

The majority of black householders aged 25 to 39 were family heads in 2003 (Generation Xers were aged 27 to 38 in that year), but female-headed families outnumbered married couples by a considerable margin. Female-headed families account for 38 percent of households headed by blacks aged 25 to 39, while married couples head a smaller 30 percent. Male-headed families account for only 6 percent of black households in the 25-to-39 age group.

A substantial 26 percent of black householders aged 25 to 39 head nonfamily households, meaning they live alone or with nonrelatives. One in five black householders in the age group lives alone.

■ During the past few decades, female-headed families have grown steadily as a proportion of black households. Today, black children are more likely to be raised by a single parent than by two parents.

Married couples head few black households

(percent distribution of black households headed by people aged 25 to 39, by household type, 2003)

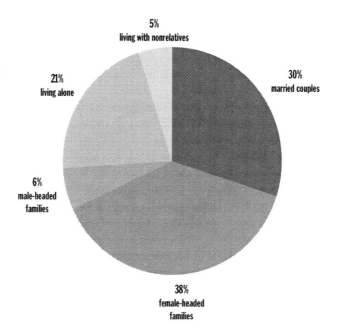

5%
living with nonrelatives

21%
living alone

30%
married couples

6%
male-headed
families

38%
female-headed
families

Table 6.4 Households Headed by People Aged 25 to 39 by Household Type, 2003: Black Households

(number and percent distribution of total households headed by blacks and households headed by blacks aged 25 to 39, by household type, 2003; numbers in thousands)

	total	aged 25 to 39 total	25 to 29	30 to 34	35 to 39
Total black households	**13,778**	**4,219**	**1,214**	**1,481**	**1,524**
Family households	9,128	3,125	880	1,091	1,154
Married couples	4,268	1,285	275	483	527
Female householder, no spouse present	4,069	1,604	528	526	550
Male householder, no spouse present	791	236	77	82	77
Nonfamily households	4,650	1,094	334	389	371
Female householder	2,550	479	151	183	145
Living alone	2,318	413	126	161	126
Male householder	2,100	615	183	206	226
Living alone	1,753	481	136	162	183
PERCENT DISTRIBUTION BY TYPE					
Total black households	**100.0%**	**100.0%**	**100.0%**	**100.0%**	**100.0%**
Family households	66.3	74.1	72.5	73.7	75.7
Married couples	31.0	30.5	22.7	32.6	34.6
Female householder, no spouse present	29.5	38.0	43.5	35.5	36.1
Male householder, no spouse present	5.7	5.6	6.3	5.5	5.1
Nonfamily households	33.7	25.9	27.5	26.3	24.3
Female householder	18.5	11.4	12.4	12.4	9.5
Living alone	16.8	9.8	10.4	10.9	8.3
Male householder	15.2	14.6	15.1	13.9	14.8
Living alone	12.7	11.4	11.2	10.9	12.0
PERCENT DISTRIBUTION BY AGE					
Total black households	**100.0%**	**30.6%**	**8.8%**	**10.7%**	**11.1%**
Family households	100.0	34.2	9.6	12.0	12.6
Married couples	100.0	30.1	6.4	11.3	12.3
Female householder, no spouse present	100.0	39.4	13.0	12.9	13.5
Male householder, no spouse present	100.0	29.8	9.7	10.4	9.7
Nonfamily households	100.0	23.5	7.2	8.4	8.0
Female householder	100.0	18.8	5.9	7.2	5.7
Living alone	100.0	17.8	5.4	6.9	5.4
Male householder	100.0	29.3	8.7	9.8	10.8
Living alone	100.0	27.4	7.8	9.2	10.4

Note: Number of black households includes both those identifying themselves as black alone and those identifying themselves as black in combination with other races.
Source: Bureau of the Census, 2003 Current Population Survey, Annual Social and Economic Supplement, Internet site http:// ferret.bls.census.gov/macro/032003/hhinc/new02_000.htm; calculations by New Strategist

Married Life Is Popular among Hispanic Gen Xers

Few Hispanic Gen Xers live alone.

Married couples accounted for the 57 percent majority of Hispanic households headed by 25-to-39-year-olds in 2003 (Generation Xers were aged 27 to 38 in that year). Even among householders aged 25 to 29, married couples are the 52 percent majority. Female-headed families account for only 18 percent of Hispanic householders aged 25 to 39, and male-headed families account for an even smaller 8 percent.

Nonfamily households are much less common among Hispanic Gen Xers than among their non-Hispanic white counterparts. Only 17 percent of Hispanic households headed by 25-to-39-year-olds are nonfamilies (meaning they live alone or with nonrelatives) versus a much larger 29 percent of non-Hispanic white households in the age group. Only 10 percent of Hispanic householders aged 25 to 39 live alone versus 20 percent of non-Hispanic whites.

■ The Hispanic population is more traditional than the non-Hispanic white population because many are immigrants from Mexico.

Among Hispanic Gen Xers, most householders are married couples

(percent distribution of households headed by Hispanics aged 25 to 39, by household type, 2003)

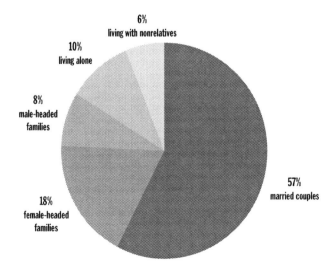

Table 6.5 **Households Headed by People Aged 25 to 39 by Household Type, 2003: Hispanic Households**

(number and percent distribution of total households headed by Hispanics and households headed by Hispanics aged 25 to 39, by household type, 2003; numbers in thousands)

			aged 25 to 39		
	total	total	25 to 29	30 to 34	35 to 39
Total Hispanic households	**11,339**	**4,605**	**1,368**	**1,612**	**1,625**
Family households	9,090	3,841	1,101	1,331	1,409
Married couples	6,189	2,639	715	930	994
Female householder, no spouse present	2,029	822	248	270	304
Male householder, no spouse present	872	381	139	131	111
Nonfamily households	2,249	765	267	282	216
Female householder	1,021	231	92	79	60
Living alone	791	162	56	58	48
Male householder	1,228	533	174	203	156
Living alone	809	318	91	117	110
PERCENT DISTRIBUTION BY TYPE					
Total Hispanic households	**100.0%**	**100.0%**	**100.0%**	**100.0%**	**100.0%**
Family households	80.2	83.4	80.5	82.6	86.7
Married couples	54.6	57.3	52.3	57.7	61.2
Female householder, no spouse present	17.9	17.9	18.1	16.7	18.7
Male householder, no spouse present	7.7	8.3	10.2	8.1	6.8
Nonfamily households	19.8	16.6	19.5	17.5	13.3
Female householder	9.0	5.0	6.7	4.9	3.7
Living alone	7.0	3.5	4.1	3.6	3.0
Male householder	10.8	11.6	12.7	12.6	9.6
Living alone	7.1	6.9	6.7	7.3	6.8
PERCENT DISTRIBUTION BY AGE					
Total Hispanic households	**100.0%**	**40.6%**	**12.1%**	**14.2%**	**14.3%**
Family households	100.0	42.3	12.1	14.6	15.5
Married couples	100.0	42.6	11.6	15.0	16.1
Female householder, no spouse present	100.0	40.5	12.2	13.3	15.0
Male householder, no spouse present	100.0	43.7	15.9	15.0	12.7
Nonfamily households	100.0	34.0	11.9	12.5	9.6
Female householder	100.0	22.6	9.0	7.7	5.9
Living alone	100.0	20.5	7.1	7.3	6.1
Male householder	100.0	43.4	14.2	16.5	12.7
Living alone	100.0	39.3	11.2	14.5	13.6

Source: Bureau of the Census, 2003 Current Population Survey, Annual Social and Economic Supplement, Internet site http:// ferret.bls.census.gov/macro/032003/hhinc/new02_000.htm; calculations by New Strategist

Many Non-Hispanic White Gen Xers Live Alone

Married couples account for the majority of their households, however.

Married couples accounted for the 57 percent majority of non-Hispanic white household-ers aged 25 to 39 in 2003 (Generation Xers were aged 27 to 38 in that year). But many in the age group live alone—especially among those still in their twenties. Nearly one in four non-Hispanic white householders aged 25 to 29 lives by him or herself. The proportion drops with age, but even among 35-to-39-year-olds a substantial 18 percent live alone.

Female-headed families accounted for only 11 percent of households headed by non-Hispanic whites in the 25-to-39 age group. This figure is far below the 38 percent female-headed family share among blacks and the 18 percent share among Hispanics in the age group. It exceeds the 7 percent share among Asians, however.

■ Married couples account for the 47 percent minority of non-Hispanic white household-ers aged 25-to-29. The figure rises to the 61 percent majority among 35-to-39-year-olds as marriage and family become priorities.

Although married couples head the majority of households, many non-Hispanic white Gen Xers live alone

(percent distribution of households headed by non-Hispanic whites aged 25 to 39, by household type, 2003)

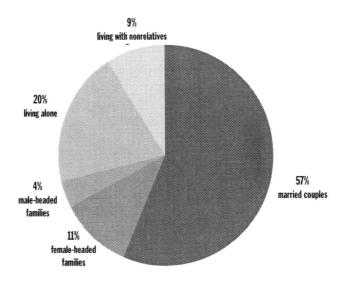

Table 6.6 Households Headed by People Aged 25 to 39 by Household Type, 2003: Non-Hispanic White Households

(number and percent distribution of total households headed by non-Hispanic whites and households headed by non-Hispanic whites aged 25 to 39, by household type, 2003; numbers in thousands)

		aged 25 to 39			
	total	total	25 to 29	30 to 34	35 to 39
Total non-Hispanic white households	**81,166**	**19,949**	**5,465**	**6,782**	**7,702**
Family households	53,845	14,232	3,427	4,913	5,892
Married couples	44,101	11,305	2,589	3,998	4,718
Female householder, no spouse present	7,070	2,155	584	663	908
Male householder, no spouse present	2,674	771	253	252	266
Nonfamily households	27,321	5,717	2,038	1,869	1,810
Female householder	15,353	2,265	875	708	682
Living alone	13,233	1,622	541	532	549
Male householder	11,968	3,452	1,163	1,161	1,128
Living alone	9,421	2,370	709	823	838
PERCENT DISTRIBUTION BY TYPE					
Total non-Hispanic white households	**100.0%**	**100.0%**	**100.0%**	**100.0%**	**100.0%**
Family households	66.3	71.3	62.7	72.4	76.5
Married couples	54.3	56.7	47.4	59.0	61.3
Female householder, no spouse present	8.7	10.8	10.7	9.8	11.8
Male householder, no spouse present	3.3	3.9	4.6	3.7	3.5
Nonfamily households	33.7	28.7	37.3	27.6	23.5
Female householder	18.9	11.4	16.0	10.4	8.9
Living alone	16.3	8.1	9.9	7.8	7.1
Male householder	14.7	17.3	21.3	17.1	14.6
Living alone	11.6	11.9	13.0	12.1	10.9
PERCENT DISTRIBUTION BY AGE					
Total non-Hispanic white households	**100.0%**	**24.6%**	**6.7%**	**8.4%**	**9.5%**
Family households	100.0	26.4	6.4	9.1	10.9
Married couples	100.0	25.6	5.9	9.1	10.7
Female householder, no spouse present	100.0	30.5	8.3	9.4	12.8
Male householder, no spouse present	100.0	28.8	9.5	9.4	9.9
Nonfamily households	100.0	20.9	7.5	6.8	6.6
Female householder	100.0	14.8	5.7	4.6	4.4
Living alone	100.0	12.3	4.1	4.0	4.1
Male householder	100.0	28.8	9.7	9.7	9.4
Living alone	100.0	25.2	7.5	8.7	8.9

Note: Number of non-Hispanic white households includes only those identifying themselves as white alone and non-Hispanic.
Source: Bureau of the Census, 2003 Current Population Survey, Annual Social and Economic Supplement, Internet site http://ferret.bls.census.gov/macro/032003/hhinc/new02_000.htm; calculations by New Strategist

Gen X Households Are Growing

Household size peaks in the 35-to-39 age group.

The average American household was home to 2.58 people in 2002. Household size grows as householders age through their twenties and into their thirties. It peaks among householders aged 35 to 39—at 3.29 people—because this age group is most likely to have at least one child at home. As householders age into their forties, the nest empties and household size shrinks.

Households headed by Gen Xers (aged 26 to 37 in 2002) are growing as they marry and have children. The average household headed by a 25-to-29-year-old has fewer than one child in the home. But the average household headed by a 30-to-34-year-old has more than one child as they enter the crowded nest stage of life. Householders aged 35 to 39 have an average of 1.42 children in the home.

■ Generation Xers are marrying, having children, buying houses, and taking on the responsibilities of home and family.

The nest is emptying for householders in their thirties

(average household size by age of householder, 2002)

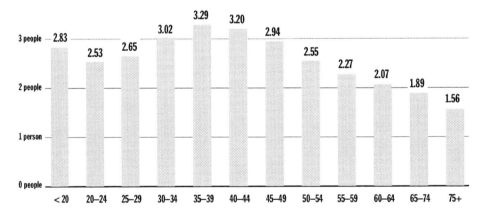

Table 6.7 Average Size of Household by Age of Householder, 2002

(number of households, average number of people per household, and average number of people under age 18 per household, by age of householder, 2002; numbers in thousands)

	number	average number of people	average number of people under age 18
Total households	**109,297**	**2.58**	**0.66**
Under age 20	907	2.83	0.80
Aged 20 to 24	5,484	2.53	0.58
Aged 25 to 29	8,412	2.65	0.86
Aged 30 to 34	10,576	3.02	1.22
Aged 35 to 39	11,599	3.29	1.42
Aged 40 to 44	12,432	3.20	1.20
Aged 45 to 49	11,754	2.94	0.78
Aged 50 to 54	10,455	2.55	0.39
Aged 55 to 59	8,611	2.27	0.20
Aged 60 to 64	6,592	2.07	0.14
Aged 65 to 74	11,472	1.89	0.09
Aged 75 or older	11,004	1.56	0.03

Source: Bureau of the Census, 2002 Current Population Survey Annual Demographic Supplement, http://www.census.gov/population/www/socdemo/hh-fam/cps2002.html

The Majority of Gen Xers Have Children at Home

Female-headed families are most likely to have children.

More than half the households headed by people aged 25 to 34 (Generation X was aged 26 to 37 in 2002) include children under age 18. The proportion with children rises from the 45 percent minority of those aged 25 to 29 to the 59 percent majority of those aged 30 to 34.

Seventy-two percent of married couples aged 25 to 34 have children at home. Families headed by women are even more likely to have children, at 92 percent. Among families headed by men, a smaller 58 percent include children under age 18.

■ The presence of children drives the spending of households headed by 25-to-34-year-olds, especially those headed by married couples and women without a spouse.

Male-headed families are least likely to have children at home

(percent of households headed by people aged 25 to 34 with children under age 18 at home, 2002)

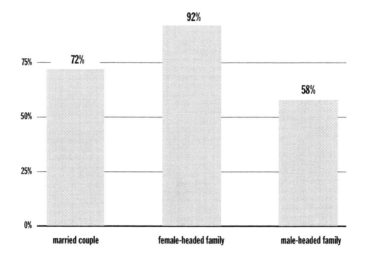

Table 6.8 Households by Type, Age of Householder, and Presence of Children, 2002: Total Households

(total number of households and number and percent with own children under age 18 at home, by household type and age of householder, 2002; numbers in thousands)

	total	with children under age 18	
		number	percent
Total households	**109,297**	**35,705**	**32.7%**
Under age 25	6,391	2,026	31.7
Aged 25 to 34	18,988	9,990	52.6
Aged 25 to 29	8,412	3,789	45.0
Aged 30 to 34	10,576	6,201	58.6
Aged 35 to 39	11,599	7,716	66.5
Aged 40 to 44	12,432	7,433	59.8
Aged 45 to 54	22,208	7,438	33.5
Aged 55 to 64	15,203	923	6.1
Aged 65 or older	22,476	180	0.8
Married couples	**56,747**	**25,792**	**45.5**
Under age 25	1,535	887	57.8
Aged 25 to 34	9,385	6,795	72.4
Aged 25 to 29	3,620	2,365	65.3
Aged 30 to 34	5,765	4,430	76.8
Aged 35 to 39	6,804	5,707	83.9
Aged 40 to 44	7,374	5,678	77.0
Aged 45 to 54	13,137	5,839	44.4
Aged 55 to 64	8,922	744	8.3
Aged 65 or older	9,591	141	1.5
Female householder, no spouse present	**13,143**	**8,010**	**60.9**
Under age 25	1,359	964	70.9
Aged 25 to 34	2,854	2,627	92.1
Aged 25 to 29	1,313	1,180	89.9
Aged 30 to 34	1,541	1,447	93.9
Aged 35 to 39	1,828	1,666	91.1
Aged 40 to 44	1,768	1,401	79.2
Aged 45 to 54	2,530	1,218	48.1
Aged 55 to 64	1,188	105	8.8
Aged 65 or older	1,616	29	1.8
Male householder, no spouse present	**4,438**	**1,903**	**42.9**
Under age 25	724	175	24.2
Aged 25 to 34	976	569	58.3
Aged 25 to 29	489	245	50.1
Aged 30 to 34	487	324	66.5
Aged 35 to 39	492	342	69.5
Aged 40 to 44	553	354	64.0
Aged 45 to 54	873	381	43.6
Aged 55 to 64	389	74	19.0
Aged 65 or older	431	10	2.3

Source: Bureau of the Census, Children's Living Arrangements and Characteristics: March 2002, Detailed Tables, *Internet site http://www.census.gov/population/www/socdemo/hh-fam/cps2002.html; calculations by New Strategist*

Hispanic Gen Xers Are Most Likely to Have Children

Households headed by Asian Gen Xers are least likely to include children.

More than two-thirds of Hispanic households headed by 25-to-34-year-olds include children under age 18. The proportion is a slightly smaller 63 percent among black households in the age group. For non-Hispanic whites, a 48 percent minority of households headed by 25-to-34-year-olds include children. Among Asian householders in the age group, just 37 percent have children in their home. Hispanics and blacks become parents at a younger age than non-Hispanic whites or Asians, in part because non-Hispanic whites and Asians are more likely to go to college and postpone childbearing.

Regardless of race, the majority of households headed by married couples aged 25 to 34 include children under age 18, with the proportion ranging from 65 percent among Asians to 86 percent among Hispanics. The same is true for families headed by women, with the proportion that have children ranging from just 51 percent among Asians to fully 94 percent among blacks.

■ Because blacks and Hispanics have children at a younger age than non-Hispanic whites or Asians, there are important lifestyle differences by race and Hispanic origin among adults in their twenties and thirties.

Asians are most likely to delay childbearing

(percent of households headed by people aged 25 to 34 with children under age 18 at home, by race and Hispanic origin, 2002)

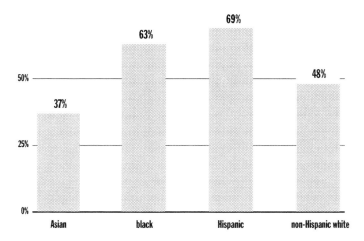

Table 6.9 Households by Type, Age of Householder, and Presence of Children, 2002: Asian Households

(total number of Asian households and number and percent with own children under age 18 at home, by household type and age of householder, 2002; numbers in thousands)

	total	with children under age 18	
		number	percent
Total Asian households	**4,071**	**1,582**	**38.9%**
Under age 25	327	37	11.3
Aged 25 to 34	999	369	36.9
Aged 25 to 29	426	95	22.3
Aged 30 to 34	573	274	47.8
Aged 35 to 39	513	349	68.0
Aged 40 to 44	498	325	65.3
Aged 45 to 54	879	444	50.5
Aged 55 to 64	436	45	10.3
Aged 65 or older	419	14	3.3
Married couples	**2,378**	**1,362**	**57.3**
Under age 25	58	22	37.9
Aged 25 to 34	493	321	65.1
Aged 25 to 29	141	81	57.4
Aged 30 to 34	352	240	68.2
Aged 35 to 39	351	287	81.8
Aged 40 to 44	334	288	86.2
Aged 45 to 54	627	392	62.5
Aged 55 to 64	301	40	13.3
Aged 65 or older	214	13	6.1
Female householder, no spouse present	**415**	**190**	**45.8**
Under age 25	53	14	26.4
Aged 25 to 34	78	40	51.3
Aged 25 to 29	40	12	30.0
Aged 30 to 34	38	28	73.7
Aged 35 to 39	65	55	84.6
Aged 40 to 44	47	32	68.1
Aged 45 to 54	81	43	53.1
Aged 55 to 64	43	4	9.3
Aged 65 or older	49	–	–
Male householder, no spouse present	**187**	**30**	**16.0**
Under age 25	44	1	2.3
Aged 25 to 34	58	9	15.5
Aged 25 to 29	38	3	7.9
Aged 30 to 34	20	6	30.0
Aged 35 to 39	16	7	43.8
Aged 40 to 44	21	4	19.1
Aged 45 to 54	27	9	33.3
Aged 55 to 64	11	1	9.1
Aged 65 or older	11	–	–

Note: (–) means number is less than 500 or sample is too small to make a reliable estimate.
Source: Bureau of the Census, Children's Living Arrangements and Characteristics: March 2002, Detailed Tables. Internet site http://www.census.gov/population/www/socdemo/hh-fam/cps2002.html; calculations by New Strategist

Table 6.10 Households by Type, Age of Householder, and Presence of Children, 2002: Black Households

(total number of black households and number and percent with own children under age 18 at home, by household type and age of householder, 2002; numbers in thousands)

	total	with children under age 18 number	with children under age 18 percent
Total black households	**13,315**	**5,065**	**38.0%**
Under age 25	1,109	540	48.7
Aged 25 to 34	2,655	1,674	63.1
Aged 25 to 29	1,185	734	61.9
Aged 30 to 34	1,470	940	63.9
Aged 35 to 39	1,583	1,016	64.2
Aged 40 to 44	1,603	902	56.3
Aged 45 to 54	2,739	787	28.7
Aged 55 to 64	1,648	113	6.9
Aged 65 or older	1,976	33	1.7
Married couples	**4,233**	**2,148**	**50.7**
Under age 25	141	91	64.5
Aged 25 to 34	769	610	79.3
Aged 25 to 29	278	225	80.9
Aged 30 to 34	491	385	78.4
Aged 35 to 39	572	471	82.3
Aged 40 to 44	599	471	78.6
Aged 45 to 54	970	419	43.2
Aged 55 to 64	577	64	11.1
Aged 65 or older	606	22	3.6
Female householder, no spouse present	**3,838**	**2,593**	**67.6**
Under age 25	498	409	82.1
Aged 25 to 34	1,029	970	94.3
Aged 25 to 29	493	459	93.1
Aged 30 to 34	536	511	95.3
Aged 35 to 39	545	494	90.6
Aged 40 to 44	495	370	74.7
Aged 45 to 54	650	307	47.2
Aged 55 to 64	315	33	10.5
Aged 65 or older	307	10	3.3
Male householder, no spouse present	**773**	**324**	**41.9**
Under age 25	129	40	31.0
Aged 25 to 34	158	94	59.5
Aged 25 to 29	87	50	57.5
Aged 30 to 34	71	44	62.0
Aged 35 to 39	88	52	59.1
Aged 40 to 44	103	60	58.3
Aged 45 to 54	147	61	41.5
Aged 55 to 64	75	16	21.3
Aged 65 or older	73	1	1.4

Source: Bureau of the Census, Children's Living Arrangements and Characteristics: March 2002, Detailed Tables, Internet site http://www.census.gov/population/www/socdemo/hh-fam/cps2002.html; calculations by New Strategist

Table 6.11 Households by Type, Age of Householder, and Presence of Children, 2002: Hispanic Households

(total number of Hispanic households and number and percent with own children under age 18 at home, by household type and age of householder, 2002; numbers in thousands)

	total	with children under age 18	
		number	percent
Total Hispanic households	**10,499**	**5,343**	**50.9%**
Under age 25	1,036	487	47.0
Aged 25 to 34	2,957	2,027	68.5
Aged 25 to 29	1,353	860	63.6
Aged 30 to 34	1,604	1,167	72.8
Aged 35 to 39	1,410	1,076	76.3
Aged 40 to 44	1,265	856	67.7
Aged 45 to 54	1,748	756	43.2
Aged 55 to 64	1,020	108	10.6
Aged 65 or older	1,062	32	3.0
Married couples	**5,778**	**3,754**	**65.0**
Under age 25	353	267	75.6
Aged 25 to 34	1,662	1,423	85.6
Aged 25 to 29	689	574	83.3
Aged 30 to 34	973	849	87.3
Aged 35 to 39	887	789	89.0
Aged 40 to 44	743	603	81.2
Aged 45 to 54	1,046	566	54.1
Aged 55 to 64	590	85	14.4
Aged 65 or older	497	21	4.2
Female householder, no spouse present	**1,922**	**1,259**	**65.5**
Under age 25	251	175	69.7
Aged 25 to 34	427	372	87.1
Aged 25 to 29	190	158	83.2
Aged 30 to 34	237	214	90.3
Aged 35 to 39	269	243	90.3
Aged 40 to 44	270	210	77.8
Aged 45 to 54	322	150	46.6
Aged 55 to 64	161	17	10.6
Aged 65 or older	143	6	4.2
Male householder, no spouse present	**817**	**330**	**40.4**
Under age 25	207	44	21.3
Aged 25 to 34	283	148	52.3
Aged 25 to 29	161	72	44.7
Aged 30 to 34	122	76	62.3
Aged 35 to 39	90	44	48.9
Aged 40 to 44	76	43	56.6
Aged 45 to 54	91	40	44.0
Aged 55 to 64	39	5	12.8
Aged 65 or older	31	4	12.9

Source: Bureau of the Census, Children's Living Arrangements and Characteristics: March 2002, Detailed Tables, *Internet site http://www.census.gov/population/www/socdemo/hh-fam/cps2002.html; calculations by New Strategist*

Table 6.12 Households by Type, Age of Householder, and Presence of Children, 2002: Non-Hispanic White Households

(total number of non-Hispanic white households and number and percent with own children under age 18 at home, by household type and age of householder, 2002; numbers in thousands)

	total	with children under age 18	
		number	percent
Total non-Hispanic white households	**80,818**	**23,532**	**29.1%**
Under age 25	3,885	954	24.6
Aged 25 to 34	12,321	5,889	47.8
Aged 25 to 29	5,421	2,084	38.4
Aged 30 to 34	6,900	3,805	55.1
Aged 35 to 39	8,006	5,226	65.3
Aged 40 to 44	8,995	5,319	59.1
Aged 45 to 54	16,676	5,395	32.4
Aged 55 to 64	12,010	652	5.4
Aged 65 or older	18,925	99	0.5
Married couples	**44,117**	**18,415**	**41.7**
Under age 25	978	503	51.4
Aged 25 to 34	6,431	4,422	68.8
Aged 25 to 29	2,494	1,475	59.1
Aged 30 to 34	3,937	2,947	74.9
Aged 35 to 39	4,962	4,135	83.3
Aged 40 to 44	5,660	4,292	75.8
Aged 45 to 54	10,420	4,429	42.5
Aged 55 to 64	7,414	552	7.4
Aged 65 or older	8,252	83	0.1
Female householder, no spouse present	**6,884**	**3,927**	**57.1**
Under age 25	558	365	65.4
Aged 25 to 34	1,241	1,158	93.3
Aged 25 to 29	539	492	91.3
Aged 30 to 34	702	666	94.9
Aged 35 to 39	932	859	92.2
Aged 40 to 44	946	781	82.6
Aged 45 to 54	1,455	704	48.4
Aged 55 to 64	658	49	7.4
Aged 65 or older	1,094	12	1.1
Male householder, no spouse present	**2,618**	**1,190**	**45.5**
Under age 25	342	85	24.9
Aged 25 to 34	472	308	65.3
Aged 25 to 29	205	117	57.1
Aged 30 to 34	267	191	71.5
Aged 35 to 39	292	232	79.5
Aged 40 to 44	348	246	70.7
Aged 45 to 54	594	262	44.1
Aged 55 to 64	253	52	20.6
Aged 65 or older	315	4	1.3

Source: Bureau of the Census, Children's Living Arrangements and Characteristics: March 2002, Detailed Tables, *Internet site http://www.census.gov/population/www/socdemo/hh-fam/cps2002.html; calculations by New Strategist*

Many Households Headed by Gen Xers include Preschoolers

Gen Xers head more than half of all households with infants.

During their twenties and early thirties, most people become parents. Only 32 percent of householders under age 25 have children under age 18 at home. The proportion rises to the 53 percent majority in the 25-to-34 age group.

Among householders aged 25 to 34, 8 percent—or about one in 12—have infants under age 1 at home. This age group accounts for the 54 percent majority of all households with infants. The proportion of households with preschoolers (under age 6) peaks at 39 percent in the 30-to-34 age group. The proportion with school-aged children (aged 6 to 17) rises from 22 percent among householders aged 25 to 29 to 38 percent of those aged 30 to 34. The majority of householders aged 35 to 44 have school-aged children at home.

■ As people have children, their priorities shift from pursuing their own wants and needs to meeting the needs of their children.

Children are the norm for householders aged 25 to 34

(percent of households headed by people aged 25 to 34 with children at home, by age of child, 2002)

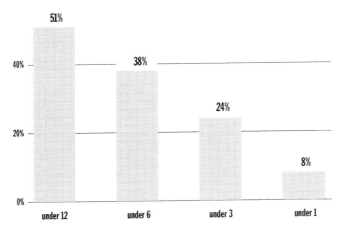

Table 6.13 Households by Presence and Age of Children and Age of Householder, 2002

(number and percent distribution of total households and households with children at home, by age of children and age of householder, 2002; numbers in thousands)

	total	under 25	aged 25 to 34 total	25 to 29	30 to 34	35 to 39	40 to 44	45 or older
Total households	**109,297**	**6,391**	**18,988**	**8,412**	**10,576**	**11,599**	**12,432**	**59,887**
With children of any age	45,812	2,047	10,048	3,816	6,232	7,883	8,212	17,621
Under age 25	40,967	2,045	10,031	3,806	6,225	7,873	8,163	12,855
Under age 18	35,705	2,026	9,990	3,789	6,201	7,716	7,433	8,541
Under age 12	26,376	2,010	9,615	3,741	5,874	6,343	4,885	3,525
Under age 6	15,376	1,922	7,178	3,058	4,120	3,493	1,820	962
Under age 3	8,909	1,446	4,575	2,047	2,528	1,789	750	349
Under age 1	2,958	528	1,608	783	825	505	220	95
Aged 6 to 17	27,438	356	5,874	1,874	4,000	6,355	6,779	8,076

PERCENT DISTRIBUTION BY AGE OF CHILD

Total households	**100.0%**	**100.0%**	**100.0%**	**100.0%**	**100.0%**	**100.0%**	**100.0%**	**100.0%**
With children of any age	41.9	32.0	52.9	45.4	58.9	68.0	66.1	29.4
Under age 25	37.5	32.0	52.8	45.2	58.9	67.9	65.7	21.5
Under age 18	32.7	31.7	52.6	45.0	58.6	66.5	59.8	14.3
Under age 12	24.1	31.5	50.6	44.5	55.5	54.7	39.3	5.9
Under age 6	14.1	30.1	37.8	36.4	39.0	30.1	14.6	1.6
Under age 3	8.2	22.6	24.1	24.3	23.9	15.4	6.0	0.6
Under age 1	2.7	8.3	8.5	9.3	7.8	4.4	1.8	0.2
Aged 6 to 17	25.1	5.6	30.9	22.3	37.8	54.8	54.5	13.5

PERCENT DISTRIBUTION BY AGE OF HOUSEHOLDER

Total households	**100.0%**	**5.8%**	**17.4%**	**7.7%**	**9.7%**	**10.6%**	**11.4%**	**54.8%**
With children of any age	100.0	4.5	21.9	8.3	13.6	17.2	17.9	38.5
Under age 25	100.0	5.0	24.5	9.3	15.2	19.2	19.9	31.4
Under age 18	100.0	5.7	28.0	10.6	17.4	21.6	20.8	23.9
Under age 12	100.0	7.6	36.5	14.2	22.3	24.1	18.5	13.4
Under age 6	100.0	12.5	46.7	19.9	26.8	22.7	11.8	6.3
Under age 3	100.0	16.2	51.4	23.0	28.4	20.1	8.4	3.9
Under age 1	100.0	17.8	54.4	26.5	27.9	17.1	7.4	3.2
Aged 6 to 17	100.0	1.3	21.4	6.8	14.6	23.2	24.7	29.4

Source: Bureau of the Census, Children's Living Arrangements and Characteristics: March 2002, *Detailed Tables, Internet site http://www.census.gov/population/www/socdemo/hh-fam/cps2002.html; calculations by New Strategist*

Two-Child Families Are Most Common

Many Gen X couples have more than two children, however.

Smaller families have been growing in popularity for decades. Most Americans now consider two children the ideal number. But many Gen X couples have three or more children. Among households headed by married couples aged 25 to 34, 26 percent have one child under age 18, 30 percent have two, and 17 percent have three or more.

Among couples aged 25 to 29, the largest share (35 percent) do not yet have children. Twenty-seven percent have one child under age 18 at home, a smaller 25 percent have two, and 13 percent have three or more. Among couples aged 30 to 34, only 23 percent have no children in the household. The largest share (32 percent) have two children and a substantial 20 percent have three or more.

■ The percentage of couples with three or more children peaks in the 35-to-39 age group at 25 percent.

Most Gen X couples have one or two children

(percent of married couples aged 25 to 34, by number of children under age 18 at home, 2002)

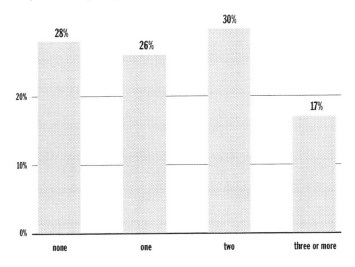

Table 6.14 Married Couples by Presence and Number of Children and Age of Householder, 2002

(number and percent distribution of married couples by presence and number of own children under age 18 at home, by age of householder, 2002; numbers in thousands)

	total	under 25	aged 25 to 34 total	25 to 29	30 to 34	35 to 39	40 to 44	45 to 54	55 to 64
Total married couples	**56,747**	**1,535**	**9,385**	**3,620**	**5,765**	**6,804**	**7,374**	**13,137**	**18,513**
Without children under18	30,955	648	2,590	1,255	1,335	1,096	1,695	7,298	17,627
With children under 18	25,792	887	6,795	2,365	4,430	5,707	5,678	5,839	885
One	9,832	502	2,415	992	1,423	1,401	1,767	3,122	624
Two	10,440	282	2,787	915	1,872	2,613	2,592	1,969	197
Three	4,058	74	1,183	341	842	1,216	958	582	46
Four or more	1,461	29	410	117	293	477	361	166	19
PERCENT DISTRIBUTION BY NUMBER OF CHILDREN									
Total married couples	**100.0%**	**100.0%**	**100.0%**	**100.0%**	**100.0%**	**100.0%**	**100.0%**	**100.0%**	**100.0%**
Without children under18	54.5	42.2	27.6	34.7	23.2	16.1	23.0	55.6	95.2
With children under 18	45.5	57.8	72.4	65.3	76.8	83.9	77.0	44.4	4.8
One	17.3	32.7	25.7	27.4	24.7	20.6	24.0	23.8	3.4
Two	18.4	18.4	29.7	25.3	32.5	38.4	35.2	15.0	1.1
Three	7.2	4.8	12.6	9.4	14.6	17.9	13.0	4.4	0.2
Four or more	2.6	1.9	4.4	3.2	5.1	7.0	4.9	1.3	0.1

Source: Bureau of the Census, Children's Living Arrangements and Characteristics: March 2002, Detailed Tables, *Internet site http://www.census.gov/population/www/socdemo/hh-fam/cps2002.html; calculations by New Strategist*

Most Female-Headed Families include Children

Male-headed families are much less likely to include children.

Most Gen X women who head families without a spouse are single mothers. Among female family householders aged 25 to 34, only 8 percent head families that do not include children under age 18. Among male family heads aged 25 to 34, a much smaller 58 percent have children under age 18 at home. The remaining 42 percent live with other relatives, such as siblings or parents.

Among women aged 25 to 34 who head families, the largest share (35 percent) have one child living with them, 33 percent have two, and a substantial 24 percent have three or more. Among their male counterparts, 36 percent have one child, 18 percent have two, and just 5 percent have three or more.

■ Single-parent families have less flexibility in choosing jobs since they need work that meshes with their children's schedules.

Many female-headed families headed by Gen Xers include three or more children

(percent distribution of female-headed families headed by people aged 25 to 34, by number of children under age 18 age home, 2002)

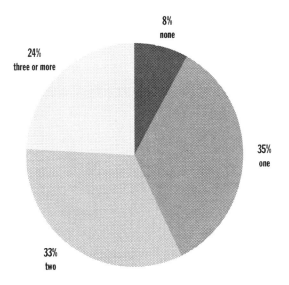

Table 6.15 Female-Headed Families by Presence and Number of Children and Age of Householder, 2002

(number and percent distribution of female-headed families by presence and number of own children under age 18 at home, by age of householder, 2002; numbers in thousands)

	total	under 25	aged 25 to 34 total	25 to 29	30 to 34	35 to 39	40 to 44	45 to 54	55 to 64
Total female-headed families	**13,143**	**1,359**	**2,854**	**1,313**	**1,541**	**1,828**	**1,768**	**2,530**	**2,805**
Without children under18	5,133	395	227	133	94	162	367	1,312	2,671
With children under 18	8,010	964	2,627	1,180	1,447	1,666	1,401	1,218	134
One	3,967	597	1,012	476	536	695	751	803	109
Two	2,580	241	931	426	505	598	467	326	17
Three	1,085	112	470	189	281	275	144	78	7
Four or more	378	13	215	90	125	99	39	12	2

PERCENT DISTRIBUTION BY NUMBER OF CHILDREN

	total	under 25	aged 25 to 34 total	25 to 29	30 to 34	35 to 39	40 to 44	45 to 54	55 to 64
Total female-headed families	**100.0%**	**100.0%**	**100.0%**	**100.0%**	**100.0%**	**100.0%**	**100.0%**	**100.0%**	**100.0%**
Without children under18	39.1	29.1	8.0	10.1	6.1	8.9	20.8	51.9	95.2
With children under 18	60.9	70.9	92.1	89.9	93.9	91.1	79.2	48.1	4.8
One	30.2	43.9	35.5	36.3	34.8	38.0	42.5	31.7	3.9
Two	19.6	17.7	32.6	32.4	32.8	32.7	26.4	12.9	0.6
Three	8.3	8.2	16.5	14.4	18.2	15.0	8.1	3.1	0.2
Four or more	2.9	1.0	7.5	6.9	8.1	5.4	2.2	0.5	0.1

Source: Bureau of the Census, Children's Living Arrangements and Characteristics: March 2002, Detailed Tables, *Internet site http://www.census.gov/population/www/socdemo/hh-fam/cps2002.html; calculations by New Strategist*

Table 6.16 Male-Headed Families by Presence and Number of Children and Age of Householder, 2002

(number and percent distribution of male-headed families by presence and number of own children under age 18 at home, by age of householder, 2002; numbers in thousands)

	total	under 25	aged 25 to 34 total	25 to 29	30 to 34	35 to 39	40 to 44	45 to 54	55 to 64
Total male-headed families	**4,438**	**724**	**976**	**489**	**487**	**492**	**553**	**873**	**820**
Without children under18	2,535	548	407	244	163	150	199	493	738
With children under 18	1,903	175	569	245	324	342	354	381	84
One	1,162	128	347	163	184	159	197	271	61
Two	538	32	172	65	107	123	105	91	15
Three	157	12	42	16	26	44	38	13	8
Four or more	45	3	8	2	6	16	13	5	–
PERCENT DISTRIBUTION BY NUMBER OF CHILDREN									
Total male-headed families	**100.0%**	**100.0%**	**100.0%**	**100.0%**	**100.0%**	**100.0%**	**100.0%**	**100.0%**	**100.0%**
Without children under18	57.1	75.7	41.7	49.9	33.5	30.5	36.0	56.5	90.0
With children under 18	42.9	24.2	58.3	50.1	66.5	69.5	64.0	43.6	10.2
One	26.2	17.7	35.6	33.3	37.8	32.3	35.6	31.0	7.4
Two	12.1	4.4	17.6	13.3	22.0	25.0	19.0	10.4	1.8
Three	3.5	1.7	4.3	3.3	5.3	8.9	6.9	1.5	1.0
Four or more	1.0	0.4	0.8	0.4	1.2	3.3	2.4	0.6	–

Note: (–) means number is less than 500 or sample is too small to make a reliable estimate.
Source: Bureau of the Census, Children's Living Arrangements and Characteristics: March 2002, *Detailed Tables, Internet site http://www.census.gov/population/www/socdemo/hh-fam/cps2002.html; calculations by New Strategist*

The Living Arrangements of Gen Xers Are Changing

Most men and women live with a spouse by their early thirties.

The majority of men and women aged 25 to 39 were living with a spouse in 2002 (Generation Xers were aged 26 to 37 in that year). But there are dramatic differences in living arrangements within the age group. Among 25–to-29-year-olds, only 37 percent of men and 47 percent of women live with a spouse. In the 30-to-34 age group, the proportions rise to the 54 and 61 percent majorities, respectively.

A large share of men and women aged 25 to 29 live alone or with nonrelatives—32 percent of men and 22 percent of women. These figures fall to 21 and 12 percent, respectively, among 35-to-39-year-olds. Fully 18 percent of men and 11 percent of women aged 25 to 29 still live with their parents. By the 35-to-39 age group, only 7 percent of men and 4 percent of women still live with mom and dad.

■ Women establish their own households sooner than men because they marry at a younger age.

Gen Xers are in transition

(percent of people aged 25 to 39 who live with a spouse, by age and sex, 2002)

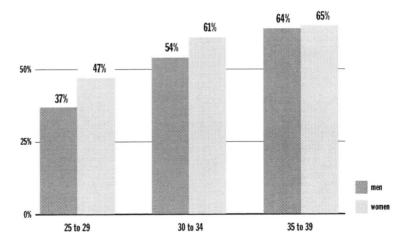

Table 6.17 Living Arrangements of Men Aged 25 to 39, 2002

(number and percent distribution of men aged 15 or older and aged 25 to 39 by living arrangement, 2002; numbers in thousands)

		aged 25 to 39			
	total	total	25 to 29	30 to 34	35 to 39
Total men	**106,819**	**29,913**	**9,141**	**10,079**	**10,693**
In family household	84,724	21,983	6,176	7,374	8,433
Living with spouse	56,747	15,671	3,374	5,489	6,808
Other family householder	4,439	1,467	489	487	491
Living with parents	18,077	3,380	1,649	961	770
Other family member	5,461	1,465	664	437	364
In nonfamily household	22,096	7,932	2,966	2,705	2,261
Living alone	12,004	3,553	1,088	1,234	1,231
Living with nonrelatives	10,092	4,379	1,878	1,471	1,030
PERCENT DISTRIBUTION BY LIVING ARRANGEMENT					
Total men	**100.0%**	**100.0%**	**100.0%**	**100.0%**	**100.0%**
In family household	79.3	73.5	67.6	73.2	78.9
Living with spouse	53.1	52.4	36.9	54.5	63.7
Other family householder	4.2	4.9	5.3	4.8	4.6
Living with parents	16.9	11.3	18.0	9.5	7.2
Other family member	5.1	4.9	7.3	4.3	3.4
In nonfamily household	20.7	26.5	32.4	26.8	21.1
Living alone	11.2	11.9	11.9	12.2	11.5
Living with nonrelatives	9.4	14.6	20.5	14.6	9.6
PERCENT DISTRIBUTION BY AGE					
Total men	**100.0%**	**28.0%**	**8.6%**	**9.4%**	**10.0%**
In family household	100.0	25.9	7.3	8.7	10.0
Living with spouse	100.0	27.6	5.9	9.7	12.0
Other family householder	100.0	33.1	11.0	11.0	11.1
Living with parents	100.0	18.7	9.1	5.3	4.3
Other family member	100.0	26.8	12.2	8.0	6.7
In nonfamily household	100.0	35.9	13.4	12.2	10.2
Living alone	100.0	29.6	9.1	10.3	10.3
Living with nonrelatives	100.0	43.4	18.6	14.6	10.2

Source: Bureau of the Census, 2002 Current Population Survey Annual Demographic Supplement, Internet site http://www.census.gov/population/www/socdemo/hh-fam/cps2002.html; calculations by New Strategist

Table 6.18 Living Arrangements of Women Aged 25 to 39, 2002

(number and percent distribution of women aged 15 or older and aged 25 to 39 by living arrangement, 2002; numbers in thousands)

	total	aged 25 to 39			
		total	25 to 29	30 to 34	35 to 39
Total women	**114,639**	**30,375**	**9,158**	**10,270**	**10,947**
In family household	90,451	25,534	7,116	8,744	9,674
Living with spouse	56,747	17,700	4,295	6,301	7,104
Other family householder	13,143	4,682	1,313	1,541	1,828
Living with parents	14,475	2,009	1,046	572	391
Other family member	6,086	1,143	462	330	351
In nonfamily household	24,188	4,841	2,041	1,526	1,274
Living alone	16,771	2,253	826	775	652
Living with nonrelatives	7,417	2,588	1,215	751	622
PERCENT DISTRIBUTION BY LIVING ARRANGEMENT					
Total women	**100.0%**	**100.0%**	**100.0%**	**100.0%**	**100.0%**
In family household	78.9	84.1	77.7	85.1	88.4
Living with spouse	49.5	58.3	46.9	61.4	64.9
Other family householder	11.5	15.4	14.3	15.0	16.7
Living with parents	12.6	6.6	11.4	5.6	3.6
Other family member	5.3	3.8	5.0	3.2	3.2
In nonfamily household	21.1	15.9	22.3	14.9	11.6
Living alone	14.6	7.4	9.0	7.5	6.0
Living with nonrelatives	6.5	8.5	13.3	7.3	5.7
PERCENT DISTRIBUTION BY AGE					
Total women	**100.0%**	**26.5%**	**8.0%**	**9.0%**	**9.5%**
In family household	100.0	28.2	7.9	9.7	10.7
Living with spouse	100.0	31.2	7.6	11.1	12.5
Other family householder	100.0	35.6	10.0	11.7	13.9
Living with parents	100.0	13.9	7.2	4.0	2.7
Other family member	100.0	18.8	7.6	5.4	5.8
In nonfamily household	100.0	20.0	8.4	6.3	5.3
Living alone	100.0	13.4	4.9	4.6	3.9
Living with nonrelatives	100.0	34.9	16.4	10.1	8.4

Source: Bureau of the Census, 2002 Current Population Survey Annual Demographic Supplement, Internet site http:// www.census.gov/population/www/socdemo/hh-fam/cps2002.html; calculations by New Strategist

Generation Xers Are at the Age of Marriage

Most 30-to-34-year-olds are currently married.

Women marry at a younger age than men. Consequently, among 25-to-34-year-olds in 2002, men were less likely than women to be currently married and living with their spouse (Generation Xers were aged 26 to 37 in that year)—48 percent of men versus 56 percent of women. For both men and women, a minority of 25-to-29-year-olds are currently married (38 percent of men and 48 percent of women). But among 30-to-34-year-olds, the majority is currently married, spouse present (56 percent of men and 63 percent of women). Still, even among 30-to-34-year-olds, a substantial 34 percent of men and 23 percent of women have never married.

With most Gen Xers just reaching the age of first marriage, few are currently divorced. Only 8 percent of women and 5 percent of men aged 25 to 34 are currently divorced. The percentage of people who are currently divorced peaks among women aged 45 to 64 at 18 percent.

■ The median age at first marriage is rising because today's young adults are more likely to attend college and start a career before committing to family life.

Most people are married by their early thirties

(percent of people aged 25 to 34 who are currently married and living with their spouse, by age and sex, 2003)

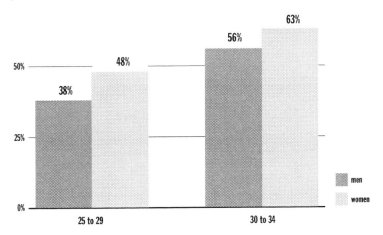

Table 6.19 Marital Status by Sex and Age, 2002: Total People

(number and percent distribution of people aged 15 or older by sex, age, and current marital status, 2002; numbers in thousands)

	total	never married	married, spouse present	married, spouse absent	separated	divorced	widowed
Total people	**221,459**	**63,090**	**115,838**	**2,926**	**4,606**	**20,955**	**14,044**
Under age 25	39,435	34,986	3,607	229	288	303	21
Aged 25 to 34	38,648	14,395	19,990	672	1,013	2,449	129
Aged 25 to 29	18,299	8,604	7,945	371	459	880	40
Aged 30 to 34	20,349	5,791	12,045	301	554	1,569	89
Aged 35 to 44	44,256	7,039	29,328	640	1,377	5,456	415
Aged 45 to 54	39,511	3,913	26,749	568	1,075	6,320	887
Aged 55 to 64	25,859	1,533	17,796	343	542	3,921	1,725
Aged 65 or older	33,750	1,224	18,368	474	311	2,506	10,867
Total women	**114,639**	**28,861**	**57,919**	**1,376**	**2,808**	**12,268**	**11,408**
Under age 25	19,529	16,659	2,328	140	175	210	14
Aged 25 to 34	19,428	6,062	10,852	302	635	1,470	108
Aged 25 to 29	9,158	3,700	4,431	182	288	524	33
Aged 30 to 34	10,270	2,362	6,421	120	347	946	75
Aged 35 to 44	22,453	2,933	14,984	270	872	3,079	317
Aged 45 to 54	20,209	1,799	13,261	257	654	3,566	672
Aged 55 to 64	13,497	715	8,530	157	305	2,384	1,407
Aged 65 or older	19,523	693	7,964	250	167	1,559	8,890
Total men	**106,819**	**34,229**	**57,919**	**1,551**	**1,798**	**8,686**	**2,636**
Under age 25	19,905	18,326	1,279	91	113	89	6
Aged 25 to 34	19,220	8,333	9,138	371	377	979	22
Aged 25 to 29	9,141	4,904	3,514	190	170	356	7
Aged 30 to 34	10,079	3,429	5,624	181	207	623	15
Aged 35 to 44	21,802	4,107	14,345	370	506	2,378	98
Aged 45 to 54	19,302	2,113	13,488	310	421	2,755	215
Aged 55 to 64	12,363	818	9,265	186	237	1,538	318
Aged 65 or older	14,227	532	10,404	223	144	947	1,977

PERCENT DISTRIBUTION	total	never married	married, spouse present	married, spouse absent	separated	divorced	widowed
Total people	**100.0%**	**28.5%**	**52.3%**	**1.3%**	**2.1%**	**9.5%**	**6.3%**
Under age 25	100.0	88.7	9.1	0.6	0.7	0.8	0.1
Aged 25 to 34	100.0	37.2	51.7	1.7	2.6	6.3	0.3
Aged 25 to 29	100.0	47.0	43.4	2.0	2.5	4.8	0.2
Aged 30 to 34	100.0	28.5	59.2	1.5	2.7	7.7	0.4
Aged 35 to 44	100.0	15.9	66.3	1.4	3.1	12.3	0.9
Aged 45 to 54	100.0	9.9	67.7	1.4	2.7	16.0	2.2
Aged 55 to 64	100.0	5.9	68.8	1.3	2.1	15.2	6.7
Aged 65 or older	100.0	3.6	54.4	1.4	0.9	7.4	32.2
Total women	**100.0**	**25.2**	**50.5**	**1.2**	**2.4**	**10.7**	**10.0**
Under age 25	100.0	85.3	11.9	0.7	0.9	1.1	0.1
Aged 25 to 34	100.0	31.2	55.9	1.6	3.3	7.6	0.6
Aged 25 to 29	100.0	40.4	48.4	2.0	3.1	5.7	0.4
Aged 30 to 34	100.0	23.0	62.5	1.2	3.4	9.2	0.7
Aged 35 to 44	100.0	13.1	66.7	1.2	3.9	13.7	1.4
Aged 45 to 54	100.0	8.9	65.6	1.3	3.2	17.6	3.3
Aged 55 to 64	100.0	5.3	63.2	1.2	2.3	17.7	10.4
Aged 65 or older	100.0	3.5	40.8	1.3	0.9	8.0	45.5
Total men	**100.0**	**32.0**	**54.2**	**1.5**	**1.7**	**8.1**	**2.5**
Under age 25	100.0	92.1	6.4	0.5	0.6	0.4	0.0
Aged 25 to 34	100.0	43.4	47.5	1.9	2.0	5.1	0.1
Aged 25 to 29	100.0	53.6	38.4	2.1	1.9	3.9	0.1
Aged 30 to 34	100.0	34.0	55.8	1.8	2.1	6.2	0.1
Aged 35 to 44	100.0	18.8	65.8	1.7	2.3	10.9	0.4
Aged 45 to 54	100.0	10.9	69.9	1.6	2.2	14.3	1.1
Aged 55 to 64	100.0	6.6	74.9	1.5	1.9	12.4	2.6
Aged 65 or older	100.0	3.7	73.1	1.6	1.0	6.7	13.9

Source: Bureau of the Census, 2002 Current Population Survey Annual Demographic Supplement, Internet site http:// www.census.gov/population/www/socdemo/hh-fam/cps2002.html

Black Gen Xers Are Least Likely to Be Married

Non-Hispanic white Gen Xers are most likely to be currently divorced.

Among Asians, Hispanics, and non-Hispanic whites aged 25 to 34, the percentage who are currently married and living with their spouse is about the same—ranging from 46 to 51 percent among men and from 59 to 61 percent among women. Blacks in the age group are far less likely to be currently married—only 35 percent of black men and 32 percent of black women are married and living with their spouse. The majority of black men (56 percent) and women (53 percent) in the age group have never married.

Non-Hispanic whites aged 25 to 34 are more likely than Asians, blacks, or Hispanics to be currently divorced. Among non-Hispanic white women in the age group, 9 percent are divorced. The comparable figure is 3 percent for Asian women and 6 percent for black and Hispanic women. The pattern is the same for men, although men are less likely to be currently divorced than women.

■ As the nation has become more diverse racially and ethnically, it has also become more diverse in its living arrangements.

Among 25-to-34-year-olds, blacks are least likely to be married

(percent of people aged 25 to 34 who are currently married and living with their spouse, by race, Hispanic origin, and sex, 2003)

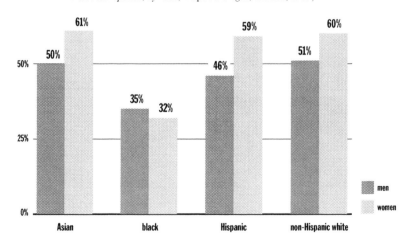

Table 6.20   Marital Status by Sex and Age, 2002: Asians

(number and percent distribution of Asians aged 15 or older by sex, age, and current marital status, 2002; numbers in thousands)

	total	never married	married, spouse present	married, spouse absent	separated	divorced	widowed
Total Asians	**9,837**	**3,229**	**5,246**	**318**	**137**	**488**	**418**
Under age 25	1,974	1,809	137	12	11	7	1
Aged 25 to 34	2,232	949	1,106	77	25	72	2
Aged 25 to 29	1,064	597	380	42	12	31	1
Aged 30 to 34	1,168	352	726	35	13	41	1
Aged 35 to 44	2,071	267	1,538	71	45	135	13
Aged 45 to 54	1,723	124	1,321	73	26	139	40
Aged 55 to 64	938	53	664	41	18	77	85
Aged 65 or older	899	27	480	44	12	58	277
Asian women	**5,079**	**1,363**	**2,822**	**139**	**93**	**316**	**346**
Under age 25	956	841	99	9	5	1	1
Aged 25 to 34	1,135	329	695	37	19	53	2
Aged 25 to 29	525	205	269	19	9	23	1
Aged 30 to 34	610	124	426	18	10	30	1
Aged 35 to 44	1,063	98	806	28	30	91	10
Aged 45 to 54	908	48	692	26	18	89	34
Aged 55 to 64	510	27	324	22	13	52	73
Aged 65 or older	507	20	206	17	8	30	226
Asian men	**4,758**	**1,866**	**2,423**	**180**	**44**	**172**	**72**
Under age 25	1,019	965	36	2	6	9	–
Aged 25 to 34	1,096	620	411	41	6	18	–
Aged 25 to 29	538	392	111	23	3	8	–
Aged 30 to 34	558	228	300	18	3	10	–
Aged 35 to 44	1,008	169	733	44	15	44	3
Aged 45 to 54	815	76	629	47	7	50	6
Aged 55 to 64	428	27	340	19	5	25	12
Aged 65 or older	392	9	274	27	5	26	51

	total	never married	married, spouse present	married, spouse absent	separated	divorced	widowed
PERCENT DISTRIBUTION							
Total Asians	**100.0%**	**32.8%**	**53.3%**	**3.2%**	**1.4%**	**5.0%**	**4.2%**
Under age 25	100.0	91.6	6.9	0.6	0.6	0.4	0.1
Aged 25 to 34	100.0	42.5	49.6	3.4	1.1	3.2	0.1
Aged 25 to 29	100.0	56.1	35.7	3.9	1.1	2.9	0.1
Aged 30 to 34	100.0	30.1	62.2	3.0	1.1	3.5	0.1
Aged 35 to 44	100.0	12.9	74.3	3.4	2.2	6.5	0.6
Aged 45 to 54	100.0	7.2	76.7	4.2	1.5	8.1	2.3
Aged 55 to 64	100.0	5.7	70.8	4.4	1.9	8.2	9.1
Aged 65 or older	100.0	3.0	53.4	4.9	1.3	6.5	30.8
Asian women	**100.0**	**26.8**	**55.6**	**2.7**	**1.8**	**6.2**	**6.8**
Under age 25	100.0	88.0	10.4	0.9	0.5	0.1	0.1
Aged 25 to 34	100.0	29.0	61.2	3.3	1.7	4.7	0.2
Aged 25 to 29	100.0	39.1	51.2	3.6	1.7	4.4	0.2
Aged 30 to 34	100.0	20.3	69.8	3.0	1.6	4.9	0.2
Aged 35 to 44	100.0	9.2	75.8	2.6	2.8	8.6	0.9
Aged 45 to 54	100.0	5.3	76.2	2.9	2.0	9.8	3.7
Aged 55 to 64	100.0	5.3	63.5	4.3	2.5	10.2	14.3
Aged 65 or older	100.0	3.9	40.6	3.4	1.6	5.9	44.6
Asian men	**100.0**	**39.2**	**50.9**	**3.8**	**0.9**	**3.6**	**1.5**
Under age 25	100.0	94.7	3.5	0.2	0.6	0.9	–
Aged 25 to 34	100.0	56.6	37.5	3.7	0.5	1.6	–
Aged 25 to 29	100.0	72.9	20.6	4.3	0.6	1.5	–
Aged 30 to 34	100.0	40.9	53.8	3.2	0.5	1.8	–
Aged 35 to 44	100.0	16.8	72.7	4.4	1.5	4.4	0.3
Aged 45 to 54	100.0	9.3	77.2	5.8	0.9	6.1	0.7
Aged 55 to 64	100.0	6.3	79.4	4.4	1.2	5.8	2.8
Aged 65 or older	100.0	2.3	69.9	6.9	1.3	6.6	13.0

Note: (–) means number is less than 500 or sample is too small to make a reliable estimate.
Source: Bureau of the Census, 2002 Current Population Survey Annual Demographic Supplement, Internet site http:// www.census.gov/population/www/socdemo/hh-fam/cps2002.html

Table 6.21   Marital Status by Sex and Age, 2002: Blacks

(number and percent distribution of blacks aged 15 or older by sex, age, and current marital status, 2002; numbers in thousands)

	total	never married	married, spouse present	married, spouse absent	separated	divorced	widowed
Total blacks	**26,137**	**11,334**	**8,640**	**522**	**1,241**	**2,727**	**1,673**
Under age 25	5,807	5,398	283	37	45	46	–
Aged 25 to 34	5,030	2,732	1,676	131	227	248	17
Aged 25 to 29	2,432	1,540	640	78	87	84	4
Aged 30 to 34	2,598	1,192	1,036	53	140	164	13
Aged 35 to 44	5,491	1,781	2,461	136	343	696	72
Aged 45 to 54	4,462	957	1,931	120	341	914	199
Aged 55 to 64	2,495	305	1,137	59	182	504	308
Aged 65 or older	2,852	161	1,152	39	103	319	1,077
Black women	**14,442**	**6,068**	**4,216**	**272**	**772**	**1,758**	**1,354**
Under age 25	3,022	2,774	171	24	29	22	–
Aged 25 to 34	2,794	1,481	902	81	159	155	17
Aged 25 to 29	1,353	829	366	48	64	44	4
Aged 30 to 34	1,441	652	536	33	95	111	13
Aged 35 to 44	3,027	981	1,228	60	229	474	54
Aged 45 to 54	2,448	547	922	56	196	576	151
Aged 55 to 64	1,421	188	536	26	99	324	248
Aged 65 or older	1,730	97	457	25	60	207	884
Black men	**11,695**	**5,266**	**4,423**	**249**	**469**	**968**	**319**
Under age 25	2,789	2,624	114	14	14	22	1
Aged 25 to 34	2,236	1,252	773	49	69	93	–
Aged 25 to 29	1,079	712	274	30	23	40	–
Aged 30 to 34	1,157	540	499	19	46	53	–
Aged 35 to 44	2,463	800	1,233	76	114	223	18
Aged 45 to 54	2,013	409	1,009	64	145	338	48
Aged 55 to 64	1,074	118	600	33	83	180	59
Aged 65 or older	1,120	63	694	13	44	112	193

	total	never married	married, spouse present	married, spouse absent	separated	divorced	widowed
PERCENT DISTRIBUTION							
Total blacks	**100.0%**	**43.4%**	**33.1%**	**2.0%**	**4.7%**	**10.4%**	**6.4%**
Under age 25	100.0	93.0	4.9	0.6	0.8	0.8	–
Aged 25 to 34	100.0	54.3	33.3	2.6	4.5	4.9	0.3
Aged 25 to 29	100.0	63.3	26.3	3.2	3.6	3.5	0.2
Aged 30 to 34	100.0	45.9	39.9	2.0	5.4	6.3	0.5
Aged 35 to 44	100.0	32.4	44.8	2.5	6.2	12.7	1.3
Aged 45 to 54	100.0	21.4	43.3	2.7	7.6	20.5	4.5
Aged 55 to 64	100.0	12.2	45.6	2.4	7.3	20.2	12.3
Aged 65 or older	100.0	5.6	40.4	1.4	3.6	11.2	37.8
Black women	**100.0**	**42.0**	**29.2**	**1.9**	**5.3**	**12.2**	**9.4**
Under age 25	100.0	91.8	5.7	0.8	1.0	0.7	–
Aged 25 to 34	100.0	53.0	32.3	2.9	5.7	5.5	0.6
Aged 25 to 29	100.0	61.3	27.1	3.5	4.7	3.3	0.3
Aged 30 to 34	100.0	45.2	37.2	2.3	6.6	7.7	0.9
Aged 35 to 44	100.0	32.4	40.6	2.0	7.6	15.7	1.8
Aged 45 to 54	100.0	22.3	37.7	2.3	0.8	23.5	6.2
Aged 55 to 64	100.0	13.2	37.7	1.8	7.0	22.8	17.5
Aged 65 or older	100.0	5.6	26.4	1.4	3.5	12.0	51.1
Black men	**100.0**	**45.0**	**37.8**	**2.1**	**4.0**	**8.3**	**2.7**
Under age 25	100.0	94.1	4.1	0.5	0.5	0.8	0.0
Aged 25 to 34	100.0	56.0	34.6	2.2	3.1	4.2	–
Aged 25 to 29	100.0	66.0	25.4	2.8	2.1	3.7	–
Aged 30 to 34	100.0	46.7	43.1	1.6	4.0	4.6	–
Aged 35 to 44	100.0	32.5	50.1	3.1	4.6	9.1	0.7
Aged 45 to 54	100.0	20.3	50.1	3.2	7.2	16.8	2.4
Aged 55 to 64	100.0	11.0	55.9	3.1	7.7	16.8	5.5
Aged 65 or older	100.0	5.6	62.0	1.2	3.9	10.0	17.2

Note: (–) means number is less than 500 or sample is too small to make a reliable estimate.
Source: Bureau of the Census, 2002 Current Population Survey Annual Demographic Supplement, Internet site http:// www.census.gov/population/www/socdemo/hh-fam/cps2002.html

Table 6.22 Marital Status by Sex and Age, 2002: Hispanics

(number and percent distribution of Hispanics aged 15 or older by sex, age, and current marital status, 2002; numbers in thousands)

	total	never married	married, spouse present	married, spouse absent	separated	divorced	widowed
Total Hispanics	**26,332**	**9,557**	**12,432**	**846**	**889**	**1,734**	**875**
Under age 25	6,679	5,538	904	107	83	37	9
Aged 25 to 34	6,992	2,476	3,667	271	225	335	19
Aged 25 to 29	3,535	1,564	1,617	146	95	112	2
Aged 30 to 34	3,457	912	2,050	125	130	223	17
Aged 35 to 44	5,432	900	3,457	217	249	549	60
Aged 45 to 54	3,393	371	2,179	130	177	443	94
Aged 55 to 64	1,939	176	1,245	73	89	228	128
Aged 65 or older	1,897	96	980	48	66	142	565
Hispanic women	**12,900**	**3,936**	**6,316**	**289**	**604**	**1,026**	**727**
Under age 25	3,146	2,415	589	56	52	27	7
Aged 25 to 34	3,268	896	1,940	73	153	190	16
Aged 25 to 29	1,604	568	869	45	65	55	2
Aged 30 to 34	1,664	328	1,071	28	88	135	14
Aged 35 to 44	2,600	330	1,677	61	179	302	49
Aged 45 to 54	1,774	161	1,102	46	121	270	75
Aged 55 to 64	1,024	80	606	29	56	143	111
Aged 65 or older	1,088	54	402	24	43	94	469
Hispanic men	**13,432**	**5,621**	**6,116**	**556**	**284**	**707**	**147**
Under age 25	3,536	3,125	316	51	30	10	2
Aged 25 to 34	3,723	1,579	1,727	199	72	145	3
Aged 25 to 29	1,931	996	748	101	30	57	–
Aged 30 to 34	1,792	583	979	98	42	88	3
Aged 35 to 44	2,830	569	1,780	155	70	247	10
Aged 45 to 54	1,619	210	1,076	85	56	173	18
Aged 55 to 64	915	96	639	44	34	85	17
Aged 65 or older	809	42	578	22	22	47	97

	total	never married	married, spouse present	married, spouse absent	separated	divorced	widowed
PERCENT DISTRIBUTION							
Total Hispanics	**100.0%**	**36.3%**	**47.2%**	**3.2%**	**3.4%**	**6.6%**	**3.3%**
Under age 25	100.0	82.9	13.5	1.6	1.2	0.6	0.1
Aged 25 to 34	100.0	35.4	52.4	3.9	3.2	4.8	0.3
Aged 25 to 29	100.0	44.2	45.7	4.1	2.7	3.2	0.1
Aged 30 to 34	100.0	26.4	59.3	3.6	3.8	6.5	0.5
Aged 35 to 44	100.0	16.6	63.6	4.0	4.6	10.1	1.1
Aged 45 to 54	100.0	10.9	64.2	3.8	5.2	13.1	2.8
Aged 55 to 64	100.0	9.1	64.2	3.8	4.6	11.8	6.6
Aged 65 or older	100.0	5.1	51.7	2.5	3.5	7.5	29.8
Hispanic women	**100.0**	**30.5**	**49.0**	**2.2**	**4.7**	**8.0**	**5.6**
Under age 25	100.0	76.8	18.7	1.8	1.7	0.9	0.2
Aged 25 to 34	100.0	27.4	59.4	2.2	4.7	5.8	0.5
Aged 25 to 29	100.0	35.4	54.2	2.8	4.1	3.4	0.1
Aged 30 to 34	100.0	19.7	64.4	1.7	5.3	8.1	0.8
Aged 35 to 44	100.0	12.7	64.5	2.3	6.9	11.6	1.9
Aged 45 to 54	100.0	9.1	62.1	2.6	6.8	15.2	4.2
Aged 55 to 64	100.0	7.8	59.2	2.8	5.5	14.0	10.8
Aged 65 or older	100.0	5.0	36.9	2.2	4.0	8.6	43.1
Hispanic men	**100.0**	**41.8**	**45.5**	**4.1**	**2.1**	**5.3**	**1.1**
Under age 25	100.0	88.4	8.9	1.4	0.8	0.3	0.1
Aged 25 to 34	100.0	42.4	46.4	5.3	1.9	3.9	0.1
Aged 25 to 29	100.0	51.6	38.7	5.2	1.6	3.0	–
Aged 30 to 34	100.0	32.5	54.6	5.5	2.3	4.9	0.2
Aged 35 to 44	100.0	20.1	62.9	5.5	2.5	8.7	0.4
Aged 45 to 54	100.0	13.0	66.5	5.3	3.5	10.7	1.1
Aged 55 to 64	100.0	10.5	69.8	4.8	3.7	9.3	1.9
Aged 65 or older	100.0	5.2	71.4	2.7	2.7	5.8	12.0

Note: (–) means number is less than 500 or sample is too small to make a reliable estimate.
Source: Bureau of the Census, 2002 Current Population Survey Annual Demographic Supplement, Internet site http:// www.census.gov/population/www/socdemo/hh-fam/cps2002.html

Table 6.23 Marital Status by Sex and Age, 2002: Non-Hispanic Whites

(number and percent distribution of non-Hispanic whites aged 15 or older by sex, age, and current marital status, 2002; numbers in thousands)

	total	never married	married, spouse present	married, spouse absent	separated	divorced	widowed
Total non-Hispanic whites	**158,188**	**38,770**	**89,082**	**1,250**	**2,327**	**15,778**	**10,981**
Under age 25	24,832	22,101	2,275	79	155	206	13
Aged 25 to 34	24,313	8,224	13,506	191	536	1,769	87
Aged 25 to 29	11,252	4,909	5,306	108	262	637	30
Aged 30 to 34	13,061	3,315	8,200	83	274	1,132	57
Aged 35 to 44	31,015	4,052	21,748	223	716	4,011	265
Aged 45 to 54	29,719	2,461	21,187	242	532	4,760	538
Aged 55 to 64	20,353	994	14,676	171	259	3,070	1,184
Aged 65 or older	27,956	938	15,690	344	129	1,962	8,894
Non-Hispanic white women	**81,625**	**17,373**	**44,303**	**667**	**1,332**	**9,045**	**8,904**
Under age 25	12,318	10,547	1,461	53	92	159	8
Aged 25 to 34	12,174	3,343	7,290	108	305	1,054	73
Aged 25 to 29	5,661	2,089	2,933	70	152	390	27
Aged 30 to 34	6,513	1,254	4,357	38	153	664	46
Aged 35 to 44	15,608	1,508	11,188	122	422	2,168	201
Aged 45 to 54	14,964	1,035	10,485	120	318	2,607	398
Aged 55 to 64	10,465	420	7,025	79	140	1,842	959
Aged 65 or older	16,096	520	6,854	185	55	1,215	7,265
Non-Hispanic white men	**76,564**	**21,397**	**44,779**	**583**	**995**	**6,733**	**2,077**
Under age 25	12,515	11,555	817	26	67	49	3
Aged 25 to 34	12,139	4,882	6,215	83	230	715	16
Aged 25 to 29	5,591	2,820	2,373	38	110	247	4
Aged 30 to 34	6,548	2,062	3,842	45	120	468	12
Aged 35 to 44	15,407	2,543	10,560	101	294	1,843	64
Aged 45 to 54	14,755	1,426	10,702	122	213	2,152	140
Aged 55 to 64	9,888	573	7,651	92	119	1,228	225
Aged 65 or older	11,860	418	8,834	159	72	746	1,629

	total	never married	married, spouse present	married, spouse absent	separated	divorced	widowed
PERCENT DISTRIBUTION							
Total non-Hispanic							
whites	**100.0%**	**24.5%**	**56.3%**	**0.8%**	**1.5%**	**10.0%**	**6.9%**
Under age 25	100.0	89.0	9.2	0.3	0.6	0.8	0.1
Aged 25 to 34	100.0	33.8	55.6	0.8	2.2	7.3	0.4
Aged 25 to 29	100.0	43.6	47.2	1.0	2.3	5.7	0.3
Aged 30 to 34	100.0	25.4	62.8	0.6	2.1	8.7	0.4
Aged 35 to 44	100.0	13.1	70.1	0.7	2.3	12.9	0.9
Aged 45 to 54	100.0	8.3	71.3	0.8	1.8	16.0	1.8
Aged 55 to 64	100.0	4.9	72.1	0.8	1.3	15.1	5.8
Aged 65 or older	100.0	3.4	56.1	1.2	0.5	7.0	31.8
Non-Hispanic							
white women	**100.0**	**21.3**	**54.3**	**0.8**	**1.6**	**11.1**	**10.9**
Under age 25	100.0	85.6	11.9	0.4	0.7	1.3	0.1
Aged 25 to 34	100.0	27.5	59.9	0.9	2.5	8.7	0.6
Aged 25 to 29	100.0	36.9	51.8	1.2	2.7	6.9	0.5
Aged 30 to 34	100.0	19.3	66.9	0.6	2.3	10.2	0.7
Aged 35 to 44	100.0	9.7	71.7	0.8	2.7	13.9	1.3
Aged 45 to 54	100.0	6.9	70.1	0.8	2.1	17.4	2.7
Aged 55 to 64	100.0	4.0	67.1	0.8	1.3	17.6	9.2
Aged 65 or older	100.0	3.2	42.6	1.1	0.3	7.5	45.1
Non-Hispanic							
white men	**100.0**	**27.9**	**58.5**	**0.8**	**1.3**	**8.8**	**2.7**
Under age 25	100.0	92.3	6.5	0.2	0.5	0.4	0.0
Aged 25 to 34	100.0	40.2	51.2	0.7	1.9	5.9	0.1
Aged 25 to 29	100.0	50.4	42.4	0.7	2.0	4.4	0.1
Aged 30 to 34	100.0	31.5	58.7	0.7	1.8	7.1	0.2
Aged 35 to 44	100.0	16.5	68.5	0.7	1.9	12.0	0.4
Aged 45 to 54	100.0	9.7	72.5	0.8	1.4	14.6	0.9
Aged 55 to 64	100.0	5.8	77.4	0.9	1.2	12.4	2.3
Aged 65 or older	100.0	3.5	74.5	1.3	0.6	6.3	13.7

Source: Bureau of the Census, 2002 Current Population Survey Annual Demographic Supplement, Internet site http:// www.census.gov/population/www/socdemo/hh-fam/cps2002.html

Population

■ The 2000 census counted 48 million members of Generation X in the U.S. population, a figure that includes all those born between 1965 and 1976, aged 24 to 35 in that year. Generation Xers account for 17 percent of the total population.

■ Sixty-four percent of Generation Xers are non-Hispanic white. Within Generation X, Hispanics outnumber blacks by more than 1 million. In fact, the number of Hispanics in Generation X surpasses the number of Hispanics in the Baby-Boom generation.

■ A substantial 12 percent of all Americans were foreign born in 2002, but the proportion is an even higher 19 percent among 25-to-34-year-olds.

■ More than 300,000 immigrants admitted to the United States in 2002 were aged 25 to 34, accounting for 29 percent of the total. The 25-to-29 and 30-to-34 age groups account for the largest share of immigrants admitted to the U.S. each year.

■ The diversity of Generation X varies greatly by state. In Maine, New Hampshire, Vermont, and West Virginia, at least 90 percent of people aged 25 to 34 are non-Hispanic white. But in California, the most populous state, the figure is just 39 percent.

Generation X Is Sandwiched between Larger Generations

The young-adult age group shrank as Generation X moved in.

The 2000 census counted 48 million members of Generation X in the U.S. population, a figure that includes all those born between 1965 and 1976, aged 24 to 35 in that year. Generation Xers account for 17 percent of the total population. They are surrounded by the two largest generations: the 78 million Boomers, accounting for 28 percent of the population, and the 73 million Millennials, accounting for 26 percent.

As Generation X moves through the age structure, age groups shrink. Between 2000 and 2002, the number of 35-to-39-year-olds fell 3 percent as Generation Xers replaced Boomers. Overall, the 25-to-39 age group shrank 1 percent between 2000 and 2002.

In the ten years between 2000 and 2010, Generation Xers will move into the 35-to-44 age group. According to Census Bureau projections, the number of adults aged 20 to 44 will remain virtually unchanged during those years.

■ Because Generation X is small, the nation focuses more of its attention on Boomers and Millennials. But Generation X is in the midst of career building, home buying, and family formation, and should not be ignored.

The number of people aged 20 to 44 will not grow during this decade

(percent change in number of people by age, 2000–10)

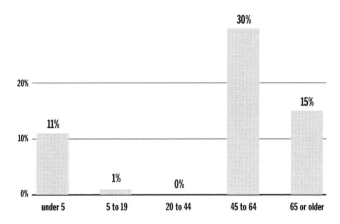

Table 7.1 Population by Age and Generation, 2000 Census

(number and percent distribution of people by age and generation, 2000; numbers in thousands)

	number	percent distribution
TOTAL PEOPLE	**281,422**	**100.0%**
Under age 5	19,176	6.8
Aged 5 to 9	20,550	7.3
Aged 10 to 14	20,528	7.3
Aged 15 to 19	20,220	7.2
Aged 20 to 24	18,964	6.7
Aged 25 to 34	39,892	14.2
Aged 25 to 29	19,381	6.9
Aged 30 to 34	20,510	7.3
Aged 35 to 39	22,707	8.1
Aged 40 to 44	22,442	8.0
Aged 45 to 49	20,092	7.1
Aged 50 to 54	17,586	6.2
Aged 55 to 59	13,469	4.8
Aged 60 to 64	10,805	3.8
Aged 65 to 69	9,534	3.4
Aged 70 to 74	8,857	3.1
Aged 75 to 79	7,416	2.6
Aged 80 to 84	4,945	1.8
Aged 85 or older	4,240	1.5
TOTAL PEOPLE	**281,422**	**100.0**
Post-Millennial (under age 6)	23,141	8.2
Millennial (aged 6 to 23)	72,655	25.8
Generation X (aged 24 to 35)	**48,049**	**17.1**
Baby Boom (aged 36 to 54)	78,310	27.8
Swing (aged 55 to 67)	30,061	10.7
World War II (aged 68 or older)	29,205	10.4

Source: Bureau of the Census, Census 2000 Summary File 1, Internet site http://factfinder.census.gov/servlet/BasicFactsServlet; calculations by New Strategist

Table 7.2 Population by Age and Sex, 2000 Census

(number of people by age and sex, and sex ratio by age, 2000; numbers in thousands)

	total	female	male	sex ratio
Total people	**281,422**	**143,368**	**138,054**	**96**
Under age 5	19,176	9,365	9,811	105
Aged 5 to 9	20,550	10,026	10,523	105
Aged 10 to 14	20,528	10,008	10,520	105
Aged 15 to 19	20,220	9,829	10,391	106
Aged 20 to 24	18,964	9,276	9,688	104
Aged 25 to 34	39,892	19,771	20,121	102
Aged 25 to 29	19,381	9,583	9,799	102
Aged 30 to 34	20,510	10,189	10,322	101
Aged 35 to 39	22,707	11,388	11,319	99
Aged 40 to 44	22,442	11,313	11,129	98
Aged 45 to 49	20,092	10,203	9,890	97
Aged 50 to 54	17,586	8,978	8,608	96
Aged 55 to 59	13,469	6,961	6,509	94
Aged 60 to 64	10,805	5,669	5,137	91
Aged 65 to 69	9,534	5,133	4,400	86
Aged 70 to 74	8,857	4,955	3,903	79
Aged 75 to 79	7,416	4,371	3,044	70
Aged 80 to 84	4,945	3,110	1,835	59
Aged 85 or older	4,240	3,013	1,227	41

Note: The sex ratio is the number of men per 100 women.
Source: Bureau of the Census, Census 2000 Summary File 1, Internet site http://factfinder.census.gov/servlet/BasicFactsServlet; calculations by New Strategist

Table 7.3 Population by Age, 2000 and 2002

(number of people by age, April 1, 2000, and July 1, 2002; percent change 2000–02; numbers in thousands)

	2000	2002	percent change 2000–02
Total people	**281,422**	**288,369**	**2.5%**
Under age 5	19,176	19,609	2.3
Aged 5 to 9	20,550	19,901	−3.2
Aged 10 to 14	20,528	21,136	3.0
Aged 15 to 19	20,220	20,376	0.8
Aged 20 to 24	18,964	20,214	6.6
Aged 25 to 39	62,598	61,843	−1.2
Aged 25 to 34	39,892	39,928	0.1
Aged 25 to 29	19,381	18,972	−2.1
Aged 30 to 34	20,510	20,956	2.2
Aged 35 to 39	22,707	21,915	−3.5
Aged 40 to 44	22,442	23,002	2.5
Aged 45 to 49	20,092	21,302	6.0
Aged 50 to 54	17,586	18,782	6.8
Aged 55 to 59	13,469	14,991	11.3
Aged 60 to 64	10,805	11,611	7.5
Aged 65 to 69	9,534	9,581	0.5
Aged 70 to 74	8,857	8,693	−1.9
Aged 75 to 79	7,416	7,420	0.1
Aged 80 to 84	4,945	5,314	7.5
Aged 85 to 89	2,790	2,943	5.5
Aged 90 to 94	1,113	1,250	12.4
Aged 95 to 99	287	342	19.2
Aged 100 or older	50	59	16.3

Source: Bureau of the Census, National Population Estimates, Internet site http://eire.census.gov/popest/data/national/tables/asro/NA-EST2002-ASRO-01.php; calculations by New Strategist

Table 7.4 Population by Age, 2000 to 2020

(number and percent distribution of people by age, 2000 to 2020; percent and percentage point change, 2000–2010 and 2010–2020; numbers in thousands)

	2000	2010	2020	percent change 2000–10	percent change 2010–20
Total people	282,125	308,936	335,805	9.5%	8.7%
Under age 5	19,218	21,426	22,932	11.5	7.0
Aged 5 to 19	61,331	61,810	65,955	0.8	6.7
Aged 20 to 44	104,075	104,444	108,632	0.4	4.0
Aged 45 to 64	62,440	81,012	83,653	29.7	3.3
Aged 65 to 84	30,794	34,120	47,363	10.8	38.8
Aged 85 or older	4,267	6,123	7,269	43.5	18.7

	2000	2010	2020	percentage point change 2000–10	percentage point change 2010–20
Percent distribution by age					
Total people	100.0%	100.0%	100.0%	–	–
Under age 5	6.8	6.9	6.8	0.1	–0.1
Aged 5 to 19	21.7	20.0	19.6	–1.7	–0.4
Aged 20 to 44	36.9	33.8	32.3	–3.1	–1.5
Aged 45 to 64	22.1	26.2	24.9	4.1	–1.3
Aged 65 to 84	10.9	11.0	14.1	0.1	3.1
Aged 85 or older	1.5	2.0	2.2	0.5	0.2

Note: (–) means not applicable.
Source: Bureau of the Census, U.S. Interim Projections by Age, Sex, Race, and Hispanic Origin, 2004, Internet site http://www.census.gov/ipc/www/usinterimproj/; calculations by New Strategist

Generation X Is More Diverse than Average

They are less diverse than children and young adults, however.

Sixty-four percent of Generation Xers are non-Hispanic white, according to the 2000 census. This figure is smaller than the 69 percent for the population as a whole, but larger than the share among the youngest Americans—only 58 percent of children under age 5 are non-Hispanic white. Older generations of Americans are much less diverse than Generation X. Among Boomers, 73 percent are non-Hispanic white. Among the World War II generation, the proportion is 84 percent.

Within Generation X, Hispanics outnumber blacks by more than 1 million. Sixteen percent of Gen Xers are Hispanic, and 13 percent are black. Twenty-two percent of the nation's Hispanics are members of Generation X. In fact, the number of Hispanics in Generation X surpasses the number of Hispanics in the Baby-Boom generation.

Among the 7 million multiracial Americans, 18 percent are members of Generation X, just slightly below the Baby Boom's 20 percent share. An enormous 36 percent of multiracial Americans are members of the Millennial generation. Two percent of Gen Xers claimed to be multiracial on the 2000 census.

■ The contrast in the racial and ethnic makeup of older versus younger generations of Americans will create political tension in the years ahead.

Fewer than two-thirds of Generation Xers are non-Hispanic white

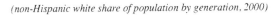

(non-Hispanic white share of population by generation, 2000)

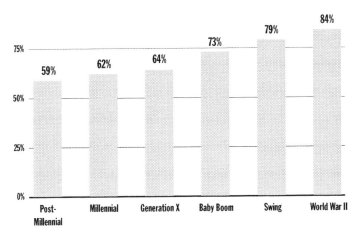

Table 7.5 Population by Age, Race, and Hispanic Origin, 2000 Census

(number and percent distribution of people by age, race, and Hispanic origin, 2000; numbers in thousands)

	total	American Indian	Asian	black	Native Hawaiian	white total	white non-Hispanic	other race	multiracial	Hispanic
Total people	**281,422**	**4,119**	**11,899**	**36,419**	**874**	**216,931**	**194,553**	**18,521**	**6,826**	**35,306**
Under age 5	19,176	359	919	3,167	88	13,656	11,194	2,017	948	3,718
Aged 5 to 14	41,078	791	1,771	6,823	175	29,533	25,186	3,648	1,533	6,787
Aged 15 to 24	39,184	697	1,878	5,853	168	28,164	24,355	3,690	1,174	6,581
Aged 25 to 34	39,892	588	2,179	5,374	140	29,096	25,356	3,578	997	6,510
Aged 35 to 44	45,149	644	1,953	5,699	126	34,984	31,801	2,693	891	5,129
Aged 45 to 54	37,678	501	1,499	4,194	86	30,494	28,387	1,553	607	3,136
Aged 55 to 64	24,275	281	839	2,429	47	20,316	19,028	718	332	1,710
Aged 65 or older	34,992	260	862	2,881	44	30,688	29,245	625	344	1,734

PERCENT DISTRIBUTION BY RACE AND HISPANIC ORIGIN

	total	American Indian	Asian	black	Native Hawaiian	white total	white non-Hispanic	other race	multiracial	Hispanic
Total people	**100.0%**	**1.5%**	**4.2%**	**12.9%**	**0.3%**	**77.1%**	**69.1%**	**6.6%**	**2.4%**	**12.5%**
Under age 5	100.0	1.9	4.8	16.5	0.5	71.2	58.4	10.5	4.9	19.4
Aged 5 to 14	100.0	1.9	4.3	16.6	0.4	71.9	61.3	8.9	3.7	16.5
Aged 15 to 24	100.0	1.8	4.8	14.9	0.4	71.9	62.2	9.4	3.0	16.8
Aged 25 to 34	100.0	1.5	5.5	13.5	0.4	72.9	63.6	9.0	2.5	16.3
Aged 35 to 44	100.0	1.4	4.3	12.6	0.3	77.5	70.4	6.0	2.0	11.4
Aged 45 to 54	100.0	1.3	4.0	11.1	0.2	80.9	75.3	4.1	1.6	8.3
Aged 55 to 64	100.0	1.2	3.5	11.0	0.2	83.7	78.4	3.0	1.4	7.1
Aged 65 or older	100.0	0.7	2.5	8.2	0.1	87.7	83.6	1.8	1.0	5.0

Note: Numbers will not add to total because each racial category includes those who identified themselves as being of the race alone and those who identified themselves as being of the race in combination with one or more other races, because the multiracial are shown, and because Hispanics may be of any race. Non-Hispanic whites include only those who identified themselves as "white alone" and non-Hispanic.

Source: Bureau of the Census, Census 2000 Summary File 1; Internet site http://factfinder.census.gov/servlet/BasicFactsServlet; calculations by New Strategist

Table 7.6 Population by Generation, Race, and Hispanic Origin, 2000 Census

(number and percent distribution of people by generation, race, and Hispanic origin, 2000; numbers in thousands)

	total	American Indian	Asian	black	Native Hawaiian	white total	white non-Hispanic	other race	Hispanic
TOTAL PEOPLE	**281,422**	**4,119**	**11,899**	**36,419**	**874**	**216,931**	**194,553**	**18,521**	**35,306**
Post-Millennial (under age 6)	23,141	432	1,100	3,833	106	16,475	13,539	2,414	4,451
Millennial (aged 6 to 23)	72,655	1,356	3,266	11,498	311	52,303	45,002	6,551	11,948
Generation X (24 to 35)	**48,049**	**711**	**2,592**	**6,486**	**169**	**35,076**	**30,585**	**4,295**	**7,812**
Baby Boom (aged 36 to 54)	78,310	1,080	3,240	9,293	198	62,074	57,154	3,919	7,652
Swing (aged 55 to 67)	30,061	337	1,024	2,999	57	25,214	23,629	859	2,085
World War II (aged 68+)	29,205	203	676	2,310	34	25,790	24,644	484	1,360
PERCENT DISTRIBUTION BY RACE AND HISPANIC ORIGIN									
TOTAL PEOPLE	**100.0%**	**100.0%**	**100.0%**	**100.0%**	**100.0%**	**100.0%**	**100.0%**	**100.0%**	**100.0%**
Post-Millennial (under age 6)	8.2	10.5	9.2	10.5	12.2	7.6	7.0	13.0	12.6
Millennial (aged 6 to 23)	25.8	32.9	27.5	31.6	35.5	24.1	23.1	35.4	33.8
Generation X (aged 24 to 35)	**17.1**	**17.3**	**21.8**	**17.8**	**19.3**	**16.2**	**15.7**	**23.2**	**22.1**
Baby Boom (aged 36 to 54)	27.8	26.2	27.2	25.5	22.6	28.6	29.4	21.2	21.7
Swing (aged 55 to 67)	10.7	8.2	8.6	8.2	6.5	11.6	12.1	4.6	5.9
World War II (aged 68+)	10.4	4.9	5.7	6.3	3.9	11.9	12.7	2.6	3.9
PERCENT DISTRIBUTION BY GENERATION									
TOTAL PEOPLE	**100.0%**	**1.5%**	**4.2%**	**12.9%**	**0.3%**	**77.1%**	**69.1%**	**6.6%**	**12.5%**
Post-Millennial (under age 6)	100.0	1.9	4.8	16.6	0.5	71.2	58.5	10.4	19.2
Millennial (aged 6 to 23)	100.0	1.9	4.5	15.8	0.4	72.0	61.9	9.0	16.4
Generation X (aged 24 to 35)	**100.0**	**1.5**	**5.4**	**13.5**	**0.4**	**73.0**	**63.7**	**8.9**	**16.3**
Baby Boom (aged 36 to 54)	100.0	1.4	4.1	11.9	0.3	79.3	73.0	5.0	9.8
Swing (aged 55 to 67)	100.0	1.1	3.4	10.0	0.2	83.9	78.6	2.9	6.9
World War II (aged 68+)	100.0	0.7	2.3	7.9	0.1	88.3	84.4	1.7	4.7

Note: Numbers will not add to total because each racial category includes those who identified themselves as being of the race alone and those who identified themselves as being of the race in combination with one or more other races, and because Hispanics may be of any race. Non-Hispanic whites include only those who identified themselves as "white alone" and non-Hispanic.
Source: Bureau of the Census, Census 2000 Summary File 2, Internet site http://factfinder.census.gov/servlet/BasicFactsServlet; calculations by New Strategist

Table 7.7 Multiracial Population by Age and Generation, 2000 Census

(number of total people and number and percent distribution of the multiracial population, by age and generation, 2000; numbers in thousands)

	total	multiracial number	multiracial percent distribution	multiracial share of total
TOTAL PEOPLE	**281,422**	**6,826**	**100.0%**	**2.4%**
Under age 5	19,176	948	13.9	4.9
Aged 5 to 9	20,550	830	12.2	4.0
Aged 10 to 14	20,528	703	10.3	3.4
Aged 15 to 19	20,220	622	9.1	3.1
Aged 20 to 24	18,964	552	8.1	2.9
Aged 25 to 29	19,381	512	7.5	2.6
Aged 30 to 34	20,510	484	7.1	2.4
Aged 35 to 39	22,707	471	6.9	2.1
Aged 40 to 44	22,442	421	6.2	1.9
Aged 45 to 49	20,092	338	5.0	1.7
Aged 50 to 54	17,586	269	3.9	1.5
Aged 55 to 59	13,469	189	2.8	1.4
Aged 60 to 64	10,805	143	2.1	1.3
Aged 65 to 69	9,534	112	1.6	1.2
Aged 70 to 74	8,857	91	1.3	1.0
Aged 75 to 79	7,416	67	1.0	0.9
Aged 80 to 84	4,945	41	0.6	0.8
Aged 85 or older	4,240	34	0.5	0.8
TOTAL PEOPLE	**281,422**	**6,826**	**100.0**	**2.4**
Post-Millennial (under 6)	23,141	1,122	16.4	4.8
Millennial (aged 6 to 23)	72,655	2,429	35.6	3.3
Generation X (24 to 35)	**48,049**	**1,200**	**17.6**	**2.5**
Baby Boom (aged 36 to 54)	78,310	1,399	20.5	1.8
Swing (aged 55 to 67)	30,061	402	5.9	1.3
World War II (68+)	29,205	274	4.0	0.9

Source: Bureau of the Census, Census 2000 Summary File 2, Internet site http://factfinder.census.gov/servlet/BasicFactsServlet; calculations by New Strategist

Nearly One in Five Gen Xers Is Foreign Born

Immigrants are making Generation X more diverse.

A substantial 12 percent of all Americans were born abroad but the proportion is an even higher 19 percent among 25-to-34-year-olds. Among the 7.5 million 25-to-34-year-olds who were born in a foreign country, only 22 percent are naturalized citizens. The 25-to-34 age group accounted for 14 percent of the total population in 2002, but it represented a much larger 23 percent of the foreign born.

Among the foreign born in the 25-to-34 age group, 47 percent were born in Central America (a region that includes Mexico in these statistics). Twenty-four percent were born in Asia, and only 8 percent are from Europe. These figures differ from those for the next older age group, which is mostly filled with Boomers in 2002. Among 35-to-44-year-olds, a much smaller share (37 percent) is from Central America and a larger share (11 percent) is from Europe.

■ The foreign-born population adds to the multicultural mix which is becoming a significant factor in American business and politics.

Nearly half of foreign-born 25-to-34-year-olds are from Central America

(percent distribution of foreign-born people aged 25 to 34 by region of birth, 2002)

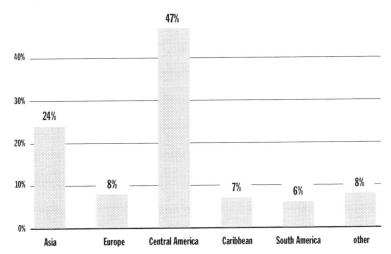

Table 7.8 Population Aged 25 to 44 by Citizenship Status, 2002

(number and percent distribution of total people and people aged 25 to 44 by citizenship status, 2002; numbers in thousands)

			foreign born		
	total	native born	total	naturalized citizen	not a citizen
TOTAL PEOPLE	282,082	249,629	32,453	11,962	20,491
Total aged 25 to 44	82,954	68,459	14,495	4,275	10,220
Aged 25 to 34	38,670	31,180	7,490	1,647	5,843
Aged 35 to 44	44,284	37,279	7,005	2,628	4,377
PERCENT DISTRIBUTION BY CITIZENSHIP STATUS					
TOTAL PEOPLE	100.0%	88.5%	11.5%	4.2%	7.3%
Total aged 25 to 44	100.0	82.5	17.5	5.2	12.3
Aged 25 to 34	100.0	80.6	19.4	4.3	15.1
Aged 35 to 44	100.0	84.2	15.8	5.9	9.9
PERCENT DISTRIBUTION BY AGE					
TOTAL PEOPLE	100.0%	100.0%	100.0%	100.0%	100.0%
Total aged 25 to 44	29.4	27.4	44.7	35.7	49.9
Aged 25 to 34	13.7	12.5	23.1	13.8	28.5
Aged 35 to 44	15.7	14.9	21.6	22.0	21.4

Source: Bureau of the Census, Foreign-Born Population of the United States, Current Population Survey, March 2002, *Internet site http://www.census.gov/population/www/socdemo/foreign/ppl-162.html; calculations by New Strategist*

Table 7.9 Foreign-Born Population Aged 25 to 44, 2002

(number and percent distribution of total people and people aged 25 to 44 by foreign-born status and region of birth, 2002; numbers in thousands)

| | | foreign born | | | | | | | |
| | | | | | Latin America | | | | |
	total	total	Asia	Europe	total	Caribbean	Central America	South America	other
TOTAL PEOPLE	282,082	32,453	8,281	4,548	16,943	3,102	11,819	2,022	2,680
Total aged 25 to 44	82,954	14,495	3,672	1,387	8,239	1,166	6,109	966	1,196
Aged 25 to 34	38,670	7,490	1,784	623	4,466	495	3,529	443	617
Aged 35 to 44	44,284	7,005	1,888	764	3,773	671	2,580	523	579
PERCENT DISTRIBUTION OF FOREIGN-BORN BY REGION OF BIRTH									
TOTAL PEOPLE	–	100.0%	25.5%	14.0%	52.2%	9.6%	36.4%	6.2%	8.3%
Total aged 25 to 44	–	100.0	25.3	9.6	56.8	8.0	42.1	6.7	8.3
Aged 25 to 34	–	100.0	23.8	8.3	59.6	6.6	47.1	5.9	8.2
Aged 35 to 44	–	100.0	27.0	10.9	53.9	9.6	36.8	7.5	8.3
PERCENT DISTRIBUTION BY AGE									
TOTAL PEOPLE	100.0%	100.0%	100.0%	100.0%	100.0%	100.0%	100.0%	100.0%	100.0%
Total aged 25 to 44	29.4	44.7	44.3	30.5	48.6	37.6	51.7	47.8	44.6
Aged 25 to 34	13.7	23.1	21.5	13.7	26.4	16.0	29.9	21.9	23.0
Aged 35 to 44	15.7	21.6	22.8	16.8	22.3	21.6	21.8	25.9	21.6

Note: Central America includes Mexico in these statistics; (–) means not applicable.
Source: Bureau of the Census, Foreign-Born Population of the United States, Current Population Survey, March 2002, Internet site http://www.census.gov/population/www/socdemo/foreign/ppl-162.html; calculations by New Strategist

Many Immigrants Are Generation Xers

Nearly three out of ten immigrants are aged 25 to 34.

The number of legal immigrants admitted to the United States numbered over 1 million in 2002. More than 300,000 were aged 25 to 34, accounting for 29 percent of the total. In fact, the 25-to-29 and 30-to-34 age groups account for the largest share of immigrants admitted to the U.S. each year as eager foreign workers seek better opportunities for themselves and their families.

Fourteen percent of immigrants to the U.S. in 2002 were aged 25 to 29, and another 15 percent were aged 30-to-34 in 2002—the largest share of any five-year age group. The figure then declines steadily with age. Just 11 percent of immigrants are aged 55 or older.

■ Because most immigrants are children and young adults, immigration has a much greater impact on the diversity of younger Americans than on the middle-aged or older population.

Immigrants aged 25 to 34 account for 29 percent of the total

(percent distribution of immigrants by age, 2002)

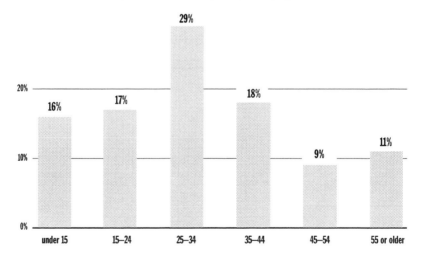

Table 7.10 Immigrants by Age, 2002

(number and percent distribution of immigrants by age, 2002)

	number	percent distribution
Total immigrants	**1,063,732**	**100.0%**
Under age 1	11,673	1.1
Aged 1 to 4	31,791	3.0
Aged 5 to 9	54,493	5.1
Aged 10 to 14	70,860	6.7
Aged 15 to 19	92,566	8.7
Aged 20 to 24	93,132	8.8
Aged 25 to 34	313,438	29.5
Aged 25 to 29	152,476	14.3
Aged 30 to 34	160,962	15.1
Aged 35 to 39	112,247	10.6
Aged 40 to 44	75,743	7.1
Aged 45 to 49	54,811	5.2
Aged 50 to 54	40,319	3.8
Aged 55 to 59	31,694	3.0
Aged 60 to 64	29,201	2.7
Aged 65 to 74	39,014	3.7
Aged 75 or older	12,541	1.2

Source: U.S. Citizenship and Immigration Services, 2002 Yearbook of Immigration Statistics, Internet site http://uscis.gov/ graphics/shared/aboutus/statistics/IMM02yrbk/IMM2002list.htm

The Largest Share of Generation Xers Lives in the South

Generation Xers account for only 11 percent of the population of Montana, but for 18 percent of the population of the District of Columbia.

The South is home to the largest share of the population, and consequently to the largest share of Generation X. The 2000 census found 36 percent of Gen Xers living in the South, where they accounted for 14 percent of the population.

The diversity of Generation X varies greatly by state. In Maine, New Hampshire, Vermont, and West Virginia, at least 90 percent of people aged 25 to 34 are non-Hispanic white. But in California, the most populous state, the figure is just 39 percent. In Texas, only 46 percent of 25-to-34-year-olds are non-Hispanic white. Hawaii, New Mexico, and the District of Columbia also have minority majorities in the 25-to-34 age group.

Because of immigration and higher fertility rates, Hispanics outnumber blacks within Generation X in many states. In California, 39 percent of 25-to-34-year-olds are Hispanic (equal to the 39 percent non-Hispanic white share), 13 percent are Asian, and 7 percent are black. In other states with large Hispanic populations such as Texas and Florida, Hispanic Gen Xers also greatly outnumber blacks. Even in states such as Illinois, however, Hispanics have the edge, 17 versus 15 percent. In the South, black Gen Xers still greatly outnumber Hispanics in the generation.

■ Although Gen Xers are more diverse in some states than others, the cultural influence of racial and ethnic diversity is shared by children and young adults.

In California, diversity is the rule among Gen Xers

(percent distribution of people aged 25 to 34 in California by race and Hispanic origin, 2000)

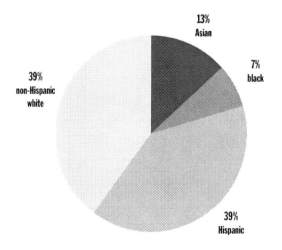

13%
Asian

7%
black

39%
non-Hispanic
white

39%
Hispanic

Table 7.11 Population Aged 25 to 34 by Region, 2000 Census

(number and percent distribution of total people and people aged 25 to 34 by age and region, 2000; numbers in thousands)

	total	Northeast	Midwest	South	West
TOTAL PEOPLE	281,422	53,594	64,393	100,237	63,198
Total aged 25 to 34	39,892	7,418	8,746	14,319	9,409
Aged 25 to 29	19,381	3,460	4,253	7,045	4,623
Aged 30 to 34	20,510	3,958	4,493	7,274	4,786
PERCENT DISTRIBUTION BY AGE					
TOTAL PEOPLE	100.0%	100.0%	100.0%	100.0%	100.0%
Total aged 25 to 34	14.2	13.8	13.6	14.3	14.9
Aged 25 to 29	6.9	6.5	6.6	7.0	7.3
Aged 30 to 34	7.3	7.4	7.0	7.3	7.6
PERCENT DISTRIBUTION BY REGION					
TOTAL PEOPLE	100.0%	19.0%	22.9%	35.6%	22.5%
Total aged 25 to 34	100.0	18.6	21.9	35.9	23.6
Aged 25 to 29	100.0	17.9	21.9	36.4	23.9
Aged 30 to 34	100.0	19.3	21.9	35.5	23.3

Source: Bureau of the Census, Census 2000 Summary File 2, Internet site http://factfinder.census.gov/servlet/BasicFactsServlet; calculations by New Strategist

Table 7.12 Regional Populations by Generation, 2000 Census

(number and percent distribution of people by generation and region, 2000; numbers in thousands)

	total	Northeast	Midwest	South	West
TOTAL PEOPLE	**281,422**	**53,594**	**64,393**	**100,237**	**63,198**
Post-Millennial (under age 6)	23,141	4,115	5,255	8,238	5,532
Millennial (aged 6 to 23)	72,655	13,059	16,826	25,834	16,936
Generation X (aged 24 to 35)	**48,049**	**8,938**	**10,547**	**17,248**	**11,315**
Baby Boom (aged 36 to 54)	78,310	15,303	17,958	27,635	17,415
Swing (aged 55 to 67)	30,061	5,957	6,863	10,995	6,246
World War II (aged 68 or older)	29,205	6,222	6,944	10,286	5,753
PERCENT DISTRIBUTION BY GENERATION					
TOTAL PEOPLE	**100.0%**	**100.0%**	**100.0%**	**100.0%**	**100.0%**
Post-Millennial (under age 6)	8.2	7.7	8.2	8.2	8.8
Millennial (aged 6 to 23)	25.8	24.4	26.1	25.8	26.8
Generation X (aged 24 to 35)	**17.1**	**16.7**	**16.4**	**17.2**	**17.9**
Baby Boom (aged 36 to 54)	27.8	28.6	27.9	27.6	27.6
Swing (aged 55 to 67)	10.7	11.1	10.7	11.0	9.9
World War II (aged 68 or older)	10.4	11.6	10.8	10.3	9.1
PERCENT DISTRIBUTION BY REGION					
TOTAL PEOPLE	**100.0%**	**19.0%**	**22.9%**	**35.6%**	**22.5%**
Post-Millennial (under age 6)	100.0	17.8	22.7	35.6	23.9
Millennial (aged 6 to 23)	100.0	18.0	23.2	35.6	23.3
Generation X (aged 24 to 35)	**100.0**	**18.6**	**22.0**	**35.9**	**23.5**
Baby Boom (aged 36 to 54)	100.0	19.5	22.9	35.3	22.2
Swing (aged 55 to 67)	100.0	19.8	22.8	36.6	20.8
World War II (aged 68 or older)	100.0	21.3	23.8	35.2	19.7

Source: Bureau of the Census, Census 2000 Summary File 2, Internet site http://factfinder.census.gov/servlet/BasicFactsServlet; calculations by New Strategist

Table 7.13 **Population Aged 25 to 34 by State, 2000 Census**

(number and percent of people aged 25 to 34 by state, 2000: numbers in thousands)

	total population	people aged 25 to 34	
		number	percent
United States	**281,422**	**39,892**	**14.2%**
Alabama	4,447	603	13.6
Alaska	627	90	14.3
Arizona	5,131	743	14.5
Arkansas	2,673	353	13.2
California	33,872	5,229	15.4
Colorado	4,301	664	15.4
Connecticut	3,406	452	13.3
Delaware	784	109	13.9
District of Columbia	572	102	17.8
Florida	15,982	2,084	13.0
Georgia	8,186	1,299	15.9
Hawaii	1,212	171	14.1
Idaho	1,294	169	13.1
Illinois	12,419	1,812	14.6
Indiana	6,080	831	13.7
Iowa	2,926	363	12.4
Kansas	2,688	349	13.0
Kentucky	4,042	568	14.1
Louisiana	4,469	601	13.5
Maine	1,275	158	12.4
Maryland	5,296	749	14.1
Massachusetts	6,349	927	14.6
Michigan	9,938	1,362	13.7
Minnesota	4,919	673	13.7
Mississippi	2,845	382	13.4
Missouri	5,595	739	13.2
Montana	902	103	11.4
Nebraska	1,711	223	13.1
Nevada	1,998	307	15.3
New Hampshire	1,236	160	13.0
New Jersey	8,414	1,189	14.1
New Mexico	1,819	234	12.9
New York	18,976	2,757	14.5
North Carolina	8,049	1,213	15.1
North Dakota	642	77	12.0
Ohio	11,353	1,520	13.4
Oklahoma	3,451	452	13.1
Oregon	3,421	471	13.8
Pennsylvania	12,281	1,561	12.7
Rhode Island	1,048	140	13.4

	total population	people aged 25 to 34	
		number	percent
South Carolina	4,012	561	14.0%
South Dakota	755	91	12.1
Tennessee	5,689	816	14.3
Texas	20,852	3,162	15.2
Utah	2,233	327	14.6
Vermont	609	75	12.2
Virginia	7,079	1,037	14.6
Washington	5,894	841	14.3
West Virginia	1,808	229	12.7
Wisconsin	5,364	706	13.2
Wyoming	494	60	12.1

Source: Bureau of the Census, Census 2000 Summary File 2, Internet site http://factfinder.census.gov/servlet/BasicFactsServlet

Table 7.14 Population Aged 25 to 34 by State, Race, and Hispanic Origin, 2000 Census

(total number of people by state, number aged 25 to 34, and percent distribution by race and Hispanic origin, by state, 2000)

	total		American Indian	Asian	black	Native Hawaiian	white		other	Hispanic
	number	percent					total	non-Hispanic		
ALABAMA										
State total	4,447,100	100.0%	1.0%	0.9%	26.3%	0.1%	72.0%	70.3%	0.9%	1.7%
Total 25 to 34	603,015	100.0	1.0	1.3	26.6	0.1	70.6	68.6	1.4	2.7
Aged 25 to 29	301,196	100.0	0.9	1.4	27.5	0.1	69.4	67.3	1.6	3.0
Aged 30 to 34	301,819	100.0	1.0	1.2	25.7	0.1	71.8	70.0	1.2	2.3
ALASKA										
State total	626,932	100.0	19.0	5.2	4.3	0.9	74.0	67.6	2.4	4.1
Total 25 to 34	89,473	100.0	17.6	5.2	4.7	0.9	73.2	67.5	2.9	4.9
Aged 25 to 29	42,987	100.0	17.7	5.2	5.1	0.9	72.9	66.9	3.1	5.2
Aged 30 to 34	46,486	100.0	17.4	5.2	4.4	0.9	73.4	68.1	2.8	4.6
ARIZONA										
State total	5,130,632	100.0	5.7	2.3	3.6	0.3	77.9	63.8	13.2	25.3
Total 25 to 34	742,665	100.0	5.6	3.2	3.9	0.3	72.8	56.7	17.2	31.2
Aged 25 to 29	374,106	100.0	5.7	3.4	3.9	0.3	71.4	54.6	18.5	33.1
Aged 30 to 34	368,559	100.0	5.5	3.0	3.9	0.3	74.1	58.8	15.9	29.2
ARKANSAS										
State total	2,673,400	100.0	1.4	1.0	16.0	0.1	81.2	78.6	1.8	3.2
Total 25 to 34	352,845	100.0	1.4	1.4	16.2	0.1	79.2	75.9	2.9	5.2
Aged 25 to 29	176,674	100.0	1.3	1.5	16.8	0.2	78.3	74.8	3.3	5.7
Aged 30 to 34	176,171	100.0	1.4	1.3	15.7	0.1	80.1	77.1	2.6	4.6
CALIFORNIA										
State total	33,871,648	100.0	1.9	12.3	7.4	0.7	63.4	46.7	19.4	32.4
Total 25 to 34	5,229,062	100.0	1.8	13.4	7.1	0.7	57.9	39.3	24.1	39.0
Aged 25 to 29	2,543,541	100.0	1.8	13.8	6.9	0.7	56.1	37.0	25.8	41.0
Aged 30 to 34	2,685,521	100.0	1.8	12.9	7.3	0.7	59.6	41.5	22.5	37.0
COLORADO										
State total	4,301,261	100.0	1.9	2.8	4.4	0.2	85.2	74.5	8.5	17.1
Total 25 to 34	664,027	100.0	1.9	3.7	4.6	0.3	81.8	70.2	10.6	20.3
Aged 25 to 29	331,795	100.0	1.9	3.9	4.5	0.3	80.8	68.4	11.6	21.8
Aged 30 to 34	332,232	100.0	1.9	3.4	4.6	0.3	82.9	72.0	9.7	18.7
CONNECTICUT										
State total	3,405,565	100.0	0.7	2.8	10.0	0.1	83.3	77.5	5.5	9.4
Total 25 to 34	451,640	100.0	0.8	4.5	11.5	0.2	77.8	70.5	7.9	13.0
Aged 25 to 29	201,467	100.0	0.8	5.1	12.2	0.2	75.7	67.6	9.0	14.7
Aged 30 to 34	250,173	100.0	0.8	4.0	10.9	0.1	79.5	72.9	7.0	11.7
DELAWARE										
State total	783,600	100.0	0.8	2.4	20.1	0.1	75.9	72.5	2.6	4.8
Total 25 to 34	108,840	100.0	0.8	3.6	21.5	0.1	71.6	67.4	4.1	7.2
Aged 25 to 29	51,219	100.0	0.8	4.0	21.2	0.1	71.1	66.3	4.7	8.4
Aged 30 to 34	57,621	100.0	0.8	3.3	21.7	0.1	72.2	68.5	3.5	6.2

	total		American			Native	white			
	number	percent	Indian	Asian	black	Hawaiian	total	non-Hispanic	other	Hispanic
DISTRICT OF COLUMBIA										
State total	572,059	100.0%	0.8%	3.1%	61.3%	0.1%	32.2%	27.8%	5.0%	7.9%
Total 25 to 34	101,762	100.0	0.8	5.0	46.6	0.2	43.9	37.7	6.7	10.6
Aged 25 to 29	52,849	100.0	0.7	5.7	44.6	0.2	45.1	38.9	7.0	10.8
Aged 30 to 34	48,913	100.0	0.8	4.3	48.8	0.1	42.7	36.5	6.4	10.4
FLORIDA										
State total	15,982,378	100.0	0.7	2.1	15.5	0.2	79.7	65.4	4.4	16.8
Total 25 to 34	2,084,100	100.0	0.8	2.9	17.4	0.2	75.3	57.5	6.3	22.0
Aged 25 to 29	995,358	100.0	0.8	3.1	18.3	0.2	73.8	55.8	6.8	22.7
Aged 30 to 34	1,088,742	100.0	0.8	2.8	16.6	0.2	76.6	59.1	5.8	21.3
GEORGIA										
State total	8,186,453	100.0	0.6	2.4	29.2	0.1	66.1	62.6	2.9	5.3
Total 25 to 34	1,299,256	100.0	0.7	3.3	29.9	0.1	63.0	58.2	4.6	8.3
Aged 25 to 29	641,750	100.0	0.7	3.5	30.1	0.2	62.0	56.7	5.3	9.4
Aged 30 to 34	657,506	100.0	0.7	3.1	29.7	0.1	63.9	59.7	3.9	7.1
HAWAII										
total	1,211,537	100.0	2.1	58.0	2.8	23.3	39.3	22.9	3.9	7.2
Total 25 to 34	171,159	100.0	2.1	53.7	4.0	23.5	40.5	24.1	4.6	8.1
Aged 25 to 29	84,000	100.0	2.2	52.7	4.4	24.3	41.3	24.1	5.0	8.8
Aged 30 to 34	87,159	100.0	2.1	54.7	3.6	22.8	39.8	24.2	4.2	7.5
IDAHO										
State total	1,293,953	100.0	2.1	1.3	0.6	0.2	92.8	88.1	5.0	7.9
Total 25 to 34	169,433	100.0	2.3	1.9	0.7	0.3	90.1	84.6	6.8	10.5
Aged 25 to 29	85,128	100.0	2.3	2.0	0.7	0.3	89.6	83.8	7.3	11.2
Aged 30 to 34	84,305	100.0	2.3	1.8	0.6	0.3	90.7	85.4	6.3	9.9
ILLINOIS										
State total	12,419,293	100.0	0.6	3.8	15.6	0.1	75.1	67.8	6.8	12.3
Total 25 to 34	1,811,674	100.0	0.6	5.3	15.4	0.1	71.2	61.9	9.5	16.9
Aged 25 to 29	891,759	100.0	0.6	5.7	15.8	0.1	69.5	59.5	10.5	18.6
Aged 30 to 34	919,915	100.0	0.6	4.9	14.9	0.1	72.9	64.3	8.4	15.3
INDIANA										
State total	6,080,485	100.0	0.6	1.2	8.8	0.1	88.6	85.8	2.0	3.5
Total 25 to 34	831,125	100.0	0.7	1.9	9.2	0.1	86.4	83.2	2.9	5.1
Aged 25 to 29	409,035	100.0	0.7	2.0	9.7	0.1	85.4	81.9	3.4	5.8
Aged 30 to 34	422,090	100.0	0.7	1.8	8.8	0.1	87.2	84.5	2.5	4.4
IOWA										
State total	2,926,324	100.0	0.6	1.5	2.5	0.1	94.9	92.6	1.6	2.8
Total 25 to 34	363,060	100.0	0.7	2.6	2.8	0.1	92.2	89.4	2.6	4.4
Aged 25 to 29	177,259	100.0	0.7	2.9	3.1	0.1	91.5	88.4	2.9	4.9
Aged 30 to 34	185,801	100.0	0.7	2.3	2.6	0.1	93.0	90.4	2.3	3.9
KANSAS										
State total	2,688,418	100.0	1.8	2.1	6.3	0.1	87.9	83.1	4.0	7.0
Total 25 to 34	348,853	100.0	1.9	3.4	6.7	0.1	83.9	78.1	6.0	10.2
Aged 25 to 29	172,975	100.0	2.0	3.8	7.0	0.2	82.8	76.6	6.5	11.1
Aged 30 to 34	175,878	100.0	1.9	2.9	6.5	0.1	84.9	79.6	5.5	9.4

	total		American			Native	white			
	number	percent	Indian	Asian	black	Hawaiian	total	non-Hispanic	other	Hispanic
KENTUCKY										
State total	4,041,769	100.0%	0.6%	0.9%	7.7%	0.1%	91.0%	89.3%	0.8%	1.5%
Total 25 to 34	568,108	100.0	0.6	1.5	7.9	0.1	89.7	87.8	1.2	2.3
Aged 25 to 29	281,134	100.0	0.6	1.5	8.3	0.1	89.1	87.1	1.4	2.6
Aged 30 to 34	286,974	100.0	0.6	1.4	7.5	0.1	90.2	88.5	1.0	2.0
LOUISIANA										
State total	4,468,976	100.0	1.0	1.4	32.9	0.1	64.8	62.5	1.1	2.4
Total 25 to 34	601,162	100.0	1.0	1.9	32.8	0.1	63.9	61.5	1.4	3.0
Aged 25 to 29	296,161	100.0	0.9	2.1	33.3	0.1	63.2	60.7	1.6	3.1
Aged 30 to 34	305,001	100.0	1.0	1.8	32.2	0.1	64.7	62.3	1.3	2.8
MAINE										
State total	1,274,923	100.0	1.0	0.9	0.7	0.1	97.9	96.5	0.4	0.7
Total 25 to 34	157,617	100.0	1.2	1.3	0.8	0.1	97.2	95.8	0.5	0.9
Aged 25 to 29	71,951	100.0	1.2	1.4	0.9	0.1	97.0	95.5	0.6	1.0
Aged 30 to 34	85,666	100.0	1.1	1.2	0.8	0.1	97.3	96.0	0.5	0.9
MARYLAND										
State total	5,296,486	100.0	0.7	4.5	28.8	0.1	65.4	62.1	2.5	4.3
Total 25 to 34	748,521	100.0	0.8	5.7	31.3	0.1	60.5	56.4	3.8	6.3
Aged 25 to 29	342,870	100.0	0.8	6.1	31.6	0.2	59.4	54.9	4.2	7.0
Aged 30 to 34	405,651	100.0	0.8	5.3	31.0	0.1	61.4	57.6	3.5	5.8
MASSACHUSETTS										
State total	6,349,097	100.0	0.6	4.2	6.3	0.1	86.2	81.9	5.1	6.8
Total 25 to 34	926,788	100.0	0.6	6.3	6.9	0.2	82.4	77.1	6.4	8.7
Aged 25 to 29	434,024	100.0	0.6	7.2	7.1	0.2	80.9	75.2	6.9	9.4
Aged 30 to 34	492,764	100.0	0.6	5.5	6.7	0.1	83.6	78.7	6.0	8.1
MICHIGAN										
State total	9,938,444	100.0	1.3	2.1	14.8	0.1	81.8	78.6	2.0	3.3
Total 25 to 34	1,362,171	100.0	1.3	3.4	16.3	0.1	78.2	74.6	2.7	4.3
Aged 25 to 29	654,629	100.0	1.3	3.7	17.4	0.1	76.6	72.7	3.1	4.8
Aged 30 to 34	707,542	100.0	1.3	3.1	15.3	0.1	79.6	76.4	2.4	3.8
MINNESOTA										
State total	4,919,479	100.0	1.6	3.3	4.1	0.1	90.8	88.2	1.8	2.9
Total 25 to 34	673,138	100.0	1.7	4.6	5.2	0.2	87.2	84.1	2.8	4.4
Aged 25 to 29	319,826	100.0	1.8	5.3	5.6	0.2	85.7	82.3	3.4	5.2
Aged 30 to 34	353,312	100.0	1.6	4.0	4.9	0.1	88.5	85.8	2.3	3.7
MISSISSIPPI										
State total	2,844,658	100.0	0.7	0.8	36.6	0.1	61.9	60.7	0.7	1.4
Total 25 to 34	381,798	100.0	0.7	1.1	37.3	0.1	60.4	59.1	1.1	2.0
Aged 25 to 29	192,526	100.0	0.7	1.1	38.2	0.1	59.4	58.0	1.2	2.2
Aged 30 to 34	189,272	100.0	0.7	1.2	36.4	0.1	61.4	60.1	0.9	1.9
MISSOURI										
State total	5,595,211	100.0	1.1	1.4	11.7	0.1	86.1	83.8	1.2	2.1
Total 25 to 34	738,733	100.0	1.1	2.2	12.7	0.1	83.6	81.1	1.7	3.0
Aged 25 to 29	362,305	100.0	1.1	2.5	13.0	0.2	82.9	80.2	1.9	3.2
Aged 30 to 34	376,428	100.0	1.1	2.0	12.4	0.1	84.2	81.9	1.5	2.7

	total		American			Native	white			
	number	percent	Indian	Asian	black	Hawaiian	total	non-Hispanic	other	Hispanic
MONTANA										
State total	902,195	100.0%	7.4%	0.8%	0.5%	0.1%	92.2%	89.5%	0.9%	2.0%
Total 25 to 34	103,279	100.0	8.1	1.1	0.5	0.1	90.7	88.0	1.1	2.4
Aged 25 to 29	51,104	100.0	8.2	1.2	0.6	0.1	90.4	87.6	1.2	2.5
Aged 30 to 34	52,175	100.0	8.0	0.9	0.5	0.1	91.1	88.5	1.0	2.2
NEBRASKA										
State total	1,711,263	100.0	1.3	1.6	4.4	0.1	90.8	87.3	3.3	5.5
Total 25 to 34	223,273	100.0	1.4	2.7	4.8	0.2	87.1	82.7	5.3	8.4
Aged 25 to 29	112,049	100.0	1.4	3.1	4.9	0.2	86.3	81.6	5.7	9.1
Aged 30 to 34	111,224	100.0	1.5	2.4	4.7	0.1	87.9	83.8	4.8	7.8
NEVADA										
State total	1,998,257	100.0	2.1	5.6	7.5	0.8	78.4	65.2	9.7	19.7
Total 25 to 34	306,611	100.0	2.1	6.2	7.6	0.9	74.1	57.9	13.2	26.3
Aged 25 to 29	148,726	100.0	2.1	6.3	7.6	1.0	73.1	55.8	14.2	28.3
Aged 30 to 34	157,885	100.0	2.1	6.1	7.6	0.9	74.9	59.9	12.2	24.4
NEW HAMPSHIRE										
State total	1,235,786	100.0	0.6	1.6	1.0	0.1	97.0	95.1	0.9	1.7
Total 25 to 34	160,061	100.0	0.6	2.6	1.2	0.1	95.3	93.2	1.3	2.3
Aged 25 to 29	71,355	100.0	0.6	3.1	1.3	0.1	94.7	92.3	1.4	2.6
Aged 30 to 34	88,706	100.0	0.6	2.2	1.1	0.1	95.8	93.9	1.2	2.1
NEW JERSEY										
State total	8,414,350	100.0	0.6	6.2	14.4	0.1	74.4	66.0	6.9	13.3
Total 25 to 34	1,189,040	100.0	0.7	8.5	15.8	0.2	68.3	57.7	9.8	17.9
Aged 25 to 29	544,917	100.0	0.7	9.1	16.3	0.2	66.3	55.1	10.8	19.5
Aged 30 to 34	644,123	100.0	0.6	8.0	15.3	0.1	69.9	60.0	8.9	16.6
NEW MEXICO										
State total	1,819,046	100.0	10.5	1.5	2.3	0.2	69.9	44.7	19.4	42.1
Total 25 to 34	234,091	100.0	11.5	2.0	2.4	0.2	64.4	38.8	23.1	46.4
Aged 25 to 29	115,387	100.0	11.8	2.1	2.5	0.2	63.3	37.4	24.0	47.3
Aged 30 to 34	118,704	100.0	11.1	1.9	2.4	0.2	65.5	40.1	22.3	45.4
NEW YORK										
State total	18,976,457	100.0	0.9	6.2	17.0	0.2	70.0	62.0	9.1	15.1
Total 25 to 34	2,757,324	100.0	1.0	8.2	17.5	0.2	65.2	55.7	11.7	18.8
Aged 25 to 29	1,304,725	100.0	1.0	8.8	17.7	0.2	63.8	54.0	12.4	19.8
Aged 30 to 34	1,452,599	100.0	0.9	7.6	17.4	0.2	66.3	57.3	11.1	17.8
NORTH CAROLINA										
State total	8,049,313	100.0	1.6	1.7	22.1	0.1	73.1	70.2	2.8	4.7
Total 25 to 34	1,213,415	100.0	1.7	2.3	22.0	0.1	70.7	66.6	4.6	7.8
Aged 25 to 29	601,522	100.0	1.8	2.4	22.1	0.1	69.7	65.0	5.4	9.1
Aged 30 to 34	611,893	100.0	1.6	2.2	21.8	0.1	71.7	68.2	3.8	6.5
NORTH DAKOTA										
State total	642,200	100.0	5.5	0.8	0.8	0.1	93.4	91.7	0.6	1.2
Total 25 to 34	76,887	100.0	6.3	1.4	1.1	0.1	91.5	89.7	0.9	1.6
Aged 25 to 29	38,792	100.0	6.3	1.5	1.2	0.1	91.2	89.3	1.0	1.8
Aged 30 to 34	38,095	100.0	6.3	1.3	0.9	0.1	91.8	90.1	0.7	1.4

	total		American			Native	white			
	number	percent	Indian	Asian	black	Hawaiian	total	non-Hispanic	other	Hispanic
OHIO										
State total	11,353,140	100.0%	0.7%	1.4%	12.1%	0.1%	86.1%	84.0%	1.1%	1.9%
Total 25 to 34	1,519,894	100.0	0.7	2.3	12.5	0.1	84.3	82.2	1.5	2.5
Aged 25 to 29	735,582	100.0	0.7	2.5	13.1	0.1	83.4	81.1	1.7	2.7
Aged 30 to 34	784,312	100.0	0.7	2.0	12.0	0.1	85.1	83.1	1.3	2.2
OKLAHOMA										
State total	3,450,654	100.0	11.4	1.7	8.3	0.1	80.3	74.1	3.0	5.2
Total 25 to 34	451,647	100.0	11.3	2.6	8.9	0.2	76.9	70.4	4.3	7.3
Aged 25 to 29	229,026	100.0	11.5	2.9	9.2	0.2	75.9	69.1	4.7	7.8
Aged 30 to 34	222,621	100.0	11.0	2.3	8.5	0.2	78.0	71.8	4.0	6.7
OREGON										
State total	3,421,399	100.0	2.5	3.7	2.1	0.5	89.3	83.5	5.2	8.1
Total 25 to 34	470,695	100.0	2.6	5.2	2.3	0.6	84.6	77.7	7.9	12.1
Aged 25 to 29	233,850	100.0	2.7	5.5	2.3	0.6	83.4	75.9	8.8	13.5
Aged 30 to 34	236,845	100.0	2.5	4.8	2.3	0.6	85.8	79.5	7.0	10.8
PENNSYLVANIA										
State total	12,281,054	100.0	0.4	2.0	10.5	0.1	86.3	84.1	1.9	3.2
Total 25 to 34	1,560,486	100.0	0.4	3.2	11.5	0.1	83.3	80.8	2.7	4.4
Aged 25 to 29	732,701	100.0	0.5	3.6	11.9	0.1	82.3	79.5	3.0	4.8
Aged 30 to 34	827,785	100.0	0.4	2.8	11.1	0.1	84.2	81.8	2.5	4.0
RHODE ISLAND										
State total	1,048,319	100.0	1.0	2.7	5.5	0.2	86.9	81.9	6.6	8.7
Total 25 to 34	140,326	100.0	1.0	3.5	6.2	0.2	83.5	77.4	8.6	11.7
Aged 25 to 29	64,732	100.0	1.0	4.0	6.6	0.2	82.0	75.4	9.4	12.7
Aged 30 to 34	75,594	100.0	0.9	3.1	5.8	0.2	84.7	79.1	8.0	10.9
SOUTH CAROLINA										
State total	4,012,012	100.0	0.7	1.1	29.9	0.1	68.0	66.1	1.3	2.4
Total 25 to 34	560,831	100.0	0.7	1.5	29.5	0.1	67.0	64.6	2.1	3.9
Aged 25 to 29	276,855	100.0	0.7	1.6	29.7	0.1	66.5	63.8	2.4	4.4
Aged 30 to 34	283,976	100.0	0.7	1.5	29.4	0.1	67.4	65.3	1.8	3.3
SOUTH DAKOTA										
State total	754,844	100.0	9.1	0.8	0.9	0.1	89.9	88.0	0.7	1.4
Total 25 to 34	91,013	100.0	9.9	1.2	1.3	0.1	87.6	85.7	1.2	2.1
Aged 25 to 29	45,084	100.0	10.3	1.4	1.4	0.1	86.9	84.9	1.3	2.2
Aged 30 to 34	45,929	100.0	9.5	1.0	1.2	0.1	88.2	86.5	1.1	1.9
TENNESSEE										
State total	5,689,283	100.0	0.7	1.2	16.8	0.1	81.2	79.2	1.3	2.2
Total 25 to 34	815,901	100.0	0.7	1.7	17.4	0.1	79.1	76.7	2.1	3.5
Aged 25 to 29	403,829	100.0	0.6	1.9	17.8	0.1	78.3	75.7	2.4	4.0
Aged 30 to 34	412,072	100.0	0.7	1.6	16.9	0.1	79.9	77.8	1.8	3.0
TEXAS										
State total	20,851,820	100.0	1.0	3.1	12.0	0.1	73.1	52.4	13.3	32.0
Total 25 to 34	3,162,083	100.0	1.0	4.1	12.3	0.2	68.6	46.1	16.5	37.0
Aged 25 to 29	1,591,522	100.0	1.0	4.2	12.2	0.2	67.5	44.4	17.5	38.6
Aged 30 to 34	1,570,561	100.0	1.0	4.1	12.3	0.2	69.6	47.8	15.4	35.3

	total		American Indian	Asian	black	Native Hawaiian	white		other	Hispanic
	number	percent					total	non-Hispanic		
UTAH										
State total	2,233,169	100.0%	1.8%	2.2%	1.1%	1.0%	91.1%	85.3%	5.1%	9.0%
Total 25 to 34	327,064	100.0	1.9	2.9	1.1	1.0	88.1	81.3	7.1	12.1
Aged 25 to 29	178,474	100.0	1.8	2.9	1.1	1.0	88.0	81.1	7.3	12.4
Aged 30 to 34	148,590	100.0	1.9	2.8	1.2	0.9	88.3	81.6	6.8	11.8
VERMONT										
State total	608,827	100.0	1.1	1.1	0.7	0.1	97.9	96.2	0.4	0.9
Total 25 to 34	74,567	100.0	1.1	1.8	0.7	0.1	97.0	95.2	0.6	1.0
Aged 25 to 29	34,182	100.0	1.1	2.1	0.9	0.0	96.5	94.7	0.6	1.1
Aged 30 to 34	40,385	100.0	1.1	1.5	0.6	0.1	97.4	95.7	0.5	0.9
VIRGINIA										
State total	7,078,515	100.0	0.7	4.3	20.4	0.1	73.9	70.2	2.7	4.7
Total 25 to 34	1,036,965	100.0	0.8	5.9	20.4	0.2	70.8	66.2	4.2	7.0
Aged 25 to 29	497,172	100.0	0.8	6.4	20.3	0.2	70.1	65.1	4.7	7.6
Aged 30 to 34	539,793	100.0	0.7	5.4	20.5	0.2	71.5	67.2	3.8	6.4
WASHINGTON										
State total	5,894,121	100.0	2.7	6.7	4.0	0.7	84.9	78.9	4.9	7.5
Total 25 to 34	841,130	100.0	2.7	8.2	4.4	0.8	80.8	74.2	6.6	10.1
Aged 25 to 29	403,652	100.0	2.8	8.8	4.5	0.9	79.5	72.3	7.4	11.3
Aged 30 to 34	437,478	100.0	2.6	7.7	4.4	0.8	82.1	76.1	5.8	9.0
WEST VIRGINIA										
State total	1,808,344	100.0	0.6	0.7	3.5	0.1	95.9	94.6	0.3	0.7
Total 25 to 34	229,094	100.0	0.6	0.9	3.5	0.1	95.4	94.2	0.4	0.8
Aged 25 to 29	113,577	100.0	0.5	1.0	3.6	0.1	95.1	93.9	0.4	0.9
Aged 30 to 34	115,517	100.0	0.6	0.8	3.3	0.1	95.6	94.5	0.3	0.8
WISCONSIN										
State total	5,363,675	100.0	1.3	1.9	6.1	0.1	90.0	87.3	2.0	3.6
Total 25 to 34	706,168	100.0	1.4	2.5	6.9	0.1	87.4	84.1	3.0	5.2
Aged 25 to 29	333,913	100.0	1.5	2.8	7.5	0.1	86.1	82.3	3.5	6.1
Aged 30 to 34	372,255	100.0	1.4	2.2	6.3	0.1	88.6	85.7	2.5	4.5
WYOMING										
State total	493,782	100.0	3.0	0.8	1.0	0.1	93.7	88.9	3.2	6.4
Total 25 to 34	59,854	100.0	3.5	1.2	1.2	0.1	91.7	86.6	4.1	7.8
Aged 25 to 29	30,084	100.0	3.4	1.3	1.2	0.2	91.4	86.0	4.4	8.2
Aged 30 to 34	29,770	100.0	3.5	1.1	1.1	0.1	92.1	87.1	3.8	7.3

Note: Percentages will not add to 100 because each race includes those who identified themselves as being of the race alone and those who identified themselves as being of the race in combination with one or more other races, and because Hispanics may be of any race. Non-Hispanic whites include only those who identified themselves as "white alone" and non-Hispanic. American Indians include Alaska natives. Native Hawaiians include other Pacific Islanders.
Source: Bureau of the Census, Census 2000 Summary File 2, Internet site http://factfinder.census.gov/servlet/BasicFactsServlet; calculations by New Strategist

8

Spending

■ Householders aged 25 to 34, an age group that was entirely filled with Generation Xers in 2002, spent only 3 percent more in 2002 than in 1997. Householders aged 35 to 44, an age group that was beginning to fill with Generation X in 2002, boosted its spending by 7 percent during those years.

■ The spending of households headed by people aged 25 to 34 almost matches spending by the average household. In 2002, householders aged 25 to 34 spent $40,318, slightly less than the $40,677 spent by the average household.

■ Households headed by people aged 35 to 44 spend 19 percent more than the average household—$48,330 in 2002. Spending by householders in the age group is particularly high for items commonly purchased by parents with children under age 18.

Householders Aged 25 to 44 Are Spending More

Spending in many categories is lower than in 1997, however.

Despite a substantial rise in overall consumer spending during the 1990s, individual house-holds have been cautious. Between 1997 and 2002, the average household boosted its spending by less than 5 percent after adjusting for inflation, despite an 11 percent increase in income. Householders aged 25 to 34, an age group that was entirely filled with Generation Xers in 2002, spent only 3 percent more in 2002 than in 1997. Householders aged 35 to 44, an age group that was beginning to fill with Generation X in 2002, boosted its spending by 7 percent during those years.

Householders aged 25 to 34 cut their spending on many discretionary items. They spent 7 percent less on alcohol, 11 percent less on furniture and appliances, 9 percent less on clothes, and 3 percent less on entertainment. One reason for these cuts in discretionary spending is that more of their budgets were devoted to necessities. Between 1997 and 2002, householders aged 25 to 34 spent 6 percent more on education, 8 percent more on pensions and Social Security, and 18 percent more on health insurance. Generation X boosted its spending on restaurant and carry-out meals, however, by a substantial 12 percent.

Householders aged 35 to 44—the age group now filling with Generation X—spent more on mortgage interest as homeownership increased, and they spent more on furniture and appliances as they outfitted their first homes. Householders aged 35 to 44 spent 6 percent less on alcoholic beverages, and their apparel spending also fell. Out-of-pocket costs for health insurance rose by 22 percent between 1997 and 2002. The age group also spent more on restaurant and carry-out meals, and—in contrast to 25-to-34-year-olds—its entertainment spending was up a substantial 13 percent.

■ The economic slowdown of the past few years has forced many young adults to devote more of their household budget to necessities.

Generation Xers have cut back on many, but not all, discretionary items

(percent change in spending by householders aged 25 to 34 on selected items, 1997 to 2002; in 2002 dollars)

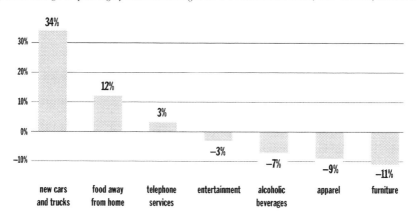

Table 8.1 Average Spending of Householders Aged 25 to 44, 1997 and 2002

(average annual spending of total consumer units and consumer units headed by people aged 25 to 44, 1997 and 2002; percent change, 1997–2002; in 2002 dollars)

	total consumer units			aged 25 to 34			aged 35 to 44		
	2002	1997	percent change 1997–02	2002	1997	percent change 1997–02	2002	1997	percent change 1997–02
Number of consumer units (in 000s)	112,108	105,576	6.2%	18,988	19,918	–4.7%	24,394	24,560	–0.7%
Average before-tax income	$49,430	$44,610	10.8	$49,133	$44,969	9.3	$61,532	$54,512	12.9
Average annual spending	40,677	38,904	4.6	40,318	38,997	3.4	48,330	45,154	7.0
FOOD	$5,375	$5,364	0.2%	$5,471	$5,196	5.3%	$6,314	$6,331	–0.3%
Food at home	3,099	3,218	–3.7	3,093	3,082	0.4	3,601	3,779	–4.7
Cereals and bakery products	450	506	–11.1	442	483	–8.4	542	603	–10.2
Cereals and cereal products	154	180	–14.4	163	188	–13.2	191	220	–13.2
Bakery products	296	326	–9.3	279	295	–5.4	351	384	–8.7
Meats, poultry, fish, and eggs	798	830	–3.9	817	784	4.2	918	967	–5.0
Beef	231	250	–7.7	253	245	3.4	271	295	–8.1
Pork	167	175	–4.8	162	161	0.7	198	194	1.8
Other meats	101	107	–5.8	96	94	2.3	122	134	–0.9
Poultry	144	162	–11.1	159	163	–2.5	164	194	–15.6
Fish and seafood	121	99	21.7	113	89	26.4	126	108	16.3
Eggs	34	37	–7.8	34	31	8.7	38	39	–2.8
Dairy products	328	351	–6.5	324	339	–4.3	392	432	–9.3
Fresh milk and cream	127	143	–11.2	130	140	–6.9	153	183	–16.5
Other dairy products	201	208	–3.3	195	198	–1.4	238	250	–4.9
Fruits and vegetables	552	532	3.8	522	485	7.6	597	587	1.8
Fresh fruits	178	168	6.2	154	153	0.6	191	180	6.2
Fresh vegetables	175	160	9.5	162	139	16.9	185	169	9.7
Processed fruits	116	114	1.8	118	108	8.9	128	131	–2.1
Processed vegetables	83	89	–7.1	88	85	3.6	93	106	–12.4
Other food at home	970	1,000	–3.0	988	991	–0.3	1,153	1,191	–3.2
Sugar and other sweets	117	127	–8.1	104	118	–12.2	139	145	–4.3
Fats and oils	85	91	–6.1	81	80	0.7	93	98	–5.4
Miscellaneous foods	472	450	4.8	512	485	5.6	572	560	2.2
Nonalcoholic beverages	254	274	–7.2	260	259	0.3	303	329	–7.8
Food prepared by household on trips	41	58	–29.4	31	48	–35.5	46	58	–20.8
Food away from home	2,276	2,146	6.0	2,378	2,115	12.4	2,712	2,551	6.3
ALCOHOLIC BEVERAGES	376	345	8.9	395	425	–7.0	367	389	–5.6
HOUSING	13,283	12,594	5.5	13,727	13,155	4.3	16,350	14,989	9.1
Shelter	7,829	7,088	10.4	8,470	7,781	8.9	9,902	8,787	12.7
Owned dwellings	5,165	4,397	17.5	4,701	3,838	22.5	7,105	5,859	21.3
Mortgage interest, charges	2,962	2,486	19.1	3,286	2,646	24.2	4,608	3,853	19.6

	total consumer units			aged 25 to 34			aged 35 to 44		
	2002	1997	percent change 1997–02	2002	1997	percent change 1997–02	2002	1997	percent change 1997–02
Property taxes	$1,242	$1,085	14.5%	$823	$714	15.3%	$1,473	$1,178	25.1%
Maintenance, repairs, insurance, other expenses	960	825	16.4	592	479	23.5	1,024	830	23.3
Rented dwellings	2,160	2,216	−2.5	3,476	3,677	−5.5	2,351	2,496	−5.8
Other lodging	505	476	6.1	293	266	10.2	446	431	3.4
Utilities, fuels, and public services	**2,684**	**2,695**	**−0.4**	**2,503**	**2,491**	**0.5**	**3,026**	**3,010**	**0.5**
Natural gas	330	336	−1.9	288	295	−2.4	369	365	1.0
Electricity	981	1,016	−3.4	864	877	−1.5	1,105	1,134	−2.6
Fuel oil and other fuels	88	121	−27.1	55	77	−28.7	86	121	−28.7
Telephone services	957	904	5.9	1,032	998	3.4	1,096	1,029	6.5
Water, other public services	328	320	2.6	263	244	8.0	369	361	2.2
Household services	**706**	**612**	**15.3**	**895**	**736**	**21.6**	**1,010**	**809**	**24.9**
Personal services	331	294	12.6	650	551	1.8	580	503	15.4
Other household services	375	318	17.8	245	187	31.3	430	306	40.5
Housekeeping supplies	**545**	**508**	**7.2**	**389**	**450**	**−13.6**	**589**	**586**	**0.6**
Laundry and cleaning supplies	131	130	1.1	125	125	−0.1	152	155	−2.1
Other household products	283	235	20.6	173	200	−13.5	295	278	6.0
Postage and stationery	131	144	−9.1	92	125	−26.5	142	152	−6.6
Household furnishings and equipment	**1,518**	**1,689**	**−10.1**	**1,469**	**1,696**	**−13.4**	**1,823**	**1,798**	**1.4**
Household textiles	136	88	54.1	128	78	63.7	137	89	53.3
Furniture	401	432	−7.3	472	531	−11.1	524	480	9.1
Floor coverings	40	87	−54.1	30	77	−61.1	44	64	−30.9
Major appliances	188	189	−0.4	148	167	−11.1	252	202	24.6
Small appliances, misc. housewares	100	103	−2.7	109	85	28.4	88	108	−18.8
Misc. household equipment	652	790	−17.5	583	758	−23.0	776	854	−9.1
APPAREL, SERVICES	**1,749**	**1,932**	**−9.5**	**1,989**	**2,187**	**−9.0**	**2,101**	**2,304**	**−8.8**
Men and boys	**409**	**455**	**−10.1**	**486**	**506**	**−4.0**	**562**	**554**	**1.4**
Men, aged 16 or older	319	361	−11.6	367	397	−7.5	383	372	2.9
Boys, aged 2 to 15	90	94	−4.1	119	110	8.7	179	182	−1.7
Women and girls	**704**	**760**	**−7.3**	**647**	**782**	**−17.3**	**787**	**886**	**−11.2**
Women, aged 16 or older	587	641	−8.5	511	648	−21.1	540	646	−16.4
Girls, aged 2 to 15	117	118	−1.2	136	134	1.4	247	240	2.8
Children under age 2	**83**	**86**	**−3.5**	**188**	**182**	**3.2**	**97**	**101**	**−3.5**
Footwear	**313**	**352**	**−11.1**	**385**	**382**	**0.8**	**382**	**436**	**−12.3**
Other apparel products and services	**240**	**279**	**−14.1**	**283**	**335**	**−15.6**	**273**	**327**	**−16.6**
TRANSPORTATION	**7,759**	**7,215**	**7.5**	**8,423**	**7,878**	**6.9**	**9,400**	**8,105**	**16.0**
Vehicle purchases	**3,665**	**3,057**	**19.9**	**4,269**	**3,618**	**18.0**	**4,592**	**3,394**	**35.3**
Cars and trucks, new	1,753	1,373	27.7	1,739	1,295	34.3	2,394	1,540	55.5
Cars and trucks, used	1,842	1,636	12.6	2,454	2,243	9.4	2,115	1,781	18.8
Gasoline and motor oil	**1,235**	**1,227**	**0.7**	**1,257**	**1,255**	**0.2**	**1,473**	**1,446**	**1.9**

	total consumer units			aged 25 to 34			aged 35 to 44		
	2002	1997	percent change 1997–02	2002	1997	percent change 1997–02	2002	1997	percent change 1997–02
Other vehicle expenses	**$2,471**	**$2,492**	**–0.8%**	**$2,505**	**$2,564**	**–2.3%**	**$2,935**	**$2,856**	**2.8%**
Vehicle finance charges	397	327	21.3	516	467	10.5	529	390	35.7
Maintenance and repairs	697	762	–8.5	609	668	–8.9	843	880	–4.3
Vehicle insurance	894	844	6.0	872	834	4.6	987	935	5.5
Vehicle rental, leases, licenses, other charges	483	560	–13.7	508	596	–14.7	576	650	–11.4
Public transportation	**389**	**439**	**–11.4**	**392**	**441**	**–11.2**	**400**	**408**	**–1.9**
HEALTH CARE	**2,350**	**2,057**	**14.2**	**1,417**	**1,381**	**2.6**	**1,980**	**1,793**	**10.4**
Health insurance	1,168	984	18.7	762	645	18.2	1,023	836	22.4
Medical services	590	593	–0.6	391	472	–17.1	556	611	–9.0
Drugs	487	358	36.2	209	189	10.7	303	235	29.1
Medical supplies	105	121	–13.0	55	75	–26.5	99	112	–11.4
ENTERTAINMENT	**2,079**	**2,026**	**2.6**	**2,027**	**2,084**	**–2.7**	**2,685**	**2,379**	**12.9**
Fees and admissions	542	526	3.0	490	474	3.4	743	641	15.9
Television, radio, sound equipment	692	645	7.3	750	691	8.6	817	750	9.0
Pets, toys, and playground equipment	369	365	1.0	368	386	–4.5	463	450	2.8
Other entertainment supplies, services	476	491	–3.0	420	533	–21.2	662	537	23.2
PERSONAL CARE PRODUCTS, SERVICES	**526**	**590**	**–10.8**	**488**	**592**	**–17.6**	**615**	**655**	**–6.1**
READING	**139**	**183**	**–24.1**	**103**	**148**	**–30.2**	**135**	**179**	**–24.5**
EDUCATION	**752**	**638**	**17.9**	**571**	**540**	**5.8**	**738**	**675**	**9.4**
TOBACCO PRODUCTS, SMOKING SUPPLIES	**320**	**295**	**8.5**	**315**	**292**	**8.0**	**376**	**368**	**2.3**
MISCELLANEOUS	**792**	**946**	**–16.3**	**678**	**846**	**–19.8**	**841**	**1,105**	**–23.9**
CASH CONTRIBUTIONS	**1,277**	**1,118**	**14.2**	**743**	**541**	**37.4**	**1,247**	**1,056**	**18.1**
PERSONAL INSURANCE AND PENSIONS	**3,899**	**3,601**	**8.3**	**3,972**	**3,733**	**6.4**	**5,183**	**4,829**	**7.3**
Life, other personal insurance	406	424	–4.1	230	267	–13.9	409	428	–4.4
Pensions and Social Security	3,493	3,178	9.9	3,742	3,466	8.0	4,774	4,401	8.5
PERSONAL TAXES	**2,496**	**3,621**	**–31.1**	**2,259**	**3,772**	**–40.1**	**3,075**	**4,780**	**–35.7**
Federal income taxes	1,843	2,758	–33.2	1,642	2,868	–42.8	2,258	3,625	–37.7
State and local income taxes	506	721	–29.8	546	840	–35.0	680	1,002	–32.2
Other taxes	147	144	2.0	71	63	13.5	136	153	–11.2
GIFTS FOR NON-HOUSEHOLD MEMBERS	**1,036**	**1,183**	**–12.4**	**688**	**851**	**–19.2**	**868**	**1,017**	**–14.6**
Food	82	76	7.9	34	34	1.4	60	83	–27.4
Alcoholic beverages	**13**	**–**	**–**	**13**	**–**	**–**	**16**	**–**	**–**
Housing	**259**	**305**	**–15.1**	**213**	**279**	**–23.7**	**231**	**275**	**–16.0**
Housekeeping supplies	42	41	1.6	32	36	–10.5	41	51	–20.2
Household textiles	14	9	56.6	13	6	132.7	11	7	64.1

	total consumer units			aged 25 to 34			aged 35 to 44		
	2002	1997	percent change 1997–02	2002	1997	percent change 1997–02	2002	1997	percent change 1997–02
Appliances and misc. housewares	$24	$30	−20.4%	$12	$25	−51.2%	$17	$20	−15.5%
Major appliances	8	7	19.3	2	6	−64.2	7	3	108.8
Small appliances and misc. housewares	16	24	−31.8	10	19	−47.4	9	17	−46.3
Misc. household equipment	65	74	−11.9	45	62	−26.8	65	67	−3.0
Other housing	114	151	−24.4	111	152	−27.0	98	129	−23.7
Apparel and services	**237**	**282**	**−15.8**	**249**	**235**	**6.1**	**208**	**256**	**−18.7**
Males, aged 2 or older	64	68	−6.1	56	59	−5.4	63	49	28.1
Females, aged 2 or older	82	91	−9.4	72	64	13.1	56	93	−39.6
Children under age 2	40	37	8.5	57	49	15.9	45	37	22.1
Other apparel products and services	52	86	−39.6	65	63	3.9	44	77	−42.9
Jewelry and watches	24	55	−56.2	44	37	19.3	20	45	−55.3
All other apparel products and services	28	32	−13.6	21	26	−18.3	23	32	−29.0
Transportation	**44**	**64**	**−30.9**	**22**	**25**	**−10.5**	**45**	**32**	**38.9**
Health care	**33**	**34**	**−1.6**	**11**	**10**	**9.4**	**21**	**21**	**−1.1**
Entertainment	**78**	**111**	**−29.5**	**60**	**96**	**−37.6**	**86**	**94**	**−8.4**
Toys, games, hobbies, and tricycles	30	46	−34.5	20	54	−62.7	29	39	−25.8
Other entertainment	48	65	−25.9	40	43	−5.8	57	55	4.1
Personal care products and services	**21**	**–**	**–**	**16**	**–**	**–**	**27**	**–**	**–**
Reading	**1**	**–**	**–**	**1**	**–**	**–**	**1**	**–**	**–**
Education	**184**	**173**	**6.2**	**27**	**31**	**−13.7**	**108**	**113**	**−4.3**
All other gifts	**84**	**140**	**−39.9**	**42**	**142**	**−70.4**	**67**	**142**	**−52.8**

Note: The Bureau of Labor Statistics uses consumer unit rather than household as the sampling unit in the Consumer Expenditure Survey. For the definition of consumer unit, see the glossary. Spending on gifts is included in the preceding product and service categories. (–) means sample is too small to make a reliable estimate or data are not available.
Source: Bureau of Labor Statistics, 1997 and 2002 Consumer Expenditure Surveys, Internet site http://www.bls.gov/cex/; calculations by New Strategist

Householders Aged 25 to 34 Are Average Spenders

They spend more than average on children, fast food, and rental housing.

The spending of households headed by people aged 25 to 34 almost matches spending by the average household. In 2002, householders aged 25 to 34 spent $40,318, slightly less than the $40,677 spent by the average household.

Judged by their spending patterns, the diets of young adults include a lot of fast-food meals and plenty of beer and snacks. Householders aged 25 to 34 spend 22 to 29 percent more than average on lunches and dinners from fast-food restaurants. They spend 11 percent more than average on snacks and nonalcoholic drinks, 26 percent more on beer and ale at home, and 14 percent more on beer and ale away from home.

What is most clearly reflected in the spending data is their status as parents. The spending of households headed by people aged 25 to 34 far exceeds the average for products and services needed by young children. They spend more than twice the average household on infants' clothing, baby food, toys, babysitting, and day care centers.

Most householders in the age group cannot yet afford to buy a home. Consequently, their spending on rent is 61 percent more than average. They also spend nearly twice the average on furniture rental.

■ The incomes of young adults don't leave much room for extravagance, and the need to buy for children limits them further.

Young adults spend big on beer, laundromats, rent, and clothes for infants

(indexed spending of householders aged 25 to 34 on selected items, 2002)

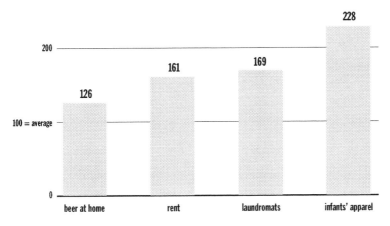

Table 8.2 Average and Indexed Spending of Householders Aged 25 to 34, 2002

(average annual spending of total consumer units (CUs) and average annual and indexed spending of consumer units headed by people aged 25 to 34, 2002)

	total consumer units	CUs headed by 25-to-34-year-olds average spending	CUs headed by 25-to-34-year-olds indexed spending
Number of consumer units (in 000s)	112,108	18,988	–
Average before-tax income	$49,430.00	$49,133.00	99
Average annual spending	40,676.60	40,318.29	99
FOOD	$5,374.80	$5,470.74	102
FOOD AT HOME	3,098.52	3,092.85	100
Cereals and bakery products	450.13	441.68	98
Cereals and cereal products	154.07	163.18	106
Flour	8.65	8.88	103
Prepared flour mixes	12.40	10.73	87
Ready-to-eat and cooked cereals	87.66	94.35	108
Rice	17.82	20.74	116
Pasta, cornmeal, and other cereal products	27.54	28.48	103
Bakery products	296.06	278.50	94
Bread	83.83	77.80	93
White bread	35.21	36.01	102
Bread, other than white	48.62	41.79	86
Crackers and cookies	70.67	63.82	90
Cookies	46.31	42.80	92
Crackers	24.36	21.02	86
Frozen and refrigerated bakery products	25.64	25.12	98
Other bakery products	115.92	111.76	96
Biscuits and rolls	41.04	36.88	90
Cakes and cupcakes	35.73	39.40	110
Bread and cracker products	3.50	3.62	103
Sweetrolls, coffee cakes, doughnuts	25.84	23.79	92
Pies, tarts, turnovers	9.82	8.08	82
Meats, poultry, fish, and eggs	798.42	817.05	102
Beef	231.17	252.70	109
Ground beef	86.29	94.03	109
Roast	40.99	41.35	101
Chuck roast	11.71	12.27	105
Round roast	10.23	7.94	78
Other roast	19.05	21.14	111
Steak	84.47	98.77	117
Round steak	13.29	17.34	130
Sirloin steak	26.62	33.57	126
Other steak	44.56	47.86	107
Pork	167.34	162.42	97
Bacon	28.45	24.97	88
Pork chops	38.43	40.11	104
Ham	37.16	35.05	94
Ham, not canned	35.66	33.77	95
Canned ham	1.50	1.28	85

	total consumer units	CUs headed by 25-to-34-year-olds	
		average spending	indexed spending
Sausage	$26.17	$26.07	100
Other pork	37.13	36.23	98
Other meats	101.08	96.36	95
Frankfurters	20.95	20.61	98
Lunch meats (cold cuts)	68.99	66.61	97
Bologna, liverwurst, salami	21.11	20.36	96
Lamb, organ meats, and others	11.14	9.14	82
Lamb and organ meats	7.99	6.56	82
Mutton, goat, and game	3.15	2.57	82
Poultry	144.13	158.75	110
Fresh and frozen chicken	113.25	124.45	110
Fresh and frozen whole chicken	32.08	34.65	108
Fresh and frozen chicken parts	81.17	89.80	111
Other poultry	30.88	34.30	111
Fish and seafood	120.97	112.79	93
Canned fish and seafood	16.13	13.20	82
Fresh fish and shellfish	69.31	68.48	99
Frozen fish and shellfish	35.53	31.10	88
Eggs	33.75	34.03	101
Dairy products	**328.34**	**324.24**	**99**
Fresh milk and cream	127.15	129.72	102
Fresh milk, all types	114.63	117.64	103
Cream	12.52	12.08	96
Other dairy products	201.19	194.52	97
Butter	18.48	16.06	87
Cheese	95.64	95.60	100
Ice cream and related products	58.74	55.86	95
Miscellaneous dairy products	28.33	27.01	95
Fruits and vegetables	**552.01**	**521.81**	**95**
Fresh fruits	178.20	153.54	86
Apples	32.59	30.32	93
Bananas	31.24	28.12	90
Oranges	20.34	19.16	94
Citrus fruits, excl. oranges	14.29	11.91	83
Other fresh fruits	79.74	64.03	80
Fresh vegetables	174.88	162.41	93
Potatoes	33.35	30.85	93
Lettuce	22.22	20.16	91
Tomatoes	33.71	32.71	97
Other fresh vegetables	85.60	78.70	92
Processed fruits	115.50	118.03	102
Frozen fruits and fruit juices	12.45	13.41	108
Frozen orange juice	6.31	6.42	102
Frozen fruits	2.79	3.20	115
Frozen fruit juices, excl. orange	3.35	3.79	113
Canned fruits	15.06	14.06	93
Dried fruits	6.06	5.56	92
Fresh fruit juice	22.20	21.87	99
Canned and bottled fruit juice	59.74	63.14	106

	total consumer units	CUs headed by 25-to-34-year-olds average spending	CUs headed by 25-to-34-year-olds indexed spending
Processed vegetables	$83.43	$87.83	105
Frozen vegetables	27.85	26.88	97
Canned and dried vegetables and juices	55.58	60.94	110
Canned beans	12.47	13.06	105
Canned corn	7.34	8.87	121
Canned miscellaneous vegetables	17.85	17.17	96
Dried peas	0.36	0.36	100
Dried beans	2.55	2.64	104
Dried miscellaneous vegetables	7.38	9.91	134
Dried processed vegetables	0.34	0.08	24
Frozen vegetable juices	0.06	–	–
Fresh and canned vegetable juices	7.23	8.86	123
Sugar and other sweets	**117.39**	**103.74**	**88**
Candy and chewing gum	75.44	66.60	88
Sugar	15.56	15.16	97
Artificial sweeteners	4.33	2.44	56
Jams, preserves, other sweets	22.06	19.55	89
Fats and oils	**85.16**	**81.00**	**95**
Margarine	9.86	7.87	80
Fats and oils	26.08	24.65	95
Salad dressings	27.01	26.28	97
Nondairy cream and imitation milk	9.33	8.24	88
Peanut butter	12.89	13.94	108
Miscellaneous foods	**471.92**	**511.81**	**108**
Frozen prepared foods	98.09	103.86	106
Frozen meals	29.88	29.79	100
Other frozen prepared foods	68.22	74.07	109
Canned and packaged soups	35.82	30.72	86
Potato chips, nuts, and other snacks	100.53	94.89	94
Potato chips and other snacks	76.37	77.66	102
Nuts	24.16	17.23	71
Condiments and seasonings	86.81	88.96	102
Salt, spices, and other seasonings	21.14	21.42	101
Olives, pickles, relishes	9.70	8.45	87
Sauces and gravies	37.78	40.03	106
Baking needs and miscellaneous products	18.19	19.06	105
Other canned/packaged prepared foods	150.67	193.39	128
Prepared salads	21.46	15.92	74
Prepared desserts	10.32	9.25	90
Baby food	31.57	73.65	233
Miscellaneous prepared foods	87.24	94.55	108
Nonalcoholic beverages	253.94	260.44	103
Cola	81.11	87.45	108
Other carbonated drinks	43.93	52.75	120
Coffee	41.59	27.73	67
Roasted coffee	27.38	18.72	68
Instant and freeze-dried coffee	14.21	9.02	63
Noncarbonated fruit-flavored drinks	18.95	23.40	123

	total consumer units	CUs headed by 25-to-34-year-olds	
		average spending	indexed spending
Tea	$15.86	$12.96	82
Nonalcoholic beer	0.64	0.49	77
Other nonalcoholic beverages and ice	51.85	55.66	107
Food prepared by CU on trips	41.20	31.08	75
FOOD AWAY FROM HOME	**2,276.29**	**2,377.89**	**104**
Meals at restaurants, carry-outs, other	**1,866.42**	**2,040.46**	**109**
Lunch	685.79	761.52	111
• At fast food, take-out, delivery, concession stands, buffet, and cafeteria (other than employer and school cafeteria)	377.71	460.31	122
• At full-service restaurants	224.82	217.71	97
• At vending machines, mobile vendors	5.50	6.67	121
• At employer and school cafeterias	77.76	76.84	99
Dinner	736.54	799.06	108
• At fast food, take-out, delivery, concession stands, buffet, and cafeteria (other than employer and school cafeteria)	213.33	276.20	129
• At full-service restaurants	518.02	517.09	100
• At vending machines, mobile vendors	1.87	2.27	121
• At employer and school cafeterias	3.32	3.50	105
Snacks and nonalcoholic beverages	262.67	292.48	111
• At fast food, take-out, delivery, concession stands, buffet, and cafeteria (other than employer and school cafeteria)	185.69	202.22	109
• At full-service restaurants	30.17	29.28	97
• At vending machines, mobile vendors	36.71	50.26	137
• At employer and school cafeterias	10.11	10.72	106
Breakfast and brunch	181.42	187.39	103
• At fast food, take-out, delivery, concession stands, buffet, and cafeteria (other than employer and school cafeteria)	87.83	106.62	121
• At full-service restaurants	87.08	75.01	86
• At vending machines, mobile vendors	1.40	1.53	109
• At employer and school cafeterias	5.11	4.22	83
Board (including at school)	**46.54**	**9.54**	**20**
Catered affairs	**69.00**	**71.86**	**104**
Food on trips	**211.49**	**168.38**	**80**
School lunches	**60.00**	**51.71**	**86**
Meals as pay	**22.86**	**35.93**	**157**
ALCOHOLIC BEVERAGES	**$375.95**	**$394.69**	**105**
At home	**228.08**	**226.96**	**100**
Beer and ale	112.34	141.39	126
Whiskey	13.90	7.47	54
Wine	77.75	56.18	72
Other alcoholic beverages	24.09	21.92	91

	total consumer units	CUs headed by 25-to-34-year-olds	
		average spending	indexed spending
Away from home	**$147.87**	**$167.73**	**113**
Beer and ale	52.86	60.13	114
• At fast food, take-out, delivery, concession			
stands, buffet, and cafeteria	7.99	12.94	162
• At full-service restaurants	41.95	46.85	112
• At vending machines, mobile vendors	0.32	0.17	53
• At catered affairs	2.59	0.16	6
Wine	25.85	30.37	117
• At fast food, take-out, delivery, concession			
stands, buffet and cafeteria	4.41	6.06	137
• At full-service restaurants	20.36	24.30	119
• At catered affairs	1.09	0.02	2
Other alcoholic beverages	69.16	77.23	112
• At fast food, take-out, delivery, concession			
stands, buffet, and cafeteria	3.50	6.32	181
• At full-service restaurants	28.94	34.73	120
• At catered affairs	3.94	0.07	2
Alcoholic beverages purchased on trips	32.78	36.11	110
HOUSING	**$13,283.08**	**$13,727.04**	**103**
SHELTER	**7,829.41**	**8,470.23**	**108**
Owned dwellings*	**5,164.96**	**4,700.64**	**91**
Mortgage interest and charges	2,962.16	3,285.94	111
Mortgage interest	2,811.49	3,183.16	113
Interest paid, home equity loan	88.61	73.32	83
Interest paid, home equity line of credit	61.88	28.52	46
Property taxes	1,242.36	822.52	66
Maintenance, repairs, insurance,			
other expenses	960.43	592.18	62
Homeowner's insurance	283.30	190.44	67
Ground rent	40.96	35.33	86
Maintenance and repair services	519.60	280.39	54
Painting and papering	55.58	30.20	54
Plumbing and water heating	46.63	26.13	56
Heat, air conditioning, electrical work	86.28	53.27	62
Roofing and gutters	71.20	23.70	33
Other repair and maintenance services	214.77	108.09	50
Repair, replacement of hard-surface flooring	43.54	36.95	85
Repair of built-in appliances	1.62	2.05	127
Maintenance and repair materials	83.75	66.07	79
Paints, wallpaper, and supplies	14.71	13.70	93
Tools, equipment for painting, wallpapering	1.58	1.47	93
Plumbing supplies and equipment	5.62	5.42	96
Electrical supplies, heating, cooling equip.	3.46	2.41	70
Hard-surface flooring, repair and replacement	8.72	7.98	92
Roofing and gutters	5.29	5.32	101
Plaster, paneling, siding, windows,			
doors, screens, awnings	13.92	9.08	65
Patio, walk, fence, driveway, masonry,			
brick, and stucco materials	1.29	0.72	56

	total consumer units	CUs headed by 25-to-34-year-olds	
		average spending	indexed spending
Landscape maintenance	$4.73	$4.37	92
Miscellaneous supplies and equipment	24.43	15.60	64
Insulation, other maintenance, repair	13.15	7.20	55
Finish basement, remodel rooms, build patios, walks, etc.	11.28	8.40	74
Property management and security	27.64	16.31	59
Property management	21.94	13.61	62
Management and upkeep services for security	5.71	2.70	47
Parking	5.17	3.63	70
Rented dwellings	**2,159.89**	**3,476.20**	**161**
Rent	2,104.66	3,397.78	161
Rent as pay	27.17	35.72	131
Maintenance, insurance, and other expenses	28.06	42.70	152
Tenant's insurance	8.90	14.01	157
Maintenance and repair services	11.16	11.41	102
Repair and maintenance services	10.58	11.11	105
Repair, replacement of hard-surface flooring	0.51	0.01	2
Repair of built-in appliances	0.07	0.29	414
Maintenance and repair materials	8.00	17.28	216
Paint, wallpaper, and supplies	1.01	1.98	196
Painting and wallpapering tools	0.11	0.21	191
Plastering, paneling, roofing, gutters, etc.	0.90	2.10	233
Plumbing supplies and equipment	0.80	0.80	100
Electrical supplies, heating, cooling equip.	0.30	0.81	270
Miscellaneous supplies and equipment	3.67	7.16	195
Insulation, other maintenance and repair	1.09	2.16	198
Materials for additions, finishing basements, remodeling rooms	2.43	4.42	182
Construction materials for jobs not started	0.15	0.57	380
Hard-surface flooring	0.73	2.24	307
Landscape maintenance	0.49	1.97	402
Other lodging	**504.56**	**293.39**	**58**
Owned vacation homes	171.55	87.80	51
Mortgage interest and charges	71.98	56.75	79
Property taxes	63.76	22.33	35
Maintenance, insurance and other expenses	35.81	8.72	24
Homeowner's insurance	9.70	4.96	51
Ground rent	2.93	2.06	70
Maintenance and repair services	16.76	0.61	4
Maintenance and repair materials	2.07	–	–
Property management and security	3.60	0.85	24
Property management	2.50	0.64	26
Management, upkeep services for security	1.10	0.21	19
Parking	0.76	0.24	32
Housing while attending school	80.14	15.66	20
Lodging on trips	252.87	189.92	75

	total consumer units	CUs headed by 25-to-34-year-olds	
		average spending	indexed spending
UTILITIES, FUELS, PUBLIC SERVICES	$2,684.32	$2,502.59	93
Natural gas	329.75	288.10	87
Natural gas (renter)	60.32	93.31	155
Natural gas (owner)	266.79	194.00	73
Natural gas (vacation)	2.54	0.50	20
Electricity	981.09	864.22	88
Electricity (renter)	223.26	347.19	156
Electricity (owner)	750.48	515.37	69
Electricity (vacation)	6.32	1.34	21
Fuel oil and other fuels	88.41	54.58	62
Fuel oil	45.98	23.88	52
Fuel oil (renter)	4.64	5.11	110
Fuel oil (owner)	40.98	18.59	45
Fuel oil (vacation)	0.36	0.18	50
Coal	0.07	–	–
Bottled/tank gas	35.27	26.15	74
Gas (renter)	5.09	7.47	147
Gas (owner)	27.19	17.08	63
Gas (vacation)	2.98	1.60	54
Wood and other fuels	7.09	4.55	64
Wood and other fuels (renter)	1.32	1.28	97
Wood and other fuels (owner)	5.68	3.27	58
Telephone services	956.74	1,032.44	108
Residential telephone and pay phones	641.00	641.89	100
Cellular phone service	293.76	360.03	123
Pager service	1.71	2.03	119
Phone cards	20.28	28.49	140
Water and other public services	328.33	263.26	80
Water and sewerage maintenance	237.16	190.31	80
Water and sewerage maintenance (renter)	32.76	45.00	137
Water and sewerage maintenance (owner)	201.79	145.09	72
Water and sewerage maintenance (vacation)	2.36	0.14	6
Trash and garbage collection	89.05	71.73	81
Trash and garbage collection (renter)	9.89	13.99	141
Trash and garbage collection (owner)	76.61	57.52	75
Trash and garbage collection (vacation)	2.53	0.21	8
Septic tank cleaning	2.12	1.22	58
HOUSEHOLD SERVICES	705.71	895.24	127
Personal services	331.02	649.96	196
Babysitting, child care in your own home	35.91	79.69	222
Babysitting, child care in someone else's home	27.48	61.86	225
Care for elderly, invalids, handicapped, etc.	50.07	29.24	58
Adult day care centers	6.81	0.21	3
Day care centers, nurseries, and preschools	210.74	478.96	227
Other household services	374.70	245.28	65
Housekeeping services	79.90	29.12	36
Gardening, lawn care service	72.38	22.49	31
Water softening service	3.15	2.83	90

	total consumer units	CUs headed by 25-to-34-year-olds	
		average spending	indexed spending
Nonclothing laundry, dry cleaning, sent out	$1.72	$1.54	90
Nonclothing laundry, dry cleaning, coin-operated	4.13	6.74	163
Termite/pest control services	13.25	8.26	62
Home security system service fee	17.40	15.34	88
Other home services	15.06	6.68	44
Termite/pest control products	0.68	0.38	56
Moving, storage, and freight express	33.13	32.41	98
Appliance repair, including service center	10.86	5.15	47
Reupholstering and furniture repair	7.40	0.98	13
Repairs/rentals of lawn/garden equipment, hand/power tools, etc.	3.62	1.66	46
Appliance rental	1.07	1.92	179
Rental of office equipment, nonbusiness use	0.41	0.22	54
Repair of misc. household equip., furnishings	0.62	0.03	5
Repair of computer systems, nonbusiness use	2.53	0.41	16
Computer information services	107.29	109.13	102
HOUSEKEEPING SUPPLIES	**545.28**	**389.49**	**71**
Laundry and cleaning supplies	**130.57**	**124.88**	**96**
Soaps and detergents	72.89	75.31	103
Other laundry cleaning products	57.68	49.57	86
Other household products	**283.28**	**172.75**	**61**
Cleansing and toilet tissue, paper towels, and napkins	76.46	63.36	83
Miscellaneous household products	96.81	71.06	73
Lawn and garden supplies	110.01	38.34	35
Postage and stationery	**131.44**	**91.86**	**70**
Stationery, stationery supplies, giftwrap	60.20	50.11	83
Postage	69.12	40.06	58
Delivery services	2.12	1.69	80
HOUSEHOLD FURNISHINGS, EQUIPMENT	**1,518.36**	**1,469.49**	**97**
Household textiles	**135.52**	**127.92**	**94**
Bathroom linens	22.35	21.44	96
Bedroom linens	65.98	65.30	99
Kitchen and dining room linens	10.11	8.45	84
Curtains and draperies	16.65	15.12	91
Slipcovers and decorative pillows	7.40	8.85	120
Sewing materials for household items	11.44	7.55	66
Other linens	1.59	1.20	75
Furniture	**401.28**	**471.70**	**118**
Mattresses and springs	52.91	70.55	133
Other bedroom furniture	68.33	88.78	130
Sofas	85.33	103.01	121
Living room chairs	39.21	34.22	87
Living room tables	18.03	17.40	97
Kitchen and dining room furniture	61.28	64.24	105
Infants' furniture	6.46	15.63	242
Outdoor furniture	16.79	11.30	67
Wall units, cabinets, and other furniture	52.94	66.57	126

	total consumer units	CUs headed by 25-to-34-year-olds	
		average spending	indexed spending
Floor coverings	**$40.49**	**$29.98**	**74**
Wall-to-wall carpeting (renter)	0.65	0.66	102
Wall-to-wall carpet (replacement) (owner)	21.04	16.48	78
Floor coverings, nonpermanent	18.79	12.83	68
Major appliances	**188.47**	**148.07**	**79**
Dishwashers (built-in), garbage disposals, range hoods (renter)	1.24	1.40	113
Dishwashers (built-in), garbage disposals, range hoods (owner)	15.28	10.18	67
Refrigerators and freezers (renter)	5.58	7.53	135
Refrigerators and freezers (owner)	46.50	32.69	70
Washing machines (renter)	4.42	8.48	192
Washing machines (owner)	17.88	17.35	97
Clothes dryers (renter)	3.17	4.82	152
Clothes dryers (owner)	13.88	13.51	97
Cooking stoves, ovens (renter)	2.86	3.05	107
Cooking stoves, ovens (owner)	28.09	16.25	58
Microwave ovens (renter)	2.14	3.36	157
Microwave ovens (owner)	8.36	5.62	67
Portable dishwasher (renter)	0.25	0.65	260
Portable dishwasher (owner)	0.51	0.03	6
Window air conditioners (renter)	1.83	3.16	173
Window air conditioners (owner)	6.07	2.46	41
Electric floor-cleaning equipment	22.80	15.35	67
Sewing machines	4.79	1.78	37
Miscellaneous household appliances	**2.81**	**0.39**	**14**
Small appliances and misc. housewares	100.43	109.00	109
Housewares	77.55	90.12	116
Plastic dinnerware	1.57	1.78	113
China and other dinnerware	14.51	24.65	170
Flatware	3.79	3.09	82
Glassware	6.51	5.58	86
Silver serving pieces	4.05	3.59	89
Other serving pieces	1.44	1.21	84
Nonelectric cookware	24.25	35.25	145
Tableware, nonelectric kitchenware	21.44	14.96	70
Small appliances	22.89	18.88	82
Small electric kitchen appliances	17.18	14.34	83
Portable heating and cooling equipment	5.70	4.54	80
Miscellaneous household equipment	**652.17**	**582.83**	**89**
Window coverings	13.91	15.86	114
Infants' equipment	12.96	16.80	130
Laundry and cleaning equipment	15.15	15.48	102
Outdoor equipment	31.52	9.76	31
Clocks	5.87	3.65	62
Lamps and lighting fixtures	11.74	7.53	64
Other household decorative items	144.94	128.94	89
Telephones and accessories	32.73	27.72	85
Lawn and garden equipment	48.16	35.43	74

	total consumer units	CUs headed by 25-to-34-year-olds	
		average spending	indexed spending
Power tools	$33.27	$46.26	139
Office furniture for home use	10.57	11.07	105
Hand tools	8.05	9.81	122
Indoor plants and fresh flowers	49.78	35.68	72
Closet and storage items	9.98	7.76	78
Rental of furniture	4.60	9.17	199
Luggage	5.98	4.66	78
Computers and computer hardware, nonbusiness use	138.58	142.09	103
Computer software and accessories, nonbusiness use	17.67	19.33	109
Telephone answering devices	1.08	1.14	106
Calculators	1.44	0.76	53
Business equipment for home use	0.97	0.87	90
Other hardware	12.85	6.74	52
Smoke alarms (owner)	1.10	1.33	121
Smoke alarms (renter)	0.39	0.17	44
Other household appliances (owner)	8.00	7.45	93
Other household appliances (renter)	1.23	1.06	86
Misc. household equipment and parts	29.62	16.34	55
APPAREL AND SERVICES	**$1,749.22**	**$1,988.99**	**114**
Men's apparel	**319.48**	**367.05**	**115**
Suits	32.96	33.93	103
Sport coats and tailored jackets	10.65	7.22	68
Coats and jackets	33.86	49.58	146
Underwear	15.27	14.40	94
Hosiery	12.22	11.33	93
Nightwear	2.98	2.53	85
Accessories	22.41	26.61	119
Sweaters and vests	15.68	15.12	96
Active sportswear	15.13	21.98	145
Shirts	78.89	94.94	120
Pants	57.64	62.43	108
Shorts and shorts sets	12.22	14.41	118
Uniforms	3.21	4.45	139
Costumes	6.35	8.13	128
Boys' (aged 2 to 15) apparel	**89.98**	**119.07**	**132**
Coats and jackets	6.38	8.76	137
Sweaters	3.65	4.86	133
Shirts	19.50	25.27	130
Underwear	5.02	6.27	125
Nightwear	2.59	2.49	96
Hosiery	4.21	5.18	123
Accessories	4.12	7.18	174
Suits, sport coats, and vests	2.37	2.52	106
Pants	22.58	30.82	136
Shorts and shorts sets	8.66	12.82	148
Uniforms	3.35	3.40	101
Active sportswear	3.84	4.98	130
Costumes	3.72	4.52	122

	total consumer units	CUs headed by 25-to-34-year-olds average spending	indexed spending
Women's apparel	**$586.91**	**$511.05**	**87**
Coats and jackets	50.06	32.29	65
Dresses	56.40	31.91	57
Sport coats and tailored jackets	6.48	3.66	56
Sweaters and vests	50.47	41.37	82
Shirts, blouses, and tops	103.24	94.29	91
Skirts	17.48	20.76	119
Pants	96.29	93.63	97
Shorts and shorts sets	16.09	14.67	91
Active sportswear	30.07	32.21	107
Nightwear	27.63	22.55	82
Undergarments	33.55	33.08	99
Hosiery	21.22	15.94	75
Suits	29.01	23.75	82
Accessories	33.37	28.92	87
Uniforms	6.12	7.74	126
Costumes	9.42	14.26	151
Girls' (aged 2 to 15) apparel	**117.21**	**135.89**	**116**
Coats and jackets	6.49	7.97	123
Dresses and suits	12.41	9.89	80
Shirts, blouses, and sweaters	29.33	32.29	110
Skirts and pants	24.07	30.22	126
Shorts and shorts sets	8.28	11.16	135
Active sportswear	9.32	9.48	102
Underwear and nightwear	7.63	10.76	141
Hosiery	4.30	4.67	109
Accessories	5.81	5.59	96
Uniforms	4.77	6.90	145
Costumes	4.80	6.97	145
Children under age 2	**82.60**	**188.24**	**228**
Coats, jackets, and snowsuits	2.43	4.68	193
Outerwear including dresses	23.71	39.47	166
Underwear	43.60	111.48	256
Nightwear and loungewear	4.07	7.06	173
Accessories	8.79	25.54	291
Footwear	**313.17**	**385.10**	**123**
Men's	102.90	121.04	118
Boys'	36.87	62.76	170
Women's	141.64	151.03	107
Girls'	31.76	50.27	158
Other apparel products and services	**239.87**	**282.60**	**118**
Material for making clothes	5.11	2.22	43
Sewing patterns and notions	8.20	5.45	66
Watches	13.62	15.52	114
Jewelry	89.65	115.99	129
Shoe repair and other shoe services	1.44	1.00	69
Coin-operated apparel laundry and dry cleaning	37.58	63.56	169
Apparel alteration, repair, and tailoring services	5.86	5.35	91
Clothing rental	2.66	3.08	116
Watch and jewelry repair	5.49	2.65	48
Professional laundry, dry cleaning	69.69	67.70	97
Clothing storage	0.55	0.08	15

	total consumer units	CUs headed by 25-to-34-year-olds	
		average spending	indexed spending
TRANSPORTATION	$7,759.29	$8,423.07	109
VEHICLE PURCHASES	3,664.93	4,268.90	116
Cars and trucks, new	1,752.96	1,739.49	99
New cars	883.08	789.03	89
New trucks	869.88	950.46	109
Cars and trucks, used	1,842.29	2,454.23	133
Used cars	1,113.46	1,315.16	118
Used trucks	728.82	1,139.07	156
Other vehicles	69.68	75.19	108
New motorcycles	36.26	41.46	114
Used motorcycles	33.42	33.73	101
GASOLINE AND MOTOR OIL	1,235.06	1,256.79	102
Gasoline	1,125.01	1,153.23	103
Diesel fuel	10.86	10.46	96
Gasoline on trips	88.24	80.63	91
Motor oil	10.05	11.65	116
Motor oil on trips	0.89	0.81	91
OTHER VEHICLE EXPENSES	2,470.55	2,505.26	101
Vehicle finance charges	397.04	516.47	130
Automobile finance charges	193.12	253.45	131
Truck finance charges	182.89	242.16	132
Motorcycle and plane finance charges	2.36	3.08	131
Other vehicle finance charges	18.67	17.77	95
Maintenance and repairs	697.30	608.61	87
Coolant, additives, brake, transmission fluids	3.82	4.20	110
Tires—purchased, replaced, installed	89.93	89.94	100
Parts, equipment, and accessories	41.70	37.50	90
Vehicle audio equipment, excl. labor	12.32	48.23	391
Vehicle products	4.92	2.09	42
Miscellaneous auto repair, servicing	43.69	20.10	46
Body work and painting	31.24	19.31	62
Clutch, transmission repair	48.68	47.61	98
Drive shaft and rear-end repair	6.51	9.54	147
Brake work	57.73	47.65	83
Repair to steering or front-end	16.91	15.05	89
Repair to engine cooling system	21.68	16.14	74
Motor tune-up	49.69	37.26	75
Lube, oil change, and oil filters	65.07	61.55	95
Front-end alignment, wheel balance, rotation	11.90	9.16	77
Shock absorber replacement	4.82	1.46	30
Gas tank repair, replacement	4.32	4.06	94
Tire repair and other repair work	39.83	28.67	72
Vehicle air conditioning repair	17.00	12.06	71
Exhaust system repair	12.56	12.15	97
Electrical system repair	28.42	21.25	75
Motor repair, replacement	76.62	58.63	77
Auto repair service policy	7.93	5.00	63

	total consumer units	CUs headed by 25-to-34-year-olds average spending	CUs headed by 25-to-34-year-olds indexed spending
Vehicle insurance	$893.50	$871.99	98
Vehicle rental, leases, licenses, other charges	482.71	508.20	105
Leased and rented vehicles	324.48	362.55	112
Rented vehicles	41.33	33.38	81
Auto rental	6.76	6.14	91
Auto rental on trips	28.28	22.72	80
Truck rental	2.21	0.44	20
Truck rental on trips	3.55	3.94	111
Leased vehicles	283.15	329.16	116
Car lease payments	149.63	188.80	126
Cash down payment (car lease)	11.13	7.92	71
Termination fee (car lease)	1.28	0.15	12
Truck lease payments	114.24	119.88	105
Cash down payment (truck lease)	4.92	10.50	213
Termination fee (truck lease)	1.94	1.91	98
Vehicle registration, state	72.82	64.33	88
Vehicle registration, local	7.76	6.17	80
Driver's license	6.26	5.98	96
Vehicle inspection	9.26	7.81	84
Parking fees	29.25	31.12	106
Parking fees in home city, excluding residence	24.24	27.20	112
Parking fees on trips	5.01	3.92	78
Tolls	10.59	12.45	118
Tolls on trips	3.94	3.75	95
Towing charges	5.60	7.55	135
Automobile service clubs	12.75	6.49	51
PUBLIC TRANSPORTATION	388.75	392.12	101
Airline fares	243.57	239.99	99
Intercity bus fares	11.48	10.01	87
Intracity mass transit fares	49.97	59.99	120
Local transportation on trips	10.91	9.37	86
Taxi fares and limousine service on trips	6.41	5.50	86
Taxi fares and limousine service	18.95	23.10	122
Intercity train fares	16.09	12.65	79
Ship fares	29.74	29.97	101
School bus	1.64	1.55	95
HEALTH CARE	$2,350.32	$1,416.55	60
HEALTH INSURANCE	1,167.71	761.86	65
Commercial health insurance	217.53	186.02	86
Traditional fee-for-service health plan (not BCBS)	68.27	41.46	61
Preferred-provider health plan (not BCBS)	149.26	144.55	97
Blue Cross, Blue Shield	315.67	221.46	70
Traditional fee-for-service health plan	53.76	27.42	51
Preferred-provider health plan	106.99	90.22	84
Health maintenance organization	101.53	87.77	86
Commercial Medicare supplement	47.35	9.62	20
Other BCBS health insurance	6.05	6.43	106

	total consumer units	CUs headed by 25-to-34-year-olds	
		average spending	indexed spending
Health maintenance plans (HMOs)	$280.47	$273.39	97
Medicare payments	186.87	21.61	12
Commercial Medicare supplements/ other health insurance	167.18	59.38	36
Commercial Medicare supplement (not BCBS)	106.32	27.63	26
Other health insurance (not BCBS)	60.86	31.75	52
MEDICAL SERVICES	589.87	390.81	66
Physician's services	147.53	120.77	82
Dental services	226.99	105.41	46
Eye care services	34.20	16.24	47
Service by professionals other than physician	42.76	23.92	56
Lab tests, X-rays	26.79	16.28	61
Hospital room	36.57	46.45	127
Hospital services other than room	51.51	51.13	99
Care in convalescent or nursing home	12.46	1.60	13
Other medical services	9.46	9.00	95
DRUGS	487.43	209.16	43
Nonprescription drugs	64.45	45.23	70
Nonprescription vitamins	49.15	34.39	70
Prescription drugs	373.83	129.53	35
MEDICAL SUPPLIES	105.31	54.72	52
Eyeglasses and contact lenses	52.26	30.28	58
Hearing aids	14.98	0.60	4
Topicals and dressings	27.56	21.06	76
Medical equipment for general use	2.69	0.76	28
Supportive, convalescent medical equipment	5.21	1.09	21
Rental of medical equipment	1.06	0.25	24
Rental of supportive, convalescent medical equipment	1.55	0.68	44
ENTERTAINMENT	**$2,078.99**	**$2,026.71**	**97**
FEES AND ADMISSIONS	**541.67**	**489.59**	**90**
Recreation expenses on trips	25.64	22.60	88
Social, recreation, civic club membership	107.92	92.90	86
Fees for participant sports	75.05	72.67	97
Participant sports on trips	29.50	23.39	79
Movie, theater, opera, ballet	98.30	101.54	103
Movie, other admissions on trips	45.57	37.68	83
Admission to sports events	36.18	43.43	120
Admission to sports events on trips	15.19	12.56	83
Fees for recreational lessons	82.69	60.20	73
Other entertainment services on trips	25.64	22.60	88
TELEVISION, RADIO, SOUND EQUIPMENT	**691.90**	**749.62**	**108**
Television	**543.66**	**559.56**	**103**
Cable service and community antenna	382.28	358.63	94
Black-and-white TV	0.80	1.38	173
Color TV, console	38.63	45.95	119
Color TV, portable, table model	39.14	45.61	117

	total consumer units	CUs headed by 25-to-34-year-olds average spending	CUs headed by 25-to-34-year-olds indexed spending
VCRs and video disc players	$23.25	$31.75	137
Video cassettes, tapes, and discs	33.13	43.74	132
Video game hardware and software	23.46	30.36	129
Repair of TV, radio, and sound equipment	2.50	1.65	66
Rental of television sets	0.46	0.49	107
Radio and sound equipment	**148.25**	**190.07**	**128**
Radios	3.98	3.19	80
Tape recorders and players	5.31	4.32	81
Sound components and component systems	20.19	20.90	104
Miscellaneous sound equipment	3.18	9.78	308
Sound equipment accessories	5.97	5.36	90
Satellite dishes	1.00	1.25	125
Compact disc, tape, record, video mail order clubs	6.53	7.82	120
Records, CDs, audio tapes, needles	36.47	43.17	118
Rental of VCR, radio, sound equipment	0.25	0.27	108
Musical instruments and accessories	24.82	37.97	153
Rental and repair of musical instruments	1.22	0.47	39
Rental of video cassettes, tapes, discs, films	39.33	55.56	141
PETS, TOYS, PLAYGROUND EQUIPMENT	**369.12**	**367.76**	**100**
Pets	**248.25**	**197.97**	**80**
Pet food	102.56	78.44	76
Pet purchase, supplies, and medicines	52.29	50.57	97
Pet services	21.95	15.24	69
Veterinarian services	71.44	53.72	75
Toys, games, hobbies, and tricycles	**117.34**	**163.50**	**139**
Playground equipment	**3.54**	**6.28**	**177**
OTHER ENTERTAINMENT SUPPLIES, EQUIPMENT, SERVICES	**476.30**	**419.74**	**88**
Unmotored recreational vehicles	**47.14**	**75.36**	**160**
Boat without motor and boat trailers	16.15	29.25	181
Trailer and other attachable campers	30.99	46.11	149
Motorized recreational vehicles	**170.19**	**86.28**	**51**
Motorized camper	40.05	–	–
Other vehicle	35.47	42.29	119
Motorboats	94.67	43.99	46
Rental of recreational vehicles	**1.99**	**1.81**	**91**
Outboard motors	**0.71**	**0.30**	**42**
Docking and landing fees	**6.66**	**2.73**	**41**
Sports, recreation, exercise equipment	**150.33**	**133.14**	**89**
Athletic gear, game tables, exercise equipment	60.51	59.03	98
Bicycles	13.45	19.46	145
Camping equipment	9.59	6.54	68
Hunting and fishing equipment	35.68	26.66	75
Winter sports equipment	5.45	3.92	72
Water sports equipment	8.95	4.77	53
Other sports equipment	14.62	12.23	84
Rental and repair of misc. sports equipment	2.07	0.54	26

	total consumer units	CUs headed by 25-to-34-year-olds	
		average spending	indexed spending
Photographic equipment and supplies	**$90.48**	**$109.61**	**121**
Film	17.74	18.99	107
Other photographic supplies	2.27	2.22	98
Film processing	26.60	29.22	110
Repair and rental of photographic equipment	0.12	–	–
Photographic equipment	23.34	26.89	115
Photographer fees	20.42	32.29	158
Fireworks	**1.52**	**4.45**	**293**
Souvenirs	**1.25**	**2.21**	**177**
Visual goods	**1.19**	**1.23**	**103**
Pinball, electronic video games	**4.84**	**2.62**	**54**
PERSONAL CARE PRODUCTS AND SERVICES	**$525.80**	**$487.53**	**93**
Personal care products	**276.65**	**260.97**	**94**
Hair care products	53.57	54.63	102
Hair accessories	6.57	7.85	119
Wigs and hairpieces	1.32	0.91	69
Oral hygiene products	27.33	23.23	85
Shaving products	15.09	18.02	119
Cosmetics, perfume, and bath products	129.13	120.36	93
Deodorants, feminine hygiene, misc. products	30.29	29.66	98
Electric personal care appliances	13.34	6.29	47
Personal care services	**249.15**	**226.56**	**91**
READING	**$138.57**	**$103.06**	**74**
Newspaper subscriptions	43.88	16.72	38
Newspaper, nonsubscription	11.30	8.69	77
Magazine subscriptions	16.59	11.22	68
Magazines, nonsubscription	9.35	11.63	124
Books purchased through book clubs	6.62	5.37	81
Books not purchased through book clubs	50.38	49.13	98
Encyclopedia and other reference book sets	0.33	0.22	67
EDUCATION	**$751.95**	**$571.41**	**76**
College tuition	444.45	375.98	85
Elementary and high school tuition	128.94	46.33	36
Other school tuition	25.53	19.19	75
Other school expenses including rentals	25.77	21.70	84
Books, supplies for college	57.93	49.53	85
Books, supplies for elementary, high school	16.14	13.88	86
Books, supplies for day care, nursery school	3.39	3.74	110
Miscellaneous school expenses and supplies	49.80	41.06	82

	total consumer units	CUs headed by 25-to-34-year-olds average spending	CUs headed by 25-to-34-year-olds indexed spending
TOBACCO PRODUCTS AND SMOKING SUPPLIES	**$320.49**	**$315.27**	**98**
Cigarettes	291.89	280.77	96
Other tobacco products	26.27	32.94	125
Smoking accessories	2.33	1.56	67
FINANCIAL PRODUCTS, SERVICES	**$788.12**	**$678.16**	**86**
Miscellaneous fees	2.25	3.40	151
Lottery and gambling losses	46.94	31.75	68
Legal fees	132.99	87.10	65
Funeral expenses	77.91	20.58	26
Safe deposit box rental	3.84	1.71	45
Checking accounts, other bank service charges	25.91	32.41	125
Cemetery lots, vaults, and maintenance fees	16.05	5.40	34
Accounting fees	57.85	41.73	72
Miscellaneous personal services	39.77	44.16	111
Finance charges, except mortgage and vehicles	271.37	342.72	126
Occupational expenses	38.46	36.88	96
Expenses for other properties	65.99	23.46	36
Credit card memberships	2.82	2.77	98
Shopping club membership fees	5.97	4.09	69
CASH CONTRIBUTIONS	**$1,277.10**	**$743.28**	**58**
Support for college students	75.94	7.17	9
Alimony expenditures	21.18	2.94	14
Child support expenditures	190.75	219.43	115
Gifts to non-CU members of stocks, bonds, and mutual funds	24.23	2.33	10
Cash contributions to charities and other organizations	137.62	45.31	33
Cash contributions to church, religious organizations	557.29	344.32	62
Cash contributions to educational institutions	33.42	8.07	24
Cash contributions to political organizations	10.90	4.32	40
Other cash gifts	225.76	109.38	48
PERSONAL INSURANCE, PENSIONS	**$3,898.62**	**$3,971.75**	**102**
Life and other personal insurance	**406.11**	**230.07**	**57**
Life, endowment, annuity, other personal insurance	391.65	220.85	56
Other nonhealth insurance	14.46	9.22	64
Pensions and Social Security	**3,492.51**	**3,741.68**	**107**
Deductions for government retirement	69.48	44.54	64
Deductions for railroad retirement	2.21	0.24	11
Deductions for private pensions	390.38	361.40	93
Nonpayroll deposit to retirement plans	426.12	303.49	71
Deductions for Social Security	2,604.32	3,032.02	116

	total consumer units	CUs headed by 25-to-34-year-olds	
		average spending	indexed spending
PERSONAL TAXES	**$2,496.26**	**$2,258.58**	**90**
Federal income taxes	1,842.57	1,642.07	89
State and local income taxes	506.45	545.80	108
Other taxes	147.24	70.71	48
GIFTS FOR NON-HOUSEHOLD MEMBERS**	**$1,036.24**	**$687.66**	**66**
FOOD	**82.18**	**34.26**	**42**
Cakes and cupcakes	2.41	2.34	97
Other fresh fruits (excl. apples, bananas, citrus)	2.26	1.51	67
Candy and chewing gum	11.69	8.38	72
Board (including at school)	21.90	2.57	12
Catered affairs	26.19	2.04	8
ALCOHOLIC BEVERAGES	**13.42**	**13.13**	**98**
Beer and ale	4.73	4.14	88
Wine	5.84	5.32	91
HOUSING	**258.69**	**213.45**	**83**
Housekeeping supplies	**42.48**	**32.04**	**75**
Laundry and cleaning supplies	2.93	1.70	58
Other household products	11.69	10.28	88
Miscellaneous household products	5.85	3.54	61
Lawn and garden supplies	4.20	5.70	136
Postage and stationery	27.86	20.06	72
Stationery, stationery supplies, giftwrap	21.13	16.78	79
Postage	6.14	3.03	49
Household textiles	**13.72**	**13.35**	**97**
Bathroom linens	2.59	2.31	89
Bedroom linens	6.10	3.84	63
Appliances and miscellaneous housewares	**23.98**	**12.21**	**51**
Major appliances	8.41	2.01	24
Electric floor-cleaning equipment	2.77	–	–
Small appliances and miscellaneous housewares	15.57	10.19	65
China and other dinnerware	2.46	2.84	115
Nonelectric cookware	3.53	1.54	44
Tableware, nonelectric kitchenware	2.63	1.24	47
Small electric kitchen appliances	2.71	1.56	58
Miscellaneous household equipment	**64.70**	**45.22**	**70**
Infants' equipment	3.82	2.11	55
Outdoor equipment	2.07	1.50	72
Other household decorative items	25.76	21.23	82
Power tools	2.80	4.75	170
Indoor plants, fresh flowers	13.43	7.55	56
Computers and computer hardware	6.59	1.49	23
Miscellaneous household equipment	2.19	2.42	111
Other housing	**113.80**	**110.63**	**97**
Repair or maintenance services	4.51	8.34	185
Housing while attending school	39.93	3.32	8

	total consumer units	CUs headed by 25-to-34-year-olds	
		average spending	indexed spending
Natural gas (renter)	$3.62	$3.46	96
Electricity (renter)	14.67	11.20	76
Water, sewer maintenance (renter)	3.04	2.22	73
Daycare centers, nurseries, and preschools	23.81	64.45	271
APPAREL AND SERVICES	**237.13**	**248.95**	**105**
Men and boys, aged 2 or older	**63.74**	**55.55**	**87**
Men's coats and jackets	5.09	3.48	68
Men's accessories	4.45	4.55	102
Men's sweaters and vests	3.06	2.66	87
Men's active sportswear	2.76	2.17	79
Men's shirts	16.79	19.16	114
Men's pants	6.93	6.94	100
Boys' shirts	3.71	1.40	38
Boys' pants	3.76	2.25	60
Women and girls, aged 2 or older	**81.76**	**71.82**	**88**
Women's coats and jackets	5.62	5.77	103
Women's dresses	7.66	5.07	66
Women's vests and sweaters	8.50	10.18	120
Women's shirts, tops, blouses	9.06	7.33	81
Women's pants	6.62	7.13	108
Women's active sportswear	4.33	8.83	204
Women's sleepwear	6.45	6.71	104
Women's accessories	5.71	5.53	97
Girls' dresses and suits	2.98	0.02	1
Girls' shirts, blouses, sweaters	4.48	2.76	62
Girls' skirts and pants	3.32	2.96	89
Girls' accessories	2.38	1.77	74
Children under age 2	**39.99**	**56.75**	**142**
Infant dresses, outerwear	15.28	15.39	101
Infant underwear	16.91	27.64	163
Infant nightwear, loungewear	2.55	2.72	107
Infant accessories	3.93	9.87	251
Other apparel products and services	**51.63**	**64.82**	**126**
Jewelry and watches	24.01	43.98	183
Watches	2.16	1.89	88
Jewelry	21.85	42.09	193
Men's footwear	8.37	8.48	101
Boys' footwear	4.46	1.82	41
Women's footwear	8.82	5.20	59
Girls' footwear	3.30	3.96	120
TRANSPORTATION	**43.87**	**21.83**	**50**
New cars	7.09	–	–
Used cars	12.21	–	–
Airline fares	6.78	4.39	65
Ship fares	2.74	2.91	106

	total consumer units	CUs headed by 25-to-34-year-olds	
		average spending	indexed spending
HEALTH CARE	**$32.59**	**$10.74**	**33**
Physician's services	3.07	0.58	19
Dental services	4.03	0.87	22
Care in convalescent or nursing home	5.19	–	–
Nonprescription vitamins	3.93	0.92	23
Prescription drugs	2.38	0.30	13
ENTERTAINMENT	**78.24**	**60.10**	**77**
Toys, games, hobbies, and tricycles	29.98	20.33	68
Other entertainment	48.26	39.77	82
Fees for recreational lessons	7.88	3.11	39
Community antenna or cable TV	6.37	4.22	66
VCRs and videodisc players	2.26	2.32	103
Video game hardware and software	2.13	1.78	84
Athletic gear, game tables, exercise equipment	6.60	3.48	53
Hunting and fishing equipment	3.06	12.25	400
Photographer fees	3.19	1.04	33
PERSONAL CARE PRODUCTS, SERVICES	**21.15**	**15.81**	**75**
Cosmetics, perfume, bath preparation	12.53	12.03	96
Electric personal care appliances	3.31	0.77	23
EDUCATION	**183.88**	**27.05**	**15**
College tuition	127.83	13.14	10
Elementary and high school tuition	25.95	1.59	6
Other school tuition	4.44	2.72	61
Other school expenses including rentals	3.99	1.61	40
College books and supplies	11.93	1.99	17
Miscellaneous school supplies	7.38	3.09	42
ALL OTHER GIFTS	**83.76**	**41.82**	**50**
Gifts of trip expenses	44.40	30.29	68
Lottery and gambling losses	2.86	0.44	15
Legal fees	5.82	0.16	3
Funeral expenses	25.25	8.81	35
Miscellaneous personal services	2.16	0.47	22

* This figure does not include the amount paid for mortgage principle, which is considered an asset.
** Expenditures on gifts are also included in the preceding product and service categories. Food spending, for example, includes the amount spent on food gifts. Only gift categories with spending of $2.00 or more by the average consumer unit are shown.
Note: The Bureau of Labor Statistics uses consumer unit rather than household as the sampling unit in the Consumer Expenditure Survey. For the definition of consumer unit, see the glossary. (–) means not applicable or the sample is too small to make a reliable estimate.
Source: Bureau of Labor Statistics, unpublished data from the 2002 Consumer Expenditure Survey; calculations by New Strategist

Householders Aged 35 to 44 Spend More than Average

Most households in the age group include children, which accounts for their above-average spending.

Households headed by people aged 35 to 44 spent 19 percent more than the average household, $48,330 versus $40,677 in 2002. Spending by householders in the age group is particularly high for items commonly purchased by parents with children under age 18. Householders aged 35 to 44 spend 22 percent more than the average household on milk, 95 percent more on day care centers, 36 percent more on dinners at fast-food restaurants, twice the average on children's clothing, 77 percent more on video games, 44 percent more on toys, 29 percent more on computer information services, and 22 percent more on cell phone service.

The age group spends less than average on some surprising items. Spending on postage, for example, is 3 percent below average (reflecting their preference for e-mailing over letter writing). Householders in the age group spend 8 percent less than average on women's clothing. They spend only 13 percent more than average on new cars, but 60 percent more than average on new trucks.

■ The spending of 35-to-44-year-olds reveals not only their lifestage needs, but also the preferences of tech-savvy Generation Xers and younger Boomers for computers and cell phones.

Householders aged 35 to 44 spend more than average on computers and cell phones

(indexed spending of householders aged 35 to 44 on selected items, 2002)

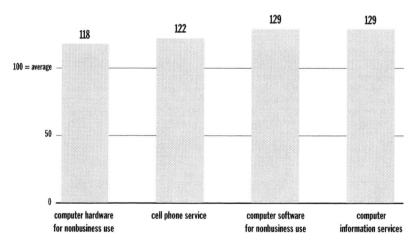

Table 8.3 Average and Indexed Spending of Householders Aged 35 to 44, 2002

(average annual spending of total consumer units (CUs) and average annual and indexed spending of consumer units headed by 35-to-44-year-olds, 2002)

	total consumer units	CUs headed by 35-to-44-year-olds	
		average spending	indexed spending
Number of consumer units (in 000s)	112,108	24,394	–
Average before-tax income	$49,430.00	$61,532.00	124
Average annual spending	40,676.60	48,330.48	119
FOOD	**$5,374.80**	**$6,313.58**	**117**
FOOD AT HOME	3,098.52	3,601.44	116
Cereals and bakery products	**450.13**	**542.20**	**120**
Cereals and cereal products	154.07	191.07	124
Flour	8.65	10.43	121
Prepared flour mixes	12.40	15.09	122
Ready-to-eat and cooked cereals	87.66	109.94	125
Rice	17.82	20.52	115
Pasta, cornmeal, and other cereal products	27.54	35.09	127
Bakery products	296.06	351.13	119
Bread	83.83	95.06	113
White bread	35.21	42.40	120
Bread, other than white	48.62	52.66	108
Crackers and cookies	70.67	87.55	124
Cookies	46.31	58.71	127
Crackers	24.36	28.84	118
Frozen and refrigerated bakery products	25.64	34.47	134
Other bakery products	115.92	134.05	116
Biscuits and rolls	41.04	48.87	119
Cakes and cupcakes	35.73	41.34	116
Bread and cracker products	3.50	3.51	100
Sweetrolls, coffee cakes, doughnuts	25.84	32.30	125
Pies, tarts, turnovers	9.82	8.02	82
Meats, poultry, fish, and eggs	**798.42**	**918.33**	**115**
Beef	231.17	270.97	117
Ground beef	86.29	103.14	120
Roast	40.99	48.90	119
Chuck roast	11.71	13.13	112
Round roast	10.23	13.32	130
Other roast	19.05	22.45	118
Steak	84.47	97.02	115
Round steak	13.29	14.25	107
Sirloin steak	26.62	29.50	111
Other steak	44.56	53.26	120
Pork	167.34	197.85	118
Bacon	28.45	33.69	118
Pork chops	38.43	46.04	120
Ham	37.16	41.55	112
Ham, not canned	35.66	39.58	111
Canned ham	1.50	1.96	131

	total consumer units	CUs headed by 35-to-44-year-olds	
		average spending	indexed spending
Sausage	$26.17	$32.79	125
Other pork	37.13	43.78	118
Other meats	101.08	121.81	121
Frankfurters	20.95	27.75	132
Lunch meats (cold cuts)	68.99	85.17	123
Bologna, liverwurst, salami	21.11	25.83	122
Lamb, organ meats, and others	11.14	8.90	80
Lamb and organ meats	7.99	7.51	94
Mutton, goat, and game	3.15	1.38	44
Poultry	144.13	164.14	114
Fresh and frozen chicken	113.25	131.29	116
Fresh and frozen whole chicken	32.08	34.89	109
Fresh and frozen chicken parts	81.17	96.41	119
Other poultry	30.88	32.84	106
Fish and seafood	120.97	125.71	104
Canned fish and seafood	16.13	16.69	103
Fresh fish and shellfish	69.31	66.56	96
Frozen fish and shellfish	35.53	42.46	120
Eggs	33.75	37.85	112
Dairy products	**328.34**	**391.66**	**119**
Fresh milk and cream	127.15	153.21	120
Fresh milk, all types	114.63	139.97	122
Cream	12.52	13.24	106
Other dairy products	201.19	238.45	119
Butter	18.48	20.60	111
Cheese	95.64	111.55	117
Ice cream and related products	58.74	72.27	123
Miscellaneous dairy products	28.33	34.04	120
Fruits and vegetables	**552.01**	**596.57**	**108**
Fresh fruits	178.20	190.56	107
Apples	32.59	38.01	117
Bananas	31.24	32.38	104
Oranges	20.34	21.07	104
Citrus fruits, excl. oranges	14.29	15.85	111
Other fresh fruits	79.74	83.25	104
Fresh vegetables	174.88	184.83	106
Potatoes	33.35	35.73	107
Lettuce	22.22	23.55	106
Tomatoes	33.71	35.13	104
Other fresh vegetables	85.60	90.42	106
Processed fruits	115.50	128.34	111
Frozen fruits and fruit juices	12.45	13.54	109
Frozen orange juice	6.31	7.50	119
Frozen fruits	2.79	2.19	78
Frozen fruit juices, excl. orange	3.35	3.85	115
Canned fruits	15.06	15.36	102
Dried fruits	6.06	5.19	86
Fresh fruit juice	22.20	22.74	102
Canned and bottled fruit juice	59.74	71.51	120

	total consumer units	CUs headed by 35-to-44-year-olds average spending	indexed spending
Processed vegetables	$83.43	$92.84	111
Frozen vegetables	27.85	31.19	112
Canned and dried vegetables and juices	55.58	61.65	111
Canned beans	12.47	15.10	121
Canned corn	7.34	8.97	122
Canned miscellaneous vegetables	17.85	18.63	104
Dried peas	0.36	0.31	86
Dried beans	2.55	2.50	98
Dried miscellaneous vegetables	7.38	7.81	106
Dried processed vegetables	0.34	0.37	109
Frozen vegetable juices	0.06	0.13	217
Fresh and canned vegetable juices	7.23	7.83	108
Sugar and other sweets	**117.39**	**138.80**	**118**
Candy and chewing gum	75.44	90.09	119
Sugar	15.56	17.46	112
Artificial sweeteners	4.33	4.59	106
Jams, preserves, other sweets	22.06	26.66	121
Fats and oils	**85.16**	**92.79**	**109**
Margarine	9.86	9.83	100
Fats and oils	26.08	29.45	113
Salad dressings	27.01	30.53	113
Nondairy cream and imitation milk	9.33	9.33	100
Peanut butter	12.89	13.65	106
Miscellaneous foods	**471.92**	**571.58**	**121**
Frozen prepared foods	98.09	126.43	129
Frozen meals	29.88	32.02	107
Other frozen prepared foods	68.22	94.41	138
Canned and packaged soups	35.82	39.06	109
Potato chips, nuts, and other snacks	100.53	127.06	126
Potato chips and other snacks	76.37	104.44	137
Nuts	24.16	22.62	94
Condiments and seasonings	86.81	100.70	116
Salt, spices, and other seasonings	21.14	25.15	119
Olives, pickles, relishes	9.70	11.28	116
Sauces and gravies	37.78	43.90	116
Baking needs and miscellaneous products	18.19	20.37	112
Other canned/packaged prepared foods	150.67	178.33	118
Prepared salads	21.46	24.08	112
Prepared desserts	10.32	13.45	130
Baby food	31.57	33.87	107
Miscellaneous prepared foods	87.24	106.60	122
Nonalcoholic beverages	253.94	303.16	119
Cola	81.11	99.86	123
Other carbonated drinks	43.93	52.53	120
Coffee	41.59	43.62	105
Roasted coffee	27.38	29.89	109
Instant and freeze-dried coffee	14.21	13.73	97
Noncarbonated fruit-flavored drinks	18.95	27.30	144

	total consumer units	CUs headed by 35-to-44-year-olds	
		average spending	indexed spending
Tea	$15.86	$18.02	114
Nonalcoholic beer	0.64	0.98	153
Other nonalcoholic beverages and ice	51.85	60.85	117
Food prepared by CU on trips	41.20	46.35	113
FOOD AWAY FROM HOME	**2,276.29**	**2,712.13**	**119**
Meals at restaurants, carry-outs, other	**1,866.42**	**2,225.31**	**119**
Lunch	685.79	863.61	126
• At fast food, take-out, delivery, concession stands, buffet, and cafeteria (other than employer and school cafeteria)	377.71	505.45	134
• At full-service restaurants	224.82	212.35	94
• At vending machines, mobile vendors	5.50	9.17	167
• At employer and school cafeterias	77.76	136.64	176
Dinner	736.54	827.67	112
• At fast food, take-out, delivery, concession stands, buffet, and cafeteria (other than employer and school cafeteria)	213.33	289.37	136
• At full-service restaurants	518.02	532.04	103
• At vending machines, mobile vendors	1.87	2.95	158
• At employer and school cafeterias	3.32	3.31	100
Snacks and nonalcoholic beverages	262.67	342.30	130
• At fast food, take-out, delivery, concession stands, buffet, and cafeteria (other than employer and school cafeteria)	185.69	242.55	131
• At full-service restaurants	30.17	30.28	100
• At vending machines, mobile vendors	36.71	53.08	145
• At employer and school cafeterias	10.11	16.39	162
Breakfast and brunch	181.42	191.74	106
• At fast food, take-out, delivery, concession stands, buffet, and cafeteria (other than employer and school cafeteria)	87.83	105.75	120
• At full-service restaurants	87.08	77.98	90
• At vending machines, mobile vendors	1.40	1.08	77
• At employer and school cafeterias	5.11	6.94	136
Board (including at school)	**46.54**	**31.31**	**67**
Catered affairs	**69.00**	**56.73**	**82**
Food on trips	**211.49**	**232.03**	**110**
School lunches	**60.00**	**142.04**	**237**
Meals as pay	**22.86**	**24.71**	**108**
ALCOHOLIC BEVERAGES	**$375.95**	**$366.91**	**98**
At home	**228.08**	**221.68**	**97**
Beer and ale	112.34	125.07	111
Whiskey	13.90	12.42	89
Wine	77.75	58.55	75
Other alcoholic beverages	24.09	25.65	106

	total consumer units	CUs headed by 35-to-44-year-olds average spending	indexed spending
Away from home	**$147.87**	**$145.23**	**98**
Beer and ale	52.86	53.57	101
• At fast food, take-out, delivery, concession stands, buffet, and cafeteria	7.99	6.79	85
• At full-service restaurants	41.95	39.06	93
• At vending machines, mobile vendors	0.32	0.14	44
• At catered affairs	2.59	7.58	293
Wine	25.85	22.70	88
• At fast food, take-out, delivery, concession stands, buffet and cafeteria	4.41	4.13	94
• At full-service restaurants	20.36	17.77	87
• At catered affairs	1.09	0.80	73
Other alcoholic beverages	69.16	68.96	100
• At fast food, take-out, delivery, concession stands, buffet, and cafeteria	3.50	3.16	90
• At full-service restaurants	28.94	26.26	91
• At catered affairs	3.94	3.34	85
Alcoholic beverages purchased on trips	32.78	36.20	110
HOUSING	**$13,283.08**	**$16,349.51**	**123**
SHELTER	**7,829.41**	**9,902.03**	**126**
Owned dwellings*	**5,164.96**	**7,105.47**	**138**
Mortgage interest and charges	2,962.16	4,608.18	156
Mortgage interest	2,811.49	4,428.51	158
Interest paid, home equity loan	88.61	116.04	131
Interest paid, home equity line of credit	61.88	63.52	103
Property taxes	1,242.36	1,473.22	119
Maintenance, repairs, insurance, other expenses	960.43	1,024.08	107
Homeowner's insurance	283.30	294.53	104
Ground rent	40.96	34.19	83
Maintenance and repair services	519.60	546.76	105
Painting and papering	55.58	62.32	112
Plumbing and water heating	46.63	46.63	100
Heat, air conditioning, electrical work	86.28	78.51	91
Roofing and gutters	71.20	77.93	109
Other repair and maintenance services	214.77	240.95	112
Repair, replacement of hard-surface flooring	43.54	38.92	89
Repair of built-in appliances	1.62	1.50	93
Maintenance and repair materials	83.75	119.20	142
Paints, wallpaper, and supplies	14.71	21.82	148
Tools, equipment for painting, wallpapering	1.58	2.34	148
Plumbing supplies and equipment	5.62	6.25	111
Electrical supplies, heating, cooling equip.	3.46	2.67	77
Hard-surface flooring, repair and replacement	8.72	14.56	167
Roofing and gutters	5.29	7.32	138
Plaster, paneling, siding, windows, doors, screens, awnings	13.92	14.42	104
Patio, walk, fence, driveway, masonry, brick, and stucco materials	1.29	2.25	174

	total consumer units	CUs headed by 35-to-44-year-olds	
		average spending	indexed spending
Landscape maintenance	$4.73	$7.43	157
Miscellaneous supplies and equipment	24.43	40.15	164
Insulation, other maintenance, repair	13.15	23.35	178
Finish basement, remodel rooms, build patios, walks, etc.	11.28	16.80	149
Property management and security	27.64	25.23	91
Property management	21.94	19.45	89
Management and upkeep services for security	5.71	5.78	101
Parking	5.17	4.17	81
Rented dwellings	**2,159.89**	**2,350.84**	**109**
Rent	2,104.66	2,297.90	109
Rent as pay	27.17	28.25	104
Maintenance, insurance, and other expenses	28.06	24.69	88
Tenant's insurance	8.90	9.40	106
Maintenance and repair services	11.16	7.42	66
Repair and maintenance services	10.58	6.96	66
Repair, replacement of hard-surface flooring	0.51	0.42	82
Repair of built-in appliances	0.07	0.04	57
Maintenance and repair materials	8.00	7.87	98
Paint, wallpaper, and supplies	1.01	1.17	116
Painting and wallpapering tools	0.11	0.13	118
Plastering, paneling, roofing, gutters, etc.	0.90	1.04	116
Plumbing supplies and equipment	0.80	1.21	151
Electrical supplies, heating, cooling equip.	0.30	0.53	177
Miscellaneous supplies and equipment	3.67	3.21	87
Insulation, other maintenance and repair	1.09	0.82	75
Materials for additions, finishing basements, remodeling rooms	2.43	2.33	96
Construction materials for jobs not started	0.15	0.06	40
Hard-surface flooring	0.73	0.30	41
Landscape maintenance	0.49	0.28	57
Other lodging	**504.56**	**445.72**	**88**
Owned vacation homes	171.55	137.67	80
Mortgage interest and charges	71.98	76.82	107
Property taxes	63.76	38.58	61
Maintenance, insurance and other expenses	35.81	22.28	62
Homeowner's insurance	9.70	9.65	99
Ground rent	2.93	0.62	21
Maintenance and repair services	16.76	8.37	50
Maintenance and repair materials	2.07	2.16	104
Property management and security	3.60	1.07	30
Property management	2.50	0.95	38
Management, upkeep services for security	1.10	0.12	11
Parking	0.76	0.41	54
Housing while attending school	80.14	31.81	40
Lodging on trips	252.87	276.23	109

	total consumer units	CUs headed by 35-to-44-year-olds	
		average spending	indexed spending
UTILITIES, FUELS, PUBLIC SERVICES	**$2,684.32**	**$3,025.84**	**113**
Natural gas	**329.75**	**369.38**	**112**
Natural gas (renter)	60.32	73.95	123
Natural gas (owner)	266.79	293.73	110
Natural gas (vacation)	2.54	1.70	67
Electricity	**981.09**	**1,105.26**	**113**
Electricity (renter)	223.26	270.64	121
Electricity (owner)	750.48	830.36	111
Electricity (vacation)	6.32	3.00	47
Fuel oil and other fuels	**88.41**	**86.14**	**97**
Fuel oil	45.98	47.75	104
Fuel oil (renter)	4.64	7.80	168
Fuel oil (owner)	40.98	39.85	97
Fuel oil (vacation)	0.36	0.10	28
Coal	0.07	0.09	129
Bottled/tank gas	35.27	32.60	92
Gas (renter)	5.09	3.64	72
Gas (owner)	27.19	26.12	96
Gas (vacation)	2.98	2.84	95
Wood and other fuels	7.09	5.70	80
Wood and other fuels (renter)	1.32	1.17	89
Wood and other fuels (owner)	5.68	4.54	80
Telephone services	**956.74**	**1,095.80**	**115**
Residential telephone and pay phones	641.00	712.52	111
Cellular phone service	293.76	358.45	122
Pager service	1.71	1.62	95
Phone cards	20.28	23.21	114
Water and other public services	**328.33**	**369.25**	**112**
Water and sewerage maintenance	237.16	272.73	115
Water and sewerage maintenance (renter)	32.76	43.20	132
Water and sewerage maintenance (owner)	201.79	228.21	113
Water and sewerage maintenance (vacation)	2.36	1.33	56
Trash and garbage collection	89.05	94.56	106
Trash and garbage collection (renter)	9.89	12.28	124
Trash and garbage collection (owner)	76.61	81.45	106
Trash and garbage collection (vacation)	2.53	0.82	32
Septic tank cleaning	2.12	1.96	92
HOUSEHOLD SERVICES	**705.71**	**1,010.38**	**143**
Personal services	**331.02**	**579.88**	**175**
Babysitting, child care in your own home	35.91	82.39	229
Babysitting, child care in someone else's home	27.48	58.09	211
Care for elderly, invalids, handicapped, etc.	50.07	27.18	54
Adult day care centers	6.81	0.30	4
Day care centers, nurseries, and preschools	210.74	411.92	195
Other household services	**374.70**	**430.50**	**115**
Housekeeping services	79.90	96.20	120
Gardening, lawn care service	72.38	64.74	89
Water softening service	3.15	4.19	133

	total consumer units	CUs headed by 35-to-44-year-olds average spending	indexed spending
Nonclothing laundry, dry cleaning, sent out	$1.72	$1.46	85
Nonclothing laundry, dry cleaning, coin-operated	4.13	4.43	107
Termite/pest control services	13.25	11.51	87
Home security system service fee	17.40	20.73	119
Other home services	15.06	11.64	77
Termite/pest control products	0.68	0.65	96
Moving, storage, and freight express	33.13	49.72	150
Appliance repair, including service center	10.86	9.79	90
Reupholstering and furniture repair	7.40	7.20	97
Repairs/rentals of lawn/garden equipment, hand/power tools, etc.	3.62	3.65	101
Appliance rental	1.07	1.77	165
Rental of office equipment, nonbusiness use	0.41	1.01	246
Repair of misc. household equip., furnishings	0.62	0.57	92
Repair of computer systems, nonbusiness use	2.53	3.09	122
Computer information services	107.29	138.15	129
HOUSEKEEPING SUPPLIES	**545.28**	**588.74**	**108**
Laundry and cleaning supplies	**130.57**	**152.11**	**116**
Soaps and detergents	72.89	86.49	119
Other laundry cleaning products	57.68	65.62	114
Other household products	**283.28**	**294.62**	**104**
Cleansing and toilet tissue, paper towels, and napkins	76.46	88.27	115
Miscellaneous household products	96.81	119.34	123
Lawn and garden supplies	110.01	87.02	79
Postage and stationery	**131.44**	**142.00**	**108**
Stationery, stationery supplies, giftwrap	60.20	74.05	123
Postage	69.12	67.05	97
Delivery services	2.12	0.90	42
HOUSEHOLD FURNISHINGS, EQUIPMENT	**1,518.36**	**1,822.52**	**120**
Household textiles	**135.52**	**137.34**	**101**
Bathroom linens	22.35	25.03	112
Bedroom linens	65.98	61.91	94
Kitchen and dining room linens	10.11	12.64	125
Curtains and draperies	16.65	20.98	126
Slipcovers and decorative pillows	7.40	2.43	33
Sewing materials for household items	11.44	12.27	107
Other linens	1.59	2.09	131
Furniture	**401.28**	**523.70**	**131**
Mattresses and springs	52.91	65.01	123
Other bedroom furniture	68.33	100.54	147
Sofas	85.33	114.43	134
Living room chairs	39.21	34.27	87
Living room tables	18.03	20.62	114
Kitchen and dining room furniture	61.28	88.11	144
Infants' furniture	6.46	9.58	148
Outdoor furniture	16.79	24.81	148
Wall units, cabinets, and other furniture	52.94	66.32	125

	total consumer units	CUs headed by 35-to-44-year-olds	
		average spending	indexed spending
Floor coverings	**$40.49**	**$44.20**	**109**
Wall-to-wall carpeting (renter)	0.65	0.94	145
Wall-to-wall carpet (replacement) (owner)	21.04	18.82	89
Floor coverings, nonpermanent	18.79	24.44	130
Major appliances	**188.47**	**252.35**	**134**
Dishwashers (built-in), garbage disposals, range hoods (renter)	1.24	2.51	202
Dishwashers (built-in), garbage disposals, range hoods (owner)	15.28	21.53	141
Refrigerators and freezers (renter)	5.58	6.72	120
Refrigerators and freezers (owner)	46.50	62.80	135
Washing machines (renter)	4.42	4.16	94
Washing machines (owner)	17.88	24.37	136
Clothes dryers (renter)	3.17	5.07	160
Clothes dryers (owner)	13.88	19.39	140
Cooking stoves, ovens (renter)	2.86	6.22	217
Cooking stoves, ovens (owner)	28.09	43.23	154
Microwave ovens (renter)	2.14	2.39	112
Microwave ovens (owner)	8.36	9.77	117
Portable dishwasher (renter)	0.25	0.08	32
Portable dishwasher (owner)	0.51	2.05	402
Window air conditioners (renter)	1.83	1.83	100
Window air conditioners (owner)	6.07	7.83	129
Electric floor-cleaning equipment	22.80	25.04	110
Sewing machines	4.79	5.52	115
Miscellaneous household appliances	**2.81**	**1.83**	**65**
Small appliances and misc. housewares	100.43	88.46	88
Housewares	77.55	63.36	82
Plastic dinnerware	1.57	1.94	124
China and other dinnerware	14.51	7.87	54
Flatware	3.79	4.30	113
Glassware	6.51	6.68	103
Silver serving pieces	4.05	5.51	136
Other serving pieces	1.44	1.29	90
Nonelectric cookware	24.25	15.54	64
Tableware, nonelectric kitchenware	21.44	20.24	94
Small appliances	22.89	25.10	110
Small electric kitchen appliances	17.18	18.21	106
Portable heating and cooling equipment	5.70	6.89	121
Miscellaneous household equipment	**652.17**	**776.47**	**119**
Window coverings	13.91	13.13	94
Infants' equipment	12.96	16.67	129
Laundry and cleaning equipment	15.15	18.50	122
Outdoor equipment	31.52	50.22	159
Clocks	5.87	11.26	192
Lamps and lighting fixtures	11.74	14.84	126
Other household decorative items	144.94	157.14	108
Telephones and accessories	32.73	27.26	83
Lawn and garden equipment	48.16	81.75	170

	total consumer units	CUs headed by 35-to-44-year-olds	
		average spending	indexed spending
Power tools	$33.27	$17.93	54
Office furniture for home use	10.57	12.41	117
Hand tools	8.05	10.23	127
Indoor plants and fresh flowers	49.78	50.36	101
Closet and storage items	9.98	16.55	166
Rental of furniture	4.60	6.89	150
Luggage	5.98	7.26	121
Computers and computer hardware, nonbusiness use	138.58	163.45	118
Computer software and accessories, nonbusiness use	17.67	22.76	129
Telephone answering devices	1.08	1.31	121
Calculators	1.44	2.00	139
Business equipment for home use	0.97	0.25	26
Other hardware	12.85	22.74	177
Smoke alarms (owner)	1.10	1.78	162
Smoke alarms (renter)	0.39	1.60	410
Other household appliances (owner)	8.00	6.18	77
Other household appliances (renter)	1.23	2.89	235
Misc. household equipment and parts	29.62	39.12	132
APPAREL AND SERVICES	**$1,749.22**	**$2,100.89**	**120**
Men's apparel	**319.48**	**382.72**	**120**
Suits	32.96	38.73	118
Sport coats and tailored jackets	10.65	10.00	94
Coats and jackets	33.86	43.02	127
Underwear	15.27	21.16	139
Hosiery	12.22	18.14	148
Nightwear	2.98	3.77	127
Accessories	22.41	24.63	110
Sweaters and vests	15.68	17.05	109
Active sportswear	15.13	16.67	110
Shirts	78.89	95.35	121
Pants	57.64	67.69	117
Shorts and shorts sets	12.22	14.77	121
Uniforms	3.21	3.77	117
Costumes	6.35	7.96	125
Boys' (aged 2 to 15) apparel	**89.98**	**179.14**	**199**
Coats and jackets	6.38	11.69	183
Sweaters	3.65	7.29	200
Shirts	19.50	41.07	211
Underwear	5.02	11.29	225
Nightwear	2.59	4.09	158
Hosiery	4.21	9.96	237
Accessories	4.12	6.57	159
Suits, sport coats, and vests	2.37	3.45	146
Pants	22.58	43.04	191
Shorts and shorts sets	8.66	17.05	197
Uniforms	3.35	7.50	224
Active sportswear	3.84	7.56	197
Costumes	3.72	8.58	231

	total consumer units	CUs headed by 35-to-44-year-olds	
		average spending	indexed spending
Women's apparel	**$586.91**	**$540.45**	**92**
Coats and jackets	50.06	32.35	65
Dresses	56.40	38.73	69
Sport coats and tailored jackets	6.48	6.78	105
Sweaters and vests	50.47	55.20	109
Shirts, blouses, and tops	103.24	82.74	80
Skirts	17.48	20.17	115
Pants	96.29	89.05	92
Shorts and shorts sets	16.09	17.21	107
Active sportswear	30.07	28.68	95
Nightwear	27.63	32.20	117
Undergarments	33.55	35.37	105
Hosiery	21.22	22.99	108
Suits	29.01	28.83	99
Accessories	33.37	35.11	105
Uniforms	6.12	7.03	115
Costumes	9.42	8.02	85
Girls' (aged 2 to 15) apparel	**117.21**	**246.96**	**211**
Coats and jackets	6.49	13.02	201
Dresses and suits	12.41	23.32	188
Shirts, blouses, and sweaters	29.33	65.89	225
Skirts and pants	24.07	48.25	200
Shorts and shorts sets	8.28	18.27	221
Active sportswear	9.32	18.89	203
Underwear and nightwear	7.63	14.53	190
Hosiery	4.30	9.51	221
Accessories	5.81	14.58	251
Uniforms	4.77	10.95	230
Costumes	4.80	9.74	203
Children under age 2	**82.60**	**97.16**	**118**
Coats, jackets, and snowsuits	2.43	2.88	119
Outerwear including dresses	23.71	25.32	107
Underwear	43.60	54.66	125
Nightwear and loungewear	4.07	4.12	101
Accessories	8.79	10.18	116
Footwear	**313.17**	**381.78**	**122**
Men's	102.90	108.10	105
Boys'	36.87	76.07	206
Women's	141.64	142.91	101
Girls'	31.76	54.70	172
Other apparel products and services	**239.87**	**272.68**	**114**
Material for making clothes	5.11	4.50	88
Sewing patterns and notions	8.20	6.98	85
Watches	13.62	18.63	137
Jewelry	89.65	94.74	106
Shoe repair and other shoe services	1.44	1.51	105
Coin-operated apparel laundry and dry cleaning	37.58	42.71	114
Apparel alteration, repair, and tailoring services	5.86	6.09	104
Clothing rental	2.66	2.32	87
Watch and jewelry repair	5.49	5.10	93
Professional laundry, dry cleaning	69.69	89.19	128
Clothing storage	0.55	0.92	167

	total consumer units	CUs headed by 35-to-44-year-olds	
		average spending	indexed spending
TRANSPORTATION	**$7,759.29**	**$9,399.89**	**121**
VEHICLE PURCHASES	**3,664.93**	**4,591.97**	**125**
Cars and trucks, new	**1,752.96**	**2,393.58**	**137**
New cars	883.08	997.89	113
New trucks	869.88	1,395.68	160
Cars and trucks, used	**1,842.29**	**2,115.23**	**115**
Used cars	1,113.46	1,189.73	107
Used trucks	728.82	925.50	127
Other vehicles	**69.68**	**83.16**	**119**
New motorcycles	36.26	35.58	98
Used motorcycles	33.42	47.58	142
GASOLINE AND MOTOR OIL	**1,235.06**	**1,472.79**	**119**
Gasoline	1,125.01	1,356.47	121
Diesel fuel	10.86	14.58	134
Gasoline on trips	88.24	89.54	101
Motor oil	10.05	11.30	112
Motor oil on trips	0.89	0.90	101
OTHER VEHICLE EXPENSES	**2,470.55**	**2,934.96**	**119**
Vehicle finance charges	**397.04**	**528.69**	**133**
Automobile finance charges	193.12	231.92	120
Truck finance charges	182.89	265.51	145
Motorcycle and plane finance charges	2.36	4.42	187
Other vehicle finance charges	18.67	26.84	144
Maintenance and repairs	**697.30**	**843.38**	**121**
Coolant, additives, brake, transmission fluids	3.82	4.82	126
Tires—purchased, replaced, installed	89.93	103.48	115
Parts, equipment, and accessories	41.70	43.94	105
Vehicle audio equipment, excl. labor	12.32	11.02	89
Vehicle products	4.92	8.66	176
Miscellaneous auto repair, servicing	43.69	63.51	145
Body work and painting	31.24	36.21	116
Clutch, transmission repair	48.68	60.61	125
Drive shaft and rear-end repair	6.51	7.73	119
Brake work	57.73	76.39	132
Repair to steering or front-end	16.91	18.15	107
Repair to engine cooling system	21.68	25.09	116
Motor tune-up	49.69	63.87	129
Lube, oil change, and oil filters	65.07	70.49	108
Front-end alignment, wheel balance, rotation	11.90	11.63	98
Shock absorber replacement	4.82	6.38	132
Gas tank repair, replacement	4.32	3.74	87
Tire repair and other repair work	39.83	47.90	120
Vehicle air conditioning repair	17.00	18.43	108
Exhaust system repair	12.56	11.25	90
Electrical system repair	28.42	33.85	119
Motor repair, replacement	76.62	106.31	139
Auto repair service policy	7.93	9.91	125

	total consumer units	CUs headed by 35-to-44-year-olds	
		average spending	indexed spending
Vehicle insurance	$893.50	$986.86	110
Vehicle rental, leases, licenses, other charges	482.71	576.03	119
Leased and rented vehicles	324.48	390.19	120
Rented vehicles	41.33	45.29	110
Auto rental	6.76	5.95	88
Auto rental on trips	28.28	31.73	112
Truck rental	2.21	2.94	133
Truck rental on trips	3.55	3.87	109
Leased vehicles	283.15	344.91	122
Car lease payments	149.63	134.16	90
Cash down payment (car lease)	11.13	8.14	73
Termination fee (car lease)	1.28	1.08	84
Truck lease payments	114.24	188.52	165
Cash down payment (truck lease)	4.92	9.17	186
Termination fee (truck lease)	1.94	3.83	197
Vehicle registration, state	72.82	84.64	116
Vehicle registration, local	7.76	10.11	130
Driver's license	6.26	5.90	94
Vehicle inspection	9.26	10.76	116
Parking fees	29.25	38.96	133
Parking fees in home city, excluding residence	24.24	32.38	134
Parking fees on trips	5.01	6.58	131
Tolls	10.59	13.72	130
Tolls on trips	3.94	4.33	110
Towing charges	5.60	5.60	100
Automobile service clubs	12.75	11.83	93
PUBLIC TRANSPORTATION	388.75	400.18	103
Airline fares	243.57	257.73	106
Intercity bus fares	11.48	11.77	103
Intracity mass transit fares	49.97	73.27	147
Local transportation on trips	10.91	10.57	97
Taxi fares and limousine service on trips	6.41	6.21	97
Taxi fares and limousine service	18.95	9.98	53
Intercity train fares	16.09	12.04	75
Ship fares	29.74	16.74	56
School bus	1.64	1.88	115
HEALTH CARE	$2,350.32	$1,979.69	84
HEALTH INSURANCE	1,167.71	1,022.89	88
Commercial health insurance	217.53	263.07	121
Traditional fee-for-service health plan (not BCBS)	68.27	51.56	76
Preferred-provider health plan (not BCBS)	149.26	211.51	142
Blue Cross, Blue Shield	315.67	316.45	100
Traditional fee-for-service health plan	53.76	36.50	68
Preferred-provider health plan	106.99	137.68	129
Health maintenance organization	101.53	124.15	122
Commercial Medicare supplement	47.35	13.34	28
Other BCBS health insurance	6.05	4.78	79

	total consumer units	CUs headed by 35-to-44-year-olds	
		average spending	indexed spending
Health maintenance plans (HMOs)	$280.47	$331.70	118
Medicare payments	186.87	32.57	17
Commercial Medicare supplements/ other health insurance	167.18	79.10	47
Commercial Medicare supplement (not BCBS)	106.32	35.66	34
Other health insurance (not BCBS)	60.86	43.44	71
MEDICAL SERVICES	589.87	555.71	94
Physician's services	147.53	137.83	93
Dental services	226.99	231.37	102
Eye care services	34.20	51.84	152
Service by professionals other than physician	42.76	40.17	94
Lab tests, X-rays	26.79	20.65	77
Hospital room	36.57	18.94	52
Hospital services other than room	51.51	41.30	80
Care in convalescent or nursing home	12.46	1.53	12
Other medical services	9.46	4.75	50
DRUGS	487.43	302.53	62
Nonprescription drugs	64.45	60.01	93
Nonprescription vitamins	49.15	28.79	59
Prescription drugs	373.83	213.74	57
MEDICAL SUPPLIES	105.31	98.56	94
Eyeglasses and contact lenses	52.26	56.86	109
Hearing aids	14.98	2.52	17
Topicals and dressings	27.56	30.25	110
Medical equipment for general use	2.69	2.40	89
Supportive, convalescent medical equipment	5.21	5.50	106
Rental of medical equipment	1.06	0.22	21
Rental of supportive, convalescent medical equipment	1.55	0.80	52
ENTERTAINMENT	$2,078.99	$2,685.22	129
FEES AND ADMISSIONS	541.67	742.60	137
Recreation expenses on trips	25.64	30.60	119
Social, recreation, civic club membership	107.92	131.61	122
Fees for participant sports	75.05	91.61	122
Participant sports on trips	29.50	40.57	138
Movie, theater, opera, ballet	98.30	123.41	126
Movie, other admissions on trips	45.57	60.68	133
Admission to sports events	36.18	53.00	146
Admission to sports events on trips	15.19	20.23	133
Fees for recreational lessons	82.69	160.29	194
Other entertainment services on trips	25.64	30.60	119
TELEVISION, RADIO, SOUND EQUIPMENT	691.90	817.37	118
Television	543.66	625.16	115
Cable service and community antenna	382.28	425.26	111
Black-and-white TV	0.80	1.18	148
Color TV, console	38.63	50.00	129
Color TV, portable, table model	39.14	36.58	93

	total consumer units	CUs headed by 35-to-44-year-olds	
		average spending	indexed spending
VCRs and video disc players	$23.25	$26.38	113
Video cassettes, tapes, and discs	33.13	40.34	122
Video game hardware and software	23.46	41.48	177
Repair of TV, radio, and sound equipment	2.50	3.06	122
Rental of television sets	0.46	0.89	193
Radio and sound equipment	**148.25**	**192.21**	**130**
Radios	3.98	1.96	49
Tape recorders and players	5.31	8.36	157
Sound components and component systems	20.19	23.95	119
Miscellaneous sound equipment	3.18	4.95	156
Sound equipment accessories	5.97	7.83	131
Satellite dishes	1.00	0.78	78
Compact disc, tape, record, video mail order clubs	6.53	8.11	124
Records, CDs, audio tapes, needles	36.47	45.11	124
Rental of VCR, radio, sound equipment	0.25	0.32	128
Musical instruments and accessories	24.82	30.46	123
Rental and repair of musical instruments	1.22	2.95	242
Rental of video cassettes, tapes, discs, films	39.33	57.42	146
PETS, TOYS, PLAYGROUND EQUIPMENT	**369.12**	**462.79**	**125**
Pets	**248.25**	**288.01**	**116**
Pet food	102.56	124.32	121
Pet purchase, supplies, and medicines	52.29	59.41	114
Pet services	21.95	23.74	108
Veterinarian services	71.44	80.54	113
Toys, games, hobbies, and tricycles	**117.34**	**169.49**	**144**
Playground equipment	**3.54**	**5.29**	**149**
OTHER ENTERTAINMENT SUPPLIES, EQUIPMENT, SERVICES	**476.30**	**662.46**	**139**
Unmotored recreational vehicles	**47.14**	**42.86**	**91**
Boat without motor and boat trailers	16.15	11.76	73
Trailer and other attachable campers	30.99	31.10	100
Motorized recreational vehicles	**170.19**	**251.86**	**148**
Motorized camper	40.05	93.26	233
Other vehicle	35.47	39.93	113
Motorboats	94.67	118.66	125
Rental of recreational vehicles	**1.99**	**2.96**	**149**
Outboard motors	**0.71**	**0.33**	**46**
Docking and landing fees	**6.66**	**5.32**	**80**
Sports, recreation, exercise equipment	**150.33**	**221.28**	**147**
Athletic gear, game tables, exercise equipment	60.51	79.11	131
Bicycles	13.45	25.96	193
Camping equipment	9.59	14.71	153
Hunting and fishing equipment	35.68	51.51	144
Winter sports equipment	5.45	7.32	134
Water sports equipment	8.95	11.39	127
Other sports equipment	14.62	27.13	186
Rental and repair of misc. sports equipment	2.07	4.15	200

	total consumer units	CUs headed by 35-to-44-year-olds average spending	indexed spending
Photographic equipment and supplies	**$90.48**	**$121.38**	**134**
Film	17.74	23.38	132
Other photographic supplies	2.27	0.01	0
Film processing	26.60	34.48	130
Repair and rental of photographic equipment	0.12	0.13	108
Photographic equipment	23.34	30.55	131
Photographer fees	20.42	32.82	161
Fireworks	**1.52**	**1.86**	**122**
Souvenirs	**1.25**	**2.59**	**207**
Visual goods	**1.19**	**2.62**	**220**
Pinball, electronic video games	**4.84**	**9.40**	**194**
PERSONAL CARE PRODUCTS			
AND SERVICES	**$525.80**	**$614.64**	**117**
Personal care products	**276.65**	**344.16**	**124**
Hair care products	53.57	73.46	137
Hair accessories	6.57	8.87	135
Wigs and hairpieces	1.32	1.59	120
Oral hygiene products	27.33	33.34	122
Shaving products	15.09	17.78	118
Cosmetics, perfume, and bath products	129.13	150.78	117
Deodorants, feminine hygiene, misc. products	30.29	37.83	125
Electric personal care appliances	13.34	20.53	154
Personal care services	**249.15**	**270.47**	**109**
READING	**$138.57**	**$134.57**	**97**
Newspaper subscriptions	43.88	33.10	75
Newspaper, nonsubscription	11.30	13.39	118
Magazine subscriptions	16.59	14.30	86
Magazines, nonsubscription	9.35	11.10	119
Books purchased through book clubs	6.62	7.69	116
Books not purchased through book clubs	50.38	54.53	108
Encyclopedia and other reference book sets	0.33	0.11	33
EDUCATION	**$751.95**	**$738.35**	**98**
College tuition	444.45	282.97	64
Elementary and high school tuition	128.94	229.46	178
Other school tuition	25.53	36.22	142
Other school expenses including rentals	25.77	39.26	152
Books, supplies for college	57.93	34.97	60
Books, supplies for elementary, high school	16.14	35.19	218
Books, supplies for day care, nursery school	3.39	5.92	175
Miscellaneous school expenses and supplies	49.80	74.35	149

	total consumer units	CUs headed by 35-to-44-year-olds	
		average spending	indexed spending
TOBACCO PRODUCTS AND SMOKING SUPPLIES	**$320.49**	**$375.83**	**117**
Cigarettes	291.89	347.75	119
Other tobacco products	26.27	25.51	97
Smoking accessories	2.33	2.56	110
FINANCIAL PRODUCTS, SERVICES	**$792.40**	**$841.42**	**105**
Miscellaneous fees	2.25	2.76	123
Lottery and gambling losses	46.94	24.44	52
Legal fees	132.99	137.59	103
Funeral expenses	77.91	50.45	65
Safe deposit box rental	3.84	2.70	70
Checking accounts, other bank service charges	25.91	33.38	129
Cemetery lots, vaults, and maintenance fees	16.05	3.36	21
Accounting fees	57.85	55.67	96
Miscellaneous personal services	39.77	46.49	117
Finance charges, except mortgage and vehicles	271.37	305.62	113
Occupational expenses	38.46	59.00	153
Expenses for other properties	65.99	92.94	141
Credit card memberships	2.82	3.23	115
Shopping club membership fees	5.97	7.36	123
CASH CONTRIBUTIONS	**$1,277.10**	**$1,247.46**	**98**
Support for college students	75.94	44.56	59
Alimony expenditures	21.18	15.68	74
Child support expenditures	190.75	376.22	197
Gifts to non-CU members of stocks, bonds, and mutual funds	24.23	1.36	6
Cash contributions to charities and other organizations	137.62	105.76	77
Cash contributions to church, religious organizations	557.29	542.84	97
Cash contributions to educational institutions	33.42	29.31	88
Cash contributions to political organizations	10.90	4.08	37
Other cash gifts	225.76	127.66	57
PERSONAL INSURANCE, PENSIONS	**$3,898.62**	**$5,182.53**	**133**
Life and other personal insurance	**406.11**	**408.79**	**101**
Life, endowment, annuity, other personal insurance	391.65	396.24	101
Other nonhealth insurance	14.46	12.55	87
Pensions and Social Security	**3,492.51**	**4,773.74**	**137**
Deductions for government retirement	69.48	92.65	133
Deductions for railroad retirement	2.21	6.49	294
Deductions for private pensions	390.38	576.38	148
Nonpayroll deposit to retirement plans	426.12	429.68	101
Deductions for Social Security	2,604.32	3,668.54	141

	total consumer units	CUs headed by 35-to-44-year-olds	
		average spending	indexed spending
PERSONAL TAXES	**$2,496.26**	**$3,074.86**	**123**
Federal income taxes	1,842.57	2,258.45	123
State and local income taxes	506.45	679.93	134
Other taxes	147.24	136.49	93
GIFTS FOR NON-HOUSEHOLD MEMBERS**	**$1,036.24**	**$868.25**	**84**
FOOD	**82.18**	**59.93**	**73**
Cakes and cupcakes	2.41	2.14	89
Other fresh fruits (excl. apples, bananas, citrus)	2.26	2.38	105
Candy and chewing gum	11.69	8.50	73
Board (including at school)	21.90	15.68	72
Catered affairs	26.19	13.25	51
ALCOHOLIC BEVERAGES	**13.42**	**15.68**	**117**
Beer and ale	4.73	4.52	96
Wine	5.84	6.46	111
HOUSING	**258.69**	**231.02**	**89**
Housekeeping supplies	**42.48**	**41.42**	**98**
Laundry and cleaning supplies	2.93	2.90	99
Other household products	11.69	12.21	104
Miscellaneous household products	5.85	6.92	118
Lawn and garden supplies	4.20	3.64	87
Postage and stationery	27.86	26.30	94
Stationery, stationery supplies, giftwrap	21.13	20.59	97
Postage	6.14	5.45	89
Household textiles	**13.72**	**10.68**	**78**
Bathroom linens	2.59	2.93	113
Bedroom linens	6.10	3.52	58
Appliances and miscellaneous housewares	**23.98**	**16.51**	**69**
Major appliances	8.41	7.05	84
Electric floor cleaning equipment	2.77	2.37	86
Small appliances and miscellaneous housewares	15.57	9.46	61
China and other dinnerware	2.46	0.96	39
Nonelectric cookware	3.53	0.47	13
Tableware, nonelectric kitchenware	2.63	3.29	125
Small electric kitchen appliances	2.71	1.99	73
Miscellaneous household equipment	**64.70**	**64.81**	**100**
Infants' equipment	3.82	1.31	34
Outdoor equipment	2.07	2.23	108
Other household decorative items	25.76	28.88	112
Power tools	2.80	3.57	128
Indoor plants, fresh flowers	13.43	11.24	84
Computers and computer hardware	6.59	7.46	113
Miscellaneous household equipment	2.19	1.96	89
Other housing	**113.80**	**97.62**	**86**
Repair or maintenance services	4.51	0.42	9
Housing while attending school	39.93	15.55	39

	total consumer units	CUs headed by 35-to-44-year-olds	
		average spending	indexed spending
Natural gas (renter)	$3.62	$3.98	110
Electricity (renter)	14.67	20.07	137
Water, sewer maintenance (renter)	3.04	3.66	120
Day-care centers, nurseries, and preschools	23.81	32.80	138
APPAREL AND SERVICES	**237.13**	**208.27**	**88**
Men and boys, aged 2 or older	**63.74**	**63.44**	**100**
Men's coats and jackets	5.09	8.45	166
Men's accessories	4.45	2.62	59
Men's sweaters and vests	3.06	3.11	102
Men's active sportswear	2.76	2.73	99
Men's shirts	16.79	15.89	95
Men's pants	6.93	6.08	88
Boys' shirts	3.71	5.26	142
Boys' pants	3.76	3.55	94
Women and girls, aged 2 or older	**81.76**	**55.82**	**68**
Women's coats and jackets	5.62	0.63	11
Women's dresses	7.66	2.32	30
Women's vests and sweaters	8.50	3.35	39
Women's shirts, tops, blouses	9.06	3.84	42
Women's pants	6.62	2.01	30
Women's active sportswear	4.33	2.09	48
Women's sleepwear	6.45	9.05	140
Women's accessories	5.71	4.23	74
Girls' dresses and suits	2.98	1.92	64
Girls' shirts, blouses, sweaters	4.48	3.17	71
Girls' skirts and pants	3.32	3.76	113
Girls' accessories	2.38	5.86	246
Children under age 2	**39.99**	**45.31**	**113**
Infant dresses, outerwear	15.28	14.55	95
Infant underwear	16.91	23.53	139
Infant nightwear, loungewear	2.55	2.06	81
Infant accessories	3.93	3.51	89
Other apparel products and services	**51.63**	**43.70**	**85**
Jewelry and watches	24.01	20.36	85
Watches	2.16	2.18	101
Jewelry	21.85	18.19	83
Men's footwear	8.37	4.41	53
Boys' footwear	4.46	6.75	151
Women's footwear	8.82	7.98	90
Girls' footwear	3.30	2.60	79
TRANSPORTATION	**43.87**	**44.93**	**102**
New cars	7.09	19.18	271
Used cars	12.21	12.17	100
Airline fares	6.78	6.36	94
Ship fares	2.74	1.91	70

	total consumer units	CUs headed by 35-to-44-year-olds	
		average spending	indexed spending
HEALTH CARE	**$32.59**	**$20.64**	**63**
Physician's services	3.07	1.03	34
Dental services	4.03	3.85	96
Care in convalescent or nursing home	5.19	0.08	2
Nonprescription vitamins	3.93	1.50	38
Prescription drugs	2.38	1.32	55
ENTERTAINMENT	**78.24**	**85.78**	**110**
Toys, games, hobbies, and tricycles	29.98	29.00	97
Other entertainment	48.26	56.78	118
Fees for recreational lessons	7.88	10.19	129
Community antenna or cable TV	6.37	8.35	131
VCRs and videodisc players	2.26	2.14	95
Video game hardware and software	2.13	2.13	100
Athletic gear, game tables, exercise equipment	6.60	8.85	134
Hunting and fishing equipment	3.06	2.18	71
Photographer fees	3.19	1.79	56
PERSONAL CARE PRODUCTS, SERVICES	**21.15**	**27.07**	**128**
Cosmetics, perfume, bath preparation	12.53	13.53	108
Electric personal care appliances	3.31	6.17	186
EDUCATION	**183.88**	**107.53**	**58**
College tuition	127.83	56.74	44
Elementary and high school tuition	25.95	32.89	127
Other school tuition	4.44	1.85	42
Other school expenses including rentals	3.99	3.73	93
College books and supplies	11.93	4.24	36
Miscellaneous school supplies	7.38	5.02	68
ALL OTHER GIFTS	**83.76**	**66.84**	**80**
Gifts of trip expenses	44.40	32.28	73
Lottery and gambling losses	2.86	0.03	1
Legal fees	5.82	2.20	38
Funeral expenses	25.25	24.28	96
Miscellaneous personal services	2.16	2.98	138

*This figure does not include the amount paid for mortgage principle, which is considered an asset.

** Expenditures on gifts are also included in the preceding product and service categories. Food spending, for example, includes the amount spent on food gifts. Only gift categories with spending of $2.00 or more by the average consumer unit are shown.

Note: The Bureau of Labor Statistics uses consumer unit rather than household as the sampling unit in the Consumer Expenditure Survey. For the definition of consumer unit, see the glossary. (–) means not applicable or the sample is too small to make a reliable estimate.

Source: Bureau of Labor Statistics, unpublished data from the 2002 Consumer Expenditure Survey; calculations by New Strategist

9

Wealth

■ During the 1990s, a strong economy boosted the net worth of the average household. But young adults did not see much of a gain. The median net worth of households headed by people under age 35 rose only 8 percent between 1989 and 2001, from $10,700 to $11,600, after adjusting for inflation.

■ The median value of financial assets owned by householders under age 35 grew 68 percent between 1989 and 2001, to a modest $6,250 after adjusting for inflation. This rise was much less than the 80 percent gain enjoyed by the average household.

■ The median value of nonfinancial assets owned by young adults stood at $30,538 in 2001, well below the $113,500 held by the average household.

■ The debt of householders under age 35 rose more slowly than that of the average household between 1989 and 2001, up 59 percent to a median of $24,898.

■ The proportion of workers under age 45 covered by a pension plan ranges from a low of 13 percent for those under age 25 to 47 percent among those aged 25 to 44.

Householders under Age 35 Have the Lowest Net Worth

Since 1989, their net worth has grown much slower than average.

Net worth, one of the most important measures of wealth, is what remains after a household's debts are subtracted from its assets. The net worth of householders under age 35 rose a modest 8 percent between 1989 and 2001, much less than the 33 percent increase in net worth for the average household, after adjusting for inflation. Although the net worth of householders under age 35 has been growing faster than average since 1998, their $11,600 median net worth in 2001 was less than what it was in 1995.

The net worth of young adults is much less than that of older householders primarily because their homeownership rate is lower. Homes account for the largest share of the net worth of Americans. Also, householders under age 35 typically have education loans, car loans, and credit card balances, all of which reduce their net worth. Net worth rises in middle age as people buy homes and pay off debts.

■ The net worth of young adults will always be less than that of older householders. Their low incomes, coupled with the costs of setting up a household and starting a family, leave young adults with little money for saving.

The net worth of the youngest householders is well below average

(median net worth of total households and householders under age 35, 2001)

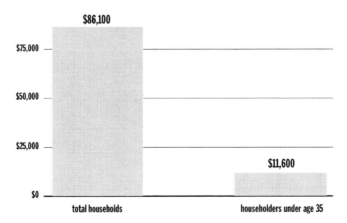

Table 9.1 **Net Worth of Households by Age of Householder, 1989 to 2001**

(median net worth of households by age of householder, 1989 to 2001; percent change, 1989–2001 and 1998–2001; in 2001 dollars)

	2001	1998	1995	1992	1989	percent change 1998–01	percent change 1989–01
Total households	**$86,100**	**$78,000**	**$66,400**	**$61,200**	**$64,600**	**10.4%**	**33.3%**
Under age 35	11,600	9,900	13,900	11,400	10,700	17.2	8.4
Aged 35 to 44	77,600	69,000	60,300	55,100	77,000	12.5	0.8
Aged 45 to 54	132,900	114,800	107,500	96,800	135,900	15.8	–2.2
Aged 55 to 64	181,500	139,200	133,200	141,100	134,700	30.4	34.7
Aged 65 to 74	176,300	159,500	128,000	121,700	105,000	10.5	67.9
Aged 75 or older	151,400	136,700	107,500	107,500	99,700	10.8	51.9

Source: Federal Reserve Board, results from the Survey of Consumer Finances; Internet site http://www.federalreserve.gov/pubs/oss/oss2/2001/scf2001home.html; calculations by New Strategist

Most Young Adults Own Financial Assets

The value of their assets has grown more slowly than average since 1989.

The value of financial assets owned by householders under age 35 grew 68 percent between 1989 and 2001, after adjusting for inflation. The increase was considerably less than the 80 percent gain in asset value for the average household. The median value of financial assets owned by young adults stood at just $6,250 in 2001 compared with $28,000 for the average household.

Behind the rise in financial asset values since 1989 was the soaring stock market. Forty-nine percent of householders under age 35 owned stock in 2001, up from 22 percent in 1989. Their stock was valued at just $7,000, however, and the market decline since 2001 is certain to have reduced the figure somewhat. Stocks account for more than half of the value of the financial assets of householders under age 35.

According to the Investment Company Institute and the Securities Industry Association, households headed by Gen Xers account for 25 percent of the nation's equity owners. Much of the stock owned by Gen Xers is in employer-sponsored retirement plans.

■ The proportion of Gen X households that own stock is likely to rise with age as they search for bigger gains for their retirement savings.

The financial assets of young adults are worth little

(median financial assets of total households and householders under age 35, 2001)

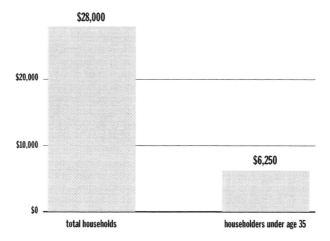

Table 9.2 Financial Assets of Households by Age of Householder, 1989 to 2001

(percentage of households owning financial assets and median value of assets for owners, by age of householder, 1989 to 2001; percentage point change in ownership and percent change in value of asset, 1989–2001 and 1998–2001; in 2001 dollars)

	2001	1998	1995	1992	1989	percentage point change 1998–01	percentage point change 1989–01
PERCENT OWNING ANY FINANCIAL ASSET							
Total households	**93.1%**	**92.9%**	**91.0%**	**90.2%**	**88.7%**	**0.2**	**4.4**
Under age 35	89.2	88.6	86.9	85.7	84.8	0.6	4.4
Aged 35 to 44	90.2	91.0	91.8	93.3	93.3	–0.8	–3.1
Aged 45 to 54	94.4	94.9	92.8	92.5	90.6	–0.5	3.8
Aged 55 to 64	94.8	95.6	90.8	92.5	87.5	–0.8	7.3
Aged 65 to 74	94.6	95.6	92.6	91.2	92.0	–1.0	2.6
Aged 75 or older	95.1	92.1	94.2	92.1	91.4	3.0	3.7

	2001	1998	1995	1992	1989	percent change 1998–01	percent change 1989–01
MEDIAN VALUE OF FINANCIAL ASSET							
Total households	**$28,000**	**$24,498**	**$17,992**	**$14,230**	**$15,554**	**14.3%**	**80.0%**
Under age 35	6,250	5,002	6,242	4,578	3,716	25.0	68.2
Aged 35 to 44	26,900	24,890	15,922	12,374	19,339	8.1	39.1
Aged 45 to 54	45,700	41,127	32,363	23,634	25,052	11.1	82.4
Aged 55 to 64	56,630	49,634	37,911	35,265	35,981	14.1	57.4
Aged 65 to 74	51,400	49,852	24,504	31,553	26,772	3.1	92.0
Aged 75 or older	40,000	39,882	26,469	26,047	40,537	0.3	–1.3

Source: Federal Reserve Board, results from the Survey of Consumer Finances; Internet site http://www.federalreserve.gov/pubs/oss/oss2/2001/scf2001home.html; calculations by New Strategist

Table 9.3 Financial Assets of Households by Type of Asset and Age of Householder, 2001

(percent of household owning selected financial assets, and median value of asset for owners, by type of asset and age of householder, 2001)

	total	under 35	35 to 44	45 to 54	55 to 64	65 to 74	75 or older
PERCENT OWNING ASSET							
Any financial asset	**93.1%**	**89.2%**	**93.3%**	**94.4%**	**94.8%**	**94.6%**	**95.1%**
Transaction accounts	90.9	86.0	90.7	92.2	93.6	93.8	93.7
Certificates of deposit	15.7	6.3	9.8	15.2	14.4	29.7	36.5
Savings bonds	16.7	12.7	22.6	21.0	14.3	11.3	12.5
Bonds	3.0	–	2.1	2.8	6.1	3.9	5.7
Stocks	21.3	17.4	21.6	22.0	26.7	20.5	21.8
Mutual funds	17.7	11.5	17.5	20.2	21.3	19.9	19.5
Retirement accounts	52.2	45.1	61.4	63.4	59.1	44.0	25.7
Life insurance	28.0	15.0	27.0	31.1	35.7	36.7	33.3
Other managed assets	6.6	2.1	3.1	6.4	13.0	11.8	11.2
Other financial assets	9.3	10.4	9.5	8.5	10.6	8.5	7.3
MEDIAN VALUE OF ASSET							
Total financial assets	**$28,000**	**$6,300**	**$26,900**	**$45,700**	**$56,600**	**$51,400**	**$40,000**
Transaction accounts	4,000	1,800	3,400	4,600	5,500	8,000	7,300
Certificates of deposit	15,000	4,000	6,000	12,000	19,000	20,000	25,000
Savings bonds	1,000	300	1,000	1,000	2,500	2,000	3,000
Bonds	43,500	–	13,600	60,000	60,000	71,400	35,000
Stocks	20,000	5,700	15,000	15,000	37,500	85,000	60,000
Mutual funds	35,000	9,000	17,500	38,500	60,000	70,000	70,000
Retirement accounts	29,000	6,600	28,500	48,000	55,000	60,000	46,000
Life insurance	10,000	10,000	9,000	11,000	10,000	8,800	7,000
Other managed assets	70,000	40,000	50,000	60,000	55,000	120,000	100,000
Other financial assets	4,000	1,300	2,000	5,000	10,000	8,000	17,500

Note: (–) means sample is too small to make a reliable estimate.
Source: Federal Reserve Board, results from the Survey of Consumer Finances; Internet site http://www.federalreserve.gov/pubs/oss/oss2/2001/scf2001home.html

Table 9.4 Stock Ownership of Households by Age of Householder, 1989 to 2001

(percentage of householders owning stocks directly or indirectly, median value of stocks for owners, and share of total household financial assets accounted for by stock holdings, by age of householder, 1989 to 2001; percent and percentage point change, 1989–2001 and 1998–2001; in 2001 dollars)

	2001	1998	1995	1992	1989	percentage point change 1998–01	percentage point change 1989–01
PERCENT OWNING STOCK							
Total households	**51.9%**	**48.9%**	**40.4 %**	**36.7%**	**31.7%**	**3.0**	**20.2**
Under age 35	48.9	40.8	36.6	28.4	22.4	8.1	26.5
Aged 35 to 44	59.5	56.7	46.4	42.4	39.0	2.8	20.5
Aged 45 to 54	59.2	58.6	48.9	46.4	41.8	0.6	17.4
Aged 55 to 64	57.1	55.9	40.0	45.3	36.2	1.2	20.9
Aged 65 to 74	39.2	42.7	34.4	30.2	26.7	−3.5	12.5
Aged 75 or older	34.2	29.4	27.9	25.7	25.9	4.8	8.3

	2001	1998	1995	1992	1989	percent change 1998–01	percent change 1989–01
MEDIAN VALUE OF STOCK							
Total households	**$34,250**	**$27,212**	**$16,875**	**$12,992**	**$11,700**	**54.6%**	**240.0%**
Under age 35	7,000	7,619	5,895	4,331	4,129	−8.1	69.5
Aged 35 to 44	27,500	21,769	11,558	9,280	7,089	26.3	287.9
Aged 45 to 54	50,000	41,362	29,986	18,561	18,100	20.9	176.2
Aged 55 to 64	81,200	51,158	35,831	30,934	25,327	58.7	220.6
Aged 65 to 74	150,000	60,954	39,298	19,798	27,942	146.1	436.8
Aged 75 or older	120,000	65,308	23,117	30,934	34,412	83.7	248.7

	2001	1998	1995	1992	1989	percentage point change 1998–01	percentage point change 1989–01
STOCK AS SHARE OF FINANCIAL ASSETS							
Total households	**56.0%**	**53.9%**	**39.9%**	**33.7%**	**27.8%**	**2.1**	**28.2**
Under age 35	52.6	44.8	27.2	24.8	20.2	7.8	32.4
Aged 35 to 44	57.3	54.6	39.5	31.0	29.2	2.7	28.1
Aged 45 to 54	59.1	55.7	42.6	40.8	33.5	3.4	25.6
Aged 55 to 64	56.1	58.4	44.2	37.3	27.6	−2.3	28.5
Aged 65 to 74	55.1	51.3	35.8	31.6	26.0	3.8	29.1
Aged 75 or older	51.4	48.7	39.8	25.5	25.0	2.7	26.4

Source: Federal Reserve Board, results from the Survey of Consumer Finances; Internet site http://www.federalreserve.gov/pubs/oss/oss2/2001/scf2001home.html; calculations by New Strategist

Table 9.5 Characteristics of Equity Owners by Generation, 2002

(selected characteristics of equity owners by generation, 2002)

	total	Generation X (born 1965 or later)	Baby Boom (born between 1946 and 1964)	Silent or GI (born in 1945 or earlier)
Percent of all equity investors	100%	25%	48%	27%
Median age*	47	30	46	65
Median household income	$62,500	$60,000	$70,000	$50,000
Median household financial assets**	100,000	35,000	125,000	350,000
Median household financial assets in equities	50,000	25,000	51,000	69,600
Median number of individual stocks and stock mutual funds owned	4	3	5	5
Percent of equity-owning households				
Married or living with partner*	71%	66%	76%	66%
College or postgraduate degree*	50	52	49	48
Employed*	77	93	91	38
Own individual stock (net)***	49	43	49	54
Inside employer-sponsored retirement plans	17	18	20	11
Outside employer-sponsored retirement plans	41	34	41	48
Stock mutual funds (net)***	89	86	92	88
Inside employer-sponsored retirement plans	66	69	76	43
Outside employer-sponsored retirement plans	56	48	53	68

* Refers to the household's responding financial decisionmaker for investments.
** Includes assets in employer-sponsored retirement plans but excludes value of primary residence.
*** Multiple responses included.
Note: Number of respondents varies.
Source: Investment Company Institute and the Securities Industry Association, Equity Ownership in America, 2002; Internet sites http://www.ici.org and http://www.sia.com

Young Adults Made Gains in Nonfinancial Assets

But the value of their nonfinancial assets is well below average.

Between 1989 and 2001, the value of nonfinancial assets owned by householders under age 35 rose 29 percent, after adjusting for inflation—greater than the 22 percent national increase. The median value of nonfinancial assets owned by householders under age 35 stood at $30,538 in 2001, well below the $113,500 held by the average household.

Households headed by people under age 35 have modest nonfinancial assets because few are homeowners, and home values account for the bulk of nonfinancial assets. In 2001, only 40 percent were homeowners versus 68 percent of all households. Younger adults are almost as likely as the average American to own a vehicle, however. Seventy-nine percent of householders under age 35 owned a vehicle in 2001, only 6 percentage points less than among all households.

■ Homeownership is the primary force behind gains in nonfinancial assets. The value of nonfinancial assets of householders under age 35 will rise only as their homeownership rate increases.

Nonfinancial assets of young adults are modest

(median value of nonfinancial assets owned by total households and householders under age 35, 2001)

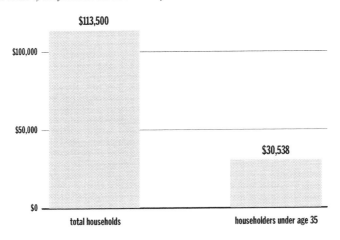

Table 9.6 Nonfinancial Assets of Households by Age of Householder, 1989 to 2001

(percentage of households owning nonfinancial assets and median value of assets for owners, by age of householder, 1989 to 2001; percentage point change in ownership and percent change in value of asset, 1989–2001 and 1998–2001; in 2001 dollars)

	2001	1998	1995	1992	1989	percentage point change 1998–01	percentage point change 1989–01
PERCENT OWNING ANY NONFINANCIAL ASSET							
Total households	**90.7%**	**89.9%**	**90.9%**	**90.8%**	**89.3%**	**0.8**	**1.4**
Under age 35	83.0	83.3	87.1	85.6	83.9	–0.3	–0.9
Aged 35 to 44	93.2	92.1	90.6	92.3	91.8	1.1	1.4
Aged 45 to 54	95.2	92.9	93.6	94.4	93.2	2.3	2.0
Aged 55 to 64	95.4	93.8	93.9	92.7	91.2	1.6	4.2
Aged 65 to 74	91.6	92.0	92.6	91.6	92.7	–0.4	–1.1
Aged 75 or older	86.4	87.2	89.9	91.3	85.4	–0.8	1.0

	2001	1998	1995	1992	1989	percent change 1998–01	percent change 1989–01
MEDIAN VALUE OF NONFINANCIAL ASSET							
Total households	**$113,500**	**$106,398**	**$96,050**	**$85,379**	**$92,911**	**6.7%**	**22.2%**
Under age 35	30,538	24,654	25,486	21,468	23,606	23.9	29.4
Aged 35 to 44	117,806	112,602	111,211	102,003	116,035	4.6	1.5
Aged 45 to 54	141,558	137,991	130,593	116,777	148,554	2.6	–4.7
Aged 55 to 64	147,863	138,154	124,830	131,687	129,249	7.0	14.4
Aged 65 to 74	149,211	119,568	109,631	97,474	86,717	24.8	72.1
Aged 75 or older	122,619	104,575	91,311	86,090	71,129	17.3	72.4

Source: Federal Reserve Board, results from the Survey of Consumer Finances; Internet site http://www.federalreserve.gov/pubs/oss/oss2/2001/scf2001home.html; calculations by New Strategist

Table 9.7 Nonfinancial Assets of Households by Type of Asset and Age of Householder, 2001

(percent of household owning selected nonfinancial assets, and median value of asset for owners, by type of asset and age of householder, 2001)

	total	under 35	35 to 44	45 to 54	55 to 64	65 to 74	75 or older
PERCENT OWNING ASSET							
Any nonfinancial asset	**90.7%**	**83.0%**	**93.2%**	**95.2%**	**95.4%**	**91.6%**	**86.4%**
Vehicles	84.8	78.8	88.9	90.5	90.7	81.3	73.9
Primary residence	67.7	39.9	67.8	76.2	83.2	82.5	76.2
Other residential property	11.3	3.4	9.2	14.7	18.3	13.7	15.2
Equity in nonresidential property	8.3	2.8	7.6	10.0	12.3	12.9	8.3
Business equity	11.8	7.0	14.2	17.1	15.6	11.6	2.4
Other nonfinancial assets	7.6	6.9	8.0	7.2	7.9	9.7	6.2
MEDIAN VALUE OF ASSET							
Total nonfinancial assets	**$113,200**	**$30,500**	**$117,800**	**$140,300**	**$147,900**	**$149,200**	**$122,600**
Vehicles	13,500	11,300	14,800	15,700	15,100	13,600	8,800
Primary residence	122,000	95,000	125,000	135,000	130,000	129,000	111,000
Other residential property	80,000	75,000	75,000	65,000	80,000	145,000	80,000
Equity in nonresidential property	49,000	33,300	39,500	56,400	78,500	50,000	28,000
Business equity	100,000	50,000	100,000	102,000	100,000	100,000	510,900
Other nonfinancial assets	12,000	10,000	9,000	11,000	30,000	20,000	15,000

Source: Federal Reserve Board, results from the Survey of Consumer Finances; Internet site http://www.federalreserve.gov/pubs/oss/oss2/2001/scf2001home.html

Table 9.8 Household Ownership of Primary Residence by Age of Householder, 1989 to 2001

(percentage of households owning primary residence, median value of asset for owners, and median value of home-secured debt for owners, by age of householder, 1989 to 2001; percentage point change in ownership and percent change in value of asset, 1989–2001 and 1998–2001; in 2001 dollars)

						percentage point change	
	2001	1998	1995	1992	1989	1998–01	1989–01
PERCENT OWNING PRIMARY RSESIDENCE							
Total households	**67.7%**	**66.2%**	**64.7%**	**63.9%**	**63.9%**	**1.5**	**3.8**
Under age 35	39.9	38.9	37.9	36.9	39.4	1.0	0.5
Aged 35 to 44	67.8	67.1	64.7	64.5	66.1	0.7	1.7
Aged 45 to 54	76.2	74.4	75.3	75.4	76.5	1.8	–0.3
Aged 55 to 64	83.2	80.3	82.0	77.5	80.1	2.9	3.1
Aged 65 to 74	82.5	81.5	79.5	79.3	77.7	1.0	4.8
Aged 75 or older	76.2	77.0	72.8	77.2	69.9	–0.8	6.3

						percent change	
	2001	1998	1995	1992	1989	1998–01	1989–01
MEDIAN VALUE OF PRIMARY RESIDENCE							
Total households	**$123,000**	**$108,847**	**$104,025**	**$98,990**	**$96,352**	**1.3%**	**27.7%**
Under age 35	95,000	91,431	87,843	85,379	83,964	3.9	13.1
Aged 35 to 44	125,000	109,935	109,804	111,363	110,117	13.7	13.5
Aged 45 to 54	135,000	130,616	115,583	111,363	116,999	3.4	15.4
Aged 55 to 64	130,000	119,732	100,557	105,053	103,234	8.6	25.9
Aged 65 to 74	129,000	103,405	98,246	85,379	75,705	24.8	70.4
Aged 75 or older	111,000	92,520	92,467	86,616	75,625	20.0	46.8

						percent change	
	2001	1998	1995	1992	1989	1998–01	1989–01
MEDIAN VALUE OF HOME-SECURED DEBT							
Total households	**$70,000**	**$67,485**	**$59,119**	**$53,207**	**$44,047**	**3.7%**	**58.9%**
Under age 35	77,000	77,281	71,662	63,106	60,564	–0.4	27.1
Aged 35 to 44	80,000	76,193	69,350	68,055	55,058	5.0	45.3
Aged 45 to 54	75,000	74,016	56,636	49,495	35,788	1.3	109.6
Aged 55 to 64	55,000	52,247	42,766	37,121	27,529	5.3	99.8
Aged 65 to 74	39,000	28,300	21,961	21,035	12,527	37.8	211.3
Aged 75 or older	44,800	23,106	13,523	34,646	9,635	93.9	365.0

Source: Federal Reserve Board, results from the Survey of Consumer Finances; Internet site http://www.federalreserve.gov/pubs/oss/oss2/2001/scf2001home.html; calculations by New Strategist

Most Householders under Age 35 Are in Debt

But they owe less than older householders.

The debt of householders under age 35 increased more slowly than that of the average household between 1989 and 2001. The amount of money owed by householders under age 35 rose 59 percent during those years versus an 88 percent increase for the average household, after adjusting for inflation. Although 83 percent of households headed by people under age 35 are in debt compared with 75 percent of all households, they owe less than average—$24,898 versus the $38,775 average.

Mortgages and home equity loans account for the largest share of debt for most households. The low homeownership rate of householders under age 35 explains their lower debt load. But those with mortgages have larger-than-average mortgage debt—$77,000 versus the $70,000 average. The difference results from the fact that younger householders are more recent home buyers and have had less time to pay down their mortgage debt.

Sixty-four percent of householders under age 35 have installment debt—typically, car loans. They owe a median of $9,500 on their installment loans. Half carry a balance on their credit card, owing a median of $2,000.

■ Between 1998 and 2001, the debt of householders under age 35 grew twice as fast as that of the average household. Behind the growing debt load of the age group are rising homeownership rates and increased mortgage debt.

Householders under age 35 owe less than the average household

(median amount of debt held by total households and householders under age 35, 2001)

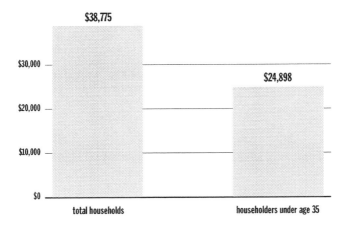

Table 9.9   Debt of Households by Age of Householder, 1989 to 2001

(percentage of households with debts and median amount of debt for debtors, by age of householder, 1989 to 2001; percentage point change in households with debt and percent change in amount of debt, 1989–2001 and 1998–2001; in 2001 dollars)

						percentage point change	
	2001	1998	1995	1992	1989	1998–01	1989–01
PERCENT WITH DEBT							
Total households	**75.1%**	**74.1%**	**74.5%**	**73.3%**	**72.3%**	**1.0**	**2.8**
Under age 35	82.7	81.2	83.5	81.5	80.0	1.5	2.7
Aged 35 to 44	88.6	87.6	87.0	86.4	88.6	1.0	0.0
Aged 45 to 54	84.6	87.0	86.3	85.4	85.3	–2.4	–0.7
Aged 55 to 64	75.4	76.4	73.7	70.1	70.8	–1.0	4.6
Aged 65 to 74	56.8	51.4	53.4	51.5	49.6	5.4	7.2
Aged 75 or older	29.2	24.6	28.4	31.6	21.0	4.6	8.2

						percent change	
	2001	1998	1995	1992	1989	1998–01	1989–01
MEDIAN AMOUNT OF DEBT							
Total households	**$38,775**	**$35,368**	**$24,987**	**$21,163**	**$20,647**	**9.6%**	**87.8%**
Under age 35	24,898	20,942	17,373	12,876	15,692	18.9	58.7
Aged 35 to 44	61,539	60,577	42,841	44,125	41,412	1.6	48.6
Aged 45 to 54	54,255	52,225	45,221	33,409	32,562	3.9	66.6
Aged 55 to 64	34,615	37,204	24,273	23,681	13,170	–7.0	162.8
Aged 65 to 74	13,100	12,964	8,146	5,974	6,882	1.1	90.3
Aged 75 or older	5,000	8,761	2,196	2,908	3,839	–42.9	30.2

Source: Federal Reserve Board, results from the Survey of Consumer Finances; Internet site http://www.federalreserve.gov/pubs/oss/oss2/2001/scf2001home.html; calculations by New Strategist

Table 9.10 Debt of of Households by Type of Debt and Age of Householder, 2001

(percent of householders with debt, and median value of debt for those with debts, by type of debt and age of householder, 2001)

	total	under 35	35 to 44	45 to 54	55 to 64	65 to 74	75 or older
PERCENT WITH DEBT							
Any debt	**75.1%**	**82.7%**	**88.6%**	**84.6%**	**75.4%**	**56.8%**	**29.2%**
Mortgage and home equity	44.6	35.7	59.6	59.8	49.0	32.0	9.5
Other residential property	4.7	2.7	4.9	6.5	8.0	3.4	2.0
Installment loans	45.2	63.8	57.1	45.9	39.3	21.1	9.5
Credit card balances	44.4	49.6	54.1	50.4	41.6	30.0	18.4
Other lines of credit	1.5	1.7	1.7	1.5	3.1	–	–
Other debt	7.2	8.8	8.0	7.4	7.4	5.0	3.6
MEDIAN VALUE OF DEBT FOR DEBTOR HOUSEHOLDS							
Total debt	**$38,800**	**$24,900**	**$61,500**	**$54,300**	**$34,600**	**$13,100**	**$5,000**
Mortgage, home equity	70,000	77,000	80,000	75,000	55,000	39,000	44,800
Other residential property	40,000	52,000	45,500	33,500	40,000	77,000	42,000
Installment loans	9,700	9,500	11,100	9,600	9,000	7,000	5,800
Credit card balances	1,900	2,000	2,000	2,300	1,900	1,000	700
Other lines of credit	3,900	500	700	5,300	20,500	–	–
Other debt	3,000	2,000	3,100	5,000	5,000	2,500	2,500

Note: (–) means sample is too small to make a reliable estimate.
Source: Federal Reserve Board, results from the Survey of Consumer Finances; Internet site http://www.federalreserve.gov/pubs/oss/oss2/2001/scf2001home.html

Most Workers under Age 45 Do Not Have Pension Coverage

Gen Xers are not overly concerned about their economic security in retirement, however.

Fewer than half—43 percent—of American workers were included in their employer's pension plan in 2001. Pension coverage peaks at 55 percent among workers aged 45 to 64. But among workers aged 25 to 44, coverage was a lower 47 percent. Among those participating in a plan, most are in defined-contribution (funded by the employee) rather than defined-benefit (funded by the employer) plans, according to the Bureau of Labor Statistics' 2003 National Compensation Survey. Younger workers are less likely than older workers to participate in a pension plan for a variety of reasons. Some do not have enough years of service to be vested in a plan, others cannot afford the contributions.

Despite their lack of pension coverage, Gen Xers are not overly concerned with funding their retirement. Fully 68 percent say they are "very" or "somewhat" confident in having enough money to afford a comfortable retirement, according to the Employee Benefit Research Institute's 2003 Retirement Confidence Survey. And they're not depending on an inheritance to help them out, either. Only 18 percent of Gen Xers expect to receive an inheritance, and 11 percent have already received one, according to an AARP study of the Federal Reserve Board's Survey of Consumer Finances. Of those receiving an inheritance, just 2 percent got $100,000 or more.

■ Gen Xers are optimistic about retirement because they have many years to prepare. But if they do not force themselves to save now, they may find themselves approaching retirement with little to show for it.

Pension coverage peaks among workers aged 45 to 64

(percent of workers whose employer offers a pension plan who are included in the plan, by age, 2001)

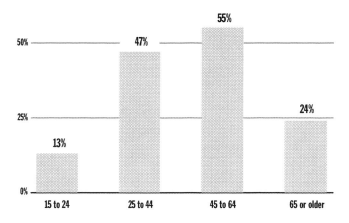

Table 9.11 Pension Coverage by Sex and Age, 2001

(total number of workers, number and percent whose employer offers a pension plan, and number and percent included in the plan, by sex and age, 2001; numbers in thousands)

| | | with employer-offered plan | | | |
| | | | | included in plan | |
	total	number	percent	number	percent
Total workers	**151,608**	**84,059**	**55.4%**	**65,445**	**43.2%**
Aged 15 to 24	24,593	8,597	35.0	3,135	12.7
Aged 25 to 44	71,281	41,904	58.8	33,534	47.0
Aged 45 to 64	50,230	31,462	62.6	27,476	54.7
Aged 65 or older	5,504	2,096	38.1	1,301	23.6
Men	**80,300**	**44,358**	**55.2**	**35,916**	**44.7**
Aged 15 to 24	12,816	4,375	34.1	1,732	13.5
Aged 25 to 44	38,048	22,223	58.4	18,417	48.4
Aged 45 to 64	26,313	16,579	63.0	14,990	57.0
Aged 65 or older	3,123	1,181	37.8	776	24.9
Women	**71,308**	**39,701**	**55.7**	**29,529**	**41.1**
Aged 15 to 24	11,777	4,223	35.9	1,403	11.9
Aged 25 to 44	33,232	19,680	59.2	15,117	45.5
Aged 45 to 64	23,917	14,883	62.2	12,485	52.2
Aged 65 or older	2,382	915	38.4	525	22.0

Source: Bureau of the Census, 2002 Current Population Survey Annual Demographic Supplement, Internet site http:// ferret.bls.census.gov/macro/032002/noncash/nc8_000.htm

Table 9.12 Retirement Confidence by Generation, 2003

(percent responding by generation, 2003)

	total	Gen X	younger Boomers	older Boomers	pre-retirees
Overall confidence in having enough money to live comfortably throughout retirement					
Very confident	21%	19%	23%	19%	29%
Somewhat confident	45	49	49	39	35
Not too confident	17	17	16	18	21
Not at all confident	16	15	12	23	14
Have saved for retirement					
Self	68	64	74	66	64
Household	71	68	78	69	68
Have done a retirement savings needs calculation					
Self	37	36	38	37	39
Household	43	41	45	41	42
Contribute to a retirement savings plan at work					
Yes	78	78	78	78	72
No	22	22	22	21	28
Expected retirement age					
Less than 55	6	8	7	4	–
Aged 55 to 59	10	11	10	11	0
Aged 60 to 64	21	19	22	22	24
Aged 65	25	28	28	21	17
Aged 66 or older	24	23	22	24	28
Never retire	6	4	5	7	10
Percentage expecting to work for pay in retirement	70	68	73	70	65

Note: Pre-retirees were born in 1945 or earlier; older Boomers were born between 1946 and 1954; younger Boomers were born between 1955 and 1964; Generation Xers were born in 1965 to 1978; (–) means data not available.
Source: 2003 Retirement Confidence Survey, EBRI/ASEC/Greenwald. Internet site http://www.ebri.org/

Table 9.13 Inheritance Receipt and Expectations by Generation, 1989 to 2001

(percent responding by generation and year, 1989 to 2001)

	pre-Boomers	Boomers	post-Boomers
Percent of households that have received at least one inheritance			
2001	24.0%	17.3%	11.0%
1998	29.1	16.9	11.8
1995	27.7	18.0	11.8
1992	27.1	15.5	9.9
1989	29.1	17.4	12.4
Percent of households that expect to receive an inheritance			
2001	5.8	14.9	18.4
1998	6.2	16.4	19.3
1995	6.4	18.1	20.7
1992	8.4	19.3	24.6
1989	10.8	26.9	20.6
Percent of households by amount inherited			
Total	**100.0**	**100.0**	**100.0**
No inheritance	76.0	82.7	89.0
$1 to $20,000	3.2	5.2	4.9
$20,001 to $50,000	3.8	3.6	2.4
$50,001 to $100,000	4.2	3.1	1.7
$100,000 or more	12.8	5.4	2.0
Median value of inheritances received (in 2002 dollars)			
2001	$108,885	$47,909	$22,167
1998	79,849	49,062	24,844
1995	78,499	41,833	20,325
1992	89,831	44,654	17,232
1989	105,165	44,692	27,635

Note: Pre-Boomers were born before 1946; Boomers were born from 1946 through 1964; post-Boomers were born after 1964.
Source: © 2003, AARP. Reprinted with permission. "Pennies from Heaven: Will Inheritances Bail Out the Boomers?" Mitja Ng-Baumhackl, John Gist, and Carlos Figueiredo, Data Digest, *DD Number 90, AARP Public Policy Institute*

For More Information

The federal government is a rich source of data on almost every aspect of American life. Below are the Internet addresses of federal and other agencies collecting the demographic data analyzed in this book. Also shown are phone numbers of the agencies and of the subject specialists at the Census Bureau and the Bureau of Labor Statistics, organized alphabetically by name of agency or specialty topic. A list of State Data Centers and Small Business Development Centers is also below to help you track down demographic and economic information for your state or local area. E-mail addresses are shown when available. Note: Telephone numbers at the Census Bureau change regularly. If the numbers below do not allow you to reach the specialists you need, go to http://www. census.gov/contacts/www/contacts.html for the most up-to-date lists.

Internet Addresses

- AARP, http://www.aarp.org
- Agency for Healthcare Research and Quality, www.meps.ahrq.gov/Data_Public.htm
- Behavioral Risk Factor Surveillance System, http://apps.nccd.cdc.gov/brfss/index.asp
- Bureau of the Census, www.census.gov
- Bureau of Labor Statistics, www.bls.gov
- Centers for Disease Control and Prevention,www .cdc.gov
- Consumer Expenditure Survey, www.bls.gov/cex/
- Current Population Survey, www.bls.census.gov/cps/ cpsmain.htm
- Employee Benefit Research Institute, www.ebri.org
- Federal Interagency Forum on Child and Family Statistics, http://childstats.gov/
- Higher Education Research Institute, www.gseis.ucla.edu/heri/heri.html
- Institute for Social Research, University of Michigan, http://monitoringthefuture.org
- Investment Company Institute, http://www.ici.org
- National Center for Education Statistics, http:// nces.ed.gov
- National Center for Health Statistics, www.cdc.gov/ nchs
- National Sporting Goods Association, www.nsga.org
- Securities Industry Association, www.sia.com
- Sourcebook of Criminal Justice Statistics,www .albany.edu/sourcebook/

- Sporting Goods Manufacturers Association, www.sgma.com
- Survey of Consumer Finances, www.federalreserve .gov/pubs/oss/oss2/scfindex.html
- U.S. Substance Abuse and Mental Health Services Administrations, www.samhsa.gov
- U.S. Citizenship and Immigration Services, http:// uscis.gov/graphics/shared/aboutus/statistics/index.htm
- Youth Risk Behavior Surveillance System, www.cdc .gov/nccdphp/dash/yrbs/results.htm

Subject Specialists

Absences from work, Staff 202-691-6378
Aging population, Staff 301-763-2378
American Community Survey/C2SS Results,
　Larry McGinn 301-763-8050
Ancestry, Staff 301-763-2403
Apportionment, Edwin Byerly 301-763-2381
Apportionment and redistricting,
　Cathy McCully 301-763-4039
Business expenditures, Sheldon Ziman 301-763-3315
Business investment, Charles Funk 301-763-3324
Business owners, characteristics of,
　Valerie Strang 301-763-3316
Census 1990 and earlier, Staff 301-763-2422
Census 2000
- American Factfinder, Staff 301-763-INFO (4636)
- Annexations/boundary changes,
　Joe Marinucci 301-763-1099
- Apportionment, Edwin Byerly 301-763-2381
- Census 2000 Briefs, Staff 301-763-2437
- Census 2000 tabulations, Staff 301-763-2422
- Census 2010, Ed Gore 301-763-3998
- Census history, Dave Pemberton 301-763-1167
- Citizenship, Staff 301-763-2411
- Commuting and place of work, Clara Reschovsky/ Celia Boertlein 301-763-2454
- Confidentiality and privacy, Jerry Gates 301-763-2515
- Count question resolution, Staff 866-546-0527
- Count review, Paul Campbell 301-763-2381
- Data dissemination, Staff 301-763-INFO (4636)
- Disability, Staff 301-763-3242
- Education, Staff 301-763-2464
- Employment/unemployment, Staff 301-763-3230
- Foreign born, Staff 301-763-2411
- Geographic entities, Staff 301-763-1099

- Grandparents as caregivers, Staff 301-763-2416
- Group quarters population, Denise Smith 301-763-2378
- Hispanic origin, ethnicity, ancestry, Staff 301-763-2403
- Homeless, Annetta Clark 301-763-2378
- Housing, Staff 301-763-3237
- Immigration/emigration, Staff 301-763-2411
- Income, Staff 301-763-3243
- Island areas, Idabelle Hovland 301-763-8443
- Labor force status/work experience, Staff 301-763-3230
- Language spoken in home, Staff 301-763-2464
- Living arrangements, Staff 301-763-2416
- Maps, customer services 301-763-INFO (4636)
- Marital status, Staff 301-763-2416
- Metropolitan areas, concepts and standards,
  Michael Ratcliffe 301-763-2419
- Microdata files, Amanda Shields 301-763-1326
- Migration, Carol Faber 301-763-2454
- Occupation/industry, Staff 301-763-3239
- Place of birth/native born, Carol Faber 301-763-2454
- Population (general information), Staff 301-763-2422
- Poverty, Alemayehu Bishaw 301-763-3213
- Race, Staff 301-763-2402
- Redistricting, Cathy McCully 301-763-4039
- Residence rules, Karen Mills 301-763-2381
- Small area income and poverty estimates,
  David Waddington 301-763-3195
- Special censuses, Mike Stump 301-763-3577
- Special populations, Staff 301-763-2378
- Special tabulations, Linda Showalter 301-763-2429
- Undercount, Phil Gbur 301-763-4206
  - Demographic analysis, Greg Robinson 301-763-2110
- Unmarried partners, Staff 301-763-2416
- Urban/rural, Ryan Short 301-763-1099
- U.S. citizens abroad, Staff 301-763-2422
- Veteran status, Staff 301-763-3230
- Voting districts, John Byle 301-763-1099
- Women, Renee Spraggins 301-763-2378
- ZIP codes, Staff 301-763-2422
Census Bureau customer service,
  Staff 301-763-INFO (4636)
Child care, Martin O'Connell/Kristin Smith
  301-763-2416
Children, Staff 301-763-2416
Citizenship status, Staff 301-763-2411
Communications and Utilities
- Current programs, Ruth Bramblett 301-763-2787
- Economic census, Jim Barron 301-763-2786
Commuting, means of transportation, and place of work,
  Clara Reschovsky/Celia Boertlein 301-763-2454

Construction
- Building permits, Staff 301-763-5160
- Economic census, Susan Bucci, Staff 301-763-4680
- Housing starts and completions, Staff 301-763-5160
- Manufactured housing, Lisa Feldman 301-763-1605
- Residential characteristics, price index, and sales,
  Staff 301-763-5160
- Residential improvements and repairs,
  Joe Huesman 301-763-1605
- Value of new construction, Mike Davis 301-763-1605
Consumer Expenditure Survey, Staff
  202-691-6900, cexinfo@bls.gov
Contingent workers, Staff 202-691-6378
County Business Patterns, Phillip Thompson
  301-763-2580
County populations, Staff 301-763-2422
Crime, Marilyn Monahan 301-763-5315
Current Population Survey, general information,
  Staff, 301-763-3806
Demographic surveys, demographic statistics,
  Staff 301-763-2422
Disability, Staff 301-763-3242
Discouraged workers, Staff 202-691-6378
Displaced workers, Staff 202-691-6378
Economic census 1997
- Accommodations and food services,
  Fay Dorsett 301-763-2687
- Construction, Staff 301-763-4680
- Finance and insurance, Faye Jacobs 301-763-2824
- General information, Robert Marske 301-763-2547
- Internet dissemination, Paul Zeisset 301-763-4151
- Manufacturing:
  - Consumer goods industries, Robert Reinard
    301-763-4810
  - Investment goods industries, Kenneth Hansen
    301-763-4755
  - Primary goods industries, Nat Shelton 301-763-6614
- Mining, Susan Bocci 301-763-4680
- Minority/women-owned businesses, Valerie Strang
  301-763-3316
- North American Industry Class. System,
  Wanda Dougherty 301-763-2790
- Puerto Rico and the Island Areas, Irma Harahush
  301-763-3319
- Real estate and rental/leasing, Pam Palmer
  301-763-2824
- Retail trade, Fay Dorsett 301-763-2687
- Services:
  - Administrative, waste management, remediation,
    Dan Wellwood 301-763-5181

Housing
- American Housing Survey data, Paul Harble 301-763-3235
- Census, Staff 301-763-3237
- Homeownership, vacancy data, Linda Cavanaugh/ Robert Callis 301-763-3199
- Housing affordability, Howard Savage 301-763-3199
- Market absorption, Alan Friedman/Mary Schwartz 301-763-3199
- New York City Housing and Vacancy Survey, Alan Friedman/Robert Callis 301-763-3199
- Residential finance, Howard Savage 301-763-3199

Immigration and Emigration
- General information, Staff 301-763-2422
- Concepts and analysis, Staff 301-763-2411

Income statistics, Staff 301-763-3243

Industry and commodity classification, James Kristoff 301-763-5179

International Statistics:
- Africa, Asia, Latin Am., North Am., and Oceania, Staff 301-763-1358
- Aging population, Staff 301-763-1371
- China, People's Republic, Staff 301-763-1360
- Europe, former Soviet Union, Staff 301-763-1360
- Health, Staff 301-763-1433
- International data base, Pat Dickerson/Peter Johnson 301-763-1351/1410
- Technical assistance and training, Staff 301-763-1444
- Women in development, Victoria Velkoff 301-763-1371

Job tenure, Staff 202-691-6378

Journey to work, Phil Salopek/Celia Boertlein 301-763-2454

Labor force concepts, Staff 202-691-6378

Language, Staff 301-763-2464

Longitudinal surveys, Ron Dopkowski 301-763-3801

Manufacturing and mining:
- Concentration, Patrick Duck 301-763-4699
- Exports from manufacturing establishments, John Gates 301-763-4589
- Financial statistics (Quarterly Financial Report), Yolando St. George 301-763-3343
- Foreign direct investment, Julius Smith 301-763-4683
- Fuels, electric energy consumed and prod. index, Susan Bucci 301-763-4680
- General information and data requests, Nishea Quash 301-763-4673
- Industries:
  - Electrical and trans. equip., instruments, machinery, Kenneth Hansen 301-763-4755

- Food, textiles, and apparel, Robert Reinard 301-763-4810
- Furniture, printing, and misc., Robert Reinard 301-763-4810
- Metals, Nat Shelton 301-763-6614
- Wood, paper, chemicals, petroleum prod., rubber, plastics, Nat Shelton 301-763-6614
- Mining, Susan Bucci 301-763-4680
- Monthly shipments, inventories, and orders, Dan Sansbury 301-763-4832
- Plant capacity utilization, Julius Smith 301-763-4683
- Research and development, Julius Smith 301-763-4683

Marital and family characteristics of workers, Staff 202-691-6378

Metropolitan areas, Staff 301-763-2422

Metropolitan standards, Michael Ratcliffe 301-763-2419

Migration
- General information, Staff 301-763-2422
- Domestic/internal, Carol Faber 301-763-2454
- International, Staff 301-763-2411

Minimum wage data, Steven Haugen 202-691-6378

Minority/women-owned businesses, Valerie Strang 301-763-3316

Minority workers, Staff 202-691-6378

Multiple jobholders, Staff 202-691-6373

National Center for Education Statistics, Staff 202-502-7300

National Center for Health Statistics, Staff 301-458-4000

National Compensation Survey, Staff 202-691-6199; ocltinfo@bls.gov

National Opinion Research Center, Staff 773-256-6000; norcinfo@norcmail.uchicago.edu

Nonemployer statistics, Staff 301-763-5184

North Am. Industry Class. System (NAICS), Wanda Dougherty 301-763-2790

Occupational and industrial statistics, Staff 301-763-3239

Occupational data, Staff 202-691-6378

Occupational employment statistics, Staff 202-691-6569; oesinfo@bls.gov

Occupational Outlook Quarterly, Kathleen Green 202-691-5717

Occupational projections:
- College graduate outlook, Arlene Dohm/Ian Wyatt 202-691-5727/5690
- Education and training, Chet Levine/Jon Sargent 202-691-5715/5722
- General information, Chet Levine/Jon Sargent 202-691-5715/5722
- Industry-occupation matrix, David Frank 202-691-5708

- Projections:
  - Computer, Chet Levine/Roer Moncarz 202-691-5715/5694
  - Construction, Doug Braddock/William Lawhorn 202-691-5695/5093
  - Education, Arlene Dohm 202-691-5727
  - Engineering, Doug Braddock 202-691-5695
  - Food and lodging, Theresa Cosca/Jon Kelinson 202-691-5712/5688
  - Health, Theresa Cosca/Alan Lacey/Terry Schau 202-601-5712/5731/5720
  - Legal, Tamara Dillon 202-691-5733
  - Mechanics and repairers, Theresa Cosca 202-691-5712
  - Sales, Doug Braddock/Andrew Alpert 202-691-5695/5754
  - Scientific, Henry Kasper 292-691-5696
- Replacement and separation rates, Alan Lacey/ Lynn Shniper 202-691-5731/5732

Older workers, Staff 202-691-6378

Outlying areas, Michael Levin 301-763-1444

Part-time workers, Staff 202-691-6378

Place of birth, Staff 301-763-2422

Population estimates and projections, Staff 301-763-2422

Population information, Staff 301-763-2422

Poverty statistics, Staff 301-763-3242

Prisoner surveys, Marilyn Monahan 301-763-5315

Puerto Rico, Idabelle Hovland 301-763-8443

Quarterly Financial Report, Yolando St. George 301-763-3343

Race, concepts and interpretation, Staff 301-763-2402

Race statistics, Staff 301-763-2422

Retail trade
- Advance monthly, Scott Scheleur 301-763-2713; svsd@census.gov
- Annual retail, Scott Scheleur 301-763-2713; svsd@census.gov
- Economic census, Fay Dorsett 301-763-5180; rcb@census.gov
- Monthly sales and inventory, Nancy Piesto 301-763-2747; retail.trade@census.gov
- Quarterly Financial Report, Yolando St. George 301-763-3343; cad@census.gov

School enrollment, Staff 301-763-2464

Seasonal adjustment methodology, Richard Tiller/Thomas Evans 202-691-6370/6354

Services
- Current Reports, Ruth Bramblett 301-763-2787; svsd@census.gov

- Economic census, Jack Moody 301-763-5181; scb@census.gov
- General information, Staff 1-800-541-8345; scb@census.gov

Small area income and poverty estimates, Staff 301-763-3193

Special censuses, Mike Stump 301-763-3577

Special surveys, Ron Dopkowski 301-763-3801

Special tabulations, Linda Showalter 301-763-2429

State population estimates, Staff 301-763-2422

Statistics of U.S. businesses, Melvin Cole 301-763-3321

Survey of Income and Program Participation (SIPP), Staff 301-763-3242

Transportation
- Commodity Flow Survey, John Fowler 301-763-2108; svsd@census.gov
- Establishments, James Barron 301-763-2786; ucb@census.gov
- Vehicle inventory and use survey, Thomas Zabelsky 301-763-5175; vius@census.gov
- Wholesale trade, Donna Hambric 301-763-2725; svsd@census.gov

Undercount, demographic analysis, Gregg Robinson 301-763-2110

Union membership, Staff 202-691-6378

Urban/rural population, Michael Ratcliff 301-763-2419

Veterans in labor force, Staff 202-691-6378

Veterans' status, Staff 301-763-3230

Voters, characteristics, Staff 301-763-2464

Voting age population, Staff 301-763-2464

Weekly earnings, Staff 202-691-6378

Wholesale trade
- Annual wholesale, Scott Scheleur 301-763-2713; svsd@census.gov
- Current sales and inventories, Scott Scheleur 301-763-2713; svsd@census.gov
- Economic census, Donna Hambric 301-763-2725; wcb@census.gov
- Quarterly Financial Report, Yolando St. George 301-763-3343; csd@census.gov

Women, Renee Spraggins 301-763-2378

Women in the labor force, Staff 202-691-6378

Work experience, Staff 202-691-6378

Working poor, Staff 202-691-6378

Youth, students, and dropouts in labor force, Staff 202-691-6378

Census Regional Offices

Information specialists in the Census Bureau's 12 regional offices answer thousands of questions each year. If you have questions about the Census Bureau's products and services, contact the regional office serving your state. The states served by each regional office are listed in parentheses.

- Atlanta (AL, FL, GA) 404-730-3833 www.census.gov/atlanta
- Boston, MA (CT, MA, ME, NH, NY, RI, VT) 617-424-0510; www.census.gov/boston
- Charlotte (KY, NC, SC, TN, VA) 704-424-6430 www.census.gov/charlotte
- Chicago (IL, IN, WI) 708-562-1350 www.census.gov/chicago
- Dallas (LA, MS, TX) 214-253-4481 www.census.gov/dallas
- Denver (AZ, CO, MT, NE, ND, NM, NV, SD, UT, WY) 303-969-7750; www.census.gov/denver
- Detroit (MI, OH, WV) 313-259-1875 www.census.gov/detroit
- Kansas City (AR, IA, KS, MN, MO, OK) 913-551-6711; www.census.gov/kansascity
- Los Angeles (southern CA, HI) 818-904-6339 www.census.gov/losangeles
- New York (NY, NJ-selected counties) 212-264-4730 www.census.gov/newyork
- Philadelphia (DE, DC, MD, NJ-selected counties, PA) 215-656-7578; www.census.gov/philadelphia
- Seattle (northern CA, AK, ID, OR, WA) 206-553-5835 www.census.gov/seattle
- Puerto Rico and the U.S. Virgin Islands are serviced by the Boston regional office. All other outlying areas are serviced by the Los Angeles regional office.

State Data Centers and Business and Industry Data Centers

For demographic and economic information about states and local areas, contact your State Data Center (SDC) or Business and Industry Data Center (BIDC). Every state has a State Data Center. Below are listed the leading centers for each state-usually a state government agency, university, or library that heads a network of affiliate centers. Asterisks (*) identify states that also have BIDCs. In some states, one agency serves as the lead for both the SDC and the BIDC. The BIDC is listed separately if a separate agency serves as the lead.

- Alabama, Annette Watters, University of Alabama 205-348-6191; awatters@cba.ua.edu

- Alaska, Kathryn Lizik, Department of Labor 907-465-2437; kathryn_lizik@labor.state.ak.us
- American Samoa, Vaitoelau Filiga, Department of Commerce 684-633-5155; vfiliga@doc.asg.as
- Arizona*, Betty Jeffries, Dept of Economic Security 602-542-5984; betty.jeffries@de.state.az.us
- Arkansas, Sarah Breshears, University of Arkansas/ Little Rock 501-569-8530; sgbreshears@ualr.edu
- California, Julie Hoang, Department of Finance 916-323-4086; fijhoang@dof.ca.gov
- Colorado, Rebecca Picaso, Department of Local Affairs 303-866-3120; rebecca.picaso@state.co.us
- Connecticut, Bill Kraynak, Office of Policy and Mgmt., 860-418-6230; william.kraynak@po.state.ct.us
- Delaware*, Mike Helmer, Economic Development Office 302-672-6848; michael.helmer@state.de.us
- District of Columbia, Herb Bixhorn, Mayor's Office of Planning 202-442-7603; herb.bixhorn@dc.gov
- Florida*, Pam Schenker, Florida Agency for Workforce Innovation 850-488-1048; pamela.schenker@awi.state.fl.us
- Georgia, Robert Giacomini, Office of Planning and Budget 404-656-6505; girt@mail.opb.state.ga.us
- Guam, Isabel Lujan, Bureau of Statistics and Plans 671-472-4201; idlujan@mail.gov.gu
- Hawaii, Jan Nakamoto, Dept. of Business, Ec. Dev., and Tourism 808-586-2493; jnakamot@dbedt.hawaii.gov
- Idaho, Alan Porter, Department of Commerce 208-334-2470; aporter@idoc.state.id.us
- Illinois*, Suzanne Ebetsch, Dept. of Commerce and Community Affairs 217-782-1381; sue_ebetsch@commerce.state.il.us
- Illinois BIDC, Ed Taft, Dept. of Commerce and Community Affairs 217-785-7545; ed_taft@commerce.state.il.us
- Indiana*, Roberta Brooker, State Library 317-232-3733; rbrooker@statelib.lib.in.us
- Indiana BIDC, Carol Rogers, Business Research Center 317-274-2205; rogersc@iupui.edu
- Iowa, Beth Henning, State Library 515-281-4350; beth.henning@lib.state.ia.us
- Kansas, Marc Galbraith, State Library 785-296-3296; marcg@kslib.info
- Kentucky*, Ron Crouch, University of Louisville 502-852-7990; rtcrou01@gwise.louisville.edu
- Louisiana, Karen Paterson, Office of Planning and Budget 225-219-5987; kpaters@doa.state.la.us

- Maine*, Eric VonMagnus, State Planning Office 207-287-3261; eric.vonmagnus@state.me.us
- Maryland*, Jane Traynham, Office of Planning 410-767-4450; jtraynham@mdp.state.md.us
- Massachusetts*, John Gaviglio, Institute for Social and Econ. Research 413-545-3460; miser@miser.umass.edu
- Michigan, Daarren Warner, Library of Michigan 517-373-2548; warnerd@michigan.gov
- Minnesota*, Dona Ronningen, State Demographer's Office 651-296-4886; barbara.ronningen@state.mn.us
- Mississippi*, Rachel McNeely, University of Mississippi 662-915-7288; rmcneely@olemiss.edu
- Mississippi BIDC, Deloise Tate, Dept. of Ec. and Comm. Dev. 601-359-3593; dtate@mississippi.org
- Missouri*, Debra Pitts, State Library 573-526-7648; pittsd@sosmail.state.mo.us
- Missouri BIDC, Cathy Frank, Small Business Research Information Center 573-341-6484; cfrank@umr.edu
- Montana*, Pam Harris, Department of Commerce 406-841-2740; paharris@state.mt.us
- Nebraska, Jerome Deichert, University of Nebraska at Omaha 402-554-2134; jerome_deichert@unomaha.edu
- Nevada, Ramona Reno, State Library and Archives 775-684-3326; rlreno@clan.lib.nv.us
- New Hampshire, Thomas Duffy, Office of State Planning 603-271-2155; t_duffy@osp.state.nh.us
- New Jersey*, David Joye, Department of Labor 609-984-2595; djoye@dol.state.nj.us
- New Mexico*, Kevin Kargacin, University of New Mexico 505-277-6626; kargacin@unm.edu
- New Mexico BIDC, Beth Davis, Economic Development Dept. 505-827-0264; edavis@edd.state.nm.us
- New York*, Staff, Department of Economic Development 518-292-5300; rscardamalia@empire.state.ny.us
- North Carolina*, Staff, State Library 919-733-3270; francine.stephenson@ncmail.net
- North Dakota, Richard Rathge, North Dakota State University 701-231-8621; richard.rathge@ndsu.nodak.edu
- Northern Mariana Islands, Diego A. Sasamoto, Dept. of Commerce 670-664-3033; csd@itecnmi.com
- Ohio*, Steve Kelley, Department of Development 614-466-2116; skelley@odod.state.oh.us
- Oklahoma*, Jeff Wallace, Department of Commerce 405-815-5184; jeff_wallace@odoc.state.ok.us
- Oregon, George Hough, Portland State University. 503-725-5159; houghg@mail.pdx.edu

- Pennsylvania*, Sue Copella, Pennsylvania State Univ./ Harrisburg 717-948-6336; sdc3@psu.edu
- Puerto Rico, Lillian Torres Aguirre, Planning Bd. 787-727-4444; torres_l@jp.gobierno.pr
- Rhode Island, Mark Brown, Department of Administration 401-222-6183; mbrown@planning.state.ri.us
- South Carolina, Mike MacFarlane, Budget and Control Board 803-734-3780; mmacfarl@drss.state.sc.us
- South Dakota, Nancy Nelson, University of South Dakota 605-677-5287; nnelson@usd.edu
- Tennessee, Betty Vickers, University of Tennessee, Knoxville 865-974-5441; bvickers@utk.edu
- Texas*, Steve Murdock, Texas A&M University 979-845-5115/5332; smurdock@rsocsun.tamu.edu
- Texas BIDC, Ann Griffith, Dept. of Economic Dev. 512-936-0550; bidc@txed.state.tx.us
- Utah*, Sophia DiCaro, Governor's Office of Planning and Budget 801-537-9013; sdicaro@utah.gov
- Vermont, William Sawyer, Center for Rural Studies 802-656-3021; william.sawyer@uvm.edu
- Virgin Islands, Frank Mills, University of the Virgin Islands 340-693-1027; fmills@uvi.edu
- Virginia*, Don Lillywhite, Virginia Employment Commission 804-786-7496; dlillywhite@vec.state.va.us
- Washington*, Yi Zhao, Office of Financial Management 360-902-0592; yi.zhao@ofm.wa.gov
- West Virginia*, Delphine Coffey, West Virginia Dev. Office 304-558-4010; dcoffey@wvdo.org
- West Virginia BIDC, Randy Childs, Bureau of Business & Economic Research 304-293-7832; randy.childs@mail.wvu.edu
- Wisconsin*, Robert Naylor, Demographic Services Center 608-266-1927; bob.naylor@doa.state.wi.us
- Wisconsin BIDC, Dan Veroff, University of Wisconsin 608-265-9545; dlveroff@facstaff.wisc.edu
- Wyoming, Wenlin Liu, Dept. of Administration and Information 307-777-7504; wliu@missc.state.wy.us

Glossary

adjusted for inflation Income or a change in income that has been adjusted for the rise in the cost of living, or the consumer price index (CPI-U-RS).

American Housing Survey (AHS) The AHS collects national and metropolitan-level data on the nation's housing, including apartments, single-family homes, and mobile homes. The nationally representative survey, with a sample of 55,000 homes, is conducted by the Census Bureau for the Department of Housing and Urban Development every other year.

American Indians In this book, American Indians include Alaska Natives (Eskimos and Aleuts). In tables showing 2000 census data, the term "American Indian" may include those who identified themselves as American Indian and no other race (called "American Indian alone") or those who identified themselves as American Indian and some other race (called "American Indian in combination").

Asian The term "Asian" is defined differently depending on whether census or survey data are shown. In tables showing 2000 census data, Asians do not include Native Hawaiians or other Pacific Islanders unless noted. The term "Asian" may include those who identified themselves as Asian and no other race (called "Asian alone") or those who identified themselves as Asian and some other race (called "Asian in combination"). Asian estimates from the 2003 Current Population Survey include both those who identified themselves as Asian alone and those who identified themselves as Asian in combination. Asian estimates in earlier survey data do not include the multiracial option. Also, in surveys and other noncensus data collections, Asian figures include Native Hawaiians and other Pacific Islanders.

Baby Boom Americans born between 1946 and 1964.

Baby Bust Americans born between 1965 and 1976, also known as Generation X.

Behavioral Risk Factor Surveillance System (BRFSS) The BRFSS is a collaborative project of the Centers for Disease Control and Prevention and U.S. states and territories. It is an ongoing data collection program designed to measure behavioral risk factors in the adult population aged 18 or older. All 50 states, three territories, and the District of Columbia take part in the survey, making the BRFSS the primary source of information on the health-related behaviors of Americans.

black The black racial category includes those who identified themselves as "black or African American." The term "black" is defined differently depending on whether census or survey data are shown. In tables showing 2000 census data, the term "black" may include those who identified themselves as black and no other race (called "black alone") or those who identified themselves as black and some other race (called "black in combination"). Black estimates from the 2003 Current Population Survey include both those who identified themselves as black alone and those who identified themselves as black in combination. Black estimates in earlier survey data do not include the multiracial option.

central cities The largest city in a metropolitan area is called the central city. The balance of the metropolitan area outside the central city is regarded as the "suburbs."

Consumer Expenditure Survey (CEX) The Consumer Expenditure Survey is an ongoing study of the day-to-day spending of American households administered by the Bureau of Labor Statistics. The survey is used to update prices for the Consumer Price Index. The CEX includes an interview survey and a diary survey. The average spending figures shown in this book are the integrated data from both the diary and interview components of the survey. Two separate, nationally representative samples are used for the interview and diary surveys. For the interview survey, about 7,500 consumer units are interviewed on a rotating panel basis each quarter for five consecutive quarters. For the diary survey, 7,500 consumer units keep weekly diaries of spending for two consecutive weeks.

consumer unit *(on spending tables only)* For convenience, the term consumer unit and households are used interchangeably in the spending section of this book, although consumer units are somewhat different from the Census Bureau's households. Consumer units are all related members of a household, or financially independent members of a household. A household may include more than one consumer unit.

disability *(1997 Current Population Survey data)* People aged 15 or older were identified as having a disability if they met any of the following criteria: 1) used a wheelchair, cane, crutches, or walker; 2) had difficulty performing one or more functional activities (seeing, hearing, speaking, lifting/carrying, climbing stairs, walking, or grasping small objects); 3) had difficulty with one or more activities of daily living (or ADL, which include getting around inside the home, getting in or out of bed or a chair, bathing, dressing, eating, and toileting); 4) had difficulty with one or more instrumental activities of daily living (or IADL, which include going outside the home, keeping track of money and bills, preparing meals, doing light housework, taking prescription medicines, and using the telephone); 5) had one or more specified conditions such as a learning disability, mental retardation, or another developmental disability, Alzheimer's disease, or some other type of mental or emotional condition; 6) had any other mental or emotional condition that seriously interfered with everyday activities (frequently depressed or anxious, trouble getting along with others, trouble concentrating, or trouble coping with day-to-day stress); 7) had a condition that limited the ability to work around the house; 8) if age 16 to 67, had a condition that made it difficult to work at a job or business; or 9) received federal benefits based on an inability to work. People were considered to have a severe disability if they met criteria 1, 6, or 9, or had Alzheimer's disease, mental retardation, or another developmental disability, or were unable to perform or needed help to perform one or more activities in criteria 2, 3, 4, 7, or 8. Children under age 5 were identified as disabled if they had a developmental delay or a condition that limited the ability to use arms or legs or a condition that limited walking, running, or playing. Children aged 6 to 14 were identified as severely disabled if they met any of the following criteria: 1) had a mental retardation or some other developmental disability; 2) had a developmental condition for which they had received therapy or diagnostic services; 3) used an ambulatory aid; 4) had a severe limitation in the ability to see, hear, or speak; or 5) needed personal assistance for an activity of daily living.

disability *(2000 Census data)* The 2000 Census defined the disabled as those who were blind, deaf, or had severe vision or hearing impairments, and/or had a condition that substantially limited one or more basic physical activities such as walking, climbing stairs, reaching, lifting, or carrying. It also included people who, because of a physical, mental, or emotional condition lasting six months or more, have difficulty learning, remembering, concentrating, dressing, bathing, getting around inside the home, going outside the home alone to shop or visit a doctor's office, or working at a job or business.

disability *(2001 National Health Interview Survey data)* This survey estimated the number of people aged 18 or older who had difficulty in physical and/or social functioning, probing whether respondents could perform 12 activities by themselves without using special equipment. Physical functioning questions were grouped in two categories: mobility, and flexibility/strength. The mobility category comprised difficulties in performing the following activities: walking a quarter of a mile, standing for two hours, or walking up 10 steps without resting. The flexibility/strength category comprised difficulties in performing the following activities: stooping, bending, kneeling, reaching over one's head, grasping or handling small objects, carrying a 10-pound object, or pushing/pulling a large object. Social functioning questions probed the following: difficulty in sitting for two hours, going shopping, going to movies, attending sporting events, visiting friends, attending clubs or meetings, going to parties, reading, watching television, sewing, or listening to music. Adults who indicated that the activities were "only a little difficult" or "somewhat difficult" were considered to have a moderate difficulty, and those who indicated that the activities were "very difficult" or "can't do this activity" were considered to have severe difficulty.

disability, work *(2003 Current Population Survey data)* A work disability is a specific physical or mental condition that prevents an individual from working. The disability must be so severe that it completely incapacitates the individual and prevents him/her from doing any kind of work for at least the next six months.

Current Population Survey (CPS) The CPS is a nationally representative survey of the civilian noninstitutional population aged 15 or older. It is taken monthly by the Census Bureau for the Bureau of Labor Statistics, collecting information from more than 50,000 households on employment and unemployment. In March of each year, the survey includes the Annual Social and Economic Supplement (formerly called the Annual Demographic Survey), which is the source of most national data on the characteristics of Americans, such as educational attainment, living arrangements, and incomes.

dual-earner couple A married couple in which both the householder and the householder's spouse are in the labor force.

earnings A type of income, earnings is the amount of money a person receives from his or her job. *See also* Income.

employed All civilians who did any work as a paid employee or farmer/self-employed worker, or who worked 15 hours or more as an unpaid farm worker or in a family-owned business, during the reference period. All those who have jobs but who are temporarily absent from their jobs due to illness, bad weather, vacation, labor management dispute, or personal reasons are considered employed.

expenditure The transaction cost including excise and sales taxes of goods and services acquired during the survey period. The full cost of each purchase is recorded even though full payment may not have been made at the date of purchase. Average expenditure figures may be artificially low for infrequently purchased items such as cars because figures are calculated using all consumer units within a demographic segment rather than just purchasers. Expenditure estimates include money spent on gifts for others.

family A group of two or more people (one of whom is the householder) related by birth, marriage, or adoption and living in the same household.

family household A household maintained by a householder who lives with one or more people related to him or her by blood, marriage, or adoption.

female/male householder A woman or man who maintains a household without a spouse present. May head family or nonfamily households.

foreign-born population People who are not U.S. citizens at birth.

full-time employment Full-time is 35 or more hours of work per week during a majority of the weeks worked.

full-time, year-round Indicates 50 or more weeks of full-time employment during the previous calendar year.

Generation X Americans born between 1965 and 1976, also known as the baby-bust generation.

group quarters population The group quarters population includes all people not living in households. Two general categories of people in group quarters are recognized: 1) the institutionalized population, which includes people under formally authorized, supervised care or custody in institutions at the time of enumeration such as correctional institutions, nursing homes, and juvenile institutions; and 2) the noninstitutionalized population, which includes all people who live in group quarters other than institutions such as college dormitories, military quarters, and group homes.

Hispanic Hispanic origin is self-reported in a question separate from race. Because Hispanic is an ethnic origin rather than a race, Hispanics may be of any race. While most Hispanics are white, there are black, Asian, American Indian, and even Native Hawaiian Hispanics. On the 2000 census, many Hispanics identified their race as "other" rather than white, black, and so on. In fact, 90 percent of people identifying their race as "other" also identified themselves as Hispanic. The 2000 census count of Hispanics differs from estimates in the Current Population Survey and other noncensus data collections in part due to methodological differences.

household All the persons who occupy a housing unit. A household includes the related family members and all the unrelated persons, if any, such as lodgers, foster children, wards, or employees who share the housing unit. A person living alone is counted as a household. A group of unrelated people who share a housing unit as roommates or unmarried partners is also counted as a household. Households do not include group quarters such as college dormitories, prisons, or nursing homes.

household, race/ethnicity of Households are categorized according to the race or ethnicity of the householder only.

householder The householder is the person (or one of the persons) in whose name the housing unit is owned or rented or, if there is no such person, any adult member. With married couples, the householder may be either the husband or wife. The householder is the reference person for the household.

householder, age of The age of the householder is used to categorize households into age groups such as those used in this book. Married couples, for example, are classified according to the age of either the husband or wife, depending on which one identified him or herself as the householder.

housing unit A housing unit is a house, an apartment, a group of rooms, or a single room occupied or intended for occupancy as separate living quarters. Separate living quarters are those in which the occupants do not live and eat with any other persons in the structure and that have direct access from the outside of the building or through a common hall that is used or intended for use by the occupants of another unit or by the general public. The occupants may be a single family, one person living alone, two or more families living together, or any other group of related or unrelated persons who share living arrangements.

Housing Vacancy Survey The AHS is a supplement to the Current Population Survey, providing quarterly and annual data on rental and homeowner vacancy rates, characteristics of units available for occupancy, and homeownership rates by age, household type, region, state, and metropolitan area. The Current Population Survey sample includes 51,000 occupied housing units and 9,000 vacant units.

housing value The respondent's estimate of how much his or her house and lot would sell for if it were for sale.

immigration The relatively permanent movement (change of residence) of people into the country of reference.

in-migration The relatively permanent movement (change of residence) of people into a subnational geographic entity, such as a region, division, state, metropolitan area, or county.

income Money received in the preceding calendar year by each person aged 15 or older from each of the following sources: (1) earnings from longest job (or self-employment); (2) earnings from jobs other than longest job; (3) unemployment compensation; (4) workers' compensation; (5) Social Security; (6) Supplemental Security income; (7) public assistance; (8) veterans' payments; (9) survivor benefits; (10) disability benefits; (11) retirement pensions; (12) interest; (13) dividends; (14) rents and royalties or estates and trusts; (15) educational assistance; (16) alimony; (17) child support; (18) financial assistance from outside the household, and other periodic income. Income is reported in several ways in this book. Household income is the combined income of all household members. Income of persons is all income accruing to a person from all sources. Earnings are the money a person receives from his or her job.

industry Refers to the industry in which a person worked longest in the preceding calendar year.

institutionalized population *See* Group quarters population.

job tenure The length of time a person has been employed continuously by the same employer.

labor force The labor force tables in this book show the civilian labor force only. The labor force includes both the employed and the unemployed (people who are looking for work). People are counted as in the labor force if they were working or looking for work during the reference week in which the Census Bureau fields the Current Population Survey.

labor force participation rate The percent of the civilian noninstitutional population that is in the civilian labor force, which includes both the employed and the unemployed.

married couples with or without children under age 18 Refers to married couples with or without own children under age 18 living in the same household. Couples without children under age 18 may be parents of grown children who live elsewhere, or they could be childless couples.

median The median is the amount that divides the population or households into two equal portions: one below and one above the median. Medians can be calculated for income, age, and many other characteristics.

median income The amount that divides the income distribution into two equal groups, half having incomes above the median, half having incomes below the median. The medians for households or families are based on all households or families. The median for persons are based on all persons aged 15 or older with income.

Medical Expenditure Panel Survey MEPS is a nationally representative survey that collects detailed information on the health status, access to care, health care use and expenses and health insurance coverage of the civilian noninstitutionalized population of the U.S. and nursing home residents. MEPS comprises four component surveys: the Household Component, the Medical Provider Component, the Insurance Component, and the Nursing Home Component. The Household Component is the core survey and is conducted each year, and includes 15,000 households and 37,000 people.

metropolitan statistical area (MSA) To be defined as a metropolitan statistical area (or MSA), an area must include a city with 50,000 or more inhabitants, or a Census Bureau-defined urbanized area of at least 50,000 inhabitants and a total metropolitan population of at least 100,000 (75,000 in New England). The county (or counties) that contains the largest city becomes the "central county" (counties), along with any adjacent counties that have at least 50 percent of their population in the urbanized area surrounding the largest city. Additional "outlying counties" are included in the MSA if they meet specified requirements of commuting to the central counties and other selected requirements of metropolitan character (such as population density and percent urban). In New England, MSAs are defined in terms of cities and towns rather than counties. For this reason, the concept of NECMA is used to define metropolitan areas in the New England division.

Millennial generation Americans born between 1977 and 1994.

mobility status People are classified according to their mobility status on the basis of a comparison between their place of residence at the time of the March Current Population Survey and their place of residence in March of the previous year. Nonmovers are people living in the same house at the end of the period as at the beginning of the period. Movers are people living in a different house at the end of the period than at the beginning of the period. Movers from abroad are either citizens or aliens whose place of residence is outside the United States at the beginning of the period, that is, in an outlying area under the jurisdiction of the United States or in a foreign country. The mobility status for children is fully allocated from the mother if she is in the household; otherwise it is allocated from the householder.

Monitoring the Future Project (MTF) The MTF survey is conducted by the University of Michigan Survey Research Center. The survey is administered to approximately 50,000 students in 420 public and private secondary schools every year. High school seniors have been surveyed annually since 1975. Students in 8th and 10th grade have been surveyed annually since 1991.

National Ambulatory Medical Care Survey (NAMCS) The NAMCS is an annual survey of visits to nonfederally employed office-based physicians who are primarily engaged in direct patient care. Data are collected from physicians rather than patients, with each physician assigned a one-week reporting period. During that week, a systematic random sample of visit characteristics are recorded by the physician or office staff.

National Health Interview Survey (NHIS) The NHIS is a continuing nationwide sample survey of the civilian noninstitutional population of the U.S. conducted by the Census Bureau for the National Center for Health Statistics. Each year, data are collected from more than 100,000 people about their illnesses, injuries, impairments, chronic and acute conditions, activity limitations, and the use of health services.

National Home and Hospice Care Survey These are a series of surveys of a nationally representative sample of home and hospice care agencies in the U.S., sponsored by the National Center for Health Statistics. Data on the characteristics of patients and services provided are collected through personal interviews with administrators and staff.

National Hospital Discharge Survey This survey has been conducted annually since 1965, sponsored by the National Center for Health Statistics, to collect nationally representative information on the characteristics of inpatients discharged from nonfederal, short-stay hospitals in the U.S. The survey collects data from a sample of approximately 270,000 inpatient records acquired from a national sample of about 500 hospitals.

National Household Education Survey (NHES) The NHES, sponsored by the National Center for Education Statistics, provides descriptive data on the educational activities of the U.S. population, including after-school care and adult education. The NHES is a system of telephone surveys of a representative sample of 45,000 to 60,000 households in the U.S. It has been conducted in 1991, 1993, 1995, 1996, 1999, 2001, and 2003.

National Nursing Home Survey This is a series of national sample surveys of nursing homes, their residents, and staff conducted at various intervals since 1973–74 and sponsored by the National Center for Health Statistics. The latest survey was taken in 1999. data for the survey are obtained through personal interviews with administrators and staff, and occasionally with self-administered questionnaires, in a sample of about 1,500 facilities.

National Survey on Drug Use and Health *(formerly called the National Household Survey on Drug Abuse)* This survey, sponsored by the Substance Abuse and Mental Health Services Administration, has been conducted since 1971. It is the primary source of information on the use of illegal drugs by the U.S. population. Each year, a nationally representative sample of about 70,000 individuals aged 12 or older are surveyed in the 50 states and the District of Columbia.

Native Hawaiian and other Pacific Islander The 2000 census, for the first time, identified this group as a separate racial category from Asians. The term "Native Hawaiian and other Pacific Islander" may include those who identified themselves as Native Hawaiian and other Pacific Islander and no other race (called "Native Hawaiian and other Pacific Islander alone") or those who identified themselves as Native Hawaiian and other Pacific Islander and some other race (called "Native Hawaiian and other Pacific Islander in combination").

net migration Net migration is the result of subtracting out-migration from in-migration for an area. Another way to derive net migration is to subtract natural increase (births minus deaths) from total population change in an area.

net worth The amount of money left over after a household's debts are subtracted from its assets.

nonfamily household A household maintained by a householder who lives alone or who lives with people to whom he or she is not related.

nonfamily householder A householder who lives alone or with nonrelatives.

non-Hispanic People who do not identify themselves as Hispanic are classified as non-Hispanic. Non-Hispanics may be of any race.

non-Hispanic white People who identify their race as white and who do not indicate a Hispanic origin. The 2000 census classified people as non-Hispanic white if they identified their race as "white alone" and did not indicate their ethnicity as Hispanic. This definition is close to the one used in the Current Population Survey and other government data collection efforts.

noninstitutionalized population *See* Group quarters population.

nonmetropolitan area Counties that are not classified as metropolitan areas.

occupation Occupational classification is based on the kind of work a person did at his or her job during the previous calendar year. If a person changed jobs during the year, the data refer to the occupation of the job held the longest during that year.

occupied housing units A housing unit is classified as occupied if a person or group of people is living in it or if the occupants are only temporarily absent—on vacation, example. By definition, the count of occupied housing units is the same as the count of households.

other race The 2000 census included "other race" as a racial category. The category was meant to capture the few Americans, such as Creoles, who may not consider themselves as belonging to the other five racial groups. In fact, more than 18 million Americans identified themselves as "other race," including 42 percent of the nation's Hispanics. Among the 18 million people who claim to be of "other" race, 90 percent also identified themselves as Hispanic. The government considers Hispanic to be an ethnic identification rather than a race since there are white, black, American Indian, and Asian Hispanics. But many Hispanics consider their ethnicity to be a separate race.

outside central city The portion of a metropolitan county or counties that falls outside of the central city or cities; generally regarded as the suburbs.

own children Own children are sons and daughters, including stepchildren and adopted children, of the householder. The totals include never-married children living away from home in college dormitories.

owner occupied A housing unit is "owner occupied" if the owner lives in the unit, even if it is mortgaged or not fully paid for. A cooperative or condominium unit is "owner occupied" only if the owner lives in it. All other occupied units are classified as "renter occupied."

part-time employment Part-time is less than 35 hours of work per week in a majority of the weeks worked during the year.

percent change The change (either positive or negative) in a measure that is expressed as a proportion of the starting measure. When median income changes from $20,000 to $25,000, for example, this is a 25 percent increase.

percentage point change The change (either positive or negative) in a value which is already expressed as a percentage. When a labor force participation rate changes from 70 percent of 75 percent, for example, this is a 5 percentage point increase.

poverty level The official income threshold below which families and people are classified as living in poverty. The threshold rises each year with inflation and varies depending on family size and age of householder.

proportion or share The value of a part expressed as a percentage of the whole. If there are 4 million people aged 25 and 3 million of them are white, then the white proportion is 75 percent.

race Race is self-reported and defined differently depending on the data source. On the 2000 census, respondents identified themselves as belonging to one or more of six racial groups: American Indian and Alaska Native, Asian, black, Native Hawaiian and other Pacific Islander, white, and other. In publishing the results, the Census Bureau created three new terms to distinguish one group from another. The "race alone" population is people who identified themselves as only one race. The "race in combination" population is people who identified themselves as more than one race, such as white and black. The "race, alone or in combination" population includes both those who identified themselves as one race and those who identified themselves as more than one race. Other government data collection efforts included the multira-

cial option beginning in 2003. The tables in this book that include race data from government surveys or from censuses prior to 2000 do not include the multiracial option.

regions The four major regions and nine census divisions of the United States are the state groupings as shown below:

Northeast:
—New England: Connecticut, Maine, Massachusetts, New Hampshire, Rhode Island, and Vermont
—Middle Atlantic: New Jersey, New York, and Pennsylvania

Midwest:
—East North Central: Illinois, Indiana, Michigan, Ohio, and Wisconsin
—West North Central: Iowa, Kansas, Minnesota, Missouri, Nebraska, North Dakota, and South Dakota

South:
—South Atlantic: Delaware, District of Columbia, Florida, Georgia, Maryland, North Carolina, South Carolina, Virginia, and West Virginia
—East South Central: Alabama, Kentucky, Mississippi, and Tennessee
—West South Central: Arkansas, Louisiana, Oklahoma, and Texas

West:
—Mountain: Arizona, Colorado, Idaho, Montana, Nevada, New Mexico, Utah, and Wyoming
—Pacific: Alaska, California, Hawaii, Oregon, and Washington

renter occupied *See* Owner occupied.

rounding Percentages are rounded to the nearest tenth of a percent; therefore, the percentages in a distribution do not always add exactly to 100.0 percent. The totals, however, are always shown as 100.0. Moreover, individual figures are rounded to the nearest thousand without being adjusted to group totals, which are independently rounded; percentages are based on the unrounded numbers.

self-employment A person is categorized as self-employed if he or she was self-employed in the job held longest during the reference period. Persons who report self-employment from a second job are excluded, but those who report wage-and-salary income from a second job are included. Unpaid workers in family businesses are excluded. Self-employment statistics include only nonagricultural workers and exclude people who work for themselves in incorporated business.

sex ratio The number of men per 100 women.

suburbs *See* Outside central city.

Survey of Consumer Finances The Survey of Consumer Finances is a triennial survey taken by the Federal Reserve Board. It collects data on the assets, debts, and net worth of American households. For the 2001 survey, the Federal Reserve Board interviewed more than 4,000 households.

Survey of Income and Program Participation (SIPP) SIPP is a longitudinal survey conducted at four-month intervals by the Census Bureau. The main focus of SIPP is information on labor force participation, jobs, income, and participation in federal assistance programs. Information on other topics is collected in topical modules on a rotating basis.

two or more races People who identified themselves as belonging to two or more racial groups on the 2000 Census. *See* Race.

unemployed Unemployed people are those who, during the survey period, had no employment but were available and looking for work. Those who were laid off from their jobs and were waiting to be recalled are also classified as unemployed.

white The term "white" is defined differently depending on whether census or survey data are shown. In tables showing 2000 census data, the term "white" may include those who identified themselves as white and no other race (called "white alone") or those who identified themselves as white and some other race (called "white in combination"). White estimates from the 2003 Current Population Survey include both those who identified themselves as white alone and those who identified themselves as white in combination. White estimates in earlier survey data do not include the multiracial option.

Youth Risk Behavior Surveillance System (YRBSS) The YRBSS was created by the Centers for Disease Control to monitor health risks being taken by young people at the national, state, and local level. The national survey is taken every two years based on a nationally representative sample of 16,000 students in 9th through 12th grade in public and private schools.

Bibliography

AARP

Internet site http://www.aarp.org

—*Boomers at Midlife: The AARP Life Stage Study*, A National Survey conducted by Princeton Survey Research Associates, November 2002

—"Pennies from Heaven: Will Inheritances Bail Out the Boomers? Mitja Ng-Baumhackl, John Gist, and Carlos Figueiredo, *Data Digest*, No. 90, AARP Public Policy Institute

—*Staying Ahead of the Curve 2003: The AARP Working in Retirement Study*

Bureau of Labor Statistics

Internet site http://www.bls.gov

—1997 and 2002 Consumer Expenditure Surveys, Internet site http://www.bls.gov/cex/

—2002 Consumer Expenditure Survey unpublished data

—2003 Current Population Survey, unpublished data

—*Characteristics of Minimum Wage Workers*, 2002, Internet site http://www.bls.gov/cps/minwage2002.htm

—*Contingent and Alternative Employment Arrangements, February 2001*, USDL 01-153, Internet site http://www.bls.gov/news.release/conemp.toc.htm

—*Employee Tenure in 2002*, Internet site http://www.bls.gov/news.release/tenure.toc.htm

—Employment Projections, 2002–2012, Internet site http://www.bls.gov/emp/emplab1.htm

—Labor force participation rates, historical, Public Query Data Tool, Internet site http://www.bls.gov/data

—*Workers on Flexible and Shift Schedules in 2001*, USDL 02-225, Internet site http://www.bls.gov/news.release/flex.toc.htm

Bureau of the Census

Internet site http://www.census.gov

—2003 Current Population Survey Annual Social and Economic Supplement, Internet site http://www.census.gov/hhes/income/dinctabs.html

—*Age: 2000*, Census 2000 Brief, 2001

—*American Housing Survey for the United States in 2001*, Internet site http://www.census.gov/hhes/www/ahs.html

—Census 2000, Internet site http://factfinder.census.gov/servlet/BasicFactsServlet

—*Children's Living Arrangements and Characteristics: March 2002*, detailed tables for Current Population Report P20-547, Internet site http://www.census.gov/population/www/socdemo/hh-fam/cps2002.html

—Current Population Surveys, historical data, Internet site http://www.census.gov/hhes/income/histinc/histinctb.html

—*Disability Status: 2000*, Census 2000 Brief, 2003

—*Educational Attainment in the United States: March 2002*, detailed tables (PPL-169), Internet site http://www.census.gov/population/www/socdemo/education/ppl-169.html

—*Fertility of American Women: June 2002*, detailed tables, Internet site http://www.census.gov/population/www/socdemo/fertility/cps2002.html

—*Foreign-Born Population of the United States, Current Population Survey*—March 2002, detailed tables (PPL-162), Internet site http://www.census.gov/population/www/socdemo/foreign/ppl-162.html

—*Geographic Mobility: 2003*, detailed tables for P20-549, Internet site http://www.census.gov/population/www/socdemo/migrate/p20-549.html

—Housing Vacancy Surveys, Internet site http://www.census.gov/hhes/www/housing/hvs/annual03/ann03ind.html

—National Population Estimates, Internet site http://eire.census.gov/popest/

—*School Enrollment—Social and Economic Characteristics of Students: October 2002*, detailed tables; Internet site http://www.census.gov/population/www/socdemo/school/cps2002.html

—*U.S. Interim Projections by Age, Sex, Race, and Hispanic Origin*, Internet site http://www.census.gov/ipc/www/usinterimproj/

Centers for Disease Control and Prevention
Internet site http://www.cdc.gov
—Behavioral Risk Factor Surveillance System Prevalence Data, Internet site http://apps.nccd.cdc.gov/brfss/index.asp

Employee Benefit Research Institute
Internet site http://www.ebri.org
—2003 Retirement Confidence Survey, EBRI/ASEC/Greenwald, Internet site http://www.ebri.org/

Federal Reserve Board
Internet site http://www.federalreserve.gov
—2001 Survey of Consumer Finances; Internet site http://www.federalreserve.gov/pubs/oss/oss2/2001/scf2001home.html

Investment Company Institute and Securities Industry Association
Internet sites http://www.ici.org and http://www.sia.com
—*Equity Ownership in America, 2002*; Internet sites http://www.ici.org and http://www.sia.com

National Center for Education Statistics
Internet site http://nces.ed.gov
—Adult Education and Lifelong Learning Survey of the National Household Education Surveys Program, Internet site http://nces.ed.gov/programs/coe/2003/section1/tables/t08_2.asp

National Center for Health Statistics
Internet site http://www.cdc.gov/nchs
—Births: Final Data for 2002, *National Vital Statistics Reports*, Vol. 52, No. 10, 2003
—Deaths: Leading Causes for 2001, *National Vital Statistics Report*, Vol. 52, No. 9, 2003
—Deaths: Preliminary Data for 2002, *National Vital Statistics Report*, Vol. 52, No. 13, 2004
—Health Behaviors of Adults: United States, 1999–2001, *Vital and Health Statistics*, Series 10, No. 219, 2004
—*Health, United States, 2003*, Internet site http://www.cdc.gov/nchs/hus.htm
—National Ambulatory Medical Care Survey: 2001 Summary, *Advance Data* No. 337, 2003

—National Hospital Ambulatory Medical Care Survey: 2001 Emergency Department Summary, *Advance Data* No. 335, 2003

—National Hospital Ambulatory Medical Care Survey: 2001 Outpatient Department Summary, *Advance Data* No. 338, 2003

—Revised Birth and Fertility Rates for the 1990s and New Rates for the Hispanic Populations 2000 and 2001: United States, *National Vital Statistics Report*, Vol. 51, No. 12, 2003

— *Summary Health Statistics for the U.S. Population: National Health Interview Survey, 2000,* Series 10, No. 214, 2003

—*Summary Health Statistics for U.S. Adults: National Health Interview Survey, 2001,* Series 10, No. 218, 2004

U.S. Citizenship and Immigration Services

—*2002 Yearbook of Immigration Statistics,* Internet site http://uscis.gov/graphics/shared/aboutus/statistics/index.htm

U.S. Substance Abuse and Mental Health Services Administration, Office of Applied Studies Internet site http://www.samhsa.gov/

—National Survey on Drug Use and Health, 2002

Index

in poverty, 133–134
population, 215, 221–223, 230, 235–240
bonds, 294
bronchitis, 50, 52, 54
business equity, 299

Caesarean section, 39–40
cancer:
    as cause of death, 63–64
    by type, 50, 52, 54
cash contributions:
    consumer spending by detailed category,
        264, 285
    consumer spending trends, 245
cerebrovascular disease, as cause of death, 63–64
certificates of deposit, 294
child support, as source of income, 128–132
childbearing. *See* Births.
children, presence of in households, 171, 186–200
cigarette smoking, 41–42. *See also* Tobacco
        products.
citizens, 225–226
college, as a reason for moving, 86–88
college enrollment, 5, 16–17
congenital malformations, as cause of death, 63
contractors. *See* Independent contractors.
coronary, 50, 52, 54
credit card debt, 301, 303

death, causes of, 21, 62–64
debt, household, 289, 301–303
dental problems, 50, 52, 54
depression, 50–55
diabetes:
    as cause of death, 63–64
    health condition, 50, 52, 54
dieting, 24, 26
disability:
    benefits, as source of income, 129–132
    by education, 49, 56
    work, 49, 56
dividends, as source of income, 129–132
divorce, 203–214
drinking, alcoholic beverages, 41, 43

drugs:
    consumer spending by detailed category, 261,
        267, 282, 288
    consumer spending trends, 245
    illicit, use of, 44–45
dual-income couples, 135, 144–145

earnings:
    as source of income, 128–132
    by educational attainment, 119–127
    minimum wage, 164–165
    of full-time workers, 119–127
eating away from home. *See* Food.
education:
    adult, 5, 18–19
    consumer spending by detailed category, 263,
        267, 284, 288
    consumer spending trends, 242, 245–246
    earnings by, 119–127
educational assistance, as source of income,
        129–132
educational attainment:
    births by, 32
    by race and Hispanic origin, 5, 10–13
    by sex, 5–13
    work disability status by, 49, 56
emergency department visits, 58, 61
emphysema, 50, 52, 54
employment–based health insurance, 46–48
employment, long-term, 156, 158
employment status:
    births by, 32
    by race and Hispanic origin, 135, 140–143
    by sex, 135–143
entertainment:
    consumer spending by detailed category,
        261–263, 267, 282–284, 288
    consumer spending trends, 242, 245–246
exercise, participation in, 24, 26–27

face pain, 50, 52, 54
families. *See* Households.
family, as a reason for moving, 84, 86–88
female-headed household. *See* Households,
        female-headed.

male-headed households. *See* Households,
        male-headed.
marital status:
    births by, 30, 32, 37–38
    by race and Hispanic origin, 206–214
    by sex, 203–214
married couples. *See* Households, married-couple.
Medicaid, 47–48
medical services, use of, 58–61
Medicare:
    coverage, 47
    spending on, 260–261, 281–282
men:
    drinking, 41, 43
    earnings by educational attainment, 119–123
    educational attainment, 5–8, 10–11
    employment, long-term, 154–155
    employment status, 138–141
    exercise, participation in, 27
    full-time workers, 107–112, 119–123, 152–153
    income, 89, 104–105, 107–112, 128–130
    job tenure of, 154–155
    labor force participation, 135–141, 168–169
    labor force projections, 168–169
    life expectancy, 65
    living alone, 172–173, 175, 177, 179, 181, 183
    living arrangements, 171, 200–201
    marital status, 203–214
    overweight, 24–25
    part-time workers, 152–153
    pension coverage, 305
    physician visits, 59
    population, 218
    school enrollment, 14–15
    self-employed, 128–130, 154–155
    source of income, 128–130
    unemployed, 139–141
    union membership, 166–167
    with AIDS, 49, 57
    with flexible schedules, 161–162
mental problems, 49–55
metropolitan status, women giving birth by, 32
migraines. *See* Headaches.
military health insurance, 47
minimum wage workers, 164–165
mobile homes, living in, 76–77
mobility, geographic:
    rate, 67, 84–85
    reason for, 84, 86–88

mortgage debt, 300–301, 303
movers. *See* Mobility, geographic.
multiracial population, 221–222, 224
mutual funds, 294, 296

Native Hawaiians:
    by state, 235–240
    population, 222–223, 235–240
naturalized citizens, 225–226
neck pain, 49–50, 52, 54
net worth, household, 289–291

obesity, 21, 24–25
occupations, 32, 146–151
out-of-wedlock births, 37–38
outpatient department visits, 58, 60
overweight problems, 21, 24–26. *See also*
        Weight loss.

part-time workers, 152–153
pensions:
    as source of income, 129–132
    percent covered by, 289, 304–305
    spending on, 245, 264, 285
personal care products and services:
    consumer spending by detailed category, 263,
        267, 284, 288
    consumer spending trends, 245–246
physician office visits, 21, 58–59
pneumonia, as cause of death, 64
population:
    by citizenship status, 225–226
    by generation, 215–217, 221, 223–224,
        230, 232
    by race and Hispanic origin, 215, 221–224,
        230, 235–240
    by region, 230–232
    by sex, 218
    by state, 215, 230, 233–240
    foreign-born, 215, 225–227
    multiracial, 221–222, 224
    projections, 216, 220
poverty rate, 89, 133–134
projections:
    labor force, 135, 168–169
    population, 216, 220

public assistance, as source of income, 129–132
public transportation:
    consumer spending by detailed category, 260, 266, 281, 287
    consumer spending trends, 245

reading material:
    consumer spending by detailed category, 263, 284
    consumer spending trends, 245–246
regions:
    population of, 230–232
    women giving birth by, 32
renters: *See also* Shelter.
    housing costs of, 80–81
    in new housing, 78–79
    number of, 67, 70–71
restaurants, spending on, 242–243, 247, 251, 268, 272
retirement:
    accounts, 294, 296
    age of, expected, 306
    as a reason for moving, 86–88
    attitudes, toward, 304, 306
    confidence, 304, 306
    income, 129–132
    savings, 294

savings bonds, 294
school enrollment, 14–17
self-employment:
    as alternative work arrangement, 159–160
    as source of income, 128–132
    by sex, 154–155
    percent, 135, 154–155
shelter:
    consumer spending by detailed category, 247, 252–253, 273–274
    consumer spending trends, 243
shift workers, 161, 163
single–family homes, living in, 67, 76–77
single-person households. *See* Households, single-person.
sinusitis, 49–50, 52, 54
smoking, 41–42
Social Security, as source of income, 129–132

spending:
    by detailed product category, 241, 247–288
    trends by product, 241–246
states, population of, 215, 230, 233–240
stock ownership, 292, 294–296
stroke, 50, 52, 54
suicide, as cause of death, 21, 62–64

taxes, personal:
    consumer spending by detailed category, 265, 286
    consumer spending trends, 245
temporary help workers, 159–160
tobacco products:
    consumer spending by detailed category, 264, 285
    consumer spending trends, 245
transportation:
    consumer spending by detailed category, 259–260, 266, 280–281, 287
    consumer spending trends, 242, 244–246

ulcers, 50, 52, 54
unemployment:
    compensation, as source of income, 129–132
    rate, 135, 138–143
union membership, 166–167
utilities, fuels, and public services:
    consumer spending by detailed category, 254, 266, 275, 287
    consumer spending trends, 244

vehicle purchases:
    consumer spending by detailed category, 259, 266, 280, 287
    consumer spending trends, 244
vehicles, as nonfinancial assets, 297, 299
veteran's benefits, as source of income, 129–132
visual impairments, 49–50, 52, 54

wages and salaries, as source of income, 128–132
wealth, household, 289–307
weight loss, 24, 26
welfare. *See* Public assistance.
White-American men, employment status, 140–141

White-American women:
    births to, 36, 38
    employment status, 142–143
White Americans:
    by state, 235–240
    population, 222–223, 235–240
White non-Hispanic American men:
    educational attainment, 10–11
    full-time workers, 107, 112
    income, 107, 112
    living alone, 175, 182–183
    marital status, 206, 213–214
White, non-Hispanic American women:
    births to, 32, 34, 36–38
    educational attainment, 12–13
    full-time workers, 113, 118
    income, 113, 118
    living alone, 175, 182–183
    marital status, 206, 213–214
White, non-Hispanic Americans:
    by state, 215, 230, 235–240
    educational attainment, 10–13
    homeownership of, 67, 74–75
    household income, 94, 98
    household types, 182–183, 188, 192
    households with children, 188, 192
    in poverty, 133–134
    population, 215, 221–223, 230, 235–240
widowhood, 204–214
women:
    births to, 21, 28–40
    by race and Hispanic origin, 32
    by region, 32
    drinking, 41, 43
    earnings by educational attainment, 119,
        124–127
    educational attainment, 5, 8–9, 12–13, 32
    employment, long-term, 154–155
    employment status, 30, 32–33, 138–139,
        142–143
    exercise, participation in, 27
    foreign born, 33
    full-time workers, 113–119, 124–127, 152–153
    income, 33, 89, 104, 106, 113–118, 128,
        131–132
    job tenure of, 154–155
    labor force participation, 135–139, 142–143,
        168–169

labor force projections, 168–169
life expectancy, 65
living alone, 172–173, 175, 177, 179, 181, 183
living arrangements, 171, 200, 202
marital status, 30, 32, 203–214
metropolitan status, 33
occupation, 33
overweight, 21, 24–25
part-time workers, 152–153
pension coverage, 305
physician visits, 21, 58–59
population, 218
school enrollment, 14–15
self-employed, 131–132, 154–155
source of income, 128, 131–132
unemployed, 139, 142–143
union membership, 166–167
with AIDS, 57
with flexible schedules, 161–162
work arrangements, alternative, 159–160
workers: *See also* Labor force.
    alternative, 159–160
    compensation, as source of income, 129–132
    contract, 159–160
    full-time, 107–127, 152–153
    in unions, 166–167
    independent contractors, 159–160
    minimum wage, 164–165
    on call, 159–160
    part-time, 152–153
    pension coverage of, 304–305
    self-employed, 128–132, 135, 154–155,
        159–160
    shift, 161, 163
    temporary, 159–160
    unemployed, 135, 138–143
    with flexible schedules, 161–162